Faulkner: International Perspectives
Faulkner and Yoknapatawpha
1982

Faulkner: International Perspectives

FAULKNER AND YOKNAPATAWPHA, 1982

EDITED BY
DOREEN FOWLER
AND
ANN J. ABADIE

UNIVERSITY PRESS OF MISSISSIPPI
JACKSON

Copyright © 1984 by the University Press of Mississippi
All rights reserved
Manufactured in the United States of America

The 1982 Faulkner and Yoknapatawpha Conference
was supported by grants from
The Ford Foundation
The United States International Communication Agency
and
The International Research and Exchanges Board

This volume has been sponsored by
The University of Mississippi

Library of Congress Cataloging in Publication Data
Faulkner and Yoknapatawpha Conference (9th: 1982:
 University of Mississippi)
 Faulkner, international perspectives.

 Bibliography: p.
 Includes index.
 1. Faulkner, William, 1897–1962—Congresses.
2. Faulkner, William, 1897–1962—Appreciation—Congresses.
I. Fowler, Doreen. II. Abadie, Ann J. III. University
of Mississippi. IV. Title.
PS3511.A86Z7832113   1982   813'.52   84-5096
ISBN 0-87805-216-X
ISBN 0-87805-217-8 (pbk.)

Contents

Introduction	vii
From Jefferson to the World CALVIN S. BROWN	3
Faulkner's Spanish Voice/s MYRIAM DÍAZ-DIOCARETZ	30
Yoknapatawpha in Santiago de Chile JORGE EDWARDS	60
Faulkner and the British: Episodes in a Literary Relationship MICK GIDLEY	74
From Vignette to Vision: The "Old, Fine Name of France" or Faulkner's "Western Front" from "Crevasse" to *A Fable* MICHEL GRESSET	97
Faulkner in Italy AGOSTINO LOMBARDO	121
Faulkner's Graphic Work in Historical Context LOTHAR HÖNNIGHAUSEN	139
Teaching Faulkner in the Soviet Union M. THOMAS INGE	174
The Perception of William Faulkner in the USSR ALEXANDRE VASHCHENKO	194
William Faulkner in Soviet Literary Criticism SERGEI CHAKOVSKY	212
The Hound and the Antelope: Faulkner in China H. R. STONEBACK	236
"Native Soil" and the World Beyond: William Faulkner and Japanese Novelists KENZABURO OHASHI	257

Il Penseroso and L'Allegro: The Poetics of a Faulkner Collector 276
LOUIS DANIEL BRODSKY

From the World to Jefferson 298
JOSEPH BLOTNER

Appendixes 319
  A. Selected Recent British Writing on Faulkner 319
    MICK GIDLEY
  B. Faulkner in Spanish 320
    MYRIAM DÍAZ-DIOCARETZ
  C. Spanish Criticism of Faulkner 1932–1959 324
    MYRIAM DÍAZ-DIOCARETZ
  D. Faulkner in German 325
    MONIKA BRÜCKNER
  E. A Chronology of Faulkner Translations into Russian 336
    M. THOMAS INGE
  F. A Checklist of Faulkner Translations into Chinese 338
    H. R. STONEBACK
  G. Faulkner in Japanese 339
    KENZABURO OHASHI

Contributors 343

Index 347

Introduction

The 1982 Faulkner and Yoknapatawpha Conference took a new twist. For the past eight years the University of Mississippi in Oxford has sponsored a six-day annual conference as a forum for Faulkner scholarship. In years past, invited lecturers were almost exclusively American scholars (one Canadian and one Frenchman were the two exceptions) who reported the latest research developments on such topics as "Faulkner and Film" or "Faulkner and the Southern Renaissance." In 1982, however, the conference wore a new look—a foreign look. Taking note of the way that the name William Faulkner has become a household word in far-distant countries, the Ninth Annual Faulkner and Yoknapatawpha Conference took for its theme Faulkner's international reputation, and scholars of American literature from all over the world, united by their enthusiasm for the American author, gathered in Oxford to report on the status of William Faulkner in their countries. From thousands of miles away they came to answer the questions: Is Faulkner read? Is he popular? And how is it that our William Faulkner, who writes about his own "postage stamp of native soil," is so universally accessible? As the responses came back from nine different nations, the tally, it soon became evident, was unanimous: everywhere Faulkner was a known quantity; everywhere he was read and admired. Ultimately, the 1982 conference had one finding—Faulkner speaks to the hearts of the people of the world.

Two speakers, Jorge Edwards, a Chilean novelist, and Myriam Díaz-Diocaretz, a poet and professor of English at the Universidad de Concepcion, Chile, discussed Faulkner's pervasive influence in Spanish-speaking nations. Focusing on South America in general and Chile in particular, Edwards attempted to explain the special significance Faulkner's fiction has for South American readers. According to Edwards, the history of the American South bears certain resemblances to Chile's history in the 1890s and, in some respects, to the history of many South American countries. Specifically, in Chile in 1891 a period of relative wealth and political stability was ended by a destructive and divisive civil war. The security and tranquillity of that prewar era was never recovered in Chile, and later generations of Chileans nostalgically contrasted a glorious past with an impoverished present. While insisting on distinctions among South American nations, Edwards nevertheless explains that many countries in South America have experienced similar, ravaging civil wars, which almost invariably have given rise among the populace of these nations to nostalgic recollections of an edenic prewar era. This historical similarity between the American South and South American countries, Edwards hypothesizes, to some extent explains why Faulkner's themes have been immediately accessible to the people of South America.

In her talk, Myriam Díaz-Diocaretz, a translator herself, discussed the problems inherent in translating Faulkner's fiction. Noting the number of different Spanish translations available for one Faulkner novel (there are, for example, presently four Spanish translations of *The Sound and the Fury,* two of which have different titles), Díaz-Diocaretz showed that these translations differ not only with one another but also with Faulkner's original text. Because Faulkner is an experimenter who extends the limits of rhetoric, Díaz-Diocaretz concludes, he is extremely difficult to translate; and, when one reads Faulkner in translation, one is reading "another Faulkner."

According to Agostino Lombardo, Director of the Institute of English and American Literature at the University of Rome, Faulkner's presence in Italy over the past decades has been all the more enduring because it has been "unobtrusive" and "unglamorous." Although Faulkner has never been as generally popular in Italy as, for example, Hemingway, nevertheless, Faulkner has "profoundly acted on Italian culture." Because Faulkner's novels were translated early in Italy (*Light in August* in 1939, *The Hamlet* in 1940, and *The Sound and the Fury* in 1947) while other experimental novels were not translated until much later (*Ulysses* appeared in Italian in 1960 and the first Italian edition of *Finnegans Wake* was published in 1982), Faulkner was the instrument through which technical developments in twentieth-century literature reached Italy. Faulkner is responsible, Lombardo concluded, not only for transforming the ways Italian novelists approached the novel but also for changing and creating the criticism of the novel in Italy.

The warmly enthusiastic response of the French people to Faulkner at a time when his novels were out of print in the United States has been documented frequently, so Michel Gresset, Professor of American Literature at the University of Paris VII, addresses a different subject—the uses Faulkner made of France in his fiction. By Gresset's count, Faulkner set in France seven short stories, two Hollywood scripts, and one novel, *A Fable*. Examining these works, Gresset finds a marked similarity: in all, the French landscape seems to serve a symbolic function having little to do with the real France. For Faulkner, Gresset concludes, France was an idea inextricably bound up with history, war, and tragedy.

Strangely enough, while Faulkner has been enthusiastically received by non-English speaking readers all over the world, British reviewers traditionally have responded somewhat coolly to Faulkner's fiction. From Britain, Mick Gidley, Chairman of the American Studies Board at the University of Exeter, England, read a roll-call of distinguished British literary figures who have written disparagingly about Faulkner. The list included such luminaries as Cyril Connolly, Edwin Muir, C. Day Lewis, Humbert Wolfe, Graham Greene, Philip Toynbee, and George Orwell. What caused this "peevish" British reaction to

Faulkner? Gidley offers two hypotheses. Possibly the regional nature of Faulkner's writing was not to the taste of British reviewers who, for the most part, were London-dwellers, or possibly the experimental nature of Faulkner's narrative techniques was not readily appreciated by the tradition-bound British. In either case, Gidley notes that today Faulkner receives better treatment at the hands of the British perhaps as a result of the growing American Studies movement in British universities.

Through the voices of three speakers the story of Faulkner's reception in the Soviet Union gradually emerged. Describing Soviet-Faulkner relations were two scholars of American literature from the A. M. Gorky Institute of World Literature, Alexandre Vashchenko and Sergei Chakovsky, and M. Thomas Inge, Professor of English at Clemson University, who taught American literature at Moscow State University in 1979. All three agreed that the attitude of the Soviets toward Faulkner has evolved over the past decades. Faulkner was translated and reviewed early in the Soviet Union: the first review of one of Faulkner's works—a review of *The Sound and the Fury*—appeared as early as 1933, and translations of some of Faulkner's stories were published in the Soviet journal, *Foreign Literature*, in the 1930s. However, the stories selected for translation were interpreted by the Soviets as implicitly critical of the American social system, and the Soviet reviews of Faulkner's works that appeared in these early years described Faulkner as a decadent modernist writer who celebrated "a world of rot and carrion." (Thomas Inge notes that at this same time in the United States Faulkner was often condemned by reviewers as a naturalist who dwells on Southern decay and degeneracy.) In the 1950s, however, a reversal of Soviet critical opinion occurred, and serious study of Faulkner's works began. Today in the Soviet Union all of Faulkner's novels, with the exceptions of only *Sanctuary* and *Mosquitoes*, have been translated; extensive chapters are devoted to Faulkner in Soviet textbooks; Faulkner is widely read and studied in Soviet universities; and Faulkner appears to have been accepted by the Soviets into their pantheon of classic authors of world literature.

H. R. Stoneback, Professor of English at the State University of New York and the American editor of a Chinese translation of Faulkner stories, reported on Faulkner's current status in China. According to Stoneback, Faulkner's reception in China has been largely conditioned by Soviet views. For this reason, early Chinese reactions to Faulkner's works tended to echo the hard-line stance of the Soviets, who declaimed Faulkner's "reactionary bourgeois ideology." In the '50s, however, as Soviet opinion shifted, gradually taking a more sympathetic and broadminded attitude toward Faulkner, Chinese views also changed. Today a wave of Chinese translations of Faulkner indicates a growing Chinese enthusiasm for the American writer. Finally, as a result of his own personal experience teaching Faulkner to Chinese scholars and students from Peking University, Stoneback reports that Chinese readers find themselves "at home" with Faulkner, who describes a world familiar to them—a rural country on the brink of joining a modern industrial world.

And the Chinese are not alone in feeling an affinity with the far-distant American writer. According to Kenzaburo Ohashi, Professor of American Literature at Tsurumi University in Japan, Faulkner writes about a subject that preoccupies the Japanese—the collapse of cultural and moral values following a military defeat. Although Japanese translations of Faulkner's works were almost unavailable before 1950, today, Ohashi reports, Faulkner is earnestly read by the Japanese, and especially by Japanese writers, who seem to find in Faulkner's narrative techniques an appropriate way of representing in fiction their own feelings of disorder and confusion.

While other speakers analyzed the influence the Mississippi writer had on the art of the world, Lothar Hönnighausen, Professor of English and American Literature at the University of Bonn, discussed the influence of worldwide art movements on the Mississippi author. Hönnighausen's detailed examination of

Faulkner's graphic art work in the student newspaper, *The Mississippian*, the annual, *Ole Miss*, and the humor magazine, *The Scream*, clearly reveals that Faulkner's art work conforms to the principles of art promulgated by the turn-of-the-century art movement frequently referred to as the Aesthetic movement. Hönnighausen concludes that "as a practicing artist" Faulkner "possessed the ability to feel his way into the mainstream of such art movements when given the least bit of exposure to them." Although seemingly isolated in backwoods Mississippi, Faulkner was not, Hönnighausen implies, as cut off from British and European artistic developments as has sometimes been assumed.

Along with the previously mentioned panoply of foreign experts on American literature, three Americans also played a part in the 1982 Faulkner conference. Calvin Brown, Distinguished Professor of English and Comparative Literature *Emeritus* at the University of Georgia and boyhood friend of William Faulkner, opened the conference with an attempt to assess Faulkner's knowledge of world literature and his use of other literature in his novels; L. D. Brodsky described the most recent additions to the ever-expanding Brodsky collection of Faulkner; and Joseph Blotner, Faulkner's friend and the author of the two-volume, authoritative biography of Faulkner, attempted to summarize the conference by addressing the question—what accounts for Faulkner's appeal to people of every nationality? According to Blotner, the answer is both "obvious and complex." Because Faulkner writes about man in history, about eternal questions, or, as Faulkner put it, about "the same griefs grieving on universal bones," the Mississippi author's voice transcends ephemeral, man-made boundaries and is heard by people all over the world.

Readers of this volume will note that *Faulkner: International Perspectives* contains a special section, a bibliographical appendix. Compiled by several foreign experts on Faulkner's works, this section lists translations as well as recent foreign criticism of Faulkner, providing scholars with a valuable research tool.

While the University of Mississippi's Faulkner and Yoknapatawpha Conference is, in the main, a forum for scholarship on Faulkner, a number of special events also form a part of this yearly meeting. At the ninth annual conference such events included tours of Faulkner country; exhibits of the University's Faulkner holdings and a special exhibit of L. D. Brodsky's Faulkner-Commins Archive; a slide presentation, "Knowing William Faulkner," narrated by the author's nephew; a dramatic presentation about Faulkner; and gospel music sung by Sister Thea Bowman and the Christian Unity Community Choir of Oxford. In conclusion, the editors of this collection wish to express their gratitude to all the people and the organizations who helped to make the Ninth Annual Faulkner and Yoknapatawpha Conference a successful international exchange.

Doreen Fowler
University of Mississippi
Oxford, Mississippi

Faulkner: International Perspectives
Faulkner and Yoknapatawpha
1982

From Jefferson to the World

CALVIN S. BROWN

In spite of detailed and limited studies, no one has made an overall assessment of Faulkner's knowledge and use of other literature, and that, within the severe limits of a single lecture, is what I propose to attempt here. It will be neither practicable nor desirable to present all the evidence in long lists of borrowings, but I hope that enough can be given to make generalizations convincing. Simply stated, then, we will be trying to find out what Faulkner read and remembered and how he used this material in his own work.

Offhand, this seems to be a simple, straightforward job. But anyone who thinks that any serious scholarly investigation is simple does not really understand it, and in an undertaking of this sort the problems are at least as interesting as the answers, and sometimes more illuminating. For that reason, I shall give them a good deal of attention.

In the extensive but spotty studies of Faulkner's knowledge and use of literature the concentration has been on his earlier work both because it is more derivative and because the borrowings are more obvious, but even here much remains to be done, and what a scholar finds often depends on where he decides to look. To take a simple example, Noel Polk's Introduction to Faulkner's play *The Marionettes*[1] does a good job of studying its sources in Wilde, Eliot, French poets, and the general *fin de siècle* literature of the *femme fatale*. But it completely misses the connection with the very different submissive and decorative women of the Pre-Raphaelites. Yet the borrowings from Rossetti's "The Blessed Damozel" are unmistakable. Rossetti's poem begins:

> The blessed damozel leaned out
> From the gold bar of heaven;
> Her eyes were deeper than the depth
> Of waters stilled at even.

Faulkner's heroine's "eyes are like pools in the depth of a forest at night" (44–45). Rossetti says that

> Her hair, that lay upon her back
> Was yellow like ripe corn. (ll. 12–13)

Faulkner tells us that "Her long fair hair hangs down" (32) and (translating from British to American), "her hair is like the sun upon a field of wheat" (44). Rossetti surmises that

> her bosom must have made
> The bar she leaned on warm, (ll. 45–46)

and in Faulkner "She leans her breast upon the balustrade" (32).

The next problem in a study of this sort is Faulkner's own unreliability. By now, I suppose everyone interested in him is well aware of what we may euphemistically call the inaccuracy of his claims to have been a fighter pilot in the First World War and a rum-runner not long afterward. But many may not know that these misrepresentations are not exceptions. They follow the rule, which is that no statement of Faulkner about himself can be believed without some sort of independent evidence to support it. This rule applies to the large body of interviews and class conferences in which he tells us a great deal about his reading, his literary tastes, and his critical views.[2] But a close study of these sources shows how utterly unreliable they are. Two examples, out of a great many, will make this point clear.

In an interview in French in the fall of 1955, when asked if he liked the theater, Faulkner replied, "I have been there five times in my life, to see *Ben Hur*, *Hamlet*, which I have seen three times, and *A Midsummer Night's Dream*" (*LiG*, 235; my translation). Only about two and a half years later he answered a similar question by saying, "I can count on my thumbs the plays I've seen in my life, and that's—one is *Ben Hur*, the other is—was *East Lynne*" (*FiU*, 285). We can count on it that he really did see *Ben Hur* because he goes on about the fact that it had a camel in it, and in a short story[3] he once wrote that country wagons on dusty roads had "a quality profound and dramatic, like the painted barge which they hauled across the stage in *Ben Hur*." But what else can we believe from these two conflicting statements?

In another interview, this one in 1952, while talking about French influences on his work, Faulkner said flatly, "I know neither Sartre nor Camus" (*LiG*, 72). Five years later, in Virginia, he discussed in convincing detail the reasons for Camus's superiority over Sartre (*FiU*, 161, 281–82). So far, we can think that everything is clear and that between 1952 and 1957 Faulkner had read Sartre and Camus. But wait. In another of the conferences at Virginia he said, "I haven't read a coeval book in about fifteen years" (*FiU*, 12–13), and once again we are left baffled.

I suppose Faulkner thought that the concerns of scholarship simply don't matter, just as I think that it doesn't in the least matter how many whacks it takes a golfer to knock a little ball into a hole in the ground. Or he may have been deliberately baiting his tormentors. Or perhaps both. At any rate, he was unpenitently aware of his own unreliability. When an interviewer once tried to embarrass Faulkner by pointing out that he had just contradicted something that he had said in another interview a year earlier, he chuckled and answered, "I'm liable to say anything on these occasions, and often contradict myself" (*LiG*, 276). There, at last, is a totally reliable statement made by Faulkner in an interview.

The Faulkners had a long family tradition of reading. In spite of his almost total lack of formal schooling and his busy and turbulent life, the Old Colonel, William's great-grandfather, was a really well-read man.[4] The grandfather continued the tradition, at least to the extent of reading through the whole of

Dumas every year with young William (*LiG*, 17). His father's reading was apparently similar, but the real point is that Faulkner grew up in an atmosphere of books and reading. When we begin to look into his reading in detail, Joseph Blotner's catalogue of Faulkner's library at the time of his death,[5] with its appendix of Phil Stone's book orders, is invaluable, as long as we remember that no one has read all the books in his library and everyone has read many books that he does not own.

On this matter of what books were available to Faulkner, however, the scholarly world is almost always guilty of an incredible omission. During the formative years of his reading and early writing he lived within a leisurely four-and-a-half minute stroll—I clocked it yesterday—of the University of Mississippi library, yet in practically all the discussions of whether and where Faulkner might have seen a book, or whether Phil Stone might have had a copy, that basic fact is simply ignored. Certainly the Ole Miss library about 1920 was not one of the world's finest, but its holdings were far better than those in the private possession of anyone in the area, or in practically any other. Like most university libraries, it did not usually get the very latest thing while it was still a sensation in cocktail-party chatter—and Phil Stone went in strongly for that sort of thing. But from my own extensive use of this library in the twenties, I can testify that for a young man with a serious interest in literature it was an almost inexhaustible resource.

Another source of books and knowledge which has been largely ignored is Eric Dawson. Blotner mentions him briefly as having taught French at the University, staged French plays there, given an inscribed copy of his book on Henry Becque to Faulkner, and being the guest of honor at a performance of Becque in Paris in 1924.[6] Ilse Lind, the only other Faulkner scholar I know of who pays any attention to Dawson, remarks that "during the years . . . while he and Faulkner were acquainted, Dawson was steeped in the controversies surrounding the French classical, naturalistic, and art theater."[7] This is correct, but for our purposes it calls for some elaboration. Dawson wrote his *Henry Becque, sa vie et son théâtre* (Paris, 1923) as a dissertation for the Sorbonne, but he had some sort of altercation with his academic directors, published the work without their *imprimatur*, and hence did not take his doctorate. Becque, who died in 1899, was a leading naturalistic dramatist and hence not on the symbolist side, but his career coincided with the apogee of Symbolism, and hence Dawson, during his several years of research in Paris, was thoroughly immersed in Symbolism and the entire Parisian literary life and theory of the period. It would be conservative to say that Dawson knew a thousand times as much about the French Symbolists as Phil Stone. Considering the fact of his presence at Ole Miss off and on since 1913, what are we to make of Carvel Collins's statement about "Faulkner's importing to the Mississippi campus . . . the works of French symbolists?"[8]

Another possible source of books and literary information was my father, who was for some forty years Head of the Department of Modern Languages. He discussed literary matters with Faulkner from time to time, and when *The Sound and the Fury* appeared, Faulkner gave him an inscribed copy.[9] His taste was romantic and his god in French literature was Victor Hugo—but remember that when Paul Valéry, himself a great poet and a protégé of Mallarmé, was asked who was the greatest French poet, he replied, "Victor Hugo—alas!" My father was an enthusiastic advocate of the plays of the principal Symbolist dramatist,[10] Maeterlinck, especially the short ones like *Les Aveugles*, *L'Intruse*, and *La Mort de Tintagiles*. Though I have found no specific borrowings, I am convinced that the atmosphere and tone of these plays contributed to Faulkner's *The Marionettes*.

The statement that there are no specific borrowings immediately raises another question. Just what is a specific borrowing, and how can it be identified? If one character in a novel meets another on the street and says "Good morning," that fact is, of course, no indication of borrowing from or familiarity with another novel in which the same obvious thing happens. No one would go quite that far, but I have seen things that approach it within a recognizable distance. Not long ago I ran into a note saying that a statement somewhere in Faulkner to the effect that writers tell lies was borrowed from a similar observation—with no verbal echoes—by either Sherwood Anderson or Joseph Hergesheimer. But it is obvious to any thinking person that poems and novels are not statements of historical fact, and this observation is not only obvious, but has a long and well-known tradition going back at least to Plato, who regretfully banished the poets from his ideal republic because they told lies.

A case like this brings up another consideration. There are a great many notions and clichés which float in the intellectual atmosphere like car-exhaust, without being referred to their individual sources. Faulkner's much-debated knowledge of Freud falls into this category. In fact, we now have a useful term for this sort of vague, floating knowledge. In his book on *Music, the Arts, and Ideas*,[11] Leonard B. Meyer, writing about theories of indeterminacy and stochastic principles in some contemporary composers, adds this footnote: "It should be noted that such 'composer-theorists' need not have actually read (let alone understood) the writings of Einstein, Heisenberg, *et al.* They may merely have acquired what one of my students aptly labeled 'cultural scuttlebut.'" We are all familiar with the tags of cultural scuttlebut in the arts, especially as they are proudly exhibited by journalists. Shakespeare: "to be or not to be"—Beethoven:
—Whistler: had a mother—Don Juan: chased women—Don Quixote: tilted at windmills, whatever that means. I recently noticed one journalist saying that the good Don tilted *with* windmills, and another, apparently taking the windmills for some form of pinball machines, said simply that he tilted windmills.

On a somewhat higher level, though, the existence of cultural scuttlebut creates some real problems. A couple of examples will show how. In his *Tenth Satire* (l. 81) Juvenal says that the Roman public has let all its responsibilities slide and now wants only two things: *panem et circenses*. In *The Mansion* (23), Faulkner paraphrases this famous phrase as "cake and excitement," and he uses it in its traditional English form of "bread and circuses" once in *The Hamlet* (200) and twice in *A Fable* (242, 349). Do these four uses of Juvenal prove that Faulkner read him? I don't think so. Probably not one in a hundred of the people who quote this phrase has ever seen it in its original context, or knows its source. I would put the odds on Faulkner's having read some of Juvenal at about fifty-fifty, but his use of this phrase would not enter into my handicapping at all. The gladiatorial combats of imperial Rome are the basis of our next example too. In *Childe Harold's Pilgrimage,* in his account of the Coliseum, Byron describes a statue at that time assumed to be a dying gladiator, but now thought to be a dying Gaul. He tells us that the man's last thoughts were not on the screaming crowd,

> But where his rude hut by the Danube lay,
> *There* were his young barbarians at play,
> *There* was their Dacian mother—he, their sire,
> Butcher'd to make a Roman holiday.   (IV, cxli)

Faulkner uses the expression "[a] Roman holiday" six times,[12] and in this case I feel sure that he did know it in its context and knew its source. For one thing, he always uses it in Byron's sense, to designate a morbid or vicious sort of thrill-seeking. A person who had merely picked up the phrase would be likely to apply it to something like, say, a Mardi-Gras parade, but Faulkner never does. Furthermore, he quotes Byron aptly and by name elsewhere, as will be seen later. Finally, it is inherently far more likely that he would read *Childe Harold's Pilgrimage* than Juvenal's *Tenth Satire*. Hence I have no hesitation in placing the phrases "bread and circuses" and "a Roman holiday," as Faulkner uses them, in different categories.

We can replace high probability with absolute certainty in the case of a third phrase, the "tomorrow and tomorrow and tomorrow" of Macbeth's last soliloquy (V, iv, 19). There is no need to list Faulkner's at least fifteen uses or adaptations of it. He uses several other phrases from this speech, and at the University of

Virginia he confirmed the fact that it is the source of the title of *The Sound and the Fury*, and added, "There must have been a dozen books titled from that speech. I think I had the best one" (*FiU*, 197). Even if "tomorrow and tomorrow and tomorrow" were a standard phrase like "bread and circuses"—which it is not—we would still be certain that Faulkner's use of it constitutes a deliberate literary borrowing.

The more distinctive a phrase is, of course, the less likely it is that its repetition is merely a random accident. In "Burbank with a Baedeker," T. S. Eliot referred to "defunctive music under sea." When Faulkner, in "Nympholepsy," refers twice (once near the beginning and once near the end) to "a girl like defunctive music" (*US*, 331, 336), we would have no hesitation in assigning the phrase to its source in Eliot—were it not for the fact that Shakespeare used "defunctive music" in "The Phoenix and the Turtle" (l. 14), and Faulkner shows us Horace Benbow running together in his mind two phrases from this difficult poem in *Flags in the Dust* (347).

Even a single word can be definitive if it is distinctive enough. In "Whispers of Immorality," Eliot tells us:

> Grishkin is nice: her Russian eye
> Is underlined for emphasis;
> Uncorseted, her friendly bust
> Gives promise of pneumatic bliss.

This brilliant transfer of the word *pneumatic* from the technological sphere to the erotic hemispheres is striking enough to be memorable. Thus when Faulkner describes the tall convict's girl in *The Wild Palms* (339) as "smelling of scent and soft young female flesh, slightly pneumatic," we easily pick up the allusion. It is true that Aldous Huxley, in *Brave New World*, adopted Eliot's word and used it several times,[13] but Faulkner was reading Eliot and borrowing from him long before Huxley's novel was written. He probably knew Huxley's use of *pneumatic* too, but he himself borrowed it from Eliot.

Another problem in the study of Faulkner's literary allusions and quotations is to identify them, not in the sense of finding out where they come from, but in the sense of knowing whether some phrases and passages are or are not quotations. Characters like Quentin Compson and Horace Benbow present particular difficulties. Though they are very different characters, both of them are romantic, literary, and verbal in their general orientation. They tend to have phrases running through their minds like obsessive tunes. Sometimes these are quotations, but sometimes they are phrases of their own invention, and it is very difficult to make the distinction unless one knows or can discover an external source. To give one example for each of these characters, Quentin, in his monologue in *The Sound and the Fury,* thrice uses the phrase "found not death at the salt lick(s)" (117, and twice on 126). The connection with French Lick, where Mrs. Compson had taken Caddy to find her a husband, is obvious. But did this connection call up a quotation in Quentin's mind which then haunted him, or did it lead him to create the haunting phrase? Unless we can find a source, I suppose we should assume that the expression is Quentin's, but we cannot be sure.

Horace Benbow is even more given to this sort of thing. In *Flags in the Dust* the phrase "Thou wast happier in thy cage, happier?" occurs six times within a space of eight pages (340–47): three times in the full form, once as "In thy cage, happier?" and twice simply as "Thou wast happier." Again, we do not know whether the obsessive refrain is a quotation or not. If anyone knows a source for it, he should certainly come forward with it.

Every writer who writes about artists of any sort has the problem of making their creations believable. Thomas Mann, writing the life of a fictional avant-garde composer in *Doktor Faustus,* knew that his own musical knowledge was inadequate and called in the musicologist Theodor Adorno as a consultant; and between them they created some interesting and powerful compositions—even though the works do not actually exist. The writer who deals with poets is almost compelled to write some poetry for them. All this is routine and hardly concerns us here. But

Faulkner's case presents special problems, for on a number of occasions in his fiction he quotes from or alludes to his own independently written poetry. A convenient example is a passage in *Soldiers' Pay* which occurs three times, with slight changes: "evening, like a ship with twilight-colored sails, dreamed on down the world" (291, 292, 294). This is taken from poem number XXXIV of *A Green Bough*, which begins:

> The ship of night, with twilightcolored sails
> Dreamed down the golden river of the west.[14]

This sort of self-quotation may strike some as a bit devious, but what concerns us here is the fact that Faulkner's poetry is itself highly derivative, and hence when a phrase in the fiction turns out to come from the poetry, we still cannot be sure that it is not a literary quotation or allusion in the ordinary sense. A fine example is the description of a frustrated man as chewing (or gnawing) his bitter thumbs. Faulkner uses this something like a dozen times in his fiction, all the way from *Flags in the Dust* to *The Mansion*. In one case he even has Ratliff refer to "that bitter thumb the poets say ever man once in his life has got to gnaw at" (*Mansion*, 135). But the expression goes back to Faulkner's literary beginnings in his poetry. In *Helen: A Courtship*,[15] a poem dated June 1925 contains the phrase "to remain/ And taste his bitter thumbs"; and poem XXXII of *A Green Bough* tells us that "abelard evaporates/the brow of time, and paris/tastes his bitter thumbs" (55). Are we to conclude that "the poets" cited by Ratliff are simply William Faulkner, or do these poems borrow the phrase from somewhere else? I wish I knew.

There is one really astonishing example of this sort of thing. One of Faulkner's favorite poems was Edward Fitzgerald's translation of Omar Khayyam. The tale of the planted money and the sale of the Old Frenchman Place, which, in its final form, was incorporated into *The Hamlet*, appears in an early draft with the title "Omar's Eighteenth Quatrain," and another version, entitled "Lizards in Jamshyd's Courtyard," was published in *The*

Saturday Evening Post in 1932.[16] This eighteenth quatrain (in the later editions of the poem) reads:

> They say the Lion and the Lizard keep
> The Courts where Jamshyd gloried and drank deep;
>   And Bahrám, that great Hunter—the wild Ass
> Stamps o'er his head, but cannot break his sleep.

Faulkner echoes phrases from the *Rubáiyát* frequently: "and their mouths are stopt with dust" (*Mosq.*, 26); "that inverted Bowl they call the Sky" (*US*, 469); "this battered Caravanserai/ Whose portals are alternate Night and Day." In *Absalom, Absalom!* he combines these last two when he speaks of "the little lost island beneath its down-cupped bowl of alternating day and night" (253). In one stanza, Omar describes mankind as

> But helpless Pieces of the Game He plays
> Upon the Checker-board of Nights and Days;
>   Hither and thither moves, and checks, and slays,
> And one by one back in the Closet lays.

Faulkner develops this metaphor of the Player and his pieces in two important passages, one at the end of *Flags in the Dust* (369–70) and the other in the account of Percy Grimm's pursuit of Joe Christmas in *Light in August* (436–37).[17] In *Soldiers' Pay* Januarius Jones has the *Rubáiyát* running through his mind and quotes two stanzas of it to himself (314–15). Then a third stanza follows:

> As autumn and the moon of death draw nigh
> The sad long days of summer herein lie
> And she too warm in sorrow 'neath the trees
> Turns to night and weeps and longs to die.

This stanza does not occur in any of Fitzgerald's five versions of his translation, nor does it correspond to anything in any of Omar's quatrains that Fitzgerald does not use. It is actually the third stanza of an unpublished poem by Faulkner, entitled "Adolescence,"[18] written in imitation of Fitzgerald's Omar though without Fitzgerald's metrical competence. What Faulkner did here was to take a stanza of his own fake Omar Khayyam and run it into *Soldiers' Pay* alongside two genuine ones—an admirably sneaky trick. I can only surmise that he was setting a deliberate trap for learned commentators, much as John Peale Bishop did in his acrostic sonnet.[19]

In general, Faulkner is quite uninhibited in his literary borrowing. He doubtless knew and endorsed Kipling's creed on this subject:

> When 'Omer smote 'is bloomin lyre
> He'd 'eard men sing by land an' sea;
> An' what he thought 'e might require,
> 'E went an' took—the same as me![20]

In fact, his own statement on this matter is even more ruthlessly amusing. "The writer's only responsibility is to his art. He will be completely ruthless if he is a good one. . . . If a writer has to rob his mother, he will not hesitate; the *Ode on a Grecian Urn* is worth any number of old ladies" (*LiG*, 239). When asked what constitutes the best training for a writer, he replied, "Read, read, read. Read everything—trash, classics, good and bad, and see how they do it. . . . Read! You'll absorb it" (*LiG*, 53). There is no reason to question the sincerity of these statements, for the simple reason that Faulkner himself acted on them.

We academics need to be constantly reminded that Faulkner was not a scholar. Since we admire him and admire scholarship—especially our own—we tend to try to make him one. But he had no such pretensions and habitually made a clear and accurate distinction between the writer and what he calls the "literary man"—a term which apparently includes both the man of letters and the scholar (*FiU*, 23, 150). It is very dangerous to make assumptions about what he must have known or could not have known since, like most largely self-educated men, he can astonish us by both what he knows and what he does not know. He frequently butchers Latin phrases and quotations, and when asked a question about Aristotle's *Poetics* he flounders helplessly (*FiU*, 51).[21] But these are matters for scholars. In *The Mansion* he has Chick Mallison refer to "one of the old Victorian headhunting mamas . . . in Fielding or Dickens or Smollett" (218). This is no more to be read as a reflection on Chick's chronology than the impossible repeated phrase *reducto absurdum* (*S&F*, 93, 105, 111) is a reflection on Mr. Compson's or Quentin's Latinity. In both cases Faulkner himself simply didn't know, didn't care, or both. He took from Fielding and Smollett what he thought he might require—but that did not include comparing their dates with those of Queen Victoria.

We are now in a position—at last—to attempt a general survey of Faulkner's knowledge of literature and use of it in his own writing. Some of what I shall be saying will be founded on demonstrable and documented fact, and some will be informed and responsible conclusions or surmises which are not definitely provable. Though it will be impossible to cite all the evidence or to label every opinion specifically as such, I hope, without constantly laboring the distinction, to make it reasonably apparent in what follows.

Only two books outside the Occidental tradition seem to have really interested Faulkner or meant anything to him, and they are both in the Western tradition by adoption. Enough has already been said about Omar Khayyam's *Rubáiyát*, which was primarily an influence on Faulkner's early work, though he never forgot it. The other is, of course, the Bible, which was important throughout his career. He named the Old Testament as one of his handful of favorite books (*FiU*, 150) and explained the preference by saying that the Old Testament was primarily about people, and the New about ideas, and that he was more interested in people (*LiG*, 12; *FiU*, 167–68). He owned a fourteen-volume edition of the King James version, but, strangely enough, no handy one-volume edition.[22] His thorough knowledge of the Bible is attested by his wide and apt use of it, as shown, for example, by his ability to find a suitable biblical epitaph for John Sartoris (which he later used for his own brother, Dean) and one for Eula Snopes (*Flags*, 364; *Town*, 355).

Much of his knowledge probably goes back to his childhood, when, he tells us, everyone in the family had to recite a verse from the Bible every morning at breakfast (*LiG*, 250).

Essential as the Bible is to Faulkner, we may tend to exaggerate its relative importance because of its privileged position in Faulkner's society. Gavin Stevens can give Linda Snopes a volume of John Donne's poetry (*Town*, 188), but it would be hard to find two other characters in Yoknapatawpha County between whom such a gift could be credibly passed. But the Bible is so much in the air that anyone in the country, religious or not, can use phrases and allusions drawn from it. For example, I have found only one literary allusion in the whole of *As I Lay Dying* which is *not* biblical, and that is Tull's rather unconvincing use of Faulkner's much-used "dying fall," from the fourth line of *Twelfth Night*, to describe the music at Addie's funeral (86).

Occidental literature begins, of course, with Homer, whom Faulkner certainly knew in a general way though apparently in no great detail. He had two copies each of the *Iliad* and the *Odyssey* in the prose translations of Lang, Leaf, and Myers and of Butcher and Lang, respectively, as well as one *Iliad* and two *Odyssey*s in Pope's version. Once or twice he echoes Homeric diction or epithets (*Town*, 192; *CS*, 890), and the yacht in *Mosquitoes* was presumably named for King Alkinoos's daughter Nausikaa in the *Odyssey*. His many references to Helen, of course, could have come from almost anywhere. There is only one really significant Homeric passage for Faulkner, but it constitutes a real problem. It is Agamemnon's account of his own murder, given to Odysseus in Hades (*Odyssey*, XI, 425–31). In the translation of Sir William Maris (London, 1925), this reads:

> But in mine ears
> Most piteous rang the cry of Priam's daughter
> Cassandra, whom the treacherous Clytemnestra
> Slew at my side, while I, as I lay dying
> Upon the sword, raised up my hands to smite her;
> And shamelessly she turned away, and scorned
> To draw my eyelids down or close my mouth.

By rendering a simple present participle as the phrase "as I lay dying," the translator supplied Faulkner's title. But there is a mystery attached to this passage. What is here translated "and shamelessly she," and in other versions by such phrases as "the shameless one" or, in the prose version that Faulkner owned, "and that shameless one," is, in the original, ἡ δὲ κυνῶπις, which can be literally rendered as "but she, dog-eyed." *Dog-eyed* had the standard metaphorical meaning of "shameless," and, as we have seen, is generally so translated. (If I were translating this passage, I would keep something of this metaphor by rendering it "But that bitch. . . .") In the short story "Carcassonne," Faulkner again alludes to this passage in a sort of stream of consciousness: *"where fell where I was King of Kings* [a standard title of Agamemnon] *but the woman with the woman with the dog's eyes to knock my bones together and together"* (*CS*, 898; Faulkner's italics). Where did Faulkner get this? He apparently did not know a word of Greek, unless one counts presumably having to memorize the motto of the Sigma Alpha Epsilon fraternity. This is a good example of how Faulkner can sometimes astonish one by what he does know.

We can sum up Faulkner's relationship to classical antiquity by saying that he had a generally good command of the history and the mythology, but had read very little of the literature, though he may well have read Greek tragedy in his youth as he says he did (*FiU*, 51). Faulkner scholars like to explain the myths he uses by quoting Ovid's *Metamorphoses*, but Faulkner did not own this work nor apparently does he ever mention or allude to Ovid. He seems to be more at home in the Roman Empire than in the Republic or in Greece. I would guess that he read Suetonius's *Lives of the Caesars* and Gibbon's *Decline and Fall of the Roman Empire* (he owned both, and referred to the latter in *Soldiers' Pay*) and that his extensive and accurate references to mythological characters and events were largely gleaned from their frequent use in English literature, probably aided by the old standard reference-work, *Bulfinch's Mythology*, which he owned, and other items in his library like Robert Graves's two books on the emperor Claudius.

Faulkner apparently knew very little of mediaeval literature. Of the six volumes of it which he owned, two involve duplication and another does not count. He had Chaucer's *Canterbury Tales* in a modern English version, and a volume containing the "General Prologue," "Knight's Tale," and "Nun's Priest's Tale" in the original Middle English. He had Dante's *Divine Comedy* in the excellent Carlyle-Wicksteed translation. He had two editions of Fitzgerald's *Rubáiyát* of Omar Khayyam. The sixth book does not count because he could not have read it. It was *Brennunjáls Saga (The Saga of Burnt Njál)* in the original Old Icelandic. I know of only three possible uses of actual mediaeval texts—one doubtful, one not certain, and one sure. The doubtful one, in *A Fable* (83), is *"In Christ is death at end in Adam that began."* It is doubtful because it is an inscription on a bell in Dorothy Sayers's mystery novel *The Nine Taylors*, but the fact that Dorothy Sayers was actually a mediaevalist makes it possible that she drew it from a mediaeval source. It also makes it equally possible that she invented it herself. The allusion which I consider likely describes Houston in *The Hamlet* as living "alone, without companionship" (214). The peculiar, emphatic redundancy reminds me of Arcite in Chaucer's "Knight's Tale" speaking of man's doom of ending in his cold grave, "Allone, withouten any compaignye," especially since this line is picked up and repeated a bit later, in a trivial context, by the drunk Miller (I, 2779 and 3204). I suspect that, consciously or unconsciously, Faulkner was here echoing the Knight and the Miller. The allusion of which we can be sure is Saint Francis of Assisi's "little sister death," which is used in three different works of Faulkner, "The Kid Learns" (in *New Orleans Sketches*), *Mayday*, and *The Sound and the Fury*.[23]

Except possibly for these, Faulkner's mediaeval references are all general. Those to Roland, including a whole poem on the subject (No. XXI of *A Green Bough*) follow the serious legend rather than the fantastic one of the Italian Renaissance epics, but there is nothing to tie them to any specific source. Faulkner's Dante and Beatrice do not go beyond the level of cultural scuttlebut. In general, the same thing goes for his Tristram and Iseult, but I suspect that he drew them primarily from Swinburne's long narrative poem, *Tristram of Lyonesse*. Though I have never seen any mention of it in Faulkner criticism, this is what one would expect. The assumption is bolstered by a couple of pieces of fairly good evidence which I shall not stop over, plus one very strong one. In "Delta Autumn" Uncle Ike makes a striking observation about love: "I think that every man and woman, at the instant when it dont even matter whether they marry or not, I think that whether they marry then or afterward or dont never, at that instant the two of them together were God" (*GDM*, 348). I have seen this idea in only one other place, in Swinburne's poem when, after their first night together, Tristram and Iseult are standing

> hand in amorous hand,
> Soul-satisfied, their eyes made great and bright
> By all the love of all the livelong night;
> With all its hours yet singing in their ears
> No mortal music made of thoughts and tears,
> But such a song, past conscience of man's thought,
> As hearing he grows god and knows it not.[24]

Though Faulkner evidently knew and used little mediaeval literature, he has many references to mediaeval matters—things like monks, ascetics, racks, drawbridges, and even the chastity-belt that Temple Drake imagines for herself in *Sanctuary* (210–11). These references are generally accurate and show a real grasp of mediaeval life and institutions, with none of the smug bigotry of a Mark Twain or a modern journalist to whom *mediaeval* is simply a vague term of abuse. I would hazard a guess that Faulkner's understanding was due to a combination of his own common sense and his reading of responsible historical novelists. He generally uses these references to universalize the limited local world that he ostensibly writes about. When the reporter's mother in *Pylon* is described as having a "fine big bosom like one of the walled impervious towns of the Middle Ages whose origin antedates writing, which have been taken and retaken in uncountable fierce assaults which overran them in the brief fury of a moment and vanished, leaving no trace" (57), the passage is not only funny, with its implied pun on *breastworks*, but is also a fine conceit in the best metaphysical tradition, implying the essential unity of the universe by establishing the similarity of things which are superficially unrelated. More obviously, when the narrator of *The Reivers* comments, "If we crossed the Rubicon when we crossed the Iron Bridge into another country, when we conquered Hell Creek we locked the portcullis and set the bridge on fire" (93), he is indicating that, slight and comical as the action of the novel is, the problems and issues are the great, timeless ones of human life. I suspect that *Don Quixote*, by its constant juxtaposition of the fantasy mediaeval world of the romances of chivalry and the prosaic everyday world of contemporary Spain, contributed a great deal to this technique.

This brings us to the Renaissance and to Cervantes and Shakespeare, the earliest of the small group of writers that Faulkner constantly cited as his favorites and, by implication at least, those most important to him as a writer. The others of this pantheon are Balzac, Dostoevsky, and Conrad. Close to them, but apparently not quite on the same level, are a number of others, notably Flaubert, Dickens, and Tolstoi. Since these writers are known to everyone seriously interested in Faulkner and it would be quite impossible to treat them adequately here, we will have to be satisfied with a few general remarks about them as a group. First of all, we can trust Faulkner's statements that he constantly read and reread some of the books of this group because his references to them (often in detail), allusions to their work, and uses of it in his own novels prove his well-informed respect for them. As he sometimes pointed out, he had favorite books rather than favorite authors, and we need not assume that he had read everything written by his favorites. For example, there is no reason to think that he knew anything of

Cervantes except *Don Quixote*—but we can dismiss this limitation with Dryden's remark on the *Canterbury Tales:* "'Tis sufficient to say, according to the proverb, that here is God's plenty."[25] Though there have been plenty of casual remarks, articles, and brief discussions, we need really thorough investigations of Faulkner's relationship to each of these men, but the only such work that I know is Jean Weisgerber's admirable study of Faulkner and Dostoevsky.[26]

Returning to the Renaissance—which is, of course, the beginning of the modern period—we can make a general statement that Faulkner was at home and well-read in literature in English from about 1590 on. Except for Rabelais, what he knew of French literature is largely confined to the period beginning about 1830, and it is a striking fact that the great Age of Louis XIV seems to have been a literary blank for him. Of the English writers of the Renaissance, the most important to him after Shakespeare seem to have been Marlowe (who is apparently the basis for Faulkner's Faustian references), Ben Jonson and the other lyricists of his tribe, Donne, and Milton. I rather suspect that Spenser was more a name to be dropped than a poet to be read. He may have been among the many poets whom Faulkner knew only by a few pieces in anthologies like *The Oxford Book of English Verse*, which was in his library.

In the Neo-Classical Period, it is not surprising that Dryden and Pope seem to have meant nothing to Faulkner, for during his early years the general conception of poetry was uncompromisingly romantic and Dryden and Pope were often considered to be non-poets who happened to write in mechanical verse. The men of the eighteenth century who loomed large on his horizon were the writers of prose fiction, primarily Swift, Defoe, Smollett, and Fielding. The one exception is Gray, whose "Elegy" turns up in a number of quotations and allusions beyond the possibility of mere cultural scuttlebut.

In the nineteenth century it becomes impossible even to mention all the writers who were important to Faulkner. Here we find two of his literary gods, Balzac and Dostoevsky, and two major works of another, Conrad, as well as a number of his demigods like Dickens and Flaubert. Here, in England and America, from the beginnings of romanticism to the *fin-de-siècle* decadents, we find the poets who shaped Faulkner's conception of poetry. His devotion to Keats is well known, but he knew all the English romantic poets and drew on them in his own work.

Byron will be a convenient example. Faulkner's use of the "Roman holiday" phrase has already been mentioned, but two out of a considerable number of other allusions are interesting. When "Judge Benbow of Jefferson once said of [Will Varner] that a milder-mannered man never bled a mule or stuffed a ballot box" (*Hamlet*, 5), he was, of course, adapting Byron's description of the old pirate Lambro in *Don Juan* (III, xli): "He was the mildest manner'd man/ That ever scuttled ship or cut a throat."

The other is more elaborate. Suetonius tells us that Caligula once wished that all the citizens of Rome had only one neck. In *Don Juan* Byron plays on this anecdote in his own fashion, adapting it to women:

> I love the sex, and sometimes would reverse
>   The tyrant's wish, "that mankind only had
> One neck, which he with one fell stroke might pierce:"
>   My wish is quite as wide, but not so bad,
> And much more tender on the whole than fierce;
>   It being (not *now*, but only while a lad)
> That womankind had but one rosy mouth,
> To kiss them all at once from North to South. (VI, xxvii)

This stanza so appealed to Faulkner that he rang the changes on it four times. Quentin Compson thinks, "Well, anyway Byron never had his wish, thank God" (*S&F*, 115). A character in *A Fable* simply paraphrases the remark and cites Byron as its source (259). Horace Benbow writes that he used to be sad "that all the spring couldn't be concentrated in one place, like Byron's ladies' mouths" (*Flags*, 339). And in the short story "Divorce in Naples," during a conversation about sex an unliterary bosun on the ship "paraphrased unwitting and with unprintable aptness Byron's epigram about women's mouths" (*CS*, 882).

Faulkner's real knowledge of French literature begins shortly after the great period of English romantic poetry, with Balzac and Gautier. What he knew was primarily the novelists, especially Balzac, Flaubert, and Proust, but quite a number of others too. The question of language must be raised here. Late in his life Faulkner said, "The [foreign] language I read with any ease is French" (*FIU*, 90), and that was probably true: the French that he writes here and there, though far from perfect, is good enough to support his claim. But though he *could* read French, there is no reason to believe that he habitually did so. He owned a two-volume set of Stendhal's major works in French, as well as Proust's *Un Amour de Swann* and Saint-Exupéry's *Le Petit prince*, and that is all the French literature that he owned in the original and may have read in his own library. He did have eight volumes of twentieth-century French poetry, including writers like Apollinaire, Éluard, and Prévert. But these seem to have been gifts to him—and the pages of all of them are uncut.

The case of the French Symbolists is particularly interesting. I am convinced that far too much has been made of them in Faulkner scholarship. It is true that as a beginner he showed a brief interest in them, probably under Eric Dawson's influence, to the extent of lifting a title from Mallarmé and translating— very loosely—four poems of Verlaine. The phrase "Noir(s) sur la lune" in *Soldiers' Pay* (134) is taken from one of these poems, though there is no equivalent for it in Faulkner's version. The one line of Laforgue that he alludes to came to him, in a modified form, through T. S. Eliot. He did not own, either in French or in translation, a single work of any French symbolist. His statement, "I know just a little of the French poets, but I know very little of any poetry outside of English" (*LiG*, 119) should be taken as an honest statement of fact. The question of Faulkner's knowledge of the French Symbolists has been confused by American scholars who are not at home in French literature and call almost anyone who wrote any sort of literature in French between about 1830 and 1910 a symbolist, including men like Gautier, Flaubert, and Baudelaire.[27]

The later nineteenth century in British and American literature and the early twentieth form a single unit, as far as Faulkner is concerned, with the early twentieth extending to about 1930. Faulkner did not consistently read things written after this date, and the influence of such works as he did read is negligible. But his reading from about 1850 to 1930 was vast, though sporadic, and all that can be done here is to review the highlights. For Faulkner the main poets of this period were clearly Swinburne, Housman, and Eliot, all of whom influenced him profoundly. The range of other poets extends from Dante Gabriel Rossetti to Djuna Barnes, including notably Tennyson, Browning, Whitman, Pound, and Yeats. In fiction, in addition to Dickens, Dostoevsky, and Conrad, Faulkner's reading was wide, but the primary influence, except for the problematical Joyce, came from two minor figures, Sherwood Anderson and James Branch Cabell.

So far, we have been concerned with Faulkner's reading and with his primarily verbal borrowings and allusions. Cabell supplies a convenient additional example in the Ghost of King Smoit, who tells Jurgen, "I was getting on in life, and had grown tired of killing people" (*Jurgen*, 101). Faulkner used this speech when, in *The Unvanquished*, he had the Old Colonel say, "I am tired of killing men" (266). But this is more than a borrowing of a phrase: it is the adoption of a theme. Themes, characters, situations, and events can be borrowed or adapted as well as phrases, but these influences are usually more tenuous and open to question. Here, too, Cabell's *Jurgen* can supply us with a good illustration. Before following the wraith of his wife into a cave of diabolical repute, Jurgen must take off a cross he is wearing and hang it on a bush (7). Similarly, before the boy in *Go Down, Moses* can see the bear, he must not only abandon his gun, but must hang his watch and compass on a bush and leave them (209). It seems very likely that Faulkner is following Cabell in the episode, but absolute proof is impossible.

Weisgerber gives a number of examples of this sort of thing in his work on Faulkner and Dostoevsky. A few other instances, from various sources, will further illustrate the idea.

In *The Sound and the Fury*, Quentin Compson makes the famous gesture of breaking the crystal of his watch, twisting off the hands, and leaving "the blank dial with little wheels clicking and clicking behind it, not knowing any better" (99). In James Thomson's *The City of Dreadful Night*—the most total expression of despair that I know anywhere in literature—a man was asked how life could go on without faith or love or hope.

> He answered coldly, "Take a watch, erase
> The signs and figures of the circling hours,
>   Detach the hands, remove the dial-face;
> The works proceed until run down, although
> Bereft of purpose, void of use, still go." (ll. 158–62)

The identity in Thomson and Faulkner of both the idea and the metaphor that expresses it is, to say the least, striking.

In the thirteenth chapter of Zola's *Nana*, the courtesan-heroine, in an orgy of destruction, smashes all the expensive presents that her suitors have brought her for her birthday. Though the circumstances are not identical, the resemblance to the scene in *Sanctuary* (218) in which Temple Drake hurls all her expensive gifts from Popeye into the corner seems too strong to be accidental. So does the similarity between Lord Steyne in Thackeray's *Vanity Fair* (Chapter XLVII, especially) maneuvering and bullying his womenfolk into sponsoring Becky Sharp socially, and Gavin Stevens in *The Town* doing the same thing for Linda Snopes.

So far we have been talking about serious adult literature, but Faulkner advised the young writer to "read everything—trash, classics, good and bad." It is worth while to show that he took his own advice and found it useful. Two examples will show his reading and use of children's literature. In Kipling's *Just So Stories*, the tale of "The Cat That Walked by Himself" develops the theme of the aloof independence of the feline character with the repeated "I am the cat that walks by himself, and all places are alike to me." In his talks at West Point Faulkner applies this to himself,[28] and he used it once in *Soldiers' Pay* (248), twice in *Absalom, Absalom!* (315, 318), and, most memorably, in *Light in August*, where, in describing the wanderings of Joe Christmas, he wrote, "But the street ran on: catlike, one place was the same as another to him" (213).

In Frances Hodgson Burnett's *The Secret Garden* (1911) there is an ugly, red-headed, engaging boy from the Yorkshire moors named Dickon. He is quiet and self-assured, and is the one who explains things to the other children and is generally in charge. Faulkner's Maurice, in *The Wishing Tree,* has "a thin, ugly face and hair so red that it made a glow in the room" (6), and is generally like Dickon in both character and function. The similarity is reinforced by the fact that both the stories are children's books.

These books are not "trash" or "bad" if taken on their own terms, and I don't believe that Faulkner meant them to be so considered. The trash and bad books that he was referring to were doubtless the perennial best-seller types that he described in *Knight's Gambit:* "women who were always ladies and men who were always brave, moving in a sort of immortal moonlight without anguish and with no pain from birth without foulment to death without carrion, so that you too could weep with them without having to suffer or grieve, exult with them without having to conquer or triumph" (143). Faulkner read and used these books too. He took the simile about "pipes blown drowsily by an idiot boy" (*Sart.,* 45) from *The House of Luck,* a blood-and-thunder novel by one Harris Dickson culminating in the historical revolt of the citizens of Vicksburg against the river-boat gamblers and other criminals who were terrorizing the town.[29]

When Dr. Martino, at the beginning of Faulkner's short story of that name, refers to his girl, "a kid born and bred in a Mississippi swamp" as "my swamp angel" (*CS*, 565), he is quoting Gene Stratton Porter's once-popular *Freckles,* whose unnamed heroine is regularly called "my/the Angel" and is eight times formally called "The Swamp Angel." This term is used twice more in *A Girl of the Limberlost,* a sort of loose sequel in which she is a minor character and in which the heroine shares with the Sartoris family's cook the rare name Elnora.[30] This heroine's mother's remark that "the Almighty is bound to be a gentleman" is echoed four times in Faulkner's work, in the short story "The Leg," (CS, 838), in *The Sound and the Fury* (112), in *Sanctuary* (273), and in *The Mansion* (131).

Owen Wister wrote the first—and probably the best—Western, *The Virginian,* in 1902. At the Faulkner and Yoknapatawpha Conference five years ago, Professor James Meriwether pointed out the fact that Faulkner's tall tale of Al Jackson in *Mosquitoes* (276–81) is obviously indebted to a similar tall tale in *The Virginian.* Nor was this the only Western of Wister's that Faulkner knew and used. In *The Wild Palms,* while Harry Wilbourne sat by the dying Charlotte, "He was trying to remember something out of a book, years ago, of Owen Wister's, the whore in the pink ball dress who drank the laudanum and the cowboys taking turns walking her up and down the floor keeping her on her feet, keeping her alive" (287).

This scene occurs towards the end of Wister's *Lin McLean.*[31] This is enough on these matters for the present, and possibly too much. I feel a bit guilty about subjecting Faulkner to this sort of investigation here on his home ground, but it is barely possible that his interest in the detective story might give him a sneaking sort of sympathy with the undertaking.

NOTES

1. Charlottesville: University Press of Virginia, 1977. To avoid excessive documentation, I have given references where possible by chapters, line or stanza numbers, etc., rather than page numbers, so that various editions and anthologies can be used. Citations of Faulkner's works refer to the Random House hard-cover editions unless otherwise indicated. (Many paperback editions have the same pagination.) Titles are given in full unless the abbreviations are self-explanatory, and citations are run into the text as far as possible.

2. This material is conveniently accessible in two collections: *Lion in the Garden: Interviews with William Faulkner, 1926–1962,* ed. James B. Meriwether and Michael Millgate (New York, 1968); and *Faulkner in the University: Class Conferences at the*

University of Virginia, 1957–1958, ed. Frederick L. Gwynn and Joseph L. Blotner (New York, 1965). These volumes will be cited under the abbreviations of *LiG* and *FiU*, respectively.

3. *Uncollected Stories of William Faulkner*—henceforth abbreviated as *US*—(New York, n. d.), 135.

4. See my article, "Colonel Falkner as General Reader: The White Rose of Memphis," *Mississippi Quarterly*, 30 (1977), 585–95.

5. *William Faulkner's Library—A Catalogue* (Charlottesville: University Press of Virginia, 1964).

6. Joseph Blotner, *Faulkner: A Biography* (New York: Random House, 1974), 352, 361.

7. Ilse Dusoir Lind, "Faulkner's Uses of Poetic Drama," in *Faulkner, Modernism, and Film*, ed. Evans Harrington and Ann J. Abadie (Jackson: University Press of Mississippi, 1979), 68–69. The whole article is valuable for the intellectual and literary milieu of Faulkner's early development.

8. *William Faulkner: Early Prose and Poetry*, ed. Carvel Collins (Boston: Little, Brown and Company, 1962), 13.

9. This copy is now in the William Faulkner Collection of Louis Daniel Brodsky.

10. For the connection between Maeterlinck and Mallarmé see Haskell M. Block, *Mallarmé and the Symbolist Drama* (Detroit, 1963), 107–16.

11. Chicago, 1967, p. 254, note 26.

12. *LiA*, 273; *Abs.*, 57; *Unv.*, 269; *Ham.*, 102, 200; *FiU*, 163. It is interesting to note that Faulkner wrote a poem entitled "Dying Gladiator." See *Early Prose and Poetry* (note 8, above), 113.

13. Harper's Modern Classics ed., e.g., 51, 56, 109.

14. *The Marble Faun and A Green Bough* (New York, n.d.), 57.

15. *Helen: A Courtship* and *Mississippi Poems*, Introductory Essays by Carvel Collins and Joseph Blotner (New Orleans and Oxford: Tulane University and Yoknapatawpha Press, 1981), 114. This poem can also be found in *Early Prose and Poetry* (see note 8), 119, where it is entitled "The Faun."

16. *US*, notes, 686–87.

17. The fact that James Branch Cabell also developed this metaphor in *Jurgen: A Comedy of Justice* (New York, 1919), 280–81, would have reinforced it for Faulkner.

18. This poem is in the Alderman Library of the University of Virginia. See Margaret J. Yonce, "*Soldiers' Pay*: A Critical Study of William Faulkner's First Novel" (unpublished dissertation, University of South Carolina, 1970), 265.

19. Bishop, *Collected Poems* (New York, 1948), 71–72.

20. Introduction to the "Barrack Room Ballads" in *The Seven Seas*.

21. But it is interesting to note that Mark Frost's idea of being "consistently inconsistent" (*Mosq.*, 182) echoes Aristotle's *Poetics*, XV, 6.

22. All statements about Faulkner's ownership of books refer to the time of his death and are based on Blotner's catalogue of his library (see note 5). Since this catalogue is well organized and indexed, there is no need for page references. As for books that Faulkner did not own, the citation of pages on which something does *not* occur would be a rather tempting apotheosis of pedantry.

23. Pp. 167, 87, and 94, respectively. St. Francis's phrase comes from his "Laudes Creaturarum" (*Oxford Book of Italian Verse*, Poem No. 1). It reads "sora nostra morte corporale." It must have come to Faulkner, directly or indirectly, through a modern Italian version, since St. Francis's *sora* is regularly replaced by the diminutive *sorella* ("little sister") in modern Italian.

24. Swinburne, *Tristram of Lyonesse*, II ("The Queen's Pleasance"), 15–22.

25. "Preface to the Fables," *Essays of John Dryden*, ed. W. P. Ker (Oxford, 1926), II, 262.

26. *Faulkner et Dostoïevski: confluences et influences* (Brussels and Paris, 1968). Université Libre de Bruxelles, Travaux de la Faculté de Philosophie et Lettres, XXXIX.

27. Cf. Noel Polk's introduction to Faulkner's *The Marionettes*, xi.

28. *Faulkner at West Point*, ed. Joseph L. Fant and Robert Ashley (New York, 1964), 113.

29. See my note, "Faulkner's Idiot Boy: The Source of a Simile in Sartoris," *American Literature*, 44 (1972), 474–76.

30. *Freckles* (New York, 1904), "The Characters" (a list preceding the novel) and 129, 189, 205, 264, 404, 408, and 426. *A Girl of the Limberlost* (New York, 1909), 210, 312. The remark about God is on 237.

31. I am indebted to Professor Meriwether for the identification of *Lin McLean* as the book here referred to.

Faulkner's Spanish Voice/s

MYRIAM DÍAZ-DIOCARETZ

> ... *he inwardly did pray*
> *For power to speak; but still the ruddy tide*
> *Stifled his voice* ...
>
> —Keats, *Isabella*, VI.

If we imagine, for a moment, a "real reader,"[1] that is, the person who buys and reads books; furthermore, if we envision a native Spanish-speaking reader who has no knowledge of the source-language—in this case, American English—and who wants to "know" Faulkner's work, we can ask ourselves, what kind of text is this reader most likely to find? What sort of authorial *voice* does Faulkner have? Does Faulkner have a single voice? or several?

In order to attempt to answer these questions, even if partially, I should begin with an explanation of my title which seems safely ambiguous; yet, as the promise of my text, "Faulkner's Spanish Voice/s" contains some presuppositions that serve as working hypotheses. To begin with, Faulkner has a voice in Spanish which differs considerably from his voice in English by the very fact that his voice exists in a national literature and a standard literary language different from his own.[2] Faulkner's Spanish voice—in the composite form I am describing here—belongs to a very heterogeneous community of three main geographical areas: South America, the Caribbean, and Spain. However, it should be remembered that the territory where Faulkner's voice in Spanish may exist is much wider when we take into account the Hispanic readership in a more realistic sense. For example, even within the United States with its large

Spanish speaking population, many readers apprehend Faulkner's work in translation rather than through the original texts.

At the same time, the works of Faulkner that are available in Spanish include translations by writers from different geographical areas: Cuba, Argentina, Mexico, Colombia, Spain, and probably other countries, each with very distinct national literature and norms. Although we can find systemic correspondences in the language used in the translations, these correspondences originate mainly in the Spanish standard literary language itself rather than in Faulkner's voice translated as a unified and euphonic totality. In English we observe Faulkner's changes of technique and rhetoric as he moves from one work to the other. However, the shifts in technical and rhetorical elements in Faulkner's work in translation do not reflect his stylistic development with a great deal of equivalent accuracy. Indeed, the multiplicity of translators and the number of times many of Faulkner's novels have been translated have led me to add the sign of plurality to my title: "Voice/s." It is a plurality that stands in opposition to the idea of unicity of style, of uniqueness of voice as readers of work in translation would naturally assume. This very plurality confirms the subjectivity of language and indicates that each translator performs a different reading of each text; as a consequence each translator produces substantial metamorphic elements in the transfer of the meaning potential of the text by rearranging the original structuring of different levels of signification. These points may seem obvious, but the translator, as coproducer of a work set in preexistence by the author, introduces his/her own textual strategies[3] and this important attitude eventually affects the reader's response.

This study will focus on the role of the translator as reader and coproducer of a literary work and on the most recent translation of *The Sound and the Fury* in Spanish, emphasizing some of the major transformations of the author's voice in the Spanish text.

The translator, as a sort of *omniscient reader*,[4] makes selections that determine a rearrangement and thereby modify significantly the textual design and the interrelations of componential features of the narrative text. Thus, the receptor-language text differs from its source not primarily because of the obligatory elements of the source language, but because of the translator's own decisions in the reading stage that is a vital part of the process of translation. These considerations apply, in other contexts, to Faulkner's voice/s in other languages as well.

In evaluating the translations of Faulkner's work one can see the degree to which the translators either help to introduce innovative solutions—thereby raising the standard of the existing receptor literary culture—or simply render in this receptor culture noninnovative literary transferences. The deviant components these translations propose would also reveal the translator's attempt to reach "virtual perfection,"[5] as in the case of Jorge Luis Borges's interesting equivalents to Faulkner's elongated sentences in his translation of *The Wild Palms*.

For a more accurate account of the status of an author in a foreign national literature, it is also necessary to explore the tension between the aesthetic self-orientation and the communicative function; that is, to determine how this tension is maintained, intensified, deintensified, or avoided in the translation process.

Faulkner in English is textually manifested as a recognizable style and by extension, as a recognizable *voice*. Through his elaborate narrative techniques, Faulkner, the protean experimenter, extends the word to the limits of rhetoric, deeply incorporating himself through his textual strategies into the realm of subjectivity. Whether his experimentation represents a technical achievement, or a "magnificent failure," or the characteristics of a particular style, to the mind and discursivity of the translator these features constitute "problems in translation." Specifically, these problems consist of deciding how and when to enter Faulkner's reality of discourse. Faulkner himself never stopped his search for appropriation of a language that could be his own, to contain and control, and textually assume the linguistic forms akin to his imagination. Language itself represents the very potential of subjectivity, as Emile Benveniste said.[6] Faulkner's own drive towards this eternally possible goal—the dialectic relationship of discourse as the medium of the subjective and Faulkner as a concrete subject to his discourse—drove him incessantly to enact a travesty existing only in and by means of discourse itself; the travesty of his first person, the shifting "I" as subject of his literary work. Following Jan Mukařovský's theory that "the subject is the point from which the structure of a work can be surveyed in its entire complexity and unity,"[7] we find that it is precisely in the *subject* that each translator performs the reconstruction of the fictional text through an interlinguistic movement. The translator gives a new identity to each work, thereby providing unsuspected points from which to interpret and acquire a sense of individuality of Faulkner's work.

For centuries, translators have influenced or delayed the development and progress of Western literature by quietly shaping what we are allowed to read in a given national language. The translator's role is more than an artistic one. It is inevitably linked with the author's "image" and with the influence this author may have or fail to have. Moreover, a translation is not simply a static text to be compared and contrasted with the original merely for the purpose of signaling mistakes or to lament its losses. On the contrary, the receptor-language text is part of the *process* of translation in which the translator as omniscient reader has a decisive function in text-creativity and in the semiotic process involved in the production of an aesthetic discourse.[8] It follows that the translator stands and acts between the source text and the receptor's interpretation—in the reading stage—recreating or initiating a dialogue of languages and cultures. In this way the translator can be even more influential than the critics in determining how an author's work may ultimately be received. In summary, the translator is an omniscient reader who decodes and encodes the source text to be received and interpreted by new receptors whose own language is the one introduced in the new text. Notwithstanding the close interrelation between author, translator, and receptor—or text, translation, and the reading of a translation—very seldom will the writer's mode of experience and work coincide with the mode of experience and work of the translator.

After five decades of criticism of Faulkner's work, we have learned that understanding the structure of the standard literary language of his country and the structure of his works is not enough. The difficulties of Faulkner's language, syntax, and style may be solved or complicated further; alternatives may be expanded or narrowed down; the variants may be multiplied or eliminated. The decisions are eventually determined by the translator's own cultural and ideological presuppositions and purposes. Each translator has the opportunity of heightening or weakening his style, or making him more of the Puritan, the tragedian, the morbid, the existentialist, the heretic, or the diabolic writer.

In Faulkner, as in Dostoevsky, Joyce, and Proust, the aesthetic function predominates in a more distinctive way than in traditional writers. However, to quote Mukařovský again, "a literary work does not exist for people who do not know its language, and it is only imperfectly or not completely accessible even to those who know its language but not as their mother tongue."[9] Therefore, not only the aesthetic effectiveness of a source-language text is at stake, but also its specific communicative function. In translation, communication may take over the primary function of an aesthetic work, thus losing the dramatic, narrative, or poetic impact. This seems to be the case of most translations of Faulkner's work in Spanish.

The *reading* process, the semiotic and aesthetic interaction between text and receptor, happens not only in the translation process, but also in the stage of critical interpretation. It is present even in the ways in which publishers, translators, readers, and critics ignore or emphasize certain translations and their qualities; it is also visible in the well-intentioned decision to correct Faulkner's *mauvaise grammaire*.[10] It can be detected in the area of editorial policies, in which the editor—or the publishing house as an institution that controls an important part of the literary modes of production—determines that dialectal expressions need to be "translated," the spelling and the punctuation "bettered," all for the purpose of the reader's easier understanding of the text in question. Even in the case of intra-lingual translation these conversions are not trivial in themselves. Commenting on the 1931 British edition of *The Sound and the Fury*, James B. Meriwether writes, "English readers might have had more confidence in Faulkner's skill if they had been given a better text by which to judge it."[11] A "better text" would have been Faulkner's own. Any change has a subsequent effect on the artistic arrangement of the textual components such as rhythm, rhetoric, and poetry of discourse, not to mention the semantic shiftings that can occur.

It is a known fact that every author has an editorial and critical history, especially those who are the great masters of world literature. For Faulkner in translation, this editorial and critical history gives the mapping of the writer's prominence in other national literatures.

Faulkner's novels come to us in Spanish after a considerable delay; therefore, they enter a very different scholarly and literary context from the one in which they originate. Moreover, the difference between the American and the Hispanic *milieux* is of consequence; hence, approaching Faulkner's work in other literatures is a complex task even for those who wish to deal honestly with it. The long delay in accepting Faulkner's innovations in the Hispanic culture cannot be overlooked—regardless of whether it is evaluated positively or negatively. Not until very recently are Hispanic readers reaping the benefit of his novels, as the result of a changing cultural environment more receptive to Faulkner's innovations.

The translation history of Faulkner in Spanish[12] begins in 1934, with *Santuario (Santuary)* published in Spain, translated by the Cuban short-story writer Lino Novás Calvo. Six years later, *Las palmeras salvajes (The Wild Palms)* came out in Argentina, translated by the well-known poet and fiction writer Jorge Luis Borges,[13] not at all a prominent author at that time. Thereafter, Faulkner's fate in Spanish has been rather different from, for instance, the development of his oeuvre in French. Maurice E. Coindreau and R. N. Raimbault have each translated or worked in collaboration with other translators in at least five of Faulkner's novels. Surprisingly, in Spanish, with the exception of Jorge Ferrer Vidal and Amando Lázaro Ros, no translator has worked on two of Faulkner's novels. It is noteworthy that from 1934 until today the list of translators continues to grow; as the appendix to this essay reveals, we can count at least thirty-two different individuals.

As to publications, during the '30s, Faulkner and other foreign writers had but a small impact on the literary scene in the Spanish-speaking sector of the European continent. This is particularly true because of the Spanish Civil War. From this perspective we begin to understand why the literary production in that country was so sporadic. In fact, for a period of several years following the Spanish Civil War, enforced inactivity in the publishing houses prevailed. By about 1942 Spanish authors began to publish again; however, there was little international exchange. It is not until 1947 that Faulkner reappears. He has been continuously translated in Spain ever since. In Latin America, in Argentina above all, Faulkner was translated without interruption since 1940 until the 1960s.

From what we know about the Faulkner translations in France, there was a long silence between 1939 and 1946—the time of World War II—comparable only to the editorial silence in Spain between 1934 and 1947. However, when *Pylon* was published in France in 1946, it was immediately followed by a translation in Spain in 1947. A similar situation can be cited in the case of *The Unvanquished*, which was translated in France in 1949, and in Spain in 1951. Neither of these was ever published or translated in Latin America. It is characteristic of the history of translations in Spain, indeed it is a documented fact that usually the translations from English, Russian, and other languages, since the eighteenth century, have been done in Spain from the French translations, a practice that was performed especially in the nineteenth century. The history of drama in the

Romantic period and of the realist novel in Spain offers ample proof of this literary phenomenon.[14] It would therefore seem highly likely that at least some of the Spanish translations of Faulkner's oeuvre come from the French. This is a subject to be studied further.

Faulkner has been read in Spanish especially since the 1950s with publications in Argentina, Mexico, and particularly Spain; the most important publishing houses for fiction, like Bruguera, Emecé, Losada, Plaza & Janés continue to publish new translations and reprints of his work.

The resurrection of Faulkner in Spain in the last twenty years has been notable; translations of his novels abound, and so do the new printings; while in Latin America, perhaps due to political and economic policies that have a bearing on editorial matters, they show a decrease since the 1960s.

In another important domain of Faulkner's existence in Spanish, it is interesting to note that the critical essays published between 1932 and 1950 are mainly translations of American or French criticism, or commentaries and articles by those writers who were in the process of translating Faulkner (like Lino Novás Calvo, Max Dickmann, and Maurice E. Coindreau) or by those critics who could read the texts in the original. On the whole, a close reading of Faulknerian criticism from the '30s to the '50s— when eight works had appeared in translation—reveals an obvious parallel with the development of American criticism in that period, with an emphasis on the thematic and narrative structures rather than on stylistic components.[15] Most importantly, we observe that the quality of the translations themselves is ignored in the criticism of that period, a fact that is not uncommon in the history of literature in translation in the Western world. Because of the rapidly expanding number of translations in the contemporary milieu it should be noted that the "real reader" is usually confronted with a split material: the original works, the criticism, and the translations of those works grow separately. Faulkner in Spanish is a good example of that.

As we move into the area of Faulkner's influence within the

Hispanic world, it is important to mention that since 1967, a novel by Juan Benet, *Volverás a región*, has been cited by many critics as Faulknerian *par excellence*.[16] Indeed, in that same year, Faulkner's influence on Gabriel García Márquez, particularly on his *One Hundred Years of Solitude* (1967), was beginning to be discussed. Significantly it was Juan Benet who wrote a prologue to the second edition, in 1970, of Borges's translation of *The Wild Palms*.[17] Also around that time, García Márquez admits and denies his readings of Faulkner.[18] The 1960s and '70s constitute what is known as the "Boom" of Hispanic fiction, a period in which also Juan Carlos Onetti, Juan Rulfo, José Donoso begin to be analyzed from the perspective of Faulkner's influence on their writings.[19] On the other hand, the Hispanic readership has had available, in the last five years, two new translations of Joyce's *Ulysses*, a new rendering of Proust's work in seven volumes, and translations of D. H. Lawrence and Virginia Woolf's prose in paperback editions. Not surprisingly, this availability coincides with the development of contemporary fiction in Spain.

Faulkner—"the untranslatable demon"[20]—stands among the most challenging authors to translate because he puts the translator in extreme, polarizing moments of decision. This is, to a great extent, due to his quality as "an incorrigible and restless experimenter," as Robert Penn Warren terms him in 1946. Warren writes of Faulkner as "peculiarly sensitive to the expressive possibilities of shifts of technique," and he refers to him as a writer who "has not developed . . . in a straight line."[21] This is more than relevant when dealing with Faulkner's work in translation.

Among the divergent opinions on the question of Faulkner's translatability, we must remember Maurice E. Coindreau and Talat Sait Halman's comments. For Coindreau, Faulkner's works "lose only a minimum of their original quality" in translation, while for Talat Sait Halman "no perfect Faulkner translation can exist, especially in a language like Turkish," as Necla Aytur gathers in her article "Faulkner in Turkish"; she concludes, on this point, that "the difference of opinion between these two translators of the same author is mainly due to the difference between the structures of the two languages concerned."[22] Unlike Necla Aytur, I believe that the translatability does not depend primarily on the degree of convergence in language structure and cultural backgrounds or frames of reference. The discrepancies on translatability and translations are also determined by the role of the translators as readers of Faulkner's texts. In fact, two translations of the same work into the same receptor language may differ substantially, and the very existence of two distinct versions—or three or more—of the same text gives ample proof that the divergences are not necessarily caused by cultural differences, or by the structures of the languages involved in the process.[23]

By way of example, even what Jacques Derrida calls "the margins of the text"—the titles—vary; a detail that may reveal a different overview of the text. *Requiem for a Nun*, in Jorge de Zalamea's version, retranslating the title into English, becomes *Requiem for a Woman (Requiem para una mujer)*; similarly, the title of this work changes to *Requiem for a Recluse* (or prisoner) *(Requiem para una reclusa)* in Victoria Ocampo's translation of Albert Camus's adaptation of that text; or the Brazilian version of *The Reivers* entitled *Os Desgarrados* (The Gone Astray) and the Portuguese *Os Ratoneiros* (The Ratters), each one bringing in quite a different cluster of semantic associations.

Some other dramatic examples of variations in the titles in Spanish are *Mientras yo agonizo* and *Mientras agonizo* for *As I Lay Dying*; *Victoria y otros relatos* and *Esos trece* for *These Thirteen*. As far as the total texts are concerned, there exist three versions of *The Hamlet (El villorrio)*, and two translations of *Soldiers' Pay (La paga de los soldados)*, of *Mosquitoes (Mosquitos)*, of *Sanctuary (Santuario)*, of *Go Down, Moses (Desciende Moisés!)*, of *A Fable (Una fabula)*, in addition to the ones that have different titles. Nevertheless, it is *The Sound and the Fury* that offers the most instructive editorial history with at least four different editions and two different titles. However, there are several other reasons for my choice in discussing this particular novel.

In the first place, the textual and editorial history of the source text[24] is in itself a subject not to be dismissed since more than one edition was produced in the original language (the 1929 and 1946 American editions and the 1931 British edition). It is important not only for the translator to know those editorial facts, but also the readers of the translations should know which source was used. Since the translation I will examine does not indicate which source-text edition was used, I have decided to compare it with a reprint of the first American edition, known to contain fewer errors than the 1946 setting.

Second, I have chosen the edition brought forth by Bruguera because it is the most recent version. Before this translation there had been at least three others, the latest dating from about twenty years ago. Third, *El sonido y la furia* is generally introduced in Spanish not only as Faulkner's most experimental novel, but also as Faulkner's best work. Fourth, Mariano Antolín Rato, the translator, was himself awarded the *Nouveau Critic* award (June, 1975) for his avant-garde novel *Cuando 900 mil Mach aprox.* Another reason is that Faulkner's *Obras escogidas* (Selected Works) and *Obras completas* (Complete Works), both including *The Sound and the Fury,* appeared in expensive editions that have been out of print for years; therefore the novel has not been available in those editions to a large number of readers. In contrast, Bruguera's edition is part of a popular collection of world literature, available in a much less expensive pocket edition of at least twenty-five thousand copies. This last aspect should be understood in the context of trying to discover what the "real reader" is actually receiving in the various Spanish translations themselves. Such a study should also aim at determining what is the correlative of experiment and innovation in the translations.

Rather than analyzing the sociological implications of the introduction of Faulkner's works in translation in the Hispanic culture, and instead of commenting in general terms on all of the translations of Faulkner's oeuvre in Spanish—topics for longer studies—I will limit myself to a discussion of the latest translation of *The Sound and the Fury*.

But first we should be aware of the editorial history of this novel. *El sonido y la furia* appeared for the first time in 1947, in Buenos Aires, Argentina. Six other books by Faulkner had already been published in Spanish. Quite unnaturally, this edition does not indicate the translator's name, nor does it contain the "Appendix" or any reference to its absence. Fourteen years later, in 1961, a new translation, signed by F. E. Lavalle, was produced in Buenos Aires, now with the important "Appendix." Strangely enough, a reprint of this Lavalle edition appeared two years later (1963) from the same publishing house, but with Floreal Mazía as translator. In that period, in Madrid, the important editorial house Aguilar—well-known for its collection "Biblioteca Premios Nobel"—included Amando Lázaro Ros's version of the novel, under the title of *El ruido y la furia*, in the second volume of *Obras escogidas* (Selected Works). Finally, Bruguera published, in 1981, a new translation by Mariano Antolín Rato.

Among Faulkner's textual strategies in *The Sound and the Fury* are the use of several points of view, the interplay of aesthetic functions for language in each of the sections, and a tackling of the problem of time and the word as principle for the multiple dimensions of human consciousness. However, all these innovations and techniques have been severed in the Bruguera translation. I will center on an analysis of Dilsey's speech, on the effect of omissions, on the use of aspectual elements of verbs having a direct effect on Quentin's notion of time, on the depoeticizing of Faulkner's language, and on the overall intonational characteristics of the novel. All these are important areas in which the translator, as *omniscient reader*, changes the scope of the meaning potential of the text and subsequently reduces the reader's response, both textually and in actuality.

The Bruguera translation centers its stylistic features on a monophonic, unevenly standardized language. The translator makes no attempt to create any equivalent effect that might reveal some of Faulkner's *varieties* of English usage.[25] Even the language of the black characters, so distinctive in Faulkner's actual text, becomes strangely muted in the translation. The problem of language variety and its differentiation in Faulkner is of central importance; one must see it first within the complexities of sociological and situational rather than just regional elements.

Before attempting to go any further it is important to go back to the original text, and consider some of the cultural and sociosituational circumstances in order to envision Faulkner's writing strategies in that context. As we know, in the geographical dialect of American English we find a variety of Southern English in which the dialects of blacks and whites correlate. Yet, "in spite of mutual influences, Southern white and Southern Black dialects are far from identical."[26] In Spanish there is no direct equivalent dialectal differentiation, even considering the great number of dialects in Spain and Latin America. However, we do find varieties of Afro-Antillean Spanish among the approximately one hundred dialects in Spanish that could be useful as working models for the translator. In *The Sound and the Fury*, the speaker's style and the addressee's relationship to the speaker call for the use of at least a differentiation in the formal, informal, or colloquial levels.

Functional equivalence of language varieties is essential for characterization and for the establishment of social and interpersonal relationships among characters. In the fictional text of *The Sound and the Fury*, the physical, external time and its psychic correlative are controlled, structured in such a way that not only the speakers' identity, but also age is indicated by language, as is time in memory. At least four language varieties overlap in different sociosituational contexts in the original: the language of children, adults, blacks, and whites.

It is interesting to note that although the Compson children spend more time with Dilsey than with their parents, in Faulkner's version one does not hear Dilsey's influence on the children's speech patterns. Here we do not have the bidialectal white Southern child found in actuality in the pre-Civil War period among the wealthy class;[27] nor does Dilsey speak like the Compsons. Likewise, it is true that Versh and T. P are playmates of the Compson children, yet through their speech Faulkner reminds us that they belong somewhere else, that they are to show their awareness of social boundaries over and over; the medium for that is language, and the person to teach them of their territorialized existence is Dilsey. The Compson children understand the black family's dialect, yet they do not speak it. Therefore, it is important to distinguish not only the language of Dilsey and her family from the one of the Compsons, but also the children's language from Dilsey's and the adults' for purposes of a complex chronology to be reconstructed by the reader. The language varieties have important markers since "every variety has features which are peculiar to it, and which serve as formal (and sometimes substantial) criteria";[28] these markers can be phonetic, phonological, graphological, morphological, lexical.

In the Bruguera translation, all the characters speak in standard Spanish, with occasional and inconsistent markers of changing language varieties that do not always correspond with the rest of the utterance of each speaker. By way of example, the Compson sons and daughter refer to and address their parents by calling them "madre," "padre," and by saying "dice padre," "dice madre," expressions used in Spain by uneducated rural speakers. This is misleading, particularly in Quentin's section, where his speech and, for that matter, his whole discourse differ from Benjy's or Jason's. What is more important is that the only markers of social difference between Dilsey's family and the Compsons in the translation are the expressions "señorito Quentin," "señorito Jason," and "señorita Caddy," used by the black characters; moreover, T. P. addresses Mrs. Compson, calling her "ama" (mistress), which stands as a signal of the master/mistress-servant relationship; only by further indirect references we have a slight hint at the relationship between black and white characters.

In Spanish, Dilsey's language is a neutral utterance, making her *voice* for the most part devoid of emotional expression; in addition, in the translation, her lexical register ranges rather randomly from the uneducated rural variety to a sophisticated and even *recherché* Spanish. While there are numerous examples, I will cite only one, which refers to the moment when Dilsey has taken Caddy to bed; she says "Goodnight, honey." Dilsey's expression in Spanish is "Buenas noches, cariño."[29] "Cariño" is an expression used as mockery, or for purposes of irony since it is not common, and not likely an expression a maid would use for a child in a parallel social situation. A more natural, appropriate expression could be, in the context of the standard language of Spain used in the text, "Buenas noches, sol mío," or "Hasta mañana, bonito." At other instances Dilsey's words are deemphasized. The foregoing examples illustrate how her speech loses her regional and national soil, the banters and pranks of the Southwestern tradition. Here Dilsey's resolute and energetic character becomes weakened:

109 What they change his name for if aint trying to help his luck?	83 Entonces, ¿para qué le cambian el nombre si no quieren que le cambie la suerte?
317 You aint got no business at no show.	234 No te interesan las funciones.

Thus, in this translation Dilsey's language loses its colloquialism and colorful diction. The original Dilsey is strong in inner impulse. The poetic designation of her power and her wisdom unfolds in the last section, against the background of an inscrutable time; it is her resolution and her self-determination that lead her into continuity and endurance. No risks were taken in the transposition of aesthetic components of Dilsey's speech in the Bruguera translation. The Dilsey "who holds the family together" is hardly the Dilsey in Spanish whose language crosses several dialectal levels. In truth it is not that Faulkner is untranslatable, but that the translator has to look for modes of expression to differentiate the characters, voices, situations.

The Sound and the Fury offers the translator the chance to contribute with new modes of expression, with the possibility of establishing innovative interplays of intonational nuances for an aesthetic effectiveness in character development. In contrast with the neutralized language of the Spanish translation, Coindreau, in his rendering of the novel into French, made a successful use of techniques of adjustment for a functional and dynamic equivalence in his inclusion of the colloquial language of the black characters, by marking with apostrophes the pronunciation or phonetic changes. Unfortunately, the black characters in this Spanish version speak in an unrhythmicized way, particularly Dilsey whose language is depersonalized and without idiomatic flavor and without any specific emphasis on the dramatic effect of her dialogues. The inconsistency of her speech in the source-text should not be understood, as in the Spanish version, as a dialectal *pastiche;* rather, it should be taken as a *necessary inconsistency* as part of the constant code-switching of black English in the United States. As Sidney Lanier explains, "you need not think, therefore, that in allowing the same speaker to say (for example) sometimes 'dat' and sometimes 'that'—as I arranged the dialect here and there— there is any lapsus. The Negro, especially since the war, tries hard for the *th* instead of *d* in such words as *the, that,* etc., and thus the same speaker often uses both forms. That remark applies to many other peculiarities."[30] This would be a way to approach an aesthetic equivalence in Spanish. Rato's "consistency" in the translation makes for a uniformity of speech that contributes to a neutralized effect in all the characters, and in the text as a whole. This is all the more deplorable since Faulkner was not only an extraordinary writer, he was also an exceptional listener, and the translator should, as reader, listen to the intonational qualities of his texts, with their contrasts and subtleties.

The unilinear, monotone narrative of the Bruguera translation is manifested in yet another important aspect: in the interior monologues, all three brothers could not possibly speak in a similarly unintensified tone. If we are to look for the worldvisions produced by the different levels of consciousness, we must pay careful attention to "the different levels of consciousness . . . rendered by Faulkner through variations in style ranging from the dialect of actual speech to intricate imagery and poetic rhythms of the unconscious," as Olga W. Vickery has stated.[31] Several points can be drawn from this remark. We can focus on Faulkner's imagery, with its poetic function in the narrative context of the story. In the Spanish translation, Faulkner's dynamic movement of poetic designation, as well as the way it develops, is narrowed, reduced. To explain this point, one example will suffice. Eight different images used by Faulkner in *The Sound and the Fury* to evoke the presence of birds and of objects in motion are given, in the translation, an almost identical denotation (emphasis mine):

96 in a street full of *scuttering* dead leaves	73 en mitad de una calle llena de hojas secas que *revolotean*
100 her veil *swirling* in long glints	76 su velo *revoloteando* en largos reflejos
131 They gushed like swallows *swooping* his eyelashes	99 Y ellas se lanzaban como golondrinas *revoloteando* alrededor de sus pestañas
310 a bunch of them would come *swirling around* in sight above the roof	229 una bandada aparecía *revoloteando por* encima del techo
315 they were *flying around* and blundering into the lights all night long	233 anduvieron toda la noche *revoloteando* y chocando contra ellas

331
A pair of jaybirds came up from nowhere, *whirled up* on the blast like gaudy scraps of cloth

245
Un par de arrendajos llegados desde ninguna parte, *revolotearon* dando vueltas atrapados por la ráfaga de viento como llamativos trozos de tela

335
The five jaybirds *whirled over* the house, screaming

248
Los cinco arrendajos *revolotearon* por encima de la casa, chillando

354
Outside the window he heard some jaybirds *swirl* shrieking

261
Fuera oía a unos arrendajos que *revoloteaban* chillando y alejándose

The translator has selected exactly the same verb for all of these images in which Faulkner's nuances of rhythm and associations become manifest; this is an example of the disambiguations produced by the translator. Instead of providing an unfolding of connotations, the translator has reduced them, diminishing the aesthetic quality of the text as he disarticulates the simultaneous levels of meaning of the original.

What in the source text is an imagistic variant, a subtle poeticizing of the "flight" motif, becomes in the translator's extrapolation the monotone of a repeated word. A concentration of eight occurrences cannot be overlooked; Spanish has more than the verb "revolotear" for those images created by Faulkner. "Swirling around" denotes a twisting, whirling motion, a dizzy confusion, for which the Spanish equivalent could be "volar en torbellino," or simply "en remolinos," or "vuelo turbulento." "Whirl up" stresses the birds' swiftness, their spinning, orbiting the blast, which could have easily been "subieron atrapados en el remolino," and "whirled over the house" might have been recreated with a longer expression—as it is usual in Spanish— "rodearon la casa en vuelos giratorios." As to the image "scuttering dead leaves," the same verb used to express "swirling around," "whirling up," or "swirl" cannot serve the same connotative function. The birds' lively movement is not quite the same as the hasty flight of the dead leaves; therefore, "scuttering" might have been "escabulléndose," or "en fuga precipitada." On the other hand, as to Quentin's memory of Caddy's veil "swirling," even if the translator had no presuppositions that might have led him to being poetic, two alternatives besides "revoloteando" were feasible: either to emphasize the veil's slow motion by means of the verb "ondear" or to stress the veil's faster movement with "agitar."

In the simile "like swallows swooping," the participle implies the opposite direction indicated in the other images used by Faulkner. As a semantic unit, it reveals a sudden, even violent descent, for which the Spanish language offers "abalanzarse," "arremeter," and other variants. While to some this may be a triviality in the novel, it is indeed an important component on the level of imagistic associations, as an underlying echo in the textual design of Faulkner's voice. To conclude, the translator's choice gives a repetitive, poorly descriptive quality to the text; rather than disclosing meaning, he conceals it. It is as if he had chosen to expel the poet in Faulkner.

Another recurrent componential and stylistic feature in the Spanish translation is the asymmetrical semanticizing of verbal features;[32] in Quentin's section above all, this causes a less coherent structure for important thematic developments in the Spanish version.

In the enlightening essay on "Time in Faulkner: *The Sound and the Fury,*" Jean-Paul Sartre intelligently points out that "the reader is tempted to look for points of reference and to reestablish the chronology for himself."[33] Because time can be segmented at will, each individual measures it according to his own emotions; and the rhythm of his life will depend on the intensity of those emotions; all these aspects are manifest in the original text. In the receptor-language text the crucial fragmentation of time is inconsistently rearranged. Also distorted are *perspective* and *voice.* Taking into consideration Gerard Genette's lucid distinction between the one who sees the action—perspective—and the one who narrates it—voice,[34] we realize that both correlations to the character's time concepts are severed.

In the translation this levelling of voice and perspective is caused by the translator's decisions of changing Quentin's modes of expressions with respect to time. Here many verbs from the simple past, past perfect, past conditional—paramount for the opposition between the temporal and the eternal—have been changed into the present,[35] as in:

105–6
I *used to think* that a Southerner had to be always conscious of niggers.

80
Pienso con frecuencia en que uno del Sur debe ser siempre consciente de los negros.

111
Niggers say a drowned man's shadow *was watching* for him in the water all the time.

84
Los negros dicen que la sombra de un ahogado *mira* siempre desde el agua.

Likewise, when Quentin is about to break his watch in order to be outside time and space, to become fixed and eternal, he thinks:

97–98
If we *could* just *have done* something so dreadful that they would have fled hell except us.

74
Si *pudiéramos* hacer algo tan terrible que todo el mundo escapara corriendo del infierno excepto nosotros.

In this case, the verbal form is changed from the past conditional to the present conditional tense. Thus in the Spanish version Quentin's impotence because he knows that nothing can be done to change the state of events disappears.

If Quentin's concept of time is central to his characterization, the relationship of time past and time present is crucial to cut back and forth across the years 1898 to 1928. Time is, as Perrin Lowrey has stressed, an organizing principle.[36] Quentin is continually twisting present tenses into past tenses. However, with the predominance of the present tense for Quentin's voice in this section of the novel in Spanish, the past produces an entirely different effect and changes the meaning of the structural pattern of the novel. It is Quentin's viewpoint that makes him confuse events that exist in time, with time itself. Thus he tries to destroy his own confusion, his own obsessions. He struggles against finding out "what time it is," in order to get away from it. For Quentin there is only a *before* and *after* with Caddy's loss of virginity as the pivotal point. Faulkner's careful use of two such differentials in Quentin's section reflects a deliberate contrast to Benjy's timeless present and Jason's "time-is-money" attitude, to become completed in the fourth section with Dilsey's prevailing order.

All these meaningful perceptions are lost in the Spanish version because of the translator's emphasis on the present in Quentin's section. If, as Sartre has argued, Faulkner's characters are committed to the past and are helpless, when Quentin's memory begins to enumerate his impressions of the past he is "*already dead.*"[37] Quentin's anguished speculations upon the nature of time are a salient technical feat in *The Sound and the Fury* to be taken quite seriously in any translation. With the changes of verbs into the present, Sartre's idea that "nothing happens, everything has happened,"[38] does not apply. Quentin's inner dialogue places his wish in a present that looks to the past in *The Sound and the Fury*, while in the translation, Quentin's perspective is a present that looks strongly to the future.

In addition to this effect, in the Spanish text we are discussing, Quentin's own time perspective is left without an equivalent textual logic, a change that is further stressed by other shifts of the verbal aspects:

(a) from the present tense — to the past tense (imperfecto)

216
I am. Drink. I *am* not.

161
Soy. Bebo. No *era*. (indefinido)

102
But then I *suppose* it takes at least one hour to lose time in,

77
Pero entonces *supuse* que por lo menos lleva una hora entera perder la noción de un tiempo

(b) from the future — to the present conditional

144
then you *will have* only me.

108
Entonces me *tendrías* a mí

(c) from the past — to the present perfect (pretérito perfecto)

199 | 148
Did you ever *have* a sister *did* you | *has tenido* alguna vez hermana la *has tenido*

(d) from the present perfect | to the past perfect (pluscuamperfecto)

116 | 88–89
We *have sold* Benjy's | *Habíamos vendido* el prado de Benjy

(e) from the conditional perfect tense | to the past (indefinido)

118 | 90
I *wouldn't have done* it. | No *quise* hacerlo.

(f) from the future | to the present subjunctive (subjuntivo presente)

118 | 90
I *wont have* my daughter spied on | No *quiero* que *andéis* espiando a mi hija.

Thus Faulkner's own thematic and functional use of time for the presentation of the Compson family is altered in the translation. Because of the change of tenses in the translator's version of Quentin's monologue, Quentin's present is easily confused with Benjy's timelessness.

It is also a well-known fact in Faulknerian criticism that recurring words, phrases, descriptions, and images become important symbolic patterns for the reader's comprehension of the underlying structure and chronology in *The Sound and the Fury*. This comprehension is essential to the intricate and multiple levels of signification which would otherwise be in confusion. Faulkner's technique of semantic addition—reduction and amplification of repeated fragments of thoughts—creates a dynamic organizational arrangement in the novel. Moreover, this technique builds up the psychological dimensions both of his narrative discourse, and of the events in the text; thus, as Sartre writes, "Even when the characters are aware of them, the actions, when they emerge in the present, burst into scattered fragments."[39]

Instead of structuring an equivalent reiterative mode of expression, here the translator has omitted most of Faulkner's stylistic "repetitions." He has overlooked seemingly unimportant details that in fact comprise an essential part of Faulkner's narrative techniques. He has not rearranged the key images, words, and phrases so that they recur and function as symbolic patterns by equivalence and opposition.[40] Therefore in his translation he does not create a new *equilibrant* for the ambiguities and structural points of reference or for the distinct flow of associations of the narrators.

At times Faulkner's style may seem wordy or redundant to the translator as reader of a text. Each translator will find an individual solution to this problem. For instance, when describing the hands of the woman selling bread to the little Italian girl, Mariano Antolín Rato omits the phrase "knuckled there by a blue knuckle" (156, *118?*). Because of the difficulties in translating Faulkner's more whimsical and playful descriptive phrases such as "no holds barred and gouging discretionary" (113, *80?*), many of these phrases have simply been eliminated in the Bruguera translation.

Apart from the obligatory alterations inherent in the process of transferring a text from one language to another, we may find other changes and deviations from the levels of signification of the original. By way of example, a descriptive detail may have a direct consequence in terms of characterization. To return once more to Dilsey, this time to the last section, while Faulkner's Dilsey is seen "wearing a man's felt hat" (332), the reader of this Spanish text is given the image of Dilsey as having on a "masculine felt hat" *(245)*. Subtleties of this kind constitute important factors for the semantic cohesion of the text.

Although it would be extremely time-consuming, it would be important to attempt to explain each change, to assess the deviations and departures in the translation. It is even more important to analyze the consistent substraction of elements, normally ignored or taken for granted.

In the Bruguera translation of *The Sound and the Fury* the substractions made by Rato can be grouped into six types: (1) *ideas* (verbal forms, fragments of phrases, sentences and other semantic units); (2) *descriptive details*, particularly of gestures and nuances of dramatic quality; (3) *parts of dialogues;*

(4) *repetitions* of a phrase or word when occurring in the same passage; (5) *images* that by contextualization become part of the symbolic structure of the novel; and (6) the specific and inconsistent omission of *the phrase "Father said"* in Quentin's section.[41]

Let us analyze first an omission where types 1 (ideas) and 6 ("Father said") overlap. This is a case in which one of the most crucial ideas has been eliminated:

143-44	109
O That That's Chinese I don't know Chinese. And Father said it's because you are a virgin: dont you see? Women are never virgins. Purity is a negative state and therefore contrary to nature. It's nature is hurting you not Caddy and I said That's just words	Eso es chino y yo no sé chino. .... Y padre decía: Eso solo son palabras

Quentin's tortured mind narrates the remembered and imagined conversations with his father, providing additional complexities to be interpreted by the reader. The relationships among honor, virginity, nature, love, and his own guilty feelings are Quentin's main dilemmas, condensed in this passage. On the other hand, the phrase "Father said" functions as a fundamental marker for the divergence and the clash of opinions between father and son, and as a semantic component to indicate Quentin's obsessive struggle against time. In this, his ideas differ greatly from those of his father, as in the following example (the emphasis is mine):

118	90
Where the best of thought *Father said* clings like dead ivy vines upon old dead brick.	Donde las mejores ideas se aferran como hiedra seca a viejos ladrillos muertos.

The reader of the Bruguera translation inevitably has to attribute the father's words, in this and other instances, to Quentin because of the apparently harmless substraction of the phrase "Father said."

In addition, still another element recurs in the translator's choices. When he does not omit "Father said," he turns this expression into a relative clause, producing a relativization of the dialogues; thus the semantic features of intensity disappear. The generally disambiguated syntax adds a confusion which is nonexistent in the original. The markers "I said," "Father said," and "he said" establish the dialogic nature of Quentin's inner voices; they set up not only ideas but also characters in opposition, defining Quentin's own concept of time in relation to other moral and religious principles. Yet more important is the immediacy and vividness of Quentin's narration of the last day of his life. Because Quentin's monologue in Spanish has more of the character of reported speech, the perspective and voice in his section of the text are also changed. Quentin's experience and his obsessions are distanced from himself, and subsequently from the reader. Indirect dialogue makes his discourse more objective, more detached.

In the source-language text the particular rhythm of Quentin's discourse is determined to a great extent by the syntactical fragmentation of his ideas and images. These ideas and images are, in turn, determined or regulated by *intonation*. The use of the intonational line[42] in Quentin's section is set in contradistinction with the intonational lines of the other sections. For a translator it is important to perform an accurate equivalent of Faulkner's fragmentation of semantic units or divisions of the sentence or paragraph in which the semantic units are subtly indicated by intonational nuances:

215–16
Caddy Jason Maury door I am not afraid only Mother Father Caddy Jason Maury getting so far ahead sleeping I will sleep fast when I door Door door

160
Caddy Jason Maury no tengo puerta miedo solamente Madre Padre Caddy Jason Maury tan lejos dormidos me dormiré en seguida cuando la puerta Puerta puerta

In this passage, the translator has substituted illogical ideas for Faulkner's juxtaposed broken thoughts. The fragment "door I am not afraid" of the example mentioned above is transferred as "I don't have a door fear," a mode of expression reflecting a psychological peculiarity more akin to Benjy rather than to

Quentin. Consequently, by changing the word order not only is the syntactical equivalence distorted through a different segmentation of semantic units, but also Quentin's own "logic" of thoughts and his unique poetic and dramatic rhythm as well.

Within the framework of the intonational quality of a literary work—and *The Sound and the Fury* is a precious example—punctuation has a significant textual function. The Spanish version of *The Sound and the Fury* we are discussing, like other translations of Faulkner into Spanish, contains a normalized punctuation. Passages that are ambiguous in the original become clear-cut and conventional in the receptor-language text. However, again this is inconsistent in this particular translation; in some passages the punctuation disappears while in others it follows the characteristics of the original. Therefore, there is no way for the Hispanic reader to ascertain the relationship between Faulkner's use of punctuation and normal usage accurately. The hints at the principles behind the deviations and the actual aesthetic effectiveness of punctuation, when they exist, do not lead to the original text. Moreover, the use of capital letters in Quentin's section—when he refers to his father, mother, grandfather, and uncle Maury—are signs of emphasis of his obsessed mind and of the awe they inspire in him. In the Bruguera translation, these references are not followed with a corresponding frequency.

Punctuation and capitalization are graphic signs indicating the intonational properties of discourse that Mukařovský has stressed.[43] Equally important is the division of the text into lines and paragraphs. Changes in any of these aspects bring in new types of emphasis, additions, intensifications. Faulkner's novels and short stories are especially sensitive to these changes.

When the translator incorporates new paragraphs by changing the punctuation and introduces divisions of the text that did not exist—as in the case of Rato's version of *The Sound and the Fury*—we are in the presence of a major change in the intonational elements of the novel. *The Sound and the Fury* exhibits outstanding features of intonational quality not only for the development of plot, character, atmosphere, tone, motifs, themes, and other elements of narrative structure; it provides a voice for the *concrescentia* of Faulkner's "liberated" and "energized imagination."[44] On the other hand, *El sonido y la furia* does not have the euphonic, rhythmic, and semantic organization of the original. Contrasts, overtones, repeated patterns, complex imagistic relations disappear or vary in an unequal equivalence of relationships.

Writing about Faulkner's "uncongenial techniques," Albert J. Guerard has insightfully remarked that Faulkner is "least at his ease, or least interesting, with impersonal third-person narration through one character's relatively normal consciousness." He goes on to say, "even more than Dickens, [Faulkner is] uncomfortable with realistic dialogue in standard middle-class English."[45] Curiously enough, Mariano Antolín Rato is most at ease precisely with the third-person narration and with the impersonal narrative in standard Spanish. However, this is characteristic not just of this translation, but of other versions of this book in Spanish, as well as Spanish renditions of Faulkner's other novels.

Faulkner's voice in Spanish is another Faulkner, a fragmented voice if one is to read his entire oeuvre in translation. His works have been so crucial to the reemergence of contemporary fiction in Spanish that a diachronic study of all the translations is indispensable for a critical overview of the development of the Spanish Faulknerian voice. It would also be important to begin synchronic comparisons of all of the translations of *The Sound and the Fury*, and of those multiple versions of Faulkner's other novels.

By isolating the crucial aspects of the Faulknerian voice of a particular translation into Spanish, the major components that establish the difference between the source text and its translation can be elucidated. Necessarily, this leads us to conclude that this asymmetry is determined by quite different components in each case. Subsequent studies could be made to determine the innovative componential features and the correlations of the variants in the original and the Faulknerian voice in Spanish. These studies would be most fruitful if they were centered on Faulknerian rhetoric and developed within the context of reader-response criticism. The "real reader"—as we have seen—becomes familiar with a language and an imagination molded by the translator. This translator is *the other reader*, who inscribes his or her own materials and techniques in the new text, the one who decides between imitating and adapting, between serving the author or the self, the one who submits or rebels. Eventually, when future translators become more conscious of Faulkner's language as the dynamic of *willful playfulness*,[46] and when they can fully benefit from their own exploration of previous translations, then, perhaps, the "real reader" in Spanish will be presented with a more harmonious voice.

NOTES

1. I emphasize the notion of "real reader" because in the last thirty years, the status of the reader in discourse has been an important area of investigation for several theoretical orientations in the study of poetics. For an excellent account of the different kinds of reader in textual analysis, see Jane P. Tompkins, ed., *Reader-Response Criticism: From Formalism to Post-Structuralism* (Baltimore: Johns Hopkins University Press, 1980), and Susan R. Suleiman and Inge Crosman, eds., *The Reader in the Text: Essays on Audience and Interpretation* (Princeton: Princeton University Press, 1980).

2. The concepts of "standard literary language" and "national literature" are explored by Jan Mukařovský, *The Word and Verbal Art: Selected Essays*, trans. and ed. John Burbank and Peter Steiner (New Haven: Yale University Press, 1977).

3. See the concept of textual strategy in Umberto Eco, *The Role of the Reader: Explorations in the Semiotics of Texts* (Bloomington: Indiana University Press, 1979), 10–11.

4. Iris M. Zavala's concept of "omniscient reader" in her essay "Lectores y lecturas: el lector omnisciente de los manuscritos," to be published in *Homenaje a Manuel Alvar* (Madrid, [1984]), refers to the reader of manuscripts. In my article I am expanding this term to be applied to the translator as well. Among other characteristics, as an omniscient reader, the translator must know the existence of the source-text, of its language, textual strategies, its cultural, sociohistoric, and aesthetic contexts; likewise, a knowledge of the writer's concrete circumstances is necessary. In addition, the translator must know the sociohistoric and aesthetic context of the receptor-language text, the receptor's literary tradition, and several other elements. This knowledge has its function primarily in the reading stage of the translation process. In the course of this essay it will become evident that I am greatly indebted also to Umberto Eco's theory on the Model Reader in *The Role of the Reader*, and to Mukařovský's stimulating theories in *The Word and Verbal Art*, which have allowed me to develop my own concept of the translator as an omniscient reader.

5. Jan Mukařovský provides a useful definition of this concept in the general framework of poetics in *The Word and Verbal Art*, 16.

6. On the subjectivity of language, see Emile Benveniste, *Problèmes de linguistique générale* (Paris: Gallimard, 1966).
7. Mukařovský, 149.
8. Eco's notion of the "aesthetic text as a communicational act" is extremely relevant to translation theory. See *A Theory of Semiotics* (Bloomington: Indiana University Press, First Midland Book Edition, 1979), 275–76.
9. Mukařovský, 10.
10. A good example of this attitude can be found in Stanley D. Woodworth, *William Faulkner en France: Panorama Critique, 1931–1952* (Paris: M. J. Minard, Lettres Modernes, 1959), 26–36.
11. James B. Meriwether, "The Textual History of *The Sound and the Fury*," in *The Merrill Studies in "The Sound and the Fury*," ed. James B. Meriwether (Columbus: Bell and Howell Co., 1970), 18.
12. See Appendix 1.
13. One of the few comments Borges has made on this translation is: "Traduje a Kafka y a Faulkner porque me había comprometido a hacerlo, no por placer. Traducir un cuento de un idioma a otro no produce gran satisfacción." In Fernando Sánchez Sorondo, "El oficio de traducir" (Encuesta), *Problemas de la Traducción, Sur* 338–39 (enero-diciembre 1976), 119.
14. José F. Montesinos, *Introducción a una historia de la novela en España, siglo XIX* (Madrid: Castalia, 1955).
15. For the sources consulted on this aspect, see Appendix II.
16. Juan Benet, *Volverás a región*, 2nd ed. (Barcelona: Ediciones Destino, 1967).
17. "Prólogo" to *Palmeras salvajes*, William Faulkner, trans. Jorge Luis Borges (Barcelona: E.D.H.A.S.A., 1970).
18. I refer the reader to Miguel Fernández-Braso, *Gabriel García Márquez: una conversación infinita* (Madrid: Editorial Azur, 1969).
19. A good account of his influence in Latin American literature can be found in James E. Irby, "La influencia de William Faulkner en cuatro narradores hispanoamericanos" (unpublished master's thesis, Universidad Nacional Autónoma de México, 1956). Irby concentrates on José Revueltas, Juan Carlos Onetti, Juan Rulfo, and Lino Novás Calvo.
20. For an interesting case of an Italian omniscient reader as translator, see Glauco Cambon, "My Faulkner: The Untranslatable Demon," in *William Faulkner: Prevailing Verities and World Literature*, Proceedings of the Comparative Literature Symposium, Vol. 6, ed. Wolodymyr Taras Zyla and Wendell Marshall Aycock (Lubbock, Texas: Texas Tech Press, 1973), 77–93.
21. Robert Penn Warren, "William Faulkner," in *William Faulkner: Three Decades of Criticism*, ed. Frederick J. Hoffman and Olga W. Vickery (New York and Burlingame: Harcourt, Brace & World, Inc., 1960), 122.
22. Quotations taken from Necla Aytur, "Faulkner in Turkish," in *William Faulkner: Prevailing Verities and World Literature*, 26–27.
23. Here I am specifically referring to a synchronic approach. A diachronic study brings in some additional points for discussion that are not relevant in the present essay.
24. See James B. Meriwether, "The Textual History of *The Sound and the Fury*," and Lawrance Thompson, *William Faulkner: An Introduction and Interpretation* (New York: Barnes & Noble, Inc., 1963).
25. I am following the concept of language varieties in translation outlined by J. C. Catford, *A Linguistic Theory of Translation: An Essay in Applied Linguistics* (London: Oxford University Press, 1965), 83–92.
26. Joey Lee Dillard, *Black English: Its History and Usage in the United States* (New York: Random House, Vintage Books, 1973), 215.
27. *Ibid.*, 186–228.
28. Catford, 86.
29. William Faulkner, *The Sound and the Fury* (1929; rpt. New York: Random

House, Vintage Books, 1972), 53. Further page references will be to this edition. William Faulkner, *El Sonido y la furia*, trans. Mariano Antolín Rato (Barcelona: Bruguera, 1981), 42. Further page references will be to this edition. Hereafter, page numbers quoted first will be for the original. The second will provide the pages for the translation.

30. Sidney Lanier, "Letter to *Scribner's Monthly*" (Nov. 23, 1879), *Works*, X, 156, quoted in Dillard, 207.

31. Olga W. Vickery, "The Dimensions of Consciousness: *As I Lay Dying*," in Hoffman and Vickery, 233.

32. See Robert de Beaugrande, *Factors in a Theory of Poetic Translating*, Approaches to Translation Studies, No. 5, ed. James S. Holmes (Assen, The Netherlands: Van Gorcum, 1978), 58–65.

33. Jean-Paul Sartre, "Time in Faulkner: *The Sound and the Fury*," in Hoffman and Vickery, 225–26.

34. Gérard Genette, *Figures III* (Paris: Editions du Seuil, 1972).

35. Other examples also in 94, 72; 98, 74–75; 111, 84; and 117, 89.

36. Perrin Lowrey, "Concepts of Time in *The Sound and the Fury*," *English Institute Essays*, 1952, ed. Alan S. Downer (New York: Columbia University Press, 1954), 57–82.

37. Sartre, "Time in Faulkner," in Hoffman and Vickery, 230.

38. *Ibid.*, 227.

39. *Ibid.*

40. On symbolic patterns, see Myriam Díaz-Diocaretz, "'The Waste Land' and *The Sound and the Fury*: Two Concurrent Interpretations of Contemporary Society," *Acta Literaria* (Universidad de Concepción, Chile) I, 1 (1975), 17–53.

41. Compare, for example, for type (1) pages 135, *102*; 141, *106*; 219, *169*; 277, *205*. For type (2) 97, *74*; 170, *128*; 189, *141*; 198, *148*; 214, *160*; 316, *233*; 345, *245*. For type (3) 311, *230*; 314, *232*. For type (4) 127, *96*; 160, *120*; 201, *149*. For type (5) 127, *96*; 139, *105*; 212, *158*. For type (6) compare Quentin's section, 93–222 in the original with 71–165 of the translation.

42. For an illuminating study of the intonational line see Mukařovský, 1–64.

43. *Ibid.*, 26.

44. The liberated rhythms of the writer's authorial voice are what Albert J. Guerard calls "Faulknerese." See his important study *The Triumph of the Novel: Dickens, Dostoevsky, Faulkner* (New York: Oxford University Press, 1976), especially chapter 8, 204–34.

45. *Ibid.*, 223.

46. *Ibid.*, 204.

Yoknapatawpha in Santiago de Chile

JORGE EDWARDS

It seems very strange indeed to relate the Indian name Yoknapatawpha with the Spanish name of the apostle who helped to fight the infidels, the Moors of the Spanish reconquest or the Araucanians of the extreme south of my country, to speak of Faulkner's fiction in a different and deteriorated reality. I am no literary critic, and I am not even an expert in William Faulkner. I am only a fiction and sometimes a nonfiction writer. I only intend to tell you a personal story, a story that perhaps has some meaning for the study of Faulkner's work and for the understanding of the world of Latin American fiction—Latin American fiction after Faulkner, I mean.

In the end of 1959 I was living in Santiago, Santiago de Chile, my native city, where I was in those years a young career diplomat. I had been writing poetry and fiction since 1945, since I was fourteen years old, but there was no hope for anyone who wanted to take writing as a profession in the Chile of those days. Writers, if they were lucky, went into teaching, into journalism, and, in the best of cases, into diplomacy. Almost every writer I knew in Santiago, and probably all the writers of my generation, believed that it was essential to escape from there: the only way out of mediocrity, provincial life, absolute hardship, and limitation; from the writing of five articles a day about any subject or the teaching of thirty-five hours a week. Pablo Neruda, Gabriela Mistral, Vicente Huidobro, the great Chilean poets, had spent their best creative years in distant or exotic places, in Rangoon, in Paris, in Mexico. In 1959, if I had some patience, I would have the privilege of escaping in a very traditional French and Latin American fashion, as a writer diplomat. I was waiting for my turn, in the Foreign Ministry, and using my free hours for intense reading and writing.

One morning I was called by the Chief of Protocol, a place I always tried to avoid in the Ministry, and I was told that I had to be the "attaché," the "aide-de-camp," of a Peruvian foreign minister who made an official visit to Chile, Doctor Raúl Porras Barrenechea. I didn't know a word about Doctor Porras Barrenechea, and I didn't like at all my commission. It would take the time I occupied after office hours for the parallel activity I saw as the only important one, the only justification for me to continue in that rather strange and formal institution.

It happened that Doctor Porras Barrenechea was a fine historian, a sort of cultivated conservative politician, well established in the French and Latin old style of the "homme de lettres" and of what we call the "public man." We talked very much about books, and he said that he didn't care at all for fiction. He was proud, in a certain way, of this sort of intellectual disdain. His passion was to submerge himself in the "Archivo de Indias," the archives in Sevilla where all the documents about the discovery and the conquest of America are collected, and to follow a colonial story through old papers. He escaped many times from his official duties and asked me to accompany him to the sellers of old books, who worked in the Santiago of the fifties in very dark and sordid shops towards the south of the city.

While we walked in those streets full of carts and peddlers, shouting boys and vendors, buses that seemed to crumble, insistent beggars, we talked about books, and he was very surprised to hear that I was reading the same authors and even the same short stories, the same poems, the same novels, that were being read by a small group of young Peruvian writers, young people he had known in the University of San Marcos, in Lima. Doctor Porras Barrenechea more or less accepted or tolerated the first poetry of Jorge Luis Borges, because, he said, it was simple and it reflected the charm of the modest, provincial outskirts of

Buenos Aires, the small yellow houses and the reserved and shady patios, but he thought the short stories of Borges were too complicated, too sophisticated, "intellectual," a word that he considered pejorative. Then, concerning our other readings—Franz Kafka, James Joyce, William Faulkner—he declared his absolute perplexity and his astonishment about the fact that people of the same age in Lima and in Santiago, without any sort of previous consultation, spoke with the same feverish admiration of *The Process, Ulysses, As I Lay Dying,* or "A Rose for Emily." He considered that this was a symptom of something, and he considered it thoughtfully, really without intolerance, but with astonishment and curiosity, beginning to believe, maybe, that something had escaped his understanding. He was, anyhow, a real politician, and he became sure, in those last years of his life, that something was changing in the Latin American scene. The Latin American countries had been always isolated among themselves, but now there was a remarkable similarity in reading, in tendencies, in attitudes. There was the surprising fact, also, that Fidel Castro and his "barbudos," a small group of young men, had just won their guerrilla war and had taken power in Cuba. What was the meaning of all this? Did all this mean a change in the Latin American conscience?

Doctor Porras Barrenechea did not modify in the least his literary tastes and his preference for history, for chronicles and memoirs. He was not impressed by my arguments in favor of poetry and fiction. But he was an open-minded man and tried to put me in contact with those young Peruvians. I knew later that they were José Miguel Oviedo, Mario Vargas Llosa, Julio Ramón Ribeyro, José Durán, that is to say, some of the novelists and the critics that would become, later on, part of a great renaissance of creative writing in the Spanish language.

But I will have to go further back now in this personal story. The first notice of William Faulkner reached me in the forties, in the city of Santiago, in a period when it was difficult to find any foreign books there. The Faulkner ones—*Las palmeras salvajes,*

Mientras yo agonizo, Santuario—came in some cheap Argentine and Spanish translations, even when two of the translators were writers already well known and much admired by a small minority: Lino Novás Calvo, a Cuban, and Jorge Luis Borges. The first of these books I came upon was *Mientras yo agonizo, As I Lay Dying*, and it made a devastating impression on me. I can only compare this feeling with the impression produced by the reading of *Residencia en la tierra* (Residence on Earth), by Pablo Neruda, and of *Poemas humanos* (Human Poems), by César Vallejo. I simply did not know that it was possible to write in that way, to use words in that way in narrative fiction. I concluded, when I was a fifteen or sixteen year old secret writer, that if it was possible to write in that way, it was worthwhile to become a writer, to put all one's will and all one's effort in trying to become a writer, and to organize all the rest of life, including, naturally, the need to earn a living in a place where there was not even a vague notion of what is a literary career—to organize all this in relation to the unique and extravagant purpose of becoming a writer.

I think one of the reasons, one of the hidden motives, for this decision had something to do with poetry. I will try to explain this. I had discovered poetry by myself, in a very sudden way, in a family where nobody ever talked about poetry, where the most common talk was about the stock exchange or the town's social gossip. My father had been a friend at school of Vicente Huidobro, one of our great poets, and he thought that Vicente was completely mad, writing verses that made no sense, living in Paris in a garret, on top of a cabaret that made an infernal noise all night, and neglecting his Chilean heritage, one of the best and largest vineyards in the Central Valley. My father had also a first cousin, Joaquín Edwards Bello, who was one of the best novelists of his day in Chile, and his nickname in the family was "el inútil," the "good-for-nothing." The title of his first novel, whose whole edition was bought and burnt by the family, in 1910, had been exactly that one: *El inútil.*

The fact, anyhow, is that I had discovered suddenly, through the musicality of words, the mystery and the fascination of *Residencia en la tierra*, of *Poemas humanos*, and later of the works of Arthur Rimbaud, Charles Baudelaire, and T. S. Eliot. I began to write poetry myself, I would say by contagion and imitation. But I was frustrated because my writing was always reflective, always the prolongation of a rhythm and a tone that belonged to others—to Neruda or to Federico García Lorca or to Vicente Huidobro and León Felipe.

The reading of Faulkner showed me, for the first time in my life, that there is a kind of poetry that can go into narrative fiction. After the great writers of the seventeenth century, there was no prose writing of this particular poetical force in the Spanish language. There were writers like Gabriel Miró, Azorín, Ramón del Valle Inclán, that tried to be poetical through elegance, through the use of precious adjectives, of ornamented language. Valle Inclán was the one who went further in this direction. His novels and his theater attained a fantasmagoric quality, something related with the black paintings of Goya, with the "bodegones" and the masquerade of another painter of the "goyesque" family, Gutiérrez Solana, and also with that wonderful baroque language of the seventeenth century, the language of Don Francisco de Quevedo, Luis de Góngora, or the Count of Villamediana, whose assasination was ordered, apparently, because of his too carnal devotion to the young queen. The problem was that the writing of Ramón del Valle Inclán sounded anachronistic to us, strange to our own world, a sort of cardboard prose.

The first personal consequence of my discovery of Faulkner was the writing of a completely Faulknerian novel. There was even a character called Cora, to whom I could not give a name other than Cora. The novel only made some progress for me, in my adolescent work, with that name for one of the characters, a very unusual name in our language. It was not a special preference for the Cora of *As I Lay Dying*—for her and her cooking. It was only a musical need of that sound in order to get into the atmosphere of my text. Fortunately, I had enough self-criticism and I stopped in time, in the middle of the writing.

Later I began to work with some stories that had to do with boyhood memories, with my own family, with the Jesuit school in the southern part of the city where I studied during nine years: stories that happened in the yards of that school, or during church ceremonies, or in decayed and dusty mansions, always haunted by the presence of strong and extravagant old ladies. I dared to publish some of those short stories in my first book, *El patio*, in 1952, a book financed by subscriptions of friends and printed in five hundred copies by the small private press of a Spanish republican émigré, Carmelo Soria. Afterwards I had the opportunity of meeting Pablo Neruda in his own house: the mysterious, the secret, the hermetic poet of *Residencia en la tierra*. But it happened that the Neruda of 1952 was denying the work of his youth in Rangoon and in India. He had become a sort of a Latin American Victor Hugo, an epic poet of American nature and history and also a militant communist poet. His literary search was now for clarity, for simplicity, for solidarity, and for joy, against the darkness and the anguish, the distress, the solitude, that were the true obsessions of my generation. Those first meetings with Neruda were filled with misunderstanding. I was speaking to the Neruda of *Residencia en la tierra* and he was not there, he had left that house some years ago. Anyhow, he kept a link with that Neruda of the past. The new one was not simply imposed on the old one, like a different geological layer. This Neruda–Victor Hugo kept, against all the rationality of his actual position, in the central place of his studio, the original photographs of the poetical heroes of his beginnings: Edgar Allan Poe, Charles Baudelaire, Arthur Rimbaud, and, of course, Walt Whitman. He was following now the Whitman cord, writing in free verse about our great volcanoes and forests, about our powerful rivers, about our miserable peasants and exploited coal miners, and against our petty and reactionary politicians and the huge companies coming from the North. Neruda had lived inside the Spanish civil war and he had engaged in the great fight of our century against fascism. This was the authentic origin of his communist militancy. One had to understand it that way.

But all this was not very easy to understand, especially in those years, and I am afraid I didn't understand it very well. He had become a poet of too great words, the poet of a certain fatherland that seemed to me a pure abstraction. In a party in his house, after drinking some glasses of Chilean wine, probably the wines produced in the abandoned vineyards of Vicente Huidobro, his poetical rival, I said to him, "Look, Pablo. My true fatherland is not the great volcanoes that I see only in pictures, that are at one thousand kilometers from my home, nor the great forests of the south of Chile, nor those powerful rivers, beautiful as they are, with a solemn, spacious beauty. My true native country is a dusty house where an old lady, a grandaunt, warns me against the perversity of an uncle who has indulged in alcohol, or about a corrupted woman that belonged to the best society and committed adultery; an old, trembling lady, who speaks with fiery passion about orderly conduct, about money, and about the dangers of eternal damnation, and then asks me to kneel down and pray with her. These grandaunts are my only fatherland!"

Neruda laughed, but other people that were in that house and heard us did not laugh at all. They said that I was a decadent writer and a good-for-nothing. They forgot to add: "Like Joaquín, his novelist uncle," but they could have added it in those days. In that same period, Neruda made some absurd declarations about Kafka, William Faulkner, and T. S. Eliot. Everybody can make a mistake, even a great poet, and it is not infrequent that great poets and novelists contradict themselves in their sayings to the press. This you know better than I, being experts on William Faulkner. In any case, my personal relations with Neruda became distant and rather cold for a time. Then, in the early seventies, after the death of Stalin and the publication of some poems of Neruda like the one entitled *Sonata crítica* (Critical Sonata), I said to him once, "When you made that attack, you really made the anthology of my three favorite non-Spanish writers." Neruda was silent for a moment, thoughtful and silent. Then he said, "My moustaches, you know, were excessively long, then. We all had very long moustaches in those days." He was referring, of course, to Joseph Stalin's moustaches. Neruda never wore a moustache himself.

The rereading of Faulkner now, before coming here, has been a surprising experience. I thought the only influence of Faulkner's fiction in my own work was that Faulknerian novel I started in my youth and then left unfinished. Now I also see that the traces of Faulkner's world are in all my fiction, concealed, so to say, under a mask that I myself had not recognized before as a mask, as a concealment. In *El patio,* my first short stories, there is the death of an old lady, "la señora Rosa," and the transportation of her coffin from the second floor of a big bourgeois mansion to the first floor, and there is her rigid face behind the glass cover, and the glances, the different attitudes, the greeds, and the guilts of her relatives. That coffin has certainly not been built by Cash Bundren. It has a black brilliant varnish and bronze handles. But it sways in a certain way and it hits a corner of those stairs in a form that seems suddenly dangerous, disturbing, distantly akin to the long travel of Addie Bundren's coffin.

That was written before 1952. But many years later, in my novel *Los convidados de piedra,* a title that means something like the "stone guests," one of my characters, the mad member of a traditional family, sees the disorder, the tension, the latent civil war of the Allende days, with the confused and contradictory look of a lucid idiot. Was there a recessed Faulknerian tone in this character? And then, in my last novel, *El museo de cera* (The Wax Museum), where I was conscious of a distant relation with Kafka and even with the Hoffman tales, but never dreamt of any relation with Faulkner, it happens that the main character becomes a wooden puppet. It is not a realistic text. It is a deliberate, fantastic metamorphosis. Some critics effectively mentioned Kafka and the old Valle Inclán with his "esperpentos." But I wonder, now, if this idea of a very rigid character, an old conservative gentleman that organizes an erotic game with puppets and becomes himself, in the end, a wooden puppet, has not some subconscious link with Jewel, with the wooden back and the crystal eyes of Jewel Bundren, who gets a more wooden appearance as the novel continues its progress.

I have wondered many times, I can assure you, about the impact of William Faulkner on my generation in Chile. It was, in a certain way, more than a purely literary discovery. Probably the discovery of a great writer is always like that. Entering into Faulkner's world, into Yoknapatawpha, provoked in many of us identification of nearly a religious kind. One of the young writers of my day, Claudio Giaconi, in his first press interview, declared proudly (modesty was not his distinctive quality), "I am the Chilean Faulkner." But there was a period, probably between 1948 and 1955, when the Parque Forestal, a park in the center of Santiago where we used to read in springtime and where we met and had long talks and discussions, was full of Chilean Faulkners. Yoknapatawpha was inside the Parque Forestal. The Mala Strana and the old quarters of Prague, the house of Marcel Proust's Tante Léonie in Combray, the Dublin pubs of Leopold Bloom and the tower of Stephen Dedalus, and Yoknapatawpha County, with all its complexity and its intricate history, all these spaces of the mind existed together in our Parque Forestal, in a moment of spring now isolated and lost in the past.

I only begin here to outline a possible interpretation of what Faulkner's work meant to us. I must warn you that this is a Chilean interpretation. You always tend to believe, in North America and also in Europe, that all Latin American countries are the same. You believe that once you know one of them, you know all the lot. But it happens that they are more different from one another than you can imagine. I will try to point now to some historical elements to help illustrate my point. We had in Chile a war against Perú and Bolivia in 1879. It was called the War of the Pacific, because of the Pacific Ocean, which was baptized Pacific by its discoverers, but has not been at all a peaceful sea. It was a succesful war for Chile and it gave Chile the world control of natural nitrate, a great richness during the years around the turn of the century. The War of the Pacific also produced other effects. The Chilean ruling class had been rather austere before the war; it had been able to organize a stable form of conservative government, in striking contrast with most of the other Latin American countries. The disillusioned generals of the wars of independence, especially the Argentine José de San Martín, lived long enough to see that Chile was the only country that spoke in Spanish and also knew how to be a republic. This exact sentence was written by San Martín in his last years of exile in France. Success in war was a consequence of this political stability, but sudden richness introduced a germ of dissolution in the Chilean social scene, a lethal poison that endangered that precious and rare stability. In 1891, only twelve years after the War of the Pacific, we had a terrible civil war. My generation was perhaps the first one to know clearly that both sides in Chile had lost that civil war.

This generation, which has been called the "generación del cincuenta," the generation of 1950, grew between memories of a brilliant and glorious past, in contrast with a decayed present, a present whose main quality was stagnation, frustration, poverty, underdevelopment. The main avenue of Santiago, the Alameda Bernardo O'Higgins, and all the old part of the city were full of imposing facades, built in many cases by French architects, or imitating, in a smaller scale, European monuments as the Andalousian palace of the Alhambra, but these facades, that had represented the nitrate splendor of the nineties, a sort of créole "belle époque," were now dusty, full of broken windows, literally cracking because of our earthquakes and also because of our economical decay, crumbling facades. Inside those houses there were impoverished families and in the rear dormitories, sometimes hiding from the outside world, old people that remembered and told stories about that lost splendor and about the terrible civil strife between the executive power and the members of Parliament, an internal struggle where Chile lost more people than in the War of the Pacific and where many new instruments of destruction, as, for instance, the machine gun, were introduced for the first time in that southern part of the world; houses full of dust, of humidity, of cracking walls, of rats, of yellow papers and fading photographs, where old, half-crazy people told stories about years of wonderful, incredible prosperity, legendary balls in fancy dresses, mixed with stories about a war where a certain Colonel Salvador Vergara had conducted the operations in one of the last battles against the army of Presidente Balmaceda, a former friend of his. Colonel Vergara was chosen to command what was called the Congressional Army in that particular battle because it was going to take place in the north of Valparaíso, in the lands that belonged to his family and that he knew like the palm of his own hand. A few days later, the defeated Balmaceda would commit suicide in his refuge in the house of the Argentinian diplomatic mission.

This was our immediate historical background, and through it I think you can easily understand the appeal Faulkner's writing had for us. You can ask why this appeal was also so strong in other Spanish-speaking countries. Well, this panorama of civil wars and of a certain past splendor, the legend of the past, took very different forms, and I must insist on the differences in each national case, but it existed in all of Latin America. There has been much writing already about the influence of Faulkner in, for instance, *Pedro Páramo*, a Mexican masterpiece by Juan Rulfo, and in Gabriel García Márquez. García Márquez once said that reading Faulkner changed his life and recently said that he had not read Faulkner when he wrote his first novels, something that seems to me really difficult to believe, but that could serve to prove my point about the similarities in our historical backgrounds. The fact, anyhow, is that Rulfo's and García Márquez's characters come back from a civil war they have lost and have their minds full of images of a sort of mythological past. We all tended to build a legend of the past and to see the future with utopian illusions. The great fact was dissatisfaction with the present, a fertile soil for the future instability in all the continent. From this perspective, the novelists of the generations that preceded us in our country said little to us. They were making inventories of the land, the botany and zoology of our regions, the peasants' way of speaking, as part of a project to describe our distinctive, non-European features, a program that started with Latin American romanticism; but our real and dramatic history and our actual situation did not pass into their writing. Faulkner was a completely different case. He belonged to another world, but he wrote about things that had a profound meaning to us.

This is one of the lines of interpretation I only begin to suggest to you, a possible explanation of our almost unanimous admiration and of our sense of identification with William Faulkner's fiction. But it happens that we also have in Chile a legendary South. This is another question to think about. Our South is a cold and rainy South. It is not the South of the United States of America but the South of the whole world. It was poetically discovered by some of the great poets of the Spanish language a long time ago, since the sixteenth century—poets like the Spanish soldier and courtier Alonso de Ercilla, who first heard about this South and about the Araucanian wars while he was attending, in London, the ceremonies of the wedding of King Philip the Second of Spain; poets like Pedro de Oña, the first who was born in Chilean territory, exactly in the frontier of that war, in Angol de los Confines, a name that means "Angol of the last extreme of the world," and who was a great master of the Spanish baroque language; and poets like Pablo Neruda himself, who also was born, more than three centuries after Pedro de Oña, in 1904, in what is yet called the frontier.

A legendary South has been the invention, also, of some masters of the English language, writers like Samuel Taylor Coleridge, Herman Melville, Edgar Allan Poe, Joseph Conrad. In *The Rime of the Ancient Mariner,* that beautiful and symbolic albatross, a bird that you can see on his majestic flight on the south coast of Chile, was probably killed near the Malvinas or Falkland Islands, as you prefer to call them, because Coleridge had just read the story of John Davis, the first English navigator to arrive to those islands, and the old mariner's ship, with its ghostly crew, got lost after the ecological crime in the southern seas of Argentina and Chile, that extreme south that in Poe's *Narrative of Arthur Gordon Pym* begins to get warm as you travel further north, a geographical aberration, and where the narrator finds a cat with red eyes of fire and ears that hang down as those of a dog.

It is a completely different South, but, as you can see, it also has a rich legend, and a legend created, to a great extent, by the imagination of writers and poets. Did this make us Chileans more receptive to the strong and contagious Faulknerian legend? I don't really know. I am a man of the center of Chile and I begin just now, after traveling recently to Temuco, in the heart of the ancient Araucanian country, to understand and to learn something about this extraordinary South, about the Araucanía of the ancient soldiers and poets; the only civilization in all the southern part of this continent that, although being in the Stone Age, stopped all foreign invasions, first from the Incas, the Peruvian precolumbian Indians, then from the Spanish, and finally, until the end of the nineteenth century, from the Chilean Republic—more than four centuries of ferocious resistance.

Allow me only a last word. All the short stories and novels of the writers of my generation spoke about decay, decadence of houses, places, families. A critic referred to a "novel of decrepitude." This made us adopt sometimes a point of view that perhaps was too mean, out of our pessimism. Our stories were told most of the time through the eyes of decayed or destroyed people. In all these last years I have personally begun to feel that this point of view imposes perhaps a moral limitation and also, as a long-run consequence, probably an artistic limitation. After my recent rereading of William Faulkner, I think I see a possible answer to this worry. Faulkner's final belief in dignity, in literature as a way of exalting the best part of the human condition, without any kind of complacency or of bigotry, has been for me the second lesson I have received from him. My first reading of Faulkner gave me an unforgetable literary lesson, and I somehow feel that my second reading gives me not only a wider understanding of his way of writing but also a kind of moral lesson. Is not absolute pessimism or nihilism a danger for the creative force of an artist? What is the profound artistic problem of choosing the narrative point of view of deteriorated or degraded characters? This is not very easy to explain, and my limited English does not allow me to explain it better, but I hope you understand me. The only thing I want to add is to thank you for this opportunity of visiting for the second time this land, the place that somehow created William Faulkner and that he in his turn created.

Faulkner and the British: Episodes in a Literary Relationship

MICK GIDLEY

Many of us will be familiar with the old saying that America and Britain are more divided by a common language than by the Atlantic Ocean. After Faulkner arrived by fast ferry in Newhaven from Dieppe in October 1925 he dashed off a letter to his mother: "It was an English boat and I heard my native tongue (or something kind of resembling it) on all sides for the first time in quite a while."[1] At that point in his life he could not have known that some of the least understanding, peevish, blimpish, and hostile criticism of his work was to come from the pens of British users of the language.

Gordon Price-Stephens quoted many samples in his excellently researched contribution to the Summer 1965 issue of the *Mississippi Quarterly*, "The British Reception of William Faulkner, 1929–1962."[2] On *Soldiers' Pay* (1926), the story of the tensions arising from the arrival home in Charlestown, Georgia, of Donald Mahon, a young airman horrifically wounded during the Great War, Gerald Gould wrote: "It is almost incredible that anybody should be able to treat so pitiful a theme without making it in the least degree moving; but one cannot be moved except by reality; and, in this book, to me at least . . . there appears nothing real at all. Mr. Faulkner has, I should judge, read Mr. Hemingway; but Mr. Hemingway is a master, and Mr. Faulkner is not, at this stage, even a pupil."[3] Cecil Roberts, a regular reviewer for *Sphere*, said this of *Light in August* (1932): "I have read with care—and difficulty—every page of *Light in August*. Its theme is commonplace—the adolescence and revolt of a youth in a backwoods family in Alabama," and he asked, "Is it coming to this, that, in an age when hundreds of persons can write well, the significant writer is the one who demonstrates that he cannot or will not write at all?"[4] And an unsigned review in *The Times Literary Supplement* of *The Hamlet* (1940)—a book most of us would find fairly readily comprehensible, perhaps almost conventional in structure—goes like this:

> It is not a bit of good—Mr. Faulkner's talent may be prodigious and highbrow fans of his and the critically knowing in general may be right in singing his praises, but he is difficult to read. He is, at any rate, more nearly unreadable in this new novel than in any previous one. In the past one was willing, up to a point, to put up with this terrific churning of words and his laboured passion for violence because some sort of queer illumination of mind or soul showed through. Here everything is as incomprehensibly opaque as the eyes of Flem Snopes, Mr. Faulkner's lunatic marionette of a hero.

This reviewer proceeds to complain of Faulkner's "copiousness of language," of his sense of time, and of his use of what he calls "digressions." On "Eula Varner and her aura of sexual energy, fecund nature and the rest," he adds, "Mr. Faulkner's gush of words, if one may say so, is rather silly."[5]

Now, of course, this sort of highly selective quotation is easy to do, and one could do it almost as readily with American reviewers—especially in the pre–Nobel Prize years. But let me indulge myself once more, though more seriously this time:

> The difficulty of reading [him] comes from the fact that Mr. Faulkner crams into each sentence thoughts which occur to him in passing but which have not necessarily much to do with the matter in hand. Like various other writers from Carlyle onwards, he is presenting the process of thought instead of the results. After a careful reading of *The Hamlet*, I must record that I have quite failed to discover the plot of the story. All I can say with certainty is that it is about some people somewhere in the Southern States of America, people with supremely hideous names—names like Flem Snopes and Eck Snopes—who sit about on the steps of village stores, chewing tobacco, swindling one another in small business deals, and from time to time committing a rape or a murder. A second reading . . . might

extract something more definite, but it is my honest opinion that it would not be worthwhile.

I find this distressing because it was not cobbled together by a hack reviewer, a Gerald Gould, a Cecil Roberts, or an anonymous member of the *Times Literary Supplement* club, but was composed by one of the finest British authors of his generation then writing, in 1940, at a high point in his development. It was written by Eric Blair, better known as George Orwell.[6] It is true that Orwell was always concerned to forge a very plain, if expressive, prose, so Faulkner's way of writing would always have been alien to his own practice. Nevertheless, I would have thought he would have proved more receptive to a new idiom in someone else—as he was in the case of Henry Miller, for instance, long before many others.

Orwell did not take this stand alone. As Cleanth Brooks pointed out in 1973, Price-Stephens's research provides what he dubs a "roll-call" of distinguished British literary figures who have uttered some kind of serious condemnation of Faulkner. He lists them: Cyril Connolly, Edwin Muir, C. Day Lewis, Humbert Wolfe, Graham Greene, Philip Toynbee, and, of course, George Orwell.[7] And Brooks could just as easily have added Rebecca West, Pamela Hansford Johnson, C. P. Snow, Compton Mackenzie, L. P. Hartley, Wyndham Lewis, and J. B. Priestley. I think we must wonder *why* this is. Why, for such a long time, were so many significant literary figures in Britain hostile—or, to be more accurate, essentially uncomprehending—towards the work of America's major novelist this century? In the course of this talk I intend to offer some very tentative suggestions as to why this was so.

But let me make a couple of preliminary observations. First, not all the figures I have spotlighted were equally blind to Faulkner's qualities. Some of them were sometimes blind in one eye only, as it were—or with another sense proved acutely perceptive. Graham Greene, for instance, while generally condescending towards *Absalom, Absalom!* (1936) in 1937—seeing not a tragedy but a pretentious costume romance—nevertheless recognized the superbly rendered urban and contemporary nature of the "sense of spiritual evil" which attends the gangster Popeye in *Sanctuary* (1931).[8] Greene calls Popeye a "memorable figure" and he certainly seems to have been very much remembered in the creation of Greene's own pathological criminal, Pinkie, who appeared in *Brighton Rock* (1938) the year after his review. Pinkie, if not impotent like Popeye, hates and fears what he calls "the game" of sexual love. He is a petty and violent criminal with black-suited narrow shoulders and eyes as devoid of humanity as Popeye's.[9]

George Orwell, too, was not completely unobservant. In his essay on detective fiction, "Raffles and Miss Blandish" (1944), he pointed out that James Hadley Chase, the English thriller writer, had lifted the plot of *No Orchids for Miss Blandish* (1939) almost wholesale from *Sanctuary*: in each book a young society girl is both sexually abused by underworld figures and is also attracted to them.[10] Also, even in the hostile review of *The Hamlet* which I quoted earlier, Orwell does make one remark which virtually parallels the highly developed thesis put forward at about the same time by Conrad Aiken in his seminal essay, "The Novel as Form" (1939). When Orwell points to the tentacular effect of Faulkner's sentences, the gathering in of "thoughts which occur to him in passing," his interest in "presenting the process of thought instead of the results," he very precisely describes Faulkner's associative method. Aiken puts it this way: "It is as if Mr. Faulkner had decided to try to tell us everything, absolutely everything . . . each sentence is to be, as it were, a microcosm." "The purpose," he adds, "is simply to keep the form—and the idea—fluid and unfinished, still in motion . . . and unknown, until the dropping into place of the very last syllable."[11]

Several British writers took the position that no matter how inept they might find Faulkner technically, his imagination—or, as it was often put, his subjection to obsession—was so powerful that he could not be disregarded. Kenneth Allsop, author of among other things, *Hard Travellin'* (1967), an excellent study of the hobo in American history and culture, put this position most succinctly when he imagined the response of a magazine editor when confronted by a Faulkner story: "We must take this. You can't ignore the Grand Canyon, even if it is an architectural mess."[12]

More importantly, as you may well have intuited already, I have so far presented a slightly unbalanced view of Faulkner's British reception. First, there were certain major British voices raised in appreciation during Faulkner's own lifetime, and we ought to be aware of some of them. The novelists Richard Hughes and Arnold Bennett were discoverers and promoters of his work (if not to quite the extent that they themselves believed).[13] Jacob Isaacs welcomed his output during the thirties and was notably appreciative of Faulkner's structural innovations.[14] In the forties the popular author H. E. Bates and the poet Norman Nicholson wrote on him with real discernment.[15] Bates compared Faulkner with Conrad and showed that he understood the more luxuriant "grandeur" that Faulkner's prose style, in comparison with Hemingway's, was able to achieve. Nicholson focused primarily on Faulkner's philosophical concerns and the relationships of those to his forms and intuited, some years before the Nobel speech, that a kind of dualism—what Faulkner himself termed "the human heart in conflict with itself"—lay at the root of much of his work. V. S. Pritchett, himself a masterful short story writer, built—either unconsciously or knowingly—on both Aiken's 1939 essay and Malcolm Cowley's famous introduction to *The Viking Portable Faulkner* (1946) when he wrote the following in 1951:

> Faulkner's ambition is visually poetic and he is attempting the instantaneous delivery of a total experience. In all his novels, he is trying to give each instant of experience in depth, to put not only physical life as it is seen directly on the page, but all the historical and imaginative allusions of a culture at the same time. If the reader is stunned by the slow, deliberate blow, that is precisely the effect Faulkner is seeking, for we do, in fact, live stunned and stupified by the totality of our experience and our present position in our life story is simply the little clearing we have cut and the devious fading

path we have left behind us, in the jungle. Order, or at any rate pattern, is that which comes *afterwards* to this romantic novelist who begins in the middle of the mind. . . . [This] method creates the South in depth as, I think, no other part of America has been created . . . since . . . *Huckleberry Finn*. American novelists have composed reports, records, chronicles of other regions, but the impression is of life in some passing, cynical, littered encampment; Faulkner, on the other hand, seems to be engaged in a compulsive task, as if he had undertaken awkwardly the building of a culture out of its ruins, as a one-man mission.[16]

Personally, I do not think Faulkner's relationship to Yoknapatawpha has ever been better put than this—at least not in so few words. That is, unless we count Faulkner's own when he wrote to Cowley: "I'm trying to say it all in one sentence, between one Cap and one period."[17]

The second reason why my quotations from Cecil Roberts and company constitute a somewhat unbalanced picture of Faulkner's reception in Britain is that they give no indication of the change—I am tempted to say the improvement—during the last fifteen or so years. The Winter 1952 issue of the first American journal devoted exclusively to Faulkner, *Faulkner Studies*, contained an interesting news note: "Walton Litz writes from Merton College, Oxford, that he has been 'doing a little evangelical work on Faulkner's behalf' during the past year and adds that Faulkner is 'practically unknown' there and his works are unavailable."[18] Such a sorry state of affairs contrasts sharply with that just a fast ferry ride away in France. There, not only did his work enjoy general circulation, but—as is well-known—from at least 1938 his handling of even metaphysical questions, such as his concept of time, was treated at length by figures of the stature of Jean-Paul Sartre.[19] In Britain the publication of Jacob Isaacs's "Introduction" to A. A. Mendilow's *Time and the Novel* in 1952 marks, I think, the very first real demand for such analytical scrutiny to be devoted to Faulkner's conceptual thought[20]—and it was certainly not met for quite a period.

Now, I have to confess that as far as Oxford is concerned a Faulkner enthusiast could well come to exactly the same conclusions today as did A. Walton Litz in 1952. It is one of the largest universities in Britain, yet it employs only one scholar specifically to teach American literature. Elsewhere the position is different. While in the fifties there were, at most, sixty academics teaching any American subjects—and most of this work was of an ancillary nature—there are now more than 400 teachers giving courses in various aspects of American studies in some forty British universities. The British Association for American Studies has nearly 500 members, and there are over 250 librarians in Britain who work with United States bibliography to some identifiable extent.

The rise of the American studies movement in Britain has tended, in the sphere in which we are interested, to create a divergence, even a gulf, between the kind of critical opinion which appears in newspapers and general circulation magazines and that written for academic journals. Needless to add, perhaps, there is some overlap, but much less, I suspect, than in the United States. This is partly because weekly reviewing in Britain is still predominantly the province of free-lance authors and journalists rather than of academics, while at the same time many fewer creative writers hold posts in universities than is the case in the United States. When Cleanth Brooks, in the 1973 article I mentioned earlier, looked for causes of the British reaction to Faulkner, he found one of them in what he called "poor critical theory," adding, "I mean good old British literary amateurism" which could be set against "American literary professionalism."[21] What Brooks really meant, of course, was "poor critical practice," but in any case such a charge can be levelled with much less assurance against the academically trained British critics who have written on Faulkner since the mid-sixties than it can against the earlier reviewers[22]—who, as far as I can tell, included very few academics and only two of any note, F. R. Leavis and J. Isaacs—or against the continuing band of newspaper critics.

What has happened—and this might well be expected of users

of the language which, as Faulkner put it, kind of resembles his own—is that the preconceptions of the American studies movement in Britain have inclined to be ones shared with the United States American studies scholars. British scholars have tended to assimilate to a kind of pedagogical and intellectual orthodoxy. And, like the Gulf Stream itself, the major movement is in one direction only, west to east. There may be minor eddies, some backwards spillage, and lately some strong countervailing currents from the European mainland, but the flow is basically as set as a geographical fact. This means that there may be individual British voices with interesting critical or scholarly points to make on Faulkner, but the more successful they are, the less likely they are to be identifiably British.

Michael Millgate, author of *William Faulkner* (1961), *The Achievement of William Faulkner* (1966), and many essays, is clearly the outstanding example. Professor Millgate is now a Canadian citizen, but even if he had remained throughout his career at the University of Leeds, there is very little in his Faulkner work that marks it as indelibly British. (Indeed, paradoxically, it would be easier to argue that Millgate's study of Hardy, especially the critical work *Thomas Hardy: His Career as a Novelist* [1971], has been immeasurably enriched by what he has been able to read back into Hardy from his knowledge of Faulkner's creation of an "apocryphal kingdom".)[23] In short, British academic treatment of Faulkner's work has now entered into the general stream of Anglo-American literary criticism of English and American literature. This is, of course, not comment on either the quantity or quality of British Faulkner scholarship—though both are still too low—but on its kind. In other words, I think it is possible to speak of a distinctively French contribution to Faulkner studies right down to the present in the work of Michel Gresset or André Bleikasten in a way that would be absurd or pretentious to talk of a British contribution. I am tempted to believe that this process of assimilation may even have gone too far, in that British critics and scholars have neglected some facets of Faulkner studies that they could reasonably have been expected to pioneer. Allow me to broadcast some examples.

In the field of Faulkner bibliographical studies James B. Meriwether has already done all the spadework,[24] but the Chatto and Windus editions—and, of course, all the Penguin paperback reprints—could take further annotation, at least for the benefit of British scholars and readers. Arnold Goldman, formerly of the University of Keele, pointed out to me that the 1933 Chatto and Windus first edition of *Light in August* is entered in the *British Library Catalogue* as a "facsimile" of the American Harrison Smith and Robert Haas 1932 edition. However, a comparison of page 204 in each of these editions shows that the word "taking"—and in a different typeface—has been substituted for "f——ing" in the angry outburst of Bobbie Allen, the prostitute: "Me f——ing for nothing a nigger son of a bitch that would get me in a jam with clodhopper police. At a clodhopper dance." One must wonder how many more instances there may be of hitherto undetected censorship and/or anglicization.

In the area of biographical research, much has already been achieved, especially by Joseph Blotner and Carvel Collins, but I know of no British scholars other than Millgate and Price-Stephens who have actually looked into the Chatto and Windus files, or interviewed the company's directors, its editorial staff, and their descendants. And so little is known of Faulkner's visits to England, both those in the fifties and, more crucially, the brief one in 1925. For example, on his walking trip through Kent and Sussex did he visit Conrad's grave? This ignorance is a pity, for the visit provoked one of Faulkner's most striking letters, as if he had found subject matter that entirely suited the circumlocutions of his style. He sent the letter to his mother from Tunbridge Wells in Kent:

> This is a funny place I have got to now. It is a watering place where the water tastes like hell and where earls and dukes that had too much fun while they were young, and old women of both sexes

whose families are tired of looking at them, come to drink the water. They all have those nasty fuzzy white dogs that look like worms. The dogs are so old and blind and there are so many of them that you can't stop to look in a shop window without one of them doddering up and feebly wetting your leg and ankle.[25]

Again, Faulkner's relationship with his one-time publisher Jonathan Cape is intriguing. Did Cape ever indicate an interest in publishing Faulkner in London as well as in New York? Did he ever—as was his usual practice—consult his great editor and reader, Edward Garnett, the man who had earlier promoted Joseph Conrad and D. H. Lawrence? The only British commentary that I have found is a farcical paragraph in an autobiographical book by the short story writer and drinking companion to Dylan Thomas, J. Maclaren-Ross. In his *Memoirs of the Forties* (1965) Maclaren-Ross—who boasts of "a perfect memory"— insists that Cape told him that Faulkner had "only one foot, lost the other flying with the RFC," and that when Cape had read the manuscript of *Sanctuary* he told Faulkner he would have liked to have known more of Popeye's childhood; Faulkner replied that it was there, at the beginning, but of course it was not: "'By God,' exclaimed Faulkner, 'If I haven't forgotten to write it after all.' So he went away to do it. However, because the book had gone [to press] it couldn't be placed at the beginning, so Faulkner said, 'Let's put it in last and the hell with them.'"[26] All complete fabrication.

Sufficient work has now been done on Faulkner's sources, significant literary influences and affinities—including treatment, of course, of several British writers—that it would be impossible for me to cite it in any meaningful manner. This being the case, it is surprising, perhaps, that, with one or two exceptions, British scholars have not undertaken full studies of the influence of figures of the stature of Dickens, Hardy, Conrad, and James Joyce. And then there are potentially interesting source and affinity studies to be done on such of Faulkner's contemporaries (or near-contemporaries) as Virginia Woolf and

John Cowper Powys. Woolf, for example, shared many assumptions on the nature of time with her fellow narrative experimenter; these are representative entries from her diary:

> Tuesday, November 23rd [1926] . . . One incident—say the fall of a flower—might contain all time. My theory being that the actual event practically does not exist—nor time either.
> Wednesday, November 28th [1928] . . . The idea has come to me that what I want to do now is to saturate every atom . . . to give the moment whole; whatever it includes. Say that the moment is a combination of thought; sensation; the voice of the sea. . . . I want to put practically everything in.
> Friday, January 4th [1929]. Now is life very solid or very shifting? I am haunted by the two contradictions. This has gone on for ever; will last for ever; goes down to the bottom of the world—this moment I stand on. Also it is transitory, flying, diaphanous.[27]

I think that if our previous discussion of Aiken's intuitions are borne in mind, together with the comments by various Faulkner characters that there is "no such thing as past," then just one comment from Faulkner will suffice to demonstrate a very similar concern indeed: "[Thomas Wolfe] and myself . . . tried to crowd and cram everything, all experience into each paragraph, to get the whole complete nuance of the moment's experience, of all the recaptured light rays, into each paragraph."[28]

Even less has been written on Faulkner's affinities with Cowper Powys. It has to be remembered that while Cowper Powys is now somewhat neglected, for quite a time both his mystical novels and his philosophical pantheistic commentary were very much in vogue. Faulkner himself reviewed *Ducdame* (1925), one of Powys's less successful novels, in the New Orleans *Times-Picayune* in 1925.[29] I believe he also knew at least some of Powys's expository writing—certainly an essay in *A Modern Book of Criticism* (1919), edited by Ludwig Lewisohn,[30] and probably *Visions and Revisions*, first published in 1915. This book includes a passage that, together with ones from Conrad— as suggested by Richard P. Adams many years ago[31]—may well have provided a source of both notions and words for parts of the Nobel Prize speech, at least as mediated by Faulkner's own memory so many years later. It will be remembered that in the speech he contrasts present-day universal fears with values of the past and urges young writers to address "the problems of the human heart in conflict with itself," to write of "the old verities and truths of the heart," and says that until a writer addresses these matters "he will write as though he stood among and watched the end of man," a concept he then images in apocalyptic terms as the end of the physical world, too: "the last worthless rock hanging tideless in the last red and dying evening."[32] This is the passage from Powys; it comes from a paean of praise to Hardy:

> [In Hardy] there is none of that intolerable 'ethical discussion', which obscures 'the old essential candours' of the human situation. The reactions of men and women upon one another, in the presence of the solemn and mocking elements; this will outlast all social readjustments. . . . While the sun shines and the moon draws the tides men and women will ache from jealousy, and the lover will not be the beloved! Long after a quite new set of 'interesting modern ideas' have replaced the present, children will break the hearts of their parents, . . . Hardy is indignant enough over the ridiculous conventions of Society, but he knows that, at the bottom, what we suffer from is "the dust out of which we are made"; the eternal illusion and disillusion which must drive us on and "take us off" until the planet's last hour.[33]

In other words, Powys depicts Hardy as the kind of writer Faulkner urged younger authors to become. Powys, for his part, certainly appreciated Faulkner. Soon after the appearance of *Absalom, Absalom!*, he wrote to his friend Louis Wilkinson that it was "the best novel since Conrad."[34] There is at the moment a revival of interest in Powys in Britain, best registered in the publication of a new journal, the *Powys Review*. Perhaps this revival will lead to work on other possible affinities with Faulkner.

It is highly unlikely that such influence and affinity study will ever take place with respect to those British writers whose near contemporaries in the States—figures like William Styron, Reynolds Price, and Ralph Ellison—so often reveal signs of the imprint of Faulkner's example in their styles or structures. This will seem strange only until it is remembered that it is also difficult to discern any high degree of influence among later British novelists of Virginia Woolf or, even, James Joyce. For many years there was what Rubin Rabinovitz calls "a reaction against experiment" in the English novel.[35] This passage from C. P. Snow typifies the reaction:

> Looking back, we can see what an odd affair the "experimental" novel was. To begin with, the "experiment" stayed remarkably constant for thirty years. Miss Dorothy Richardson was a great pioneer, so were Virginia Woolf and Joyce: but between *Pointed Roofs* in 1915 and its successors, largely American, in 1945, there was no significant development. In fact there could not be; because this method, the essence of which was to represent brute experience through the moments of sensation, effectively cut out precisely those aspects of the novel where a living tradition can be handed on. Reflection had to be sacrificed; so did moral awareness; so did the investigatory intelligence. That was altogether too big a price to pay and hence the "experimental" novel . . . died from starvation, because its intake of human stuff was so low.[36]

Clearly, these sorts of assumptions form one of the fundamental reasons for the hostile or uncomprehending reception offered Faulkner by the bulk of British reviewers: they were the selfsame writers as those who were rejecting, for themselves, the experimental road that Faulkner, in many of his major works, followed.

C. P. Snow's comments, published in September 1953, were quoted by the novelist and critic David Lodge in an essay with the suggestive title "The Novelist at the Crossroads" that first appeared in 1969.[37] Despite the fact that Lodge's own creative work was and is predominantly social fiction, and "realistic" in structure, he found a position like Snow's acutely discomforting. Hence the essay outlines just some of the roads contemporary writers might take. And since then, of course, some interesting or important British writers have indeed taken turnings towards increased fabulation, mythical and magical frameworks, discontinuous narrative, acute narrative self-reflexiveness, documentary fiction, and so on. I have to assume that the British readers of this generation of writers—I am thinking of Robert Nye, Ian McEwen, D. M. Thomas, and Fay Weldon, as well as of more "conservative" figures like John Fowles, Malcolm Bradbury, and David Lodge himself—will be significantly more open to the narrative advances made by Faulkner.

I realize I am in danger of over-simplifying literary history here, both the complexities of readers' responses—the degree to which such responses can be translated into receptivity to works of earlier periods—and, more importantly, the nature of Faulkner's own achievement. I do not, that is, wish to categorize him wholly as an experimental or avant-garde author. The most persuasive presentation I have seen of Faulkner's position was delivered four years ago by Hugh Kenner, at one of these Faulkner and Yoknapatawpha conferences. In "Faulkner and the Avant-Garde" he attempted to locate Faulkner's modernism very precisely.[38] His argument, as you would expect, was, to use his own expression, so "salmon-supple," and closely detailed, that I will not risk rigidifying it by summarizing it here. One of his concerns was to distinguish Faulkner's works from the productions of international modernism and to stress the qualities they share with stories, yarns, tales told orally; to some extent, they must be seen—or, better, heard—as local expressions of a familiar but indistinctly bounded community. Yet, at the same time, Faulkner could not have composed as he did without a full awareness of all the resources of international literary modernism— neologisms, eccentric punctuation, exaggerated italicization, and the like—resources heavily dependent, that is, on the highly sophisticated technology of point. Kenner views Faulkner, in other words, as a unique and paradoxical amalgam of the traditional and the avant-garde whose texts make unique demands on the reader.

Now, when you or I come to a talk like Kenner's we have the advantage of the whole modernist movement behind us. Even if we have not thought about such matters as literary and oral registers in any depth, we probably know that others have done so. Faulkner did not have this advantage. In fact, he had the task of finding and locating *himself* as a writer. And he had to undertake this task against the background of literary and cultural discussion of his own time, with the modern movement just underway, as it became available to him. I would like us now to look back briefly at some of his comments in his very early essays, especially comments on language and provincialism, because these clearly bear witness to the paradoxical situation he faced.

At the close of his essay on Eugene O'Neill—in the course of which he refers to John Millington Synge's *The Playboy of the Western World* (1907)—Faulkner writes, "Nowhere today, saving in parts of Ireland, is the English language spoken with the same earthy strength as it is in the United States."[39] A little later, in a general article on drama, he repeats the point: "One rainbow we have on our dramatic horizon: language as it is spoken in America. In comparison with it British is a Sunday night affair of bread and milk—melodious but slightly tiresome nightingales in a formal clipped hedge."[40] (This image, by the way, is especially apt, both in that nightingales and clipped privet hedges seem so emblemmatically British, but also in hinting at the kind of declension that had occurred between Keats's "Ode to a Nightingale" (1819) in which "In some melodious plot/Of beeches green, and shadows numberless" the nightingale "singest of summer in full throated ease" and T. S. Eliot's rendition of the birds in "Sweeney Among the Nightingales" (1920).) Faulkner most likely had practical experience of British English during his stint in the R.A.F. in Toronto, and it is worth remembering that even some British reviewers praised his rendering of British servicemen's idiom in *A Fable* (1954).[41]

Back in 1922 he was certainly not alone in his perception of the two languages. In his *Devil's Dictionary* (1906) Ambrose Bierce had defined English English as "a language so haughty and reserved that few writers succeed in getting on terms of familiarity with it."[42] As early as 1891, William Dean Howells had written:

For any novelists to try to write Americanly, from any motive, would be a dismal error, but being born Americans, I would have them use "Americanisms" whenever these serve their turn; and when their characters speak, I should like to hear them speak true American. . . . if we wrote the best "English" in the world, probably the English themselves would not know it, or, if they did, certainly would not own it. . . . God apparently meant languages for the common people; and the common people will use them freely as they use other gifts of God. On their lips our continental English will differ more and more from the insular English, and I believe that this is not deplorable but desirable.

In fine, I would have our American novelists be as American as they unconsciously can.[43]

Such a passage—difficult as its instructions might be to actually follow—may be taken as representative. Similar sentiments appear in works that Faulkner almost certainly knew: H. L. Mencken's famous *The American Language* (1919), in which he exhorts Americans to write in American in just the manner that Synge and others had written in Irish; Van Wyck Brooks's "America's Coming-of-Age" (1915); Joseph Warren Beach's *The Outlook for American Prose* (1926);[44] and, as James Kibler has shown, fellow Oxonian Stark Young's theatre commentary in *The New Republic*. "Synge," as Young puts it, "had the advantage over modern writers in that he found a speech ready to hand in the west of Ireland, a brave, rich, poetic idiom."[45]

There is, then, in these debates a stress on orality—"spoken with earthy strength," "language as it is spoken," "the common people will use language," and so on—but the distinction Faulkner wants to make in 1922 is also still primarily a national one, America as against England, as when, also at the end of his essay on O'Neill, he says, "A *national* literature cannot spring from folk lore." But the references to Synge do indicate that he, like Young, saw the possibility of enrichment from sub-cultures and regions. Indeed, these essays are shot through with notions of provincialism, as are the literary debates in *Mosquitoes* (1927), and in both Faulkner often seems not yet to have made up his mind what his own position is. For example, I think most of us would be very hard put to decide which characters "win" any of the arguments in *Mosquitoes,* or even what the really telling points are.

In the essay on drama Faulkner offers a verdict on Mark Twain that he was later to repudiate: "a hack writer who would not have been considered fourth rate in Europe, who tricked out a few of the old proven 'sure fire' literary skeletons with sufficient local color to intrigue the superficial and the lazy." The phrase "who would not have been considered fourth rate in Europe" betrays what Australians today, with reference to their own relationship to the British, often call "the cultural cringe," the notion that Europe somehow automatically possesses the *real* values. (And I suppose that such a view never died out totally in Faulkner, though it was transferred to much less important matters: witness his continuing regard for "aristocratic" talismans from Britain—particular kinds of pipes and jackets, old port, and the like.)

Despite the fact that "local color" is downgraded in Twain's case, the article on O'Neill opens with the following words: "Someone has said—a Frenchman probably; they have said everything—that art is preeminently provincial; i.e., it comes directly from a certain age and a certain locality. This is a very profound statement; for Lear and Hamlet . . . could never have been written anywhere save in England during Elizabeth's reign . . . nor could Madame Bovary have been written in any place other than the Rhone Valley in the nineteenth century; and just as Balzac is nineteenth century Paris. But there are exceptions to this . . . the two modern ones being Conrad and O'Neill." This paragraph, only partially quoted here, sends up a number of flares which, quite apart from whatever light they shed on Conrad and O'Neill, serve to illuminate aspects of the young Faulkner. The "Frenchman's" formulation that Faulkner most likely had in mind here was Hippolyte Taine's famous "*race, milieu, et moment,*" the trio of determinants he developed in detail in his *History of English Literature* (1864).

On the other hand, Phil Stone, in his Preface to his friend's

1924 book of poems, *The Marble Faun*, attributed the view to the English writer George Moore. "George Moore said that all universal art became great by first being provincial," writes Stone, "and the sunlight and mocking birds of North Mississippi are a part of this young man's very being."[46] It may be that both attributions could be justified. Stone does not indicate his precise source in Moore's works, so it is likely that he—and, I think, Faulkner—read Moore's views on the subject in one of the "Imaginary Conversations" Moore contributed to the *Dial* from October 5, 1918, and which were published in book form as *Conversations in Ebury Street* (1924). In one of these, a disquisition on Balzac, Moore says, "to secure great work two things, as Mr. Matthew Arnold said, are necessary, the man and the moment," and then proceeds to speak—suggestively, I think—of the currents in motion in Balzac's France and to compare that situation with Shakespeare's in Elizabethan England.[47]

Fundamentally, whether Faulkner ever read Taine's *History*, the influence of its thesis was so pervasive—as Moore's comment implies, it even got into Matthew Arnold's independent mind—that he could hardly have failed to be aware of it. For example, it appears many times in Lewisohn's *A Modern Book of Criticism*.[48]

If we take these early comments on the necessity for provincialism in the production of art as *the* predominant position Faulkner held, rather than his denigration of Twain as a "local color" writer, then it would be surprising if he really ever needed Sherwood Anderson's advice to mine the resources of his own soil. In fact, it would have been a very short leap for the author of these early essays to see himself in a similar relation to, say, New York as Synge was to London.

Another way of looking at this is to say that in thinking about the richness of oral language and the productiveness of provincialism in national terms, Faulkner—using both the fading and the avant-garde ideas of his own formative years—was in fact facing two of the fundamental questions: the appropriate language to write in and the appropriate subject matter to write about. His major works themselves *are*, as we know, his answers to these questions.

It certainly seems to me that a view like this holds good if looked at through the wrong end of the telescope, so to speak, for it was so often the regional aspect of Faulkner's subject matter that many British reviewers could not abide. "We don't know whether we're being offered Mississippi or mythology," wrote J. B. Priestley. *The Hamlet* "is about some people somewhere in the Southern States of America," muses Orwell. Or an anonymous writer for the *Cambridge Review:* "[Faulkner] is carried away by the sense, by the feeling of his geographical environment. No doubt this absorption helps resolve some conflict within himself, but it does not make for good literature."[49] Cleanth Brooks thinks that opinions like these are the product of an anti–Southern bias absorbed from the American New York or Northern literary establishment,[50] but I think it would be more appropriate to see them as reflections of an anti-regional tendency in British reviewers, themselves predominantly centered on London, which has applied as much to British writing as to Southern fiction.

It is probably no accident that several of the major British writers to welcome Faulkner's work felt themselves—or were seen by others—as regional authors. Richard Hughes was Welsh. Arnold Bennett's major works, including *Anna of the Five Towns* (1902) and *Clayhanger* (1910), the start of a family saga, were set in his native Potteries region of the Midlands. Cowper Powys was intimately associated with Dorset. H. E. Bates, despite vast national popularity, identified himself closely with the countryside of the West Midlands. And Norman Nicholson, whose own best collection of verses is appropriately titled *A Local Habitation* (1972), has spent his whole life in the same house in Millom, Cumberland. Provincial or regional orientations such as these cannot be invoked with reference to *all* of the British authors who wrote appreciatively of Faulkner's achievements; V. S. Pritchett, for example, as his own autobiographical writings reveal, is very much a Londoner. And, of course, such orientations do not, in themselves, account for the warm reception these authors gave to Faulkner.

The response of readers to writers is, ultimately, a most mysterious thing, especially when it involves a translation from one culture to another. To illustrate this point, I am going to risk concluding this talk on a personal note. I grew up in Leicester, which is located at almost the exact center of England and close to the Charnwood Forest, geologically part of one of the very oldest rock formations in England. The most significant historical figure with Leicester associations was Simon de Montfort, traditionally thought of as the father of the English parliament in the late middle ages. He is the main person carved on a large clock tower right in the middle of the city. In an earlier reincarnation I fancied myself as an author of fiction and I wanted to write about these things; they were to be the symbolic framework by which one could depict present-day chaos and loss of meaning. The only author of any note to emerge from Leicester in the twentieth century was none other than the (to me) reactionary C. P. Snow, so you will appreciate that there was no model for me to look to. By coincidence, it was while I was trying to write these things that I discovered Faulkner. My fictional protagonist—who, naturally, bore no resemblance to myself—was a little crazy and had the habit of identifying himself with Simon de Montfort. On one occasion he even succeeded in climbing into the clock tower and squeezing himself right into the stone features of Simon de Montfort's statue. The trouble was that Faulkner's images were too powerful, too obliterating, too overwhelming. I simply could not get down what *I* wanted to say. When my protagonist stared from the eyes of Simon de Montfort he would invariably see not maroon corporation buses, blue-coated butchers' boys on bicycles, and red post office vans, but mules, beaten-up farm vehicles, and, of course, one horse and buggy which persistently tries to drive the wrong way round the town square.

I kept remembering this experience while putting this talk together. And this, in turn, reminded me that, according to

Joseph Blotner's biography, when Faulkner joined the R.A.F. he actually filled in the enlistment document as if he were British, even a member of the Church of England. He claimed that he was born in Finchley in Middlesex and just happened to have been resident in Oxford, Mississippi, as a student, when the war broke out.[51] (Needless to say, it would fit the thesis of this talk better if he had not picked somewhere so close to London to be born!) Disquieting as it may seem when the tenor of his reception in Britain is remembered, I could not help wondering to myself, What would Faulkner's fiction have been like if he had in fact been born and raised in England?

NOTES

1. Joseph Blotner, ed., *Selected Letters of William Faulkner* (New York: Vintage, 1978), 28.
2. Gordon Price-Stephens, "The British Reception of William Faulkner, 1929–1962," *Mississippi Quarterly*, 18 (Summer 1965), 119–200. Where appropriate, *both* the original location of reviews, etc., and their location in Price-Stephens will be provided. Also, John Bassett's compilation, *William Faulkner: The Critical Heritage* (London: Routledge, Kegan Paul, 1975), contains a disproportionate number of British selections; this is cited instead of Price-Stephens whenever its selection is significantly fuller. I did not manage to consult James R. Fitzgerald's unpublished dissertation "William Faulkner's Literary Reputation in Britain, with a Checklist of Criticism, 1929–1972" (Ph.D. University of Georgia, 1973).
3. *The Observer*, July 13, 1930; Price-Stephens, 123.
4. *Sphere*, 132 (February 11, 1933), 200; Price-Stephens, 131.
5. *TLS*, September 1940, 481; *Critical Heritage*, 257–58.
6. *Time and Tide*, 21 (November 9, 1940), 1097; Price-Stephens, 149.
7. "The British Reception of Faulkner's Work," in W. T. Zyla and W. M. Aycock, eds., *William Faulkner: Prevailing Verities and World Literature* (Lubbock: Texas Tech University. Proceedings of the Comparative Literature Symposium, Vol. 6, 1973), 49.
8. "The Furies in Mississippi," *London Mercury*, 35 (March 1937), 517–18; *Critical Heritage*, 218–20.
9. It has been pointed out to me that Claude-Edmond Magny remarked on Faulkner's possible effect on Greene in *L'Age du roman Americain* (1948), trans. Eleanor Hochman as *The Age of the American Novel: The Film Aesthetic of Fiction Between the Two Wars* (New York: Ungar, 1972), 231.
10. "Raffles and Miss Blandish", in Orwell, *A Collection of Essays* (Garden City: Doubleday, 1954), 145. For a longer treatment of Faulkner and detective fiction, see M. Gidley, "Elements of the Detective Story in William Faulkner's Fiction," *Journal of Popular Culture*, 7 (Summer 1973), 97–123.
11. "William Faulkner: The Novel as Form," *Atlantic Monthly*, 164 (November, 1939), 650–54; in Linda W. Wagner, ed., *William Faulkner: Four Decades of Criticism* (East Lansing: Michigan State University Press, 1973), 136–37.
12. "Farmer Who Scribbled a Bit on the Side," in Allsop, *Scan* (London: Hodder and Stoughton, 1965), 57.

13. Hughes, "Faulkner and Bennett," *Encounter*, 21 (September 1963), 59–61; see also Price-Stephens, 122–23 and *Critical Heritage*, 59–60.

14. See Isaacs's series of reviews in the *Annual Register*, Part II: 1931, 35 *(Sanctuary)*; 1933, 37 *(Light in August)*; 1935, 35–36 *(Pylon)*; 1938, 347–48 *(The Unvanquished)*.

15. For Bates, see his *The Modern Short Story: A Critical Survey* (London: Nelson, 1941), 180–83; *Critical Heritage*, 262–63. For Nicholson, see his "Morals and the Modern Novel," *Theology*, 40 (June 1940), 412–20 and *Man and Literature* (London: S.C.M. Press, 1943), 62–63, 122–23, 128–38; Price-Stephens offers a summary of the latter, 155–56.

16. V. S. Pritchett, "The Vogue of Faulkner," *New Statesman and Nation*, 41 (June 2, 1951), 624 and 626; Price-Stephens, 157–58.

17. Malcolm Cowley, *The Faulkner-Cowley File: Letters and Memories, 1944–1962* (New York: Viking, 1966), 14.

18. *Faulkner Studies*, 1 (Winter 1952), 62.

19. For a comparative view of Faulkner's reception in Europe, see Heinrich Straumann, "The Early Reputation of Faulkner's Work in Europe: A Tentative Appraisal," in Ilva Cellini and Giorgio Melchiori, eds., *English Studies Today*, Fourth Series (Rome: Edizioni di Storia e Letteratura, 1966), 443–59. Of the various studies of Faulkner in France, one of the most interesting short ones is Percy G. Adams, "Faulkner, French Literature, and 'Eternal Verities,'" in Zyla and Aycock, 7–24.

20. *Time and the Novel* (New York: Humanities Press reprint edition, 1962), viii. In his review of *Light in August* in 1933 (see note 14 above) Isaacs had written: "The interest in Mr. Faulkner's work does not lie in the mere story . . . but in the spatial deployment of his motives, and in the uncanny grip of time problems."

21. Brooks, 54.

22. This exemption cannot be applied to the treatment of Faulkner in an extraordinarily eccentric book by Professor Martin Green: *Reappraisals: Some Commonsense Readings in American Literature* (London: Hugh Evelyn, 1963), 167–95. It is the kind of work which, if it represents "commonsense," makes one pleased to be eccentric. Brooks demolishes it in the essay cited here, 47–48.

23. *Thomas Hardy: His Career as a Novelist* (London: Bodley Head, 1971), especially 245–50.

24. "The Text of Faulkner's Books: An Introduction and Some Notes," *Modern Fiction Studies*, 9 (Summer 1963), 159–70 and "The Books of William Faulkner: A Guide for Students and Scholars," *Mississippi Quarterly*, 30 (Summer 1977), 417–28.

25. *Selected Letters*, 30.

26. *Memoirs of the Forties* (London: Alan Ross, 1965), 10–11. After the oral delivery of this paper in Oxford, Mississippi, Tom Dardis kindly informed me that there is some information on the Cape-Faulkner relationship in Michael S. Howard's book, *Jonathan Cape, Publisher: Herbert Jonathan Cape, G. Wren Howard* (London: Jonathan Cape, 1971), 120–21. This indicates, if extremely briefly, that Cape had a very limited understanding of Faulkner's work—though since Howard thinks that *As I Lay Dying* was still in the proof stage "early in 1932," it is difficult to know just how much credence to give *his* testimony.

27. *A Writer's Diary*, ed. Leonard Woolf (London: Hogarth Press, 1953), 102, 139, 141, respectively.

28. *Lion in the Garden: Interviews with William Faulkner, 1926–1962*, ed. James B. Meriwether and Michael Millgate (New York: Random House, 1968), 107.

29. See Carvel Collins, "A Fourth Book Review by Faulkner" and "Faulkner's Review of *Ducdame*," *Mississippi Quarterly*, 28 (Summer 1975), 339–46.

30. For evidence of Faulkner's having read *A Modern Book of Criticism* see Joseph Blotner's *Faulkner: A Biography* (New York: Random House, 1974), I, 470–71; for discussions of the implications of Faulkner's having read it see M. Gidley, "Some Notes

on Faulkner's Reading," *Journal of American Studies*, 4 (April 1970), 91–102, and "One Continuous Force: Notes on Faulkner's Extra-Literary Reading" (1970), in *Four Decades*, 55–68.

31. "The Apprenticeship of William Faulkner" (1962), in *Four Decades*, 24–25.

32. "Address upon Receiving the Nobel Prize for Literature" in *Essays, Speeches and Public Letters*, ed. James B. Meriwether (New York: Random House, 1965), 119–21.

33. *Visions and Revisions: A Book of Literary Devotions* (London: Macdonald, 1955), 166–67.

34. *Letters to Louis Wilkinson* (London: Macdonald, 1958), 32.

35. *The Reaction Against Experiment in the English Novel, 1950–1960* (New York: Columbia University Press, 1967). Rabinovitz offers no theories, but documents the reaction in terms of reviews by Snow, Kingsley Amis, Angus Wilson, and others.

36. Quoted in David Lodge, *The Novelist at the Crossroads and Other Essays on Fiction and Criticism* (London: Routledge and Kegan Paul, 1971), 18.

37. *Ibid.*, 3–34. Robert Nye makes a more vigorous claim in his "The Future of the Experimental Novel in English," *The Guardian* (September 10, 1970), 10.

38. "Faulkner and the Avant-Garde," in Evans Harrington and Ann J. Abadie, eds., *Faulkner, Modernism, and Film: Faulkner and Yoknapatawpha, 1978* (Jackson: University Press of Mississippi, 1979), 182–96.

39. "Books and Things: American Drama: Eugene O'Neill," *The Mississippian* (February 3, 1922), 5; reprinted in Carvel Collins, ed., *William Faulkner: Early Prose and Poetry* (Boston: Atlantic-Little, Brown, 1962), 86–89. Subsequent quotations from this short essay will not be page referenced.

40. "Books and Things: American Drama: Inhibitions," *The Mississippian* (March 17, 1922), 5; reprinted in *Early Prose and Poetry*, 93–97. Subsequent quotations will not be page referenced.

41. For example, J. Maclaren-Ross, in *The London Magazine*, 2 (November, 1955), 84–87; Price-Stephens, 165.

42. "English," in Bierce, *The Enlarged Devil's Dictionary*, ed. Ernest J. Hopkins (London: Gollancz, 1967), 80.

43. *Criticism and Fiction* (1891), bound with *My Literary Passions* (1895) (New York: Harpers Library Edition, 1910), 256–57.

44. For some elaboration of these connections and those with Taine treated subsequently, see Gidley, "One Continuous Force" and "Some Notes on Faulkner's Reading." *The Outlook for American Prose* (1926; reprinted, New York: Greenwood Press, 1968) contains a provocative chapter titled "English Speech and American Masters" that had earlier appeared in *The New Republic*.

45. Kibler, "William Faulkner and Provincetown Drama, 1920–1922," *Mississippi Quarterly*, 22 (Summer 1969), 226–36.

46. *The Marble Faun* and *A Green Bough* (New York: Random House, reprint edition, 1965), 7.

47. *Conversations in Ebury Street* (London: Chatto and Windus Landmark Library, 1969), 59.

48. *A Modern Book of Criticism* (New York: Modern Library, 1919), 21–22, 30, 107–11, 125, 126. For Taine's pervasiveness, see Harry Hayden Clark, "The Influence of Science on American Literary Criticism, 1860–1910, Including the Vogue of Taine," *Transactions of the Wisconsin Academy of Sciences, Arts and Letters*, 44 (1955), 109–64.

49. J. B. Priestley, *Literature and Western Man* (London: Heinemann, 1960), 436–37; Price-Stephens, 174. "J.H.P." review of *Absalom, Absalom!*, *Cambridge Review*, 59 (October 22, 1937), 34; Price-Stephens, 142.

50. Brooks, 42–44.

51. Blotner, *A Biography*, I, 210–11.

From Vignette to Vision: The "Old, Fine Name of France" or Faulkner's "Western Front" from "Crevasse" to *A Fable*

MICHEL GRESSET

A geography of the imagination would extend the shore of the Mediterranean all the way to Iowa.

Guy Davenport, *The Geography of the Imagination*

It is one thing to be dealing with a national cliché—i.e., the collective, conventional, and usually rather trite image of itself that a country finds of itself abroad; it is quite another to be dealing with a great writer's representation of a foreign country (even though it may well be familiar to him) as incorporated, if not even integrated, in his own writings. On the one hand, you have France as it is commonly seen, which I suspect is as the land of rare wines and elegant women, châteaux and perfumes, good cooking and a rather difficult language. With luck, you might add a distinguished literature. And it may well be, indeed it is likely, that on July 7, 1925, when he boarded the West Ivis bound for Genoa, young William Faulkner did not have much else in mind but these stereotypes.

However, when by late August he began to write home from Paris, his letters revealed a dramatic change in outlook: what struck him most in France was the presence of war everywhere. Hardly seven years had passed since November 1918, and the image of France which the young American carried away with him when he left in December of the same year was that of a scarred country. He had one very good reason, of course, for being particularly sensitive to whatever could "remind" him of the war: he had not made it. This was clearly a juncture when observation had to make up for experience (or the lack of it), and when imagination enlarged upon observation.

It may be useful here to recall the distinction made by Robert Penn Warren between subject and theme. Milton announces his subject in the very first line of *Paradise Lost*: "Of Man's first disobedience and the fruit/ Of the forbidden tree . . . Sing, Heavenly Muse"; but some of his themes are liberty, authority, rebellion, man and wife. In other terms, a theme is what a writer does with his subject, what and how he invests into it. And my interest here lies in what Faulkner did with France. Working upon the assumption that there would be other opportunities to discuss the existence of a "French Face of Faulkner,"[1] I have deliberately set aside two approaches to my topic, not because they are not worthy of attention, but because they have been dealt with already by other critics, whereas it seems to me that by following a "road not taken," I might perhaps hope to break some fresh ground. Besides, why shouldn't a critic be entitled to his own themes, too?

There are three possible ways of addressing oneself to the question of Faulkner's special relationship with France. The first, which might come under the title "Faulkner in France," is almost purely biographical. How often, for example, did Faulkner go to France between 1925 and 1955? The answer is nine times if you count each of the four stops he made in Paris in the winter and early spring of 1954, and the total of time he spent in France is approximately six months out of the thirteen or so he spent abroad during his whole life. But of course there was a great gap between 1925 and 1950, when he was persuaded not to decline to accept Sweden's invitation. However, we all know that a stop in Paris (so that his daughter might see it) was his excuse for going to Stockholm to receive the Nobel Prize. So while it is safe to conclude that there was no other country that Faulkner visited more, or more often, than France, it is clear that his successive trips had very different values for him, and that the first was by far the most—if not even the only—important one from a literary point of view. As for the eight other visits, I must refer the reader to the King James version of Faulkner's biography, i.e., to the work of Joseph Blotner, by whom one might wish to see an essay entitled "Faulkner in France" as there is a "Faulkner in Hollywood."[2] Chances are that one would find that France was Faulkner's favorite country indeed—or was it Paris which was his favorite city? That is, until in March 1957, he discovered Greece. But that is another matter, a uniquely interesting one in my opinion, which, for the sake of suspense, I shall keep for the end of my allotted space.

The second possible approach would come under the title "Faulkner and France," with a change in the meaning of both words—no longer the man but the writer, and no longer the physical or geographical country, but the image projected upon and reflected by the mind of the budding writer by the cultural and particularly the literary history of that country. After all, Faulkner did not hesitate to give a French title to the very first poem he published, and both the poetry and the prose he wrote after the First World War were full of echoes of the French Symbolists. It may even be that the French influence was far from limited to literature: who knows, for instance, if the impact of Cubism upon Faulkner the individual in 1925 was not in the same nature of a revelation as it had been twelve years before, at the Armory Show, for the collective body in New York City? Although well charted out by such critics as Richard P. Adams, Percy Adams, Michael Millgate, and others,[3] I do not think that the field of French influences upon Faulkner has been exhausted yet. I would be personally interested in exploring a possible debt to Victor Hugo in *A Fable*, for example.[4] However, the question "What did Faulkner owe to France?" has definitely not been my concern in this paper—nor has it been the other side of the same question, namely "What did France owe to Faulkner?" Although some good pioneering work has already been done in the latter field,[5] the span of one more generation of French Faulkner readers and their response has yet to be covered in this interesting though somewhat neglected field, which may best be described as the field of the cross-fertilization of one culture by another. I shall only offer one contribution in the form of a suggestion, which is that we consider Faulkner's early reputation in France (mostly through the work of his original "heralds": Malraux, Sartre, and Camus) in much the same light as one can see the relationship between Poe and France through the uniquely powerful filter of Baudelaire's enthusiastic reading. In both cases, one might even go as far as finding a rather remarkable case of misunderstanding as communication, or of communication through misunderstanding—depending on whether we are pessimists or optimists!

My topic, then, is yet a third one: "Faulkner's France," or what use Faulkner made of France in his fiction. Let us remember that he himself went on record as saying again and again that he used symbolism and particularly what he called the Christian "symbology" as tools for the carpenter that he liked to compare himself with. I shall therefore be concerned with the works, not with the man, with the single exception of my starting-point, which must be biographical or even autobiographical—as, I suspect, most of the so-called "facts" of fiction must be, either originally or ultimately, or both.

I am referring to two letters among the fine series of twenty-five or so which he wrote in the late summer and early fall of 1925 from Paris either to his mother, Mrs. Murry C. Falkner, or to his great-aunt, Mrs. Walter B. McLean of Memphis. The first excerpt is from a letter to his mother dated September 6, which begins with an enthusiastic statement about his having just written 2,000 words on "the Luxembourg gardens and death." Those familiar with the 350-word coda which now ends *Sanctuary* will not fail to note how Faulkner, in his account of the genesis of the piece, has associated the theme (or the motif) of death with a place, the Luxembourg gardens, which is venerable, to be sure, but hardly one to be necessarily linked with death: it is much more currently associated, in fact, with the lively though quiet games of children. Now the letter ends thus:

From Vignette to Vision 101

... near the cathedrals, in the religious stores, any number of inscriptions to dead soldiers, and always at the bottom: "Pray for him." And so many many young men on the streets, bitter and gray-faced, on crutches or with empty sleeves and scarred faces. [At this point one cannot help but recall Donald Mahon in *Soldiers' Pay*.] And now they must still fight, with a million young men already dead between Dunkirk and the Vosges mountains, in Morocco. Poor France, so beautiful and unhappy and so damn cheerful. We dont know how lucky we are, in America.[6]

The second extract is from a letter to his aunt Alabama written only four days later:

But France [as opposed to Switzerland], poor beautiful unhappy France. So innately kind, despite their racial lack of natural courtesy, so palpably keeping a stiff upper lip, with long lists of names in all the churches no matter how small, and having to fight again in Maroc.[7]

Let me immediately offer a somewhat provocative *rapprochement* between these two excerpts and one of the most extraordinary feats of Faulkner's imagination, which is to be found in the "Compson Appendix" of 1946 under the form of the highly improbable, even downright implausible *vignette* of Caddy as the mistress (probably) of a German staff-general:

—a picture, a photograph in color clipped obviously from a slick magazine—a picture filled with luxury and money and sunlight—a Riviera backdrop of mountains and cypresses and the sea, an open powerful expensive chromium-trimmed sports car, the woman's face hatless between a rich scarf and seal coat, ageless and beautiful, cold serene and damned; beside her a German staffgeneral—[8]

What strikes me here, besides the deliberately postcardish quality of the description, is the perfectly arbitrary, indeed the purely imaginative decision of the novelist to set our very last meeting with "the darling of [his] heart" in the South of France in 1943 (whereas *The Sound and the Fury* was so typically Southern, and so definitely set in the post–World War I period). Whether or not Faulkner ever visited the Côte d'Azur or (more probably) Marseille is immaterial here. Indeed there is evidence, from both typescripts of the "Appendix," that he never typed *Riviera* but *Cannebiere* (sic). The latter, being a street in Marseille, would certainly not have fitted the description, which is more evocative of Nice. It was Malcolm Cowley who thought it necessary to emend Faulkner's slight error before publication in the *Portable Faulkner*. However, my point is that both place and date come as additional proof that for Faulkner, from the very beginning of his acquaintance with France until almost thirty years later, when he made a point of visiting Verdun twice (in April 1951, and again in April 1954), France had always been associated, not with a particular geography nor even with a certain type of civilization, but much more symbolically with an historical landscape scarred by war and death-ridden—in short, with a scene of tragedy.

Of course, it is the writer's inalienable right thus to turn France into the matrix of a cluster of interrelated themes: death, war, and history. To this, Faulkner's tragic triad, we might add a fourth dimension, that of time—not, however, as the first generation of French readers, and Sartre in particular, fascinated as he was by Faulkner's technique, saw it, but under the form of a workable polarity between America-as-space and France (or Europe)-as-time. In spite of the fact that the same could perhaps be said of Melville's vision (say in *Clarel* as opposed to *Moby Dick*), it is tempting to think that this had something to do with the fact that Faulkner was a Southerner, or an American with a difference. I think we can find the evidence for this in his special interest for, if not even his sympathy with, the losing side (Vendée's) in the French civil war of 1793. I am referring here to the title he gave to the fifth chapter of *The Unvanquished* in September 1934.

Three years before, however, in his first collection of thirteen stories, he had published four stories entitled "Victory," "Ad Astra," "All the Dead Pilots," and "Crevasse," which, with the addition of "Turnabout," were to constitute the section entitled "The Wasteland" in the *Collected Stories* volume of 1950. To this set of five we may now add two stories: one, "Thrift," was published in 1930 but remained uncollected until 1979; the other, "With Caution and Dispatch," was probably written in the early 1930s but remained unpublished until 1979. In the words of Joseph Blotner, both are "predominantly comic treatments of aerial warfare in the Great War, and offer a contrast . . . to the tragicomic 'Turnabout' and the tragic 'Ad Astra' and 'All the Dead Pilots.' "[9] Thus counting these two, what we have is a total of seven World War I stories which are all, except "Turnabout," implicitly or explicitly set in France. Were it only for this reason, it might be interesting to examine them as a set (though certainly not a "cycle," as Malcolm Cowley would probably call them). I have chosen to discuss only one, "Crevasse," for two reasons: the first is that it has the most interesting imaginary landscape, and the second is that it is the one least discussed by Douglas Day in a 1961 article devoted to "The War Stories of William Faulkner."[10]

Douglas Day (himself, I believe, an aviator in World War II) began quite rightly by observing that "the description of the death of such archaic notions as gallantry and chivalry at the hands of the modern military machinery became a common *motif* in the 'lost generation' fiction of the post–World War I decade, especially in the works of John Dos Passos, E. E. Cummings, and Ernest Hemingway, where disillusionment with the war became the dominant theme" (386). He then observed that the disregard which affected the four war stories published in *These Thirteen* "has, in fact, continued through the 1950's and up to the present." And he quoted two critics who had slighted them in their writings:

In 1951, we find Irving Howe saying of the war stories that "They are specimens of a class rather than individual works of art; specimens of the war story in which a writer, facing an experience impossible to order, invokes its terror and pity through tense understatement." And for William Van O'Connor, "None of these . . . is particularly distinguishable in its harsh subject-matter or unqualified bitter irony from war stories written by John Dos Passos, Ernest Hemingway, or Harvey Allen." (386)

On the contrary, found Douglas Day, "the reader who does not turn a jaundiced eye on the disillusionment-with-war narratives is likely to find a surprising depth in these heretofore unexplored stories" (387). He was right even beyond expectation, particularly if we now turn to "Crevasse" with an eye more interested in the workings of Faulkner's imagination than in the rendition of the experience of a war which, as we know, Faulkner never had anyway.

Although no actual location is given in the text, the title itself might suffice to make the French connection rather clear. The true literary effect of the title, however, is not of setting the story in a foreign locale, but of adumbrating the main interest of the story. A party of twenty-six men led by a captain, a "subaltern," and a sergeant are trying to reach a point on the Western front in 1918 where they can be safe from an artillery barrage. After stumbling painfully along for some time, in typical Faulknerian fashion they "gain the crest of the ridge. The ridge slopes westward into a plateau slightly rolling. Southward, beneath its dun pall, the barrage still rages; westward and northward about the shining empty plain smoke rises lazily here and there above a clump of trees. But this is the smoke of burning things, burning wood and not powder."[11] We may wonder why there should be a "But" to begin the last sentence; the answer, I believe, lies in the unmistakable impression of *déjà vu* given by this scene, which is not structurally different from (indeed it might even be considered as the negative of) the original cresting-of-a-hill scene in "The Hill," the prose sketch written and published ten years before:

> At last his shadow reached the crest and fell headlong over it.
> The opposite valley rim came first into sight, azure and aloof, in the level afternoon sun. Against it, like figures rising in a dream, a white church spire rose, then house-tops, red and faded green and olive, half-hidden in budded oaks and elms. . . . Here and there a thread of smoke balanced precariously upon a chimney. The hamlet slept, wrapped in peace and quiet beneath the evening sun, as it had slept for a century; waiting, invisibly honeycombed with joys and sorrows, hopes and despairs, for the end of time.[12]

There cannot be a doubt that we are dealing here not with "realism" at all, but with an absolutely basic affective landscape, a "structural matrix" as Piaget would call it, of which perhaps the best-known recurrence is to be found in the opening chapter of *Light in August*. In "The Hill" and in "Crevasse" we find the same structure; only one version is made to connote peace like a figure "rising in a dream," whereas the other illustrates the nightmare of the selfsame landscape disfigured by war.

After reaching the bottom of the valley and passing from one small depression to another in a kind of lunar landscape, the party eventually finds this:

> This one is like a miniature valley between miniature cliffs. Overhead they can see only the drowsy and empty bowl of the sky, with a few faint smoke smudges to the northwest. The sound of the barrage is now remote and far away: a vibration in earth felt rather than heard. It is as though they had strayed suddenly into a region, a world where the war had not reached, where nothing had reached, where no life is, and silence itself is dead. . . .
>
> The valley, the depression, strays vaguely before them. They can see that it is a series of overlapping, vaguely circular basins formed by no apparent or deducible agency. Pallid grass bayonets saber at their legs, and after a time they are again among old healed scars of trees to which there cling sparse leaves neither green nor dead, as if they too had been overtaken and caught by a hiatus in time, gossiping dryly among themselves though there is no wind. (115, 468–69)

A little later, after digging up an old rotted rifle and just before finding a half-buried skull, the party are seen to "go on, across the uneven ground, among the chalky knobs thrusting up through the soil. Light, the wan and drowsy light, is laked in the valley, stagnant, bodiless, without heat" (116–17, 469–70). Now this, the second sentence about the quality of the light, could almost be excerpted from quite another story, with quite another, very well-known, landscape—that of the opening scene of *Sanctuary:*

> The spring welled up at the root of a beech tree and flowed away upon a bottom of whorled and waved sand. It was surrounded by a

thick growth of cane and brier, cypress and gum in which the broken sunlight lay sourceless. . . .
Behind him the bird sang again, three bars in monotonous repetition: a sound meaningless and profound out of a suspirant and peaceful following silence which seemed to isolate the spot. . . .
Popeye's hat jerked in a dull, vicious gleam in the twilight as he looked down the hill where the jungle already lay like a lake of ink. . . .[13]

The mere presence of the image of the *lake* in both texts is the sign of an unmistakable link between the two scenes. They seem to have the same root in Faulkner's imagination, which of course is the one and only matrix of such strange, highly disquieting scenes.

In the Gothic climax of the story, the party falls into a cave, the walls of which reveal standing or sitting "skeletons in dark tunics and bagging Zouave trousers, their moldering arms beside them; the captain recognizes them as Senegalese troops of the May fighting of 1915, surprised and killed by gas probably in the attitudes in which they had taken refuge in the chalk caverns" (120, 472). In the end, however, they succeed in digging a tunnel into the slide obstructing the mouth of the cavern. And here is a third, equally unmistakable echo of other works; the wounded man in the party "begins to laugh again, meaningless and high," and the very last sentence describes "the wounded man's gibberish . . . meaningless and unemphatic and sustained" (123, 474). At this point one cannot but recall the ending of both "The Kingdom of God" and of *The Sound and the Fury*, with Benjy's voice "mounting toward its unbelievable crescendo" of "just sound."[14]

To sum up, let me quote the conclusion of Douglas Day's too brief comment on "Crevasse": " 'Crevasse' may indeed be compared with *The Red Badge of Courage* as another example of the successful imaginative portrayal of the horror of war by a brilliant writer who has himself had no actual experience in combat" (393). I cannot but agree with this conclusion, although I feel that "Crevasse" is even more rewarding if one reads it less as a genre story than as a painting in words, a veritable "landscape of fear,"[15] in one word a nightmare. It then becomes very interesting to set it against another story with a French title, and one which, perhaps not surprisingly, mostly French critics have written about, particularly François Pitavy. Here is what he has to say about "Carcassonne," which ends the last section of *These Thirteen* just as "Crevasse" ends the first, so that the two stories stand to each other in a kind of neat symmetry:

> Without any doubt, "Carcassonne" is a key-text at the threshold of Faulkner's career as a novelist. In the paradoxical conjunction to be found at the end of a vertical movement of soaring and of a will to be rooted in the "dark and tragic figure of the Earth, his mother," one can find the structural outline of Faulkner's imagination: verticality and horizontality, the spirit and the body, etc.[16]

In all respects, then, "Crevasse" and "Carcassonne" are poles apart: while one literally tells the story of a nightmare, the horror of being buried alive, the other visualizes the aerial/ideal dream of the Pegasus-like poet; both are essentially two facets of Faulkner's imagination. In fact, although it is noteworthy that in both cases the writer should have resorted to a French title, they have little if anything to do with France, and certainly nothing to do with "realism": the "Frenchness" of their titles is entirely metaphorical.

Between the late twenties and World War II, however, France was not much in the writer's toolbox. Hollywood may have replaced it, for better or for worse. And I certainly agree with Bruce Kawin that not only the part played by Faulkner in Hollywood, but also and perhaps primarily the part played by Hollywood in Faulkner's development as a writer are much less negligible than was believed at first.[17] It may even be upheld that Hollywood was the mediator of Faulkner's second literary meeting with France. Let us bear in mind that the first assignment he received on arriving at Warner's in Burbank in the summer of 1942 was a subject which appears to have been successively entitled "Journey Toward Dawn" or "Journey Toward Hope," then "De Gaulle" or "Free France" or yet "The Free French," and finally "De Gaulle Story." By November, after writing several shorter drafts amounting to 120 pages, he had finished a 153-page first treatment under the latter title. Here is a paragraph which should draw our attention, especially if we look at it from the vantage point of *A Fable*:

> Georges represents the French individual as De Gaulle represents the abstract idea of Free France. He is a typical Frenchman, perhaps a peasant, perhaps a city-dweller, perhaps a Parisian. I see him as a member of the middle-class, with some education, the possessor of all the French middle-class virtues. He represents the class which by tradition is democratic, which is the backbone of any democracy. It has pride in its Fatherland, in the traditions. It has regard for its fellow man, especially for those who are not as well off as it is. In character he is a simple young man who looks forward to peace in which to marry and raise his children and do his work. He wants only that and no more.[18]

Needless to say, the degree of generality here almost precludes anything typically French, and I do not know what "the French middle-class virtues" are which are not also the virtues of the middle-class all over the world. However, that is precisely what is noteworthy. France is made to stand for democracy in jeopardy. Like Georges himself, it is a symbol from the start. But there is more to it if we bear in mind that this was written in the late summer of 1942, after the Battle—and the fall—of France.

After the "De Gaulle Story" was discarded, the spring of 1943 saw Faulkner at work on "Battle Cry," which also had French sequences. But in the fall of the same year came what Joseph Blotner has aptly described as "the most extended and laborious single project of his career as a creative artist."[19] First entitled "Who?" when it was only a 51-page treatment based on an idea by Henry Hathway and William Bacher, *A Fable*, the "magnum o."[20] of Faulkner's literary career, which was not completed until eleven years after it was incepted, can now be seen under a new light if one cares to look at it from the following double viewpoint: *(a)* the part played by Hollywood in Faulkner's most ambitious treatment of France as a literary subject; *(b)* the possibility that the transformation of France into an unmistakable theme is a process that can also be seen at work, although in a different mode (the autobiographical), in "Mississippi," published only a few months before *A Fable*. In the latter, Faulkner uses history (including his own) in order to modify geography (the river). In other terms, his interest in geography is only in the palimpsest of man's presence upon the earth: "People first, where second," after all. There is more, however. Why should Hitler suddenly appear in *Go Down, Moses*, if not because Faulkner was also careful to bring geography up to date, as it were? Hitler's name, more than anybody else's, seems to doom the wilderness forever. But the passage in "Delta Autumn" I am referring to may even achieve more than this. In old Ike's mouth, Faulkner has put words which take on a strangely moving, prophetic quality if one reads them from a strictly contemporary point of view (that is, bearing in mind that the date Harold Ober received the story was December 16, 1940):

> "So that's what's worrying you," the old man said. "I aint noticed this country being short of defenders yet, when it needed them. You did some of it yourself twenty-odd years ago, before you were a grown man even. This country is a little mite stronger than any one man or group of men outside of it or even inside of it either. I reckon, when the time comes and some of you have done got tired of hollering we are whipped if we dont go to war and some more are hollering we are whipped if we do, it will cope with one Austrian paper-hanger, no matter what he will be calling himself. My pappy and some other better men than any of them you named tried once to tear it in two with a war, and they failed."[21]

To put it yet another way, what I am suggesting here is that there are elements not so much of continuity as of repetition in Faulkner's vision of the South in *Go Down, Moses* and in his vision of France in *A Fable*. The prevalent agent, indeed the catalyst in his outlook on the two countries (I was about to say the two nations), is a highly idealistic, even a spiritual conception, or rather vision, of history.

Considered not as a replay of the Passion story, but as a text at least partly structured by clusters of images, and particularly by images of space and time, *A Fable* is amazingly lacking in the dimension of Faulkner's art which was overwhelmingly and magnificently present in *Go Down, Moses,* and which Cleanth Brooks has aptly called the poetry of nature.[22] The only recurrent natural image—more than an image, in fact: a symbolic motif, such as the one in the Nobel Prize speech—is that of sunset: for instance, "Wednesday Night" begins with "the saffron sunset between the violet city and the cobalt-green firmament" (212)—hardly a "realistic" picture, and hardly a typical French sunset. But of course one must not forget that sunset had been a highly favorite moment of day with Faulkner ever since the pseudo epiphany at sunset dramatized in "The Hill."[23] More broadly speaking, however, the system of images which makes *A Fable* function as a novel (or perhaps, more aptly, as an epic poem in prose) almost in spite of its being a fable, reveals a triple polarity: America vs. France (or Europe), or the New World vs. the Old; country and small town vs. city; and last but not least, individual vs. crowd, mob, or even mass (or yet, in a more abstract way, man in the singular vs. man in the plural). *A Fable* is quite abstract, after all: "nothing now but the correlative to a map" (105) one can read in the text and could use as a general description: *A Fable* stands to the rest of Faulkner's works, particularly the Yoknapatawpha novels, as a map to a landscape.

This system of images, however, is not a simple, mechanical working of oppositions. The latter (individual vs. mass) does not fit any of the former polarities, as it can be found to be distributed evenly between them. In other terms, the America vs. Europe opposition is clearcut and coincides almost exactly with the country and small town vs. city polarity (in much the same way as the Jefferson/Jackson opposition is found to work in *Requiem for a Nun*); through repetition and development, these images are gradually raised to the status of recurrent symbolic motifs. However, the theme, the grand romantic theme of the book, is at work on both sides of the Atlantic, whether in "Arkansas, in a new paint-rank hotel room in a little booming logging town itself less old than last year" (159), which is the scene of the central episode of the "Notes on a Horsethief" section (it could also be a setting out of *Huckleberry Finn*), or in Chaulnesmont, the medieval city almost out of Victor Hugo's *Notre Dame de Paris*, which, of course, is no more the real Chaumont than Jefferson is Oxford strictly speaking, and where most of the action of the book takes place.

At this point I would like to pause a while for three general remarks on the nature of *A Fable*. *(a)* I just wrote "where most of the action of the book takes place"—which is very little in fact. *A Fable* is an almost static book, not events but situations being responsible for whatever narrative energy the book possesses. As far as plot is concerned, there is a minimum of it since the only question is not even whether the men responsible for the mutiny shall be shot, but how many of them shall be: whether the whole 3,000 men of the regiment,[24] or the gang of thirteen, or just one, the corporal, the individual in the lawcourt of history—just as De Gaulle already was in Faulkner's treatment. *A Fable* is no more a novel of war than it is "a pacifist book."[25] *(b)* Whatever action there is—apart from prologue (the front) and epilogue (Douaumont)—is actually nothing but either an unceasing coming and going of individuals through innumerable doors (and gazing through windows), or a moving to and fro of crowds under "the old arch," the venerable though forbidding city gate which of course adumbrates the part played by the Arch of Triumph at the end. *(c)* From both preceding propositions the dialectic synthesis is easy enough. What is this fable which is not quite a novel nor quite a prose poem, if not a unique (others might say monstrous) cross between a play that could be set on a stage with a limited number of highly stylized characters whose main activity is verbal, and a film script (which it was to begin with) with few locations and superb crowd scenes? And if by an act of imagination one sets it to music and has the characters sing instead of talk, *A Fable* becomes an opera: the complete genre, and the nearest approach to the grand epic poem in the manner of *Paradise Lost* which Faulkner could handle as a modern (instead of, say, Stephen Vincent

Benet's somewhat conservative solution in *John Brown's Body*).

To return to the French setting of *A Fable*, however, here is the best pair of symmetrical quotations I could find in order to illustrate my point that the main theme of *A Fable* is equally distributed between the two geographical and historical scenes used. The first is from section I; it describes Chaulnesmont:

> . . . presently the ones she had passed began to overtake her in turn and pass her; soon she was running in a fading remnant of *dispersal*, panting and stumbling, seeming to run now in spent and frantic retrograde to the whole city's motion, the whole world's, so that when she reached the Place de Ville at last, and stopped, all mankind seemed to have drained away and vanished. . . . (18–19; emphasis added)

The second quotation is from the "Notes on a Horsethief" episode contained in "Tuesday":

> People were entering now not only through the judge's chambers but through the main doors at the back too, not just men and boys now but women also . . . until not just the town but the county itself, all of which had probably seen the three-legged horse run, and most of which had contributed at least one or two each of the dollars (by now the total had reached the thirty thousand) which the two men had won and which the old Negro preacher had escaped with and indubitably concealed—seemed to be *converging* steadily into the courthouse. . . .
>
> And, standing with his prize behind the railing's flimsy sanctuary, bayed, trapped in fact . . . the lawyer watched Man pouring steadily into the tabernacle, the shrine itself, of his last tribal mysteries . . . (171–72, emphasis added)

Like an organism (a word which, interestingly, on page 519 of the typescript setting copy, Faulkner seems to have confused with "orgasm"), *A Fable* can thus be seen to develop through a series of dispersals and convergences, like so many systoles and diastoles. In the two instances given above as in so many others, Faulkner chooses to pit an individual against the mass, and always the former is conceived as standing, vertical, while the latter is seen as flowing in or draining away.

Nor should this come as a surprise if one looks back to *Intruder in the Dust* and *Requiem for a Nun* as steps toward *A Fable*—which indeed they were from the point of view of the thematics implied in such a vision as in this passage from *A Fable:*

> . . . thinking how it was no wonder that man had never been able to solve the problems of his span upon earth, since he has taken no steps whatever to educate himself, not in how to manage his lusts and follies; they harm him only in sporadic, almost individual instances; but in *how to cope with his own blind mass and weight*. . . . (161; emphasis added)

Later, one reads this fantastic, quasi-cataclysmic vision of Man in the plural:

> . . . huddling still in the dusk that fading and shapeless mass which might have been Protoplasm itself, eyeless and tongueless on the floor of the first dividing of the sea, palpant and vociferant with no motion nor sound of its own but instead to some gigantic uproar of the primal air-crashing tides' mighty copulation. . . . (225)

At this point, of course, the France vs. America polarity has become utterly irrelevant. Through symbolization, the French setting has been lost sight of almost as completely as the American one in pages 151–89. Toward the end, i.e., before it is reintroduced as a highly specific setting in "Tomorrow," France is hardly more than the sound of its name, whatever meanings the book itself has piled upon it. Shouldn't this remind us of Faulkner's own meditation on the very name Sartoris at the end of his third novel? "For there is death in the sound of it, and a glamorous fatality, like silver pennons downrushing at sunset, or the dying fall of horns along the road to Roncevaux."[26] In the "De Gaulle Story" typescript, Faulkner had written of "the old fine name of France."[27] In *A Fable*, France is neither a concept nor an image, but, as so often in fiction, a concept-in-image in which the signified outcrops the signifier by far.[28]

If we look at the function of France as a narrative agent, it begins with "not just in France, but in forty kilometres of the Western front" (8), which strikes the keynote once for all: France stands for the whole West. "France? England too; the whole West" (125); "France, Europe, home" (264), etc. If this is patriotism, the word is to be taken in its strict, original meaning of the defense of one's home or fatherland. However, this is hardly typical of the West—so that the defense of France in *A Fable* becomes the defense of one's (everyman's) highest value upon earth. There can hardly be another interpretation of the semigrotesque, semisublime invention of the association entitled *Les Amis Myriades et Anonymes à la France de Tout le Monde* (146).[29]

Besides this grand idea of France-as-symbol, there are two other features in Faulkner's vision in *A Fable* that seem to be worth pointing out. One is that there is hardly a French landscape that is not a cityscape; and the other is the clear-cut distinction between Chaulnesmont, the medieval city which can be described as the epitome of whatever the word "Gothic" ever meant for Faulkner, and Paris, which is described in the most elaborate baroque terms:

> . . . that city which was the world, too, since of all cities it was supreme, dreamed after and adored by all men, and not just when she was supreme in her pride but when—as now—she was abased from it. Indeed, never more dreamed after and adored than now, while in abasement; never more so than now because of what, in any other city, would have been abasement . . . conquered—or rather, not conquered, since, France's Paris, she was inviolate and immune to the very iron heel beneath which the rest of France (and, since she was the world's Paris too, the rest of the world also) lay supine and abased—impregnable and immune: the desired, the civilised world's inviolate and forever unchaste, virgin barren and insatiable. . . . (248–49)

In this composite vision of woman both fallen and proud, Paris is definitely the *femme fatale* of Western civilization: "Eve and Lilith both to every man in his youth so fortunate and blessed as to be permitted within her omnivorous insatiable orbit" (248). There may even be something of the Cow in this vision of Paris![30]

Chaulnesmont is entirely different; in fact, it hardly exists as place—merely as the space of the action or the setting of the play, with "hovel and tenement voiding into lane and alley and nameless *cul-de-sac*, and lane and alley and *cul-de-sac* compounding into streets," up to the "broad boulevards converging like wheel spokes into the *Place de Ville*" (4). The latter quotation elicits two remarks: *(a)* as every Faulkner reader must recognize, the organization of space here is no different from what all of the Yoknapatawpha novels have made us familiar with, namely Jefferson as the "hub" of the country; *(b)* a *Place de Ville* never existed in any French city. What Faulkner meant, of course, was *Place de l'Hôtel de Ville*. But who cares? Someone did, however—and I cannot resist quoting from a letter I found in the Random House papers now at the University of Virginia Library:

> Gentlemen:
> I am preparing a book on Faulkner from a French viewpoint (you know that we pride ourselves at having discovered him), and I cannot resist bringing a little matter to your attention—if and when you re-issue *A Fable*.
>
> There are some ludicrous mistakes in the French names that amount to nonsense, like Place de Ville, Comité de Ferrovie, etc. . . .
>
> It mars an admirable book.

The letter is signed by one Anne Taillefer-Stokes; it was written in New York in May 1964. I do not know what else the lady's projected book might have told us, but it should be clear by now that this was a baseless charge, or rather a charge based upon the old, apparently ineradicable "realistic" assumption about fiction. Of course Faulkner did not want to communicate an atlas, but to convey a feeling, of France; his *Comité de Ferrovie*, for instance, is quite an interesting and charming take-off from the well-known, old *Comité des Forges*. (I only wish he had done the same with the New Testament!)

Back to Chaulnesmont, though. Here is how, after a breathtaking description of the motley crowd swarming in it as in a "tremendous bee-hive" (239), the old general sees the city from his window:

> Out of that enduring and anguished dust it rose, out of the dark Gothic dream, carrying the Gothic dream, arch- and buttress-winged, by knight and bishop, angels and saints and cherubim groined and pilastered upward into soaring spire and pinnacle where goblin and demon, gryphon and gargoyle and hermaphrodite yelped in icy soundless stone against the fading zenith. (242)

How could we not be reminded here of some of Faulkner's wonderful early letters to his mother from Europe:

> I left Genoa for Milan . . . when I looked out and saw Pavia. A bridge, where the German army got to in 1917, and a cathedral. It is a lovely place—quite old, little narrow streets, all cobbled, and only two automobiles in town. It is so quiet and provincial—you pass an old wall and a door, and carved over the door is the date—1149 or something.[31]

And again, ten days later in the same month of August 1925:

> The cathedral of Notre Dame is grand. Like the cathedral at Milan it is all covered with cardinals mitred like Assyrian kings, and knights leaning on long swords, and saints and angels, and beautiful naked Greek figures that have no religious significance what ever, and gargoyles—creatures with heads of goats and dogs, and claws and wings on men's bodies, all staring down in a jeering sardonic mirth.[32]

There is much to reap from both these passages, not only from a purely biographical point of view, but mostly from that of the imaginative process: how Faulkner was literally charmed by Pavia as, say, by a mother image, whereas he was impressed by Notre Dame (which is surprisingly identified with the cathedral of Milan) to the point of using some of the words that are to be found in his poetry when he describes his idea, or vision, of the aggressively manly personification of Death, or "Derision." Once more, we come up with a neat polarity: the romanesque, the provincial, and the motherly on the one hand; the Gothic, the urban, and the manly on the other.

Thus, whereas Chaulnesmont does not even have to be French, it is both necessary and sufficient, according to the laws of Faulkner's imagination, that it be Gothic. This brings me to my last point at last, or rather to Faulkner's, since I feel that he must have the last word with the extraordinarily revealing (and moving) account he gave on May 8, 1957, to engineering students at the University of Virginia, in answer to the very lucky question: "Mr Faulkner . . . wouldn't you mind telling us a little about your trip to Greece?" Before coming to it, however, let me sum up what I have been trying to say.

Faulkner's France has nothing to do with the France of travel agencies. It is almost always mediated by images of World War I. However, through the highly stylized, neo-epic, deliberately "grand" style of *A Fable,* France is elevated almost indefinitely to a literary status that is more than that of a metaphor: in my opinion, it stands somewhere between Hawthorne's scarlet letter and Melville's white whale. Not only is it the theatre, but the very symbol of a drama so universal as to render any kind of local color totally amiss. However, although typically Faulknerian in the manner in which it is conveyed, the symbol has also, as it must, a transindividual and highly ideological nucleus, or conceptual content, since France is no less than the *locus* where the highest values of the Western world are at stake and must be saved. So, for instance, was the France of the British writer Charles Morgan, whose *Ode to France* (dated "September 1942") ended with this stanza:

> Thou art the wisdom, O France, within all knowledge,
> The salt of delight. Who dies for thee
> Dies for mankind's perpetual redemption;
>   And none can live in thee
> That has not died the death of saints and lovers
> And been raised up, in hate and holiness,
> To beat down Satan under thy feet.[33]

It is important to realize here that the category of taste must fail to do justice to the latter association no more nor less than to Faulkner's association of Paris with Eve and Lilith both. To us, however, the France of *A Fable* is primarily the France of Faulkner's imagination, especially as it can be seen to stand in the same relationship to him as Caddy stood to Quentin with his "principle that honor must be defended whether it was or not because defended it was whether or not."[34]

It may be that no other artist has read as much into France as Faulkner did after or with the cumulative effect of two wars he did not make. And yet there was something there, as in the rest of Europe, which he was afraid of: something which he seems to have read again and again in the old world's cities and cathedrals, whether English or French or German or Italian. And this was what he called "something Gothic and in a sense a little terrifying," which only in Greece, at the age of fifty-nine, did he find himself delivered from at last. Here is the full account of his trip, which I suggest should tell us as much if not more about Europe in general—or Mississippi or even Iowa for that matter—as about Greece:

> It was a strange experience in that that was the only country that looked exactly like we had—I mean, the background, the educational background of the Anglo-Saxon had taught him to expect it to look. And sure enough there was the Hellenic light that I had heard of, had read about. And I saw Homer's wine-dark sea too. And there was a—*the only place I was in where there was a sense of a very distant past but there was nothing inimical in it.* In the other parts of the Old World there is a sense of the past but there is something Gothic and in a sense a little terrifying. . . . The people seem to function against that past that for all its remoteness in time it was still inherent in the light, the resurgence of spring, you didn't expect to see the ghosts of the old Greeks, or expect to see the actual figures of the gods, but you had a sense that they were near and they were still powerful, not inimical, just powerful. That they themselves had reached and were enjoying a kind of nirvana, they existed, but they were free of man's folly and trouble, of having to involve themselves in man's problem. That they at last had the time to watch what man did without having to be involved in it. Yes, it was very interesting. I think that two weeks is not only too short, it's an insult to that country, that one should go with no limit to his visit. That there's no end to what you can see, *and there sure enough you see something which is exactly like what you imagined.* There will be the plain and across it suddenly there is Parnassus with snow on it, and the old ruins, they look ancient but there's a sense as though it

From Vignette to Vision 119

happened only yesterday. That whether Agamemnon ever lived, ever was an actual man or not, there he was, because he had to be. It was necessary. What he was in the literary history of man's spirit, so therefore he must have existed at one time as a flesh and blood man.[35] (emphasis added)

Shall I dare offer a "translation" of this most extraordinary confession? In my reading of it, only in Greece had Faulkner found at last, at long last, the "right to dream" which is the lovely, title of Gaston Bachelard's last, posthumous book.[36]

NOTES

1. This title has been used, literally or otherwise, so many times since World War II that I must refer the reader to the forthcoming book by André Bleikasten and myself (University of Indiana Press) for a complete bibliography. For a few studies, however, see note 5.
2. Joseph Blotner, "Faulkner and Hollywood," in *Man and the Movies*, ed. W. R. Robinson (1967; rpt. Baltimore: Penguin, 1969), 261–303.
3. Richard P. Adams, "The Apprenticeship of William Faulkner," *Tulane Studies in English*, 12 (1962), 113–56. Percy Adams, "The Franco-American Faulkner," *Tennessee Studies in Literature*, 5 (1960), 1–13; "Faulkner, French Literature, and Eternal Verities," in *William Faulkner: Prevailing Verities and World Literature*, ed. W. T. Zyla and W. M. Aycock (Lubbock: Texas Tech Press, 1973), 7–24. Michael Millgate, "Faulkner's Masters," *Tulane Studies in English*, 23 (1978), 143–55.
4. See William Faulkner, *A Fable* (New York: Random House, 1954), 173, 268. All subsequent references to this novel are given between parentheses in the text and refer to this edition or to the first "Modern Library" edition of 1960, which has the same pagination.
5. Stanley Woodworth, *William Faulkner en France: Panorama critique, 1931–1952* (Paris: M. J. Minard, 1959) and Robert Weber, "Aspekte der Faulkner-Kritik in Frankreich," in *Jahrbuch für Amerikastudien*, Band 6 (Heidelberg: Carl Winter, 1961), 152–67.
6. Joseph Blotner, ed., *Selected Letters of William Faulkner* (New York: Random House, 1977), 18.
7. *Ibid.*, 19.
8. Malcolm Cowley, ed., *The Portable Faulkner* (New York: Viking Press, 1946), 746.
9. Joseph Blotner, ed., *Uncollected Stories of William Faulkner* (New York: Random House, 1979), 700–701.
10. *Georgia Review*, 10 (Winter 1961), 385–94. Further references are given in the text.
11. William Faulkner, *These Thirteen* (New York: Cape and Smith, 1931), 112; *Collected Stories* (New York: Random House, 1950), 467. Further references are given in the text, to both volumes successively.
12. Carvel Collins, ed., *William Faulkner: Early Prose and Poetry* (Boston: Little, Brown and Co., 1962), 90–92.
13. William Faulkner, *Sanctuary* (New York: Cape and Smith, 1931), 1–5.
14. William Faulkner, *The Sound and the Fury* (New York: Cape and Smith, 1929), 400.

15. See Yi-fu Tuan, *Landscapes of Fear* (Oxford: Basil Blackwell, 1979).
16. François Pitavy, "William Faulkner romancier, 1929–1939" (Diss., Paris IV, 1978), 62. My translation.
17. See Bruce Kawin, *Faulkner and Film* (New York: Frederick Ungar, 1977), and his unpublished contribution to the "Faulkner and Hollywood" conference, Boston College, November 15, 1980.
18. William Faulkner, "De Gaulle Story," screenplay, first draft (Hollywood: Warner Brothers, 1942), 5. Quoted from his notes with the kind permission of Joseph Blotner.
19. "Faulkner in Hollywood," 288.
20. Letter to Malcolm Cowley, April 23, 1946, *Selected Letters of William Faulkner,* 233.
21. William Faulkner, *Go Down, Moses* (New York: Random House, 1942), 338–39.
22. See chapter 3, "Faulkner as Nature Poet," in Cleanth Brooks, *William Faulkner: The Yoknapatawpha Country* (New Haven: Yale University Press, 1963), 29–46.
23. See my "Faulkner's 'The Hill'," *Southern Literary Journal,* 6 (1974), 3–18.
24. On page 487 of the typescript setting copy at the University of Virginia Library, there is an interesting sidelight on Faulkner's relationship to facts; instead of a number, he typed between parentheses: "(how many men in a 1918 French regt???)," and it must have been his editor, Saxe Commins, who checked and then wrote the number in red pencil.
25. William Faulkner, "A Note on *A Fable*," in *A Faulkner Miscellany,* ed. James B. Meriwether (Jackson: University Press of Mississippi, 1974), 162.
26. William Faulkner, *Sartoris* (New York: Harcourt and Brace, 1929), 380.
27. Here is the complete sentence: "Then his [Georges's, after he escapes from France] little house represents to Georges what the old fine name of France now cast into the dust represents to De Gaulle." First draft of screenplay, 6.
28. Much in the same way as with the eponyms of both *The Scarlet Letter* and *Moby Dick.*
29. Even more revealing is what Faulkner actually typed in capitals on page 209 of the setting copy: "LES AMIS MYRIADES ET ANONYMES VERS LA FRANCE DE TOUT LE MONDE," or "the myriad anonymous society of the friends *towards* everybody's France"—another example of convergence.
30. See Monique Pruvot's remarkable study of the episode about Ike and the cow in *The Hamlet:* "Le Sacre de la Vache," *Delta,* 3 (November, 1976), 105–23.
31. *Selected Letters of William Faulkner,* 8.
32. *Ibid.,* 12.
33. Charles Morgan, *Ode to France* (London: Macmillan, 1942), [7].
34. *The Portable Faulkner,* 738.
35. Frederick L. Gwynn and Joseph L. Blotner, eds., *Faulkner in the University: Class Conferences at the University of Virginia, 1957–1958* (1959; New York: Random House, 1965), 129–30.
36. Gaston Bachelard, *Le Droit de rêver* (Paris: Presses universitaires de France, 1970).

Faulkner in Italy

AGOSTINO LOMBARDO

The first article on William Faulkner appeared in Italy in 1931—and it was due, significantly, to that great critic and scholar and literary man, Mario Praz, who, while denying any competence in the field of American literature, was among the first to introduce American authors to the Italian public.[1] The first Italian translation of a Faulkner novel *(Pylon)* was published in 1937.[2] Since then, all the novels and a good number of the stories have been translated,[3] a collection of the complete works, edited by Fernanda Pivano, has been started (the "plan" was discussed with Faulkner himself),[4] and articles, essays, and books on Faulkner have been written.[5] Owing to the exceptionally intense development, in the last decades, of American studies in Italian universities, innumerable courses and seminars on Faulkner have been and are regularly being offered, dissertations have been and are regularly being written, and often are published as articles or books. Faulkner's reputation is now firmly established in Italy, and he is indeed considered the greatest American writer of our century.

This does not mean, however, that he is, in Italy, a "popular" writer. This is true of Ernest Hemingway and F. Scott Fitzgerald; it was true, in the thirties and forties, of minor writers such as Edgar Lee Masters, or William Saroyan, or John Steinbeck; it is unfortunately true, at present, of much less valuable, if more commercial, writers. But it was and is *not* true of Faulkner. There was of course a certain amount of journalistic ado in 1950, when the Nobel Prize was assigned to him; or during his rare and often silent apparitions at round tables or press conferences; and the twentieth anniversary of his death has been celebrated also in Italy with articles (some of which are penetrating) in newspapers. But there is not, in our country, a Faulkner "myth" even slightly comparable to that surrounding Hemingway or that, fostered by the movies, surrounding Fitzgerald.

Faulkner would have presumably been the first to refuse any such idealization of himself, and one scarcely needs to refer to certain passages of his letters where his refusal to become a public figure is vigorously and suggestively expressed:

> I'm old-fashioned and probably a little mad too; I dont like having my private life and affairs available to just any and everyone who has the price of the vehicle it's printed in, or a friend who bought it and will lend it to him. . . . I would have preferred nothing at all prior to the instant I began to write, as though Faulkner and Typewriter were concomitant, coadjutant and without past on the moment they first faced each other at the suitable (nameless) table. . . . I will want to blue pencil everything which even intimates that something breathing and moving sat behind the typewriter which produced the books. . . . I will protest to the last: no photographs, no recorded documents. It is my ambition to be, as a private individual, abolished and voided from history, leaving it markless, no refuse save the printed books; I wish I had enough sense to see ahead thirty years ago and, like some of the Elizabethans, not signed them. It is my aim, and every effort bent, that the sum and history of my life, which in the same sentence is my obit and epitaph too, shall be them both: He made the books and he died.[6]

I can personally bear witness to Faulkner's evasiveness, to his defensive attitude, in Rome, in front of all questions ("I am a farmer") but especially in front of those trying to delve into his personal life. And such a witness is Mario Materassi, author of an important book on Faulkner's novels, who wittily describes his nonvisit to Faulkner at Rowan Oak, the desperate and unsuccessful attempt to be asked to enter, the few words mumbled on both sides.[7] Yet another witness is Emilio Cecchi, one of Italy's most influential critics as well as most exquisite essayists, who draws a delightful portrait of the writer at a Roman party, evoking a Faulkner "not only extraordinary small and fragile but also detached from everybody, as if he were at the same time there and at an unreal distance. One had the impression of looking at him through binoculars." Faulkner, Cecchi comments, "has nothing of the professional literary man, who is capable of moving deftly among profane necessities. To his psychology, which one might call tragic but which is undoubtedly without illusions, that happy turmoil, that crowd, certainly appeared as an almost incomprehensible rite, from which, within the limits of courtesy, he chose to remain absent."[8]

But even more deeply than by his own attitude, Faulkner's lack of popularity in Italy is motivated (not to speak of the linguistic, stylistic, and intellectual complexity which makes him a "difficult" writer not only for a foreign public) by his not fitting into the particular vision from which the Italian "fortune" of American literature springs. This fortune, this myth ("there is no other myth," a critic justly observes, "comparable to it in Italian culture"),[9] this perhaps unique episode of intellectual history and cultural interchange, has been too widely studied and too minutely analyzed to render the detailed examination necessary here.[10] It is sufficient to note that the interest in American literature (an early one, born during the Italian Risorgimento and the American Civil War and already strong at the end of the nineteenth century)[11] was greatly fostered in the thirties and forties of the twentieth century (that is, under Fascism) by two opposing and complementary trends. On one side there are "literati" like Carlo Linati, Emilio Cecchi, and Mario Praz who "discover" American literature but consider it fundamentally "barbaric"; they look at it patronizingly (they would all subscribe to Linati's words: "The European mind aspires to something deeper than the ability to build machinery or to enjoy oneself in a carefree manner. It aspires to the grace of culture, the sweetness of emotion. It lives on thoughts, desires, and passions; it not only glories in but feeds on its artistic, musical and poetic genius; tradition is its second nature. . . . The American, instead, is rootless by nature")[12] but also with a fascinated dismay. Thus Mario Praz, writing in 1929 the first Italian article on Hemingway, can join illuminating observations on Hemingway's style ("His style is faithful to the outlines of things with a steadiness which has something impersonal about it . . . the greatest economy of means, as in natural processes . . . a maximum of evocative power") with remarks which are witty but substantially hard to accept ("Hemingway . . . has not read Pirandello, and his pugilists do not suffer from metaphysical languors. And he knows nothing of the history of religion, and his matadors are not thinking of the sacrifice of Mithras when they strike the bull between the horns. It is indeed hard to imagine what he has read").[13] In any case, what is stressed is the simplicity of American literature, its naturalness, its "realism," and it is such an image which is offered not only to the Italian public but also to Italian literature. In connection with the article on Hemingway, Praz himself was to write, after the war: "To a literature saturated with culture as Italian literature was around 1929, so that it came naturally to compare it with the Petrarchists, I put forward as a remedy the example of an art which seemed to be born of a virgin soil. A return to nature has been, from time to time, the panacea for an over-Alexandrinized society."[14]

But if American literature could be considered a "remedy," in spite of its "barbarism" (and in fact because of it), by the "literati," it was much more so for those writers, such as Cesare Pavese and Elio Vittorini, who were most strongly engaged socially and politically. As Pavese writes:

> Around 1930, when Fascism was beginning to look like "the hope of the world," some young Italians happened to discover America in their books—a pensive and barbaric America, happy and quarrelsome, corrupt, bountiful, heavy with the past of the whole world, and at the same time young and innocent. During several years those young Italians read, translated, and wrote, savoring the joy of discovery and rebelliousness which made official culture indignant but insured their success to the point where the regime was forced to tolerate them if it wanted to save face.[15]

This "barbaric" America, this land of "nature," this new world described with impassionate expressions by Elio Vittorini ("We say 'America,' then. We say it, and we think of the atlas with the immense spread of the crowded colors, plains, mountains, snows high on the mountains, the icebergs up north, and the miles of shoreline facing the two oceans with those two great names—Atlantic and Pacific—and within that the ancient god, the desert, and the waterways, the railways, the highways, and houses, houses, houses. . . .")[16] is also the land of liberty, of the democracy scorned by Fascism. It is the progressive America of Roosevelt and the New Deal, the America of which Italo Calvino acutely writes while introducing Pavese's literary essays:

> America. The ages of discontent have often seen the birth of a literary myth of a country offered as a point of reference, a Germany recreated by a Tacitus or a Madame de Staël. Often the discovered country is only a land of utopia, a social allegory which has very few elements in common with the real country. . . . The interest in American literature under Fascism can be described in this manner. . . . It was not evasion . . . it was, as Pavese wrote, "the gigantic theatre where our common drama was played out with greater frankness than elsewhere. . . . we discovered Italy looking for men and words in America, in Russia, in France, in Spain. . . . And really this America of the literary people became a complex symbol of all contemporary ferments and realities, a mixture of America, Russia, and Italy . . . a chaotic synthesis of all that Fascism wanted to deny, to exclude.[17]

Such being the situation, while it was inevitable that the "discovery" was characterized by brilliant intuitions joined with serious critical mistakes,[18] it was also inevitable that a writer like Faulkner, although acutely examined by Praz as well as by Pavese and Vittorini, who translated respectively *The Hamlet* and *Light in August*,[19] was not considered typical of a literature seen almost exclusively in the optics of "realism," "simplicity," "democracy," "social engagement." The writers offered both by the "literati" and by the anti-fascist writers as *exemplary* of a literature capable on one side of transfusing new blood in the sick and bloodless body of Italian literature and on the other of acting as an instrument of political protest were Hemingway, Cain, Caldwell, Steinbeck, Dos Passos. They, not Faulkner, were the writers most widely read, translated, imitated in the period between the wars, and certainly [it was] to them, not to Faulkner, that the novelist Giuseppe Berto referred when he wrote that "the influence of the American writers came in the fittest moment, that is when the events of a decaying regime and then the defeat compelled us, willy-nilly, to face reality. The American writers offered us an example not so much of style as of courage: the courage to look, without literary veils, at our life."[20]

Still, in spite of all this, and in spite of his lack of popularity, I have no hesitation in saying that Faulkner has been the American writer of this century who has most profoundly and indeed decisively acted on Italian culture. He may have been "more famous than read," as our great poet Eugenio Montale (who translated some of his stories) once said.[21] And he has certainly been less imitated than Hemingway or other writers; to quote Cecchi again: "The qualities of his imagination and of his style were such as to save him from the mechanical offenses of the imitators. It has been possible, in Italy, to be under the illusion that one could mechanically ape Hemingway's dialogue. But nobody ever could and will imitate the magical mixture of Faulkner's symphonic verbal magma; his accent of epic distance, as of trumpets in the darkness of the night; that tone which, even in his less notable fragments, gives the sense of something desolately grand."[22] And yet Faulkner has left a trace in our culture which is the more enduring because his presence has been so unglamorous and unobtrusive. And I am not referring only to the influence which all great writers exert on any culture by offering new perspectives and insights, by adding new experience to our life, and by discovering new time and space, new territories of the mind and the heart. Neither do I refer only to the understanding of modern civilization and history which Faulkner's works render possible, so that Yoknapatawpha's epics, and comedy, and tragedy are a mirror not only of Southern life but of our general *condition humaine* and of our condition as men of the twentieth century everywhere in the world. These are contributions the value of which is too obvious to be underlined. Less obvious, I believe, is a more specific contribution offered by Faulkner to Italian culture: namely the change in attitude towards American literature and the change in attitude towards the novel, and the criticism of the novel, which his works have determined.

T. S. Eliot's famous words in "Tradition and the Individual Talent" can be of help in clarifying this point. In fact, his statements on the "alterations" of tradition under the action of a new work of art (". . . what happens when a new work of art is created is something that happens simultaneously to all the works of art which preceded it. . . . The existing monuments form an ideal order among themselves, which is modified by the introduction of the new (the really new) work of art among them . . . the relations, proportions, values of each work of art toward the whole are readjusted.")[23] can be certainly applied not only to Faulkner in his general relationship with tradition but also to Faulkner in connection with the Italian (and perhaps European) vision of American literature. Through Faulkner (and through Melville) such vision has been indeed profoundly "altered," "modified"—and the more so since Faulkner (as Melville) is exactly one of those "traditional" writers who, again to use Eliot's words, write "not merely with [their] own generation in [their] bones, but with a feeling that the whole of the literature of Europe from Homer and within it the whole of the literature of [their] own country has a simultaneous existence and composes a simultaneous order"; writers with "the historical sense, which is a sense of the timeless as well as of the temporal and of the timeless and of the temporal together." Through Faulkner (and Melville) Italian culture, while still under the influence of the "myth," has assimilated a notion of American literature—of its complexity and ambiguity, of its tragic substance, of its ties with "tradition," of its constant blending of realism and symbolism—which is perhaps less exciting and surprising than the "mythical" one but is certainly nearer to historical truth.

Thus, if we look at Italian criticism on Faulkner we observe that, besides being since the very beginning much more appreciative of Faulkner's art (also owing to the authority of French writers such as Gide, Malraux, Camus, and later Sartre) than American criticism, its development coincides with an enlargement and deepening of our vision of American literature. This is true of Praz's pioneering article, where we not only find judgments which anticipate later critical achievements (for instance, introducing *Soldiers' Pay*, he notes that Faulkner, even if not alien from depicting "the most disgusting and horrid scenes" is "fundamentally a moral writer," while, writing on *The Sound and the Fury*, he recognizes, long before other critics, that "Faulkner's narrative method succeeds in intensifying the sense of mystery and hallucination of the tragedy"), but we also find a clear perception of Faulkner's strong connections with the past (it is the case of *Absalom, Absalom!* in which, for Praz, "the destiny of crime and destruction has more than vague affinities with the frightening classical fable").[24] And the same is true of Emilio Cecchi;[25] of Aldo Camerino, who in 1934 analyzed the relationships and the differences between Faulkner and French naturalism;[26] of Salvatore Rosati, who insists on the "morality" of Faulkner's art and on its Puritan "roots," tracing at the same time Faulkner's derivations from James and Conrad;[27] and of Umberto Morra.[28] These and other critics may be at times in contradiction with themselves, but there is no doubt that they move toward that "ripeness" in the Italian approach to American literature which Pavese recognized in an important essay of 1946 (dedicated to F. O. Matthiessen's *American Renaissance*):

> We were accustomed to considering the United States as a country which entered world culture with a warm, persuasive and unmistakable voice only in the ten years which followed the great war, and the names of Dewey and Mencken, Lee Masters and Sandburg, Anderson, O'Neill, Van Wyck Brooks, Waldo Frank, Gertrude

Stein, Dreiser, Carlos Williams, Hemingway and Faulkner seemed to us the sudden explosion, inexplicable and unexpected, of a social or academic crust which, in spite of occasional protests or cracks—something was known of Poe and Whitman—had remained intact from the beginnings of the colony. . . . We shared the sensation of those "young Americans" of being new Adams, alone and resolute, who had come out not from Eden but from a jungle, freed of all burdens of the past, fresh and ready to walk on the free earth. . . . But now it turns out that those young Americans were wrong. Their explosion was not the first nor, above all, the greatest in American history. . . . In reality it was not American culture which was renewed from the bottom in those years; it was we who seriously came into contact with it for the first time. Now not a day passes without voices from across the Atlantic reaching whoever cares to listen, voices which recall, evoke and explain a whole rich tradition in which at least one great revolution, one great "renaissance," had already taken place.[29]

Pavese did not nourish, at first, any particular enthusiasm for Faulkner, and some of his letters in English to his Italo-American friend and literary advisor Tony Chiuminato prove it abundantly. "As for Faulkner," he writes, "you're right: he's a tremendous bore, till now at least: I didn't as yet get through the whole book."[30] Later, writing on *Sanctuary*, which he considers "a too ambitious detective story" (and he was of course thinking of Malraux's famous statement: "*Sanctuary* is the intrusion of Greek tragedy into the detective story"),[31] he defines Faulkner "a bad pupil of Anderson," with a "stylistic *ralenti* which has no justification."[32] And yet, while noting this attitude—clearly due to the fact that, as we have seen, Faulkner did not fit into the scheme produced by the American "myth"—we must first note that Pavese's translation of *The Hamlet,* published in 1942[33] (at a later date than the remarks of above, and when Pavese's American experience had been enormously enriched by his magnificent translation of *Moby Dick*, published in 1932),[34] is so conscious of Faulkner's craftmanship and seriousness of purpose and is so strenuously engaged in the effort of penetrating every nuance of Faulkner's language that it objectively testifies to a radical change in appreciation.[35] Second, and even more important, we must note that the translation, while rigorously faithful to the letter and the spirit of the original, reveals the constant attempt, on the part of Pavese, to make of it an instrument for the introduction of new linguistic elements in the texture of Italian narrative prose[36] (so that it is not surprising that, as a critic writes, "the language of the translation often coincides with that of Pavese's fiction and poetry").[37] The fact is that in translating Faulkner Pavese not only acquires a deeper knowledge of American literature and its tradition, and not only receives new suggestions in that search for the connections between literature and myth which was to become an essential part of his artistic and critical activity,[38] but finds himself in front of a problem—that of the relationship between literary language and dialect—which has always been the fundamental problem of the Italian writer of fiction. Faulkner's solutions are not explicitly stressed by Pavese, but there is no doubt that one could apply to Faulkner certain observations he makes when drawing a parallel between the situation of the writer in Piedmont, his native "region," and some American writers:

> Since Alfieri, all Italian writers try, sometimes unconsciously, to reach a deeper national unity by penetrating more and more into their regional character, their *true* nature, thus reaching the creation of a human conscience and a language rich of all the blood of the province and of all the dignity of a renewed life. . . . In Piedmont, where the ferment of this aspiration is stronger, and the realization more distant because we are taken astray by an excessive dialect specialization . . . [we] never had that man and that work which . . . would really reach the universality and freshness which make themselves understood by all men. . . . This is our need, still unsatisfied. Such need, in their own land and province, the American writers I am speaking of have succeeded in satisfying. From them, then, we must learn.[39]

And indeed this seems to me one of the most important elements of Faulkner's influence not only on Pavese but on Italian culture. He has not offered to our writers a prose to "imitate" but a supreme linguistic lesson capable of expanding and enriching that offered by modern writers such as Verga or the Pirandello of the stories—those writers whose relationship, social and linguistic, with their region is extremely similar to that of Faulkner with Mississippi; Southern writers whose Sicily (and one can say the same of Gabriel García Márquez's Colombia), in spite of all differences, is not very far from Yoknapatawpha.[40]

Sicily is very likely to be the starting point for the interest in Faulkner by Elio Vittorini, who translated *Light in August* in 1939,[41] in a language which, even more than in other translations of his, succeeds in achieving those results which, for Vittorini, a good translation should achieve: "a good translation is that which not only succeeds in having a work pass from one language to another language, but from one literature to another literature, rendering it entirely participant of the latter one."[42] What mainly interests Vittorini, however, is not the relationship between literary language and dialect but the "poetic" impact of Faulkner's word, its evocative power—those qualities which render Vittorini's prose unique in contemporary Italian literature.[43] And it is, moreover, Faulkner's technique. Already in 1938 Vittorini had written an article ("From Conrad to Faulkner") which was one of the first and best attempts made in Italy, and not only in Italy, to grasp certain aspects of Faulkner's style and especially its "duplicity"—that is the presence, in Faulkner's prose at its best, of "a double word, nourished image by image by a double vitality. The image is always accompanied by a second incarnation . . . that seems to reinforce the first but in truth expresses another impulse of the imagination. . . . It is Faulkner's poetic imagination that needs to and does express itself a second time: and it is from such inner necessity of the imagination to create at the same time in two different realms that all the duplications, even psychological, even external, of Faulkner's art are originated."[44] And this process is further analyzed in an article of 1950, "Faulkner Like Picasso?," where the analogy with Picasso is based upon the "double existence" imposed on their creatures by both artists "because of an entirely internal necessity to grasp at the same time two or more different planes of reality, or the visible of reality together with the invisible," and where the remarks already quoted develop into a critical synthesis which seems to me of great importance:

> In a scene, in an action, in the whole of various actions, the double measure of Faulkner's imagination becomes duplicity of time, by which one moves from an immediate time to a time more or less distanced, from a time of precise evidence to a time of approximation, from a time of proved reality to a time of supposed reality, and vice versa. . . . Thus each action narrated by Faulkner, being at the same time reality and fable, and reality often of the crudest and fable often of the most enchanted or exalted, acquires the proportions of a legendary action. Just as each character of which Faulkner tells us, being a concrete, earthy thing and at the same time an apparition, acquires the towering grandiosity of the stone *commendadór*.[45]

This passage is not only significant because of the critical awareness and insight it reveals but also because it makes us perceive another aspect of Faulkner's impact on Italian culture. It is mainly through Faulkner, in fact, that certain fundamental innovations of modern fiction are known and absorbed by Italian writing—a writing developing, under Fascism, in that atmosphere of cultural stagnation and isolation of the rebellion against which the "discovery" of American literature was the most evident sign. One should not forget, for instance, that while James and Conrad were known only to some specialists (and even now, in spite of a great number of studies and translations, their "presence" in our culture is not as large as it could and should be), this was even more true of Joyce's *Ulysses*. *A Portrait of the Artist as a Young Man* had been translated in 1933 by Pavese, and the same year had seen a translation of *Dubliners,* but Italy had to wait until 1960 for the first complete translation of *Ulysses,* until then circulating only in English or French, while only in 1982 have we the translation of the first part of *Finnegans Wake*.[46] Thus, it is Faulkner who becomes the real mediator between the "new" novel and Italy: the translations, already mentioned, of *The Hamlet* and of *Light in August*, and those, in the following years, of *The Sound and the Fury* (1947), of *Intruder in the Dust* (1951), and of *Absalom, Absalom!*

Faulkner in Italy 133

(1954),[47] to mention only the most influential, are not only the instruments through which a great individual artistic experience penetrates into Italian culture (and the more deeply when the translators are Pavese and Vittorini, or Glauco Cambon, whose translation of *Absalom, Absalom!*, perhaps the best Italian translation of Faulkner, is a perfect blending of philological exactness and artistic expression); and not only the instruments through which an image of American fiction is offered which is much more complex and rich than the reduced and partial one offered by the "myth"; but the instruments, also, through which Italian culture is made aware of stylistic and technical innovations and discoveries—the stream of consciousness, a dynamic use of time, the point of view, etc.—which were later to become integral parts of our best writing, from Pavese and Vittorini to Italo Calvino and Beppe Fenoglio.

But Faulkner, while transforming in many ways the Italian novelists' approach to the novel, has also greatly helped in transforming and at times even creating our criticism of the novel. In a country where the lack of a great novel tradition has certainly not stimulated a serious reflection on the novel as a form of art, Faulkner criticism has been in fact the ground on which such reflection has most seriously and significantly been made. There are of course other reasons which make this criticism valuable: the great amount of work done in Italy on Faulkner in the decades after the Second World War has achieved—also owing to a riper vision of American literature as a whole, to the general development of American studies, and to the much closer contact established with American criticism—results which greatly contribute, I believe, to the understanding of Faulkner's art. And one should at least mention the long and stimulating essay, in 1950, by Nemi D'Agostino, which is the first Italian "portrait" of Faulkner;[48] Glauco Cambon's Introduction to his translation of *Absalom, Absalom!* (1954) as well as his article on "Old People" (1961) and on the "sacred" in that story and in Faulkner's work;[49] Nadia Fusini's subtle and impassioned analysis of "The Bear" (1968), and of its connections with the initiation theme;[50] the penetrating essays on Faulkner's language and technique collected by Angela Giannitrapani in her book *Wistaria* (1963);[51] the book by Mario Materassi on Faulkner's novels (1968), undoubtedly the most remarkable Italian critical contribution;[52] and the thorough study of Faulkner's stories offered by Rosella Mamoli Zorzi in a book of 1976.[53] Much of this critical work, however, is also important because while analyzing Faulkner it deals with "the art of the novel" in a way which is, in Italy, substantially new. Materassi's book, where the close reading of Faulkner's novels coincides with the individuation of more general technical problems, from "the art of mixed technique" *(The Sound and the Fury)* to "plurisubjectivity as objectivity" *(As I Lay Dying)*, from the relationship between "metaphorical apparatus and semantic structure" *(Pylon)* to the use of time, the construction of characters, the fictional function of imagery, etc., is a clear example of the fact that it is through Faulkner that Italian criticism has started to take, as James would say, the novel seriously.

It should be evident, at this point, that however "not popular," Faulkner has been one of the authentically creative elements of Italian contemporary culture. His influence—exactly because it was not created by the mass media nor determined by contingent, if important, social or political events—is difficult to grasp, to define precisely. But the presence is deep and rich, wide and extensive; not an episode, indeed, but a permanent value; an experience which, moving from the restricted area of the connoisseurs and then the specialists to that of the novelists, has touched the very heart of our culture. This reserved, difficult, complex writer has become, in fact, one of our classics, enriching us with the innovating and at the same time "traditional" quality of his inimitable style; his belief in the novel as an instrument for the search of truth and in the possibilities of artist to "endure" in a world like ours; the depth of his strenuous inquiry in the forest and the horror of the heart; and his desperate faith in man and in the permanence of human values. For us, too, a literary experience has thus become a fundamental human lesson. He writes in a letter:

I have been writing all the time about honor, truth, pity, consideration, the capacity to endure well grief and misfortune and injustice and then endure again, in terms of individuals who observed and adhered to them not for the reward but for virtue's own sake, not even merely because they are admirable in themselves, but in order to live with oneself and die peacefully with oneself when the time comes. I dont mean that the devil will snatch every liar and rogue and hypocrite shrieking from his deathbed. I think liars and hypocrites and rogues die peacefully every day in the odor of what he calls sanctity. I'm not talking about him. I'm not writing for him. But I believe there are some, not necessarily many, who do and will continue to read Faulkner and say, 'Yes. It's all right. I'd rather be Ratliff than Flem Snopes.'[54]

In Italy, too, there *are* some, not necessarily few, who do and will continue to read Faulkner and say, "Yes. It's all right. I'd rather be Ratliff than Flem Snopes."

NOTES

1. Mario Praz, "William Faulkner," in *La Stampa*, December 4, 1931. The article is collected in Mario Praz, *Cronache letterarie anglosassoni* (Rome: Edizioni di Storia e Letteratura, 1951), II, 246–56.
2. William Faulkner, *Oggi si vola*, trans. Lorenzo Gigli (Milan: Mondadori, 1937).
3. An up-to-date list in Rosella Mamoli Zorzi, *Invito alla lettura di Faulkner* (Milan: Mursia, 1976).
4. These volumes have appeared: II *(I negri e gli indiani)*, 1960; III–IV *(I piantatori e i poveri bianchi. Le donne del Sud)*, 1961; VI *(La famiglia Stevens)*, 1963. The publisher is Mondadori, Milan.
  Fernanda Pivano, a real pioneer of American studies in Italy, has translated *Intruder in the Dust (Non si fruga nella polvere*, Milan: Mondadori, 1951) and has written many times on Faulkner. Her essays, the most important of which is "Il Sud di Faulkner," 1951, are collected mainly in the volumes *La balena bianca e altri miti* (Milan: Mondadori, 1961), and *Mostri degli anni venti* (Milan: Rizzoli, 1982). A personal friend of Faulkner, Miss Pivano has very recently remembered him in an article ("Quando Faulkner venne alla scoperta dell'Italia," *Il Corriere della Sera*, July 5, 1982).
5. See the good bibliography in Rosella Mamoli Zorzi, note 3. Also see Mario Materassi, *I romanzi di Faulkner* (Rome: Edizioni di Storia e Letteratura, 1968), where there is also an acute, if short, history of Faulkner criticism. A good bibliography is also in the volume dedicated to Faulkner in the series: "I Nobel" and including the translations of *Sanctuary* and *Light in August* with an introduction by Emilio Cecchi (Milan: Club degli Editori, 1964). See also the *Repertorio bibliografico della letteratura americana in Italia*, ed. Biancamaria Tedeschini Lalli (Rome: Edizioni di Storia e Letteratura), I, II (1966), III (1969).
6. *Selected Letters of William Faulkner*, ed. Joseph Blotner (New York: Random House, 1977), 215, 222, 282, 285.
7. Mario Materassi, "Un incontro con William Faulkner," preface to the Italian version of Frederick J. Hoffman, *Faulkner* (Florence, 1968).

8. In the already quoted Introduction (see note 5).
9. Donald Heiney, *America in Modern Italian Literature* (New Brunswick, N.J.: Rutgers University Press, 1964), 5.
10. The author of these notes has dealt with the theme in various occasions: see Agostino Lombardo, "La critica italiana sulla letteratura americana," *Studi Americani*, 5 (1959), 9ff; the chapter "La letteratura americana in Italia," *La Ricerca del Vero* (Rome: Edizioni di Storia e Letteratura, 1961), and *L'America e la cultura letteraria italiana* in a series published by the "Istituto di Studi Nordamericani di Bologna," 1981. See also the Introduction to a special issue of *Sewanee Review* (Summer 1960), edited by Agostino Lombardo.

See also Sigmund Skard, "Italy," in *American Studies in Europe*. (Philadelphia: University of Pennsylvania Press, 1958); Sergio Pacifici, *Guide to Contemporary Italian Literature* (Cleveland: Meridian Books, 1962); Donald Heiney, (see note 9), 1964; Dominique Fernandez, *Il mito dell'America negli intellettuali italiani* (Caltanissetta-Rome: Sciascia, 1969); Nicola Carducci, *L'intellettuale e l'ideologia americana* (Bari: Lacaita, 1972); Giuseppe Massara, *Viaggiatori italiani in America (1860–1971)* (Rome: Edizioni di Storia e Letteratura, 1976); *New World Journeys*, Contemporary Italian Writers and the Experience of America, ed. and trans. Angela M. Jeannet and Louise K. Barnett (Westford-London: Greenwood Press, 1977). Bibliographies appear in each of these works.

11. On this period see Agostino Lombardo, *L'America e la cultura letteraria italiana*, cited in note 10.
12. Carlo Linati, *Scrittori anglo-americani d'oggi* (Milan, 1932), 63.
13. Now in Mario Praz, *Cronache* etc. (see note 1), II, 203ff.
14. Now in Mario Praz, *Cronache* etc. (see note 1), II, 239ff. The article had appeared in English in 1948 ("Hemingway in Italy," *Partisan Review*, October 1948).
15. Cesare Pavese, "Ieri e oggi," *La letteratura americana e altri saggi* (Turin: Einaudi, 1959), 193–96. The essay is included in the already quoted (see note 10) *New World Journeys*, 171–75 and the above translation is by the editors of the volume.
16. These notes by Vittorini belonged to a short history of American literature which was meant to introduce an anthology of American writers. The anthology was published (*Americana*, Milan: Bompiani, 1942) but the Fascist censorship eliminated Vittorini's notes, which he later included in *Diario in pubblico* (Milan: Bompiani, 1957). The above passage, too, is quoted from the translation of the editors of *New World Journeys* (158–61).
17. Italo Calvino, "Preface" to Cesare Pavese, *La letteratura americana e altri saggi*, already quoted (see note 10).
18. See the various essays by Agostino Lombardo already quoted (see note 10).
19. William Faulkner, *Il borgo* (Milan: Mondadori, 1940); *Luce d'agosto* (Milan: Mondadori, 1939).
20. In a special issue of the Italian magazine *Galleria* dedicated to American literature (December 1954). Berto's best known novel is *Il cielo è rosso* (Milan: Longanesi, 1957), translated in the U.S.A. as *The Sky Is Red* (Norfolk, Conn.: New Directions, 1950).
21. Eugenio Montale, "La morte di William Faulkner", *Il Corriere della Sera*, July 9, 1962.
22. Emilio Cecchi, "Note su William Faulkner," *William Faulkner. Venti anni di critica*, a cura di Frederick J. Hoffman e Olga W. Vickery—the Italian version, with Italian additions, of *William Faulkner: Two Decades of Criticism*—(Parma: Guanda, 1957), 114.
23. The quotation is from T. S. Eliot, *Selected Prose* (Harmondsworth: Penguin Books), 23–24.
24. See note 1. See also, with reference to *Absalom, Absalom!*, "L'ultimo Faulkner," *Omnibus*, April 3, 1937.
25. Cecchi's articles on Faulkner are included in the various, constantly enlarged, editions of *Scrittori inglesi e americani* (first edition: Lanciano: Carabba, 1935). See also

Emilio Cecchi, *America Amara* (Florence: Sansoni, 1939)—a magnificent reportage with many literary observations. On Cecchi as an "Americanist" see the studies mentioned in note 10, and also Vito Amoruso, "Cecchi, Vittorini, Pavese e la letteratura americana," *Le contraddizioni della realtà* (Bari: Dedalo, 1968), and Agostino Lombardo, "Cecchi e gli scrittori anglo-americani," *Emilio Cecchi Oggi* (Proceedings of a conference on Cecchi held in Florence in 1979), (Florence: Vallecchi, 1981), 86–134.

26. Aldo Camerino, "Novità di William Faulkner," now in *Scrittori di lingua inglese* (Milan-Naples: Ricciardi, 1968), 208–15.

27. Rosati's articles are now condensed in the essay "William Faulkner," *L'ombra dei padri* (Rome: Edizioni di Storia e Letteratura, 1958), 99–110. See also his *Storia della letteratura americana* (Turin: Eri, 1956), 99–110.

28. Umberto Morra, "William Faulkner: *Luce d'agosto,*" *Letteratura*, 3 July 1939.

29. Cesare Pavese, "F. O. Matthiessen," *La letteratura americana e altri saggi*, quoted at note 15, 177–87.

30. Cesare Pavese, *Lettere 1924–1944* (Turin: Einaudi, 1966), 326.

31. André Malraux, "A Preface for Faulkner's *Sanctuary,*" *Faulkner: A Collection of Critical Essays*, ed. Robert Penn Warren (Englewood Cliffs: Prentice-Hall, 1966), 272–74. (Malraux's essay had appeared in *La Nouvelle Revue Française*, November 1, 1933.)

32. Cesare Pavese, "Faulkner, cattivo allievo di Anderson," *La Cultura*, April 1934, now in *La letteratura americana*, etc., 167–70 with the title "Un angelo senza cura d'anime."

33. See note 19.

34. Herman Melville, *Moby Dick* (Turin: Frassinelli, 1932).

35. An excellent analysis of Pavese's translation in the third chapter ("La traduzione di *The Hamlet* di William Faulkner," 211–32) of Maria Stella, *Pavese traduttore* (Rome: Bulzoni, 1977; the book is essential for the understanding of this aspect of Pavese's activity).

36. See the acute article by Claudio Gorlier, "Tre riscontri sul mestiere di tradurre," *Sigma* 3/4, December 1964.

37. Maria Stella, 220.

38. See the third part ("Il mito"), of *La letteratura americana*.

39. Cesare Pavese, "Sherwood Anderson" (first section: "Middle West e Piemonte"), in *La letteratura americana*, 33–49.

40. See especially Nemi D'Agostino, "William Faulkner," *Studi Americani*, 1 (1955), 257–308.

41. See note 19.

42. Quoted from Mario Picchi, "Del tradurre," *La Fiera Letteraria*, June 9, 1956.

43. See Agostino Lombardo, "L'America di Vittorini," *La Ricerca del Vero* (quoted at note 10), 63–81. See also Louise K. Barnett, "Elio Vittorini and the Criticism of American literature: a reexamination," *Studi Americani*, 18 (1972), 395–412.

44. "Da Conrad a Faulkner," *Omnibus*, October 1938.

45. "Faulkner come Picasso?" *La Stampa*, December 8, 1950. Reprinted in *Faulkner. Vent'anni di critica* (quoted at note 22), 162–64.

46. James Joyce, *Ulisse*, trans. Giulio de Angelis (Milan: Mondadori, 1960); *Finnegans Wake H.C.E.*, trans. Luigi Schenoni (Milan: Mondadori, 1982).

47. William Faulkner, *L'urlo e il furore*, trans. Augusto Dauphiné (Milan: Mondadori, 1947). *Non si fruga nella polvere*, trans. Fernanda Pivano (Milan: Mondadori, 1951). *Assalonne, Assalonne!* trans. Glauco Cambon (Milan: Mondadori, 1954).

48. See note 40.

49. See note 47. Glauco Cambon, "Stile e percezione del numinoso in un racconto di Faulkner," *Studi Americani*, 7 (1961), 147–62.

50. Nadia Fusini, "La caccia all'orso di Faulkner," *Studi Americani*, 14 (1968), 289–308. In *Studi Americani* were also published Angela Giannitrapani, "Wistaria: le immagini in Faulkner," 5 (1959), 243–80; Id., "Il procedimento dello stupore in Faulkner," 6 (1960), 275–306 (both essays to be included in *Wistaria*, see note 51); Ruggero Bianchi, "Faulkner e *The Unvanquished*," 8 (1962), 129–50; Mario Materassi, "Le immagini in

Soldiers' Pay," 9 (1963), 353-70 (to be included in *I romanzi di Faulkner,* see note 5); Maria Stella, "Una traduzione di Pavese: *The Hamlet* di Faulkner," 19/20 (1973-74), 319-38 (to be included in *Pavese traduttore,* see note 35); Daniela Montanari, "Il personaggio nero nei romanzi di William Faulkner," 21/22 (1975-76), 275-308. Excellent observations on Faulkner in the more general article by Claudio Gorlier, "Il pellegrinaggio del buon ribelle," 10 (1964), 135-80.

Claudio Gorlier has contributed to the development of Italian Faulkner criticism also with "William Faulkner, la genesi e la redenzione," *Approdo letterario,* October-December 1962, 42-68, and with the "Introduction" to his anthology *Gli umoristi della frontiera* (Vicenza: Neri Pozza, 1967). As to the author of these notes, his various articles on Faulkner are now collected in Agostino Lombardo, *Il diavolo nel manoscritto* (Milan: Rizzoli, 1974), ("Note su William Faulkner", 201-237). While I refer, for additional information on Italian contributions, to the bibliographies mentioned in the previous pages, mention should be made here of three literary histories where good observations on Faulkner are made: Rolando Anzilotti, *Storia della letteratura americana* (Milan: Vallardi, 1957); Salvatore Rosati (see note 27); Carlo Izzo, *La letteratura nord-americana* (Milan: Accademia, 1957).

51. Angela Giannitrapani, *Wistaria.* Studi faulkneriani (Naples: Cymba, 1963).
52. See note 5.
53. Rosella Mamoli Zorzi, *I racconti di Faulkner* (Brescia: Paideia, 1976).
54. *Selected Letters of William Faulkner,* 142.

Faulkner's Graphic Work
in Historical Context

LOTHAR HÖNNIGHAUSEN

Over the years, Faulkner's graphic work has become increasingly known and accessible, but critics and scholars continue to be somewhat at a loss in knowing what to make of it.[1] Because Faulkner himself finally realized and conceded the limits of his talents for graphic art, Faulkner scholarship has tended to dismiss the illustrations for his one-act play *The Marionettes* and his sketches for the student annual *Ole Miss* as curiosities, as youthful "transgressions" bearing no relevance on his major work. When given serious consideration at all, they are, like the early poetry, written off as unoriginal and entirely derivative in nature.

That *The Marionettes* illustrations are influenced by Beardsley is of course obvious.[2] To view this single influence in isolation, however, is to miss the point. Beardsley is only one of many manifestations of Faulkner's affinities for a complex, far-reaching artistic movement spanning the late nineteenth and early twentieth centuries. A wide spectrum of terms has been used to designate the diverse, even heterogeneous aspects of this movement, classifying it according to art form and nationality. The extent to which labels like *Arts and Crafts, art nouveau, Aestheticism,* and *fin de siècle* make sense in regard to Faulkner must be demonstrated at each step along the way. From the outset, however, it is important to emphasize that the imprint of this international movement is not only to be found in American cultural centers like New York and Chicago. In a modish, somewhat trivialized form and with a certain provincial lateness, it had an impact on Faulkner's hometown Oxford and the campus of the University of Mississippi. It may go against the grain for anyone who still considers Faulkner the exclusive product of his native soil, but there is no denying the relationship of his calligraphic and hand-bound manuscripts to the Arts and Crafts Movement or the style of *The Marionettes* illustrations to *art nouveau*.

In view of the numerous thematic and stylistic correspondences between *The Marionettes* and *art nouveau*, it is not surprising to find that similar tendencies also influence layout, binding, illustration, and script (plate 1).[3] By no means an exceptional case among Faulkner's early works, this one-act play belongs to a whole group of handcrafted booklets: *Dawn, an Orchid, a Song* (1918), *The Lilacs* (1919–20), *Vision in Spring* (1920), *Mayday* (1926), *Helen: A Courtship* (1926), *Royal Street* (1926), and *The Wishing Tree* (1927). The drawings that Faulkner contributed to *Ole Miss* are in the same vein.

There are obvious reasons why Faulkner's earliest works took the form they did. He was a young man interested in both drawing and writing. He had little access to other means of publication. There are, however, additional circumstances not particular to Faulkner. His calligraphic manuscripts are directly in line with the Aestheticist tendencies of his time and reflect a widespread interest in handcrafted objects and artworks.

Any attempt to place Faulkner's early works within the context of his cultural milieu and at the same time within the larger context of artistic and literary movements brings with it a host of methodological and terminological problems. To maintain that art movements like *art nouveau* left an impression on Faulkner's hometown Oxford does not imply that its inhabitants and students were fully aware of their significance or gave much thought to them. Faulkner and the students who worked on the University of Mississippi yearbook *Ole Miss* must have come across diverse and fashionable art forms more by instinct than by theoretical consideration. As a critic, Faulkner would have probably had little to say about the relationship of terms like *art*

Faulkner's Graphic Work in Historical Context 141

Plate 1. William Faulkner, *The Marionettes* (cover)

Plate 2. William Faulkner, *Nocturne*, from *Ole Miss* XXV (1921)

Faulkner's Graphic Work in Historical Context

Listen! A violin
Freezes into a blade, so bright and thin
It pierces through his brain, into his heart,
And he is spitted by a pin of music on the dark.

Swift the wisps of motion blown across the moon;
Colombine flings a paper rose, —
Pierrot flits like a white moth on blue dark.

Black the taper, sharp their mouths in starlight,
The sky with icy rootless flowers gauntly glows.
They are stiffly frozen, bright and stark.

nouveau, fin de siècle, Aestheticism, and *Arts and Crafts Movement.* As a practicing artist, however, he possessed the ability to feel his way into the mainstream of such art movements when given the least bit of exposure to them. This is especially true when such influences were important to his artistic development or to his handling of form. A comparison of motifs and of style reveals that Faulkner adopted elements from Swinburne, Verlaine, Wilde, and Beardsley, modifying them to suit his own purposes. The remarkable thing in this process is that out of relatively few instances of influence, he was able to reconstruct and imitate artistic styles in their entirety. In his illustrated poem *Nocturne* (plate 2) and in the *Dramatis Personae* of *The Marionettes* (plate 3), Faulkner, in all probability knowing comparatively little about the tenets of European and American *art nouveau,* made recognizable contributions to this tradition.

It is generally acknowledged that the direct source for *The Marionettes* is Beardsley's illustrated edition of Wilde's *Salomé*. But this knowledge alone does not explain what lies behind Faulkner's attraction to *Salomé*, nor does it help to determine the channels through which he came into contact with a number of artistic directions assimilated into early American modernism. He may have learned of new trends in art and literature from Phil Stone, whom he visited at Yale in 1918, or come across them himself by way of his own reading in contemporary books and magazines. It should be emphasized, however, that Oxford, home of the University of Mississippi, was by no means as cut off from new trends in the artistic world as has generally been assumed. In this respect, the student publications of Faulkner's alma mater—the newspaper *The Mississippian,* the annual *Ole Miss,* and the humor magazine *The Scream*—are of great interest. A thorough examination of the contents of these publications shows that a number of Faulkner's fellow students shared his interests and made contributions influenced by *fin de siècle* and *art nouveau.*

In comparing these publications, some distinctions need to be made. *The Mississippian* is altogether farther from the Aesthetic

Movement than *Ole Miss*. This can be partly explained by the fact that art work, the medium in which such influences are most palpable, appears only in the annual. There Faulkner is only one of many students who contributed drawings showing the influence of Aestheticist tendencies. Immediately apparent is the use of motifs—among others, peacocks and *femme fatale* figures—which demonstrate some degree of familiarity on the part of Mississippi students with international trends in art and literature. The circle of Faulkner's friends making up the theater group The Marionettes is liberally represented in *Ole Miss*. L. R. Somerville's contribution, *A New World Symphony—Dvorak*, appears in the same volume as Faulkner's sketch *Fish, Flesh, Fowl*.[4] In his poem *To an Ole Miss Coed*, Ben Wasson related the coed to a sphinx, a motif used by Victorian painters and by Wilde in poetry.[5] The concluding compliment, with its

Plate 3. William Faulkner, illustration from *The Marionettes (Dramatis Personae)*

Plate 4. M. B. Howorth, drawing of a *Dandy*, from Ole Miss XXVI (1922)

humorous contrast of "free verse" and the "sonnet," reveals Wasson's familiarity with contemporary trends in poetry. The combination of *fin de siècle* attitudes and modernist traits, characteristic of both *Ole Miss* and the twenties in general, is clearly evident in M. B. Howorth's drawing of a dandy, a Japanese kimono thrown over his formal wear, sitting in an abstractly covered easy chair (plate 4).[6]

Howorth's dandy is suggestive of the kind of connoisseurship which made room in *Ole Miss* for a number of *art nouveau* touches. The 1917 cover vignette displays typical *art nouveau* motifs (a candle, arabesqued flames, stylized flowers) and makes an effort to unify ornament and script (plate 5). With its stylized, symmetrical treelike forms and its gothic landscape with ruins, the 1921 *Ex Libris* goes a long way toward realizing the aims of *art nouveau* (plate 6). Lettering and decoration are brought into close relationship; balance is established between geometric and organic forms.

The *art nouveau* nature of graphic work in *Ole Miss* is carried over into its advertisements. An ad for Kennington's (plate 7) shows that the business world of Mississippi was no stranger to that odd coupling of beauty in design and commercial intentions responsible for some of the finest achievements of European and American *art nouveau* (for example, Bradley's bicycle posters).[7] In typical *art nouveau* manner, it interweaves organic forms into arabesques without neglecting their symmetrical ordering. The script, beginning "The Best Styles . . ." and placed directly above the ornamentation, is made an integral part of the decoration by means of positioning—resting, as it were, on the floral arrangement—and lettering (especially the shaping of *Q, y, s,* and *B*). One of the characteristic traits of *art nouveau* scripts is the combining of latinate-curved lettering with arabesquelike gemmations. This rather subdued ensemble of word and picture is set in aesthetic contrast to the large, simple, boldface lettering which bring the store's name to prominence, "Jackson's Best Store: Kennington's."

The Kennington advertisement illustrates one of the ways in

Faulkner's Graphic Work in Historical Context 147

Plate 5. Cover vignette from *Ole Miss* XXI (1917)

Plate 6. Ex Libris from *Ole Miss* XXV (1921)

Plate 7. Advertisement for Kennington's from *Ole Miss* XXIV (1920)

which international influences in art, with their origins in the commercial and cultural centers of Europe and America, made themselves felt even in more provincial areas. The significance of such indirect channels should not be underestimated. Advertising is one medium in which *art nouveau* came to make an immediate and frequent impression on people's lives. An advertisement like that for Kennington's would have appeared somewhat earlier in Vienna or Berlin, New York or Chicago, but there would have been little difference in appearance.

The importance of supplementary material like that of the graphic work in *Ole Miss* is that it provides insight into the background behind *The Marionettes*. It helps us to visualize the artistic milieu of the young Faulkner, demonstrating that even in the Mississippi of the 1920s, a young artist sampling means of expression would have had access to *art nouveau*. Few of Faulkner's fellow students were prepared or capable of matching his preoccupation with Wilde, Beardsley, and other aspects of *fin de siècle* and *art nouveau*. Nevertheless, the same interests which spurred Faulkner were widespread enough to find their way into the college annual.

The college annual of a provincial university is of course no comparison to avant-garde magazines like *The Yellow Book, Savoy,* or *The Chapbook*. In a publication like *Ole Miss*, a certain number of adolescent elements are unavoidable: an emphasis on undergraduate club life, manifestations of social status and snobbery, attempts to assert a sense of self-importance, second-rate contributions. Just these elements, however, make the art work in *Ole Miss* representative of the taste of its time. In the process of reconstructing an artistic environment like the young Faulkner's, it is just as important to trace the indirect, diluted, often banalized effects of art modes and movements as to pinpoint direct, consequential influences like that of Beardsley's brilliant black-and-white art. A look at *Ole Miss*, where most of Faulkner's known graphic work takes its place among similar drawings from his fellow students, brings us much closer to the world of *The Marionettes*.

Faulkner's Graphic Work in Historical Context 149

Plate 8. M. B. Howorth, drawing of a *femme fatale*, from *Ole Miss* XXVI (1922)

Characteristic of the cultural environment of Faulkner's college days is its fostering of young artists, like Howorth, capable of accommodating *fin de siècle* types like the *femme fatale* and the dandy to the spirit of the twenties (plate 8).[8] In his illustration for the title page of the 1922 *Ole Miss* (plate 9), he proves just as capable of handling the neorococo style. This scene, in which a cavalier woos a lady in an eighteenth-century park, is a prelude to the neorococo decoration which throughout the volume gives an air of elegance and modish sophistication to the plainness of the seniors' photographs. The moon and the rising form of a pine tree, which finds an echo in the hanging Spanish moss, are features reminiscent of similar effects in illustrations by Beardsley and Faulkner. Two other *art nouveau* elements are clearly evident: the arabesque shape of the branches on the left and the use of leaves as organic patterns. It is hardly conceivable that Howorth or other Mississippi students sought in neorococo that which Faulkner or Wallace Stevens found in Verlaine's *Fêtes*

Plate 9. M. B. Howorth, title page from *Ole Miss* XXVI (1922)

Faulkner's Graphic Work in Historical Context   151

Galantes or in Beardsley's illustrations for *The Rape of the Lock*. Nevertheless, some shared with them, if not the artist's purpose, at least the same artistic taste.

The table of contents of the 1922 *Ole Miss* (plate 10) shows the influence of the Japanese style, which like other *fin de siècle* and *art nouveau* tendencies, reached Faulkner's Oxford with typical provincial lateness.[9] Not its Japanese motifs, however, but the ensemblelike unity of illustration and script connects this illuminated page to the *Dramatis Personae* of *The Marionettes*. Like Faulkner, the anonymous young draftsman emulates the ideals of *art nouveau* by treating the lettering as part of the decoration. Numerous details contribute to this functional integration. The rising curtain provides the overture element appropriate to a table of contents. The painted Japanese screens, in their own way as promising of things-to-come as the table of contents itself, correspond to it in format and in the decoration of the cords by which they hang.

The distinctly handwritten character of the script and the

Plate 10. Order of Books from *Ole Miss* XXVI (1922)

Plate 11. Durfey, drawing for the Clubs section of *Ole Miss* XXIV (1920)

Plate 12. Drawing for the Clubs section of *Ole Miss* XXV (1921)

Plate 13. Drawing for the Juniors section of *Ole Miss* XXV (1921)

Faulkner's Graphic Work in Historical Context 153

affinity between the floral ornamentation and the organic, uneven letters provide further parallels to *The Marionettes*. The general tendency followed in forming the letters and even particular decorative details (for example, the low position of the middle bars in *E* and *F*, the arabesquelike curves of the *S*) are reminiscent of Faulkner's ornate script. Unlike the exoticism of his literary tastes, this attraction to calligraphy was apparently shared by many of his fellow students. There are numerous examples of this common interest in *Ole Miss*. In a sketch by Durfey for the Clubs section (plate 11), the *art nouveau* script, carried up by pipe smoke, makes an effective contrast to the geometric shape and abstract patterns of the modernist furniture.[10] In another sketch for this section (plate 12), the form of the script mirrors tree and shrubbery in a quite original way.[11] A sketch accompanying the Juniors section is quite successful in capturing the spirit of the Fitzgerald generation (plate 13); by way of lengthening the tail of the initial *J* and the curve of the final *S*, the script closely connects the depicted figures of a Japanese girl and her beau.[12] This sketch provides another example of how international fashions reached provincial areas by way of advertising. The Japanese girl is obviously indebted to an advertisement for the New York dressmaking firm Homer in the 1919 *Vanity Fair*.[13]

In regard to these examples of graphic art from *Ole Miss* or to Faulkner's *Marionettes* and his other handmade volumes, particular models or influences are, however, of lesser importance. At issue here is the inspiring force that unites all these efforts: the Arts and Crafts Movement. Before and after the turn-of-the-century, this movement made a profound impact on both European and American art.

One American author exemplary of this is—perhaps unexpectedly—Carl Sandburg. In a letter to his friend and teacher Philip Green Wright, Sandburg elevates "arts-craft" to an absolute guideline.[14] In writing and designing one of his early books of poetry, *The Plaint of a Rose* (1908, plate 14), Carl Sandburg attempts to go beyond the *fin de siècle* variety and to develop a modernist version: "I will get away somewhat from the Blue Sky-Bibelot-long hair-estheticism-art and art's sake, and approximate the skyscraper rather than the Parthenon." Despite such goals, both the cover design and the stylized prose of the opening section are closer to the elegant *art nouveau* curves of William Bradley's drawings and the artificial simplicity of Wilde's prose poems than to the skyscraper art of the American cubists (Max Weber, Joseph Stella, Charles Demuth) and Sandburg's own *Chicago Poems* (1916).

The interest of the young Sandburg in printing and binding, in decorative borders and initials, his emphasis of the close relationship of picture and text, and his delight in floral ornamentation and sinuous lines—all these things leave no doubt as to the access of American writers of the twenties to the Arts and Crafts Movement. As a graphic and literary ensemble, *The Plaint of a Rose* points to the tradition behind Faulkner's own handcrafted books from *The Marionettes* to *Mayday*.

The beginnings of the Arts and Crafts tradition can be traced back to William Morris and his attempt to reconcile body and

Plate 14. Carl Sandburg, cover design for *The Plaint of a Rose*

spirit by means of an integration of art and craftsmanship; the spiritual godfather was the Victorian prophet of art, John Ruskin. As a result of such works as Roger Stein's study of the reception of Ruskin, it has become evident that in the same ways as in England, attempts were being made in America to relate art and life in a new and meaningful way.[15] As early as 1902, Oscar Lovell Trigg's *Chapters in the History of the Arts and Crafts Movement* had provided the American public with an engaged survey of the sociopolitical and aesthetic concepts of Carlyle, Ruskin, Morris, and Charles Ashbee.[16] He placed similar manifestations in America within the same tradition. More far-reaching than Trigg's book was the journal *The Craftsman*, which appeared from 1901 to 1916. Edited by the designer Gustav Stickley, this magazine gave American readers access to the entire spectrum of the Arts and Crafts Movement, encompassing both the Anglo-American variety and the continental European variation *art nouveau*.

As early as the 1893 Columbia Exhibition in Chicago, America had demonstrated to the world that it not only had an interest in English Arts and Crafts (Oscar Wilde made his famous lecture tour of America in 1882, Walter Crane in 1890), but that it was also in a position to make its own contributions. The Arts and Crafts Movement found its most important repercussion in the architecture of Frank Lloyd Wright and the Prairie School in Chicago. The glasswork and jewelry of Louis Comfort Tiffany (1848–1933) and the posters and illustrations of William H. Bradley (1868–1961) measure up to the best work of European *art nouveau*.

Catalyst for the rediscovery of the value of craftmanship as a means of expression and fulfillment for the individual was protest against the machine. This protest also brought about the revival as arts of both printing and calligraphy. Handwriting and printing, illustrating and bookbinding, were for Morris intrinsically bound together by his conviction that the spirit of the artist and craftsmanship go hand-in-hand; only so could the artist overcome the fragmentation resulting from a world of division of labor and rediscover a natural, harmonious life. The pleasure taken in handwritten and handmade books corresponds to that longing for the organic that led Ruskin to postulate an ideal of imperfection in opposition to the deadening perfection of machine-made products.[17]

The propagation of living things and organic growth manifests itself artistically in such motifs as tendrils, the necks of swans and peacocks, and in flamelike, cloudlike, and wavelike forms. A predilection for flowing, sinuous outlines characterizes many *art nouveau* types, scripts, and illustrations. It is found to an equal degree in Henry van de Velde's woodcut for Max Elskamp's book *Dominical* (plate 15) and on the cover of Faulkner's *Marionettes* (plate 1).[18] Whereas Faulkner on his cover limits the curvilinear element to the shaping of individual letters, in his sketch for the Organizations section of *Ole Miss* (plate 16), which dates from the same period, it dominates the entire page. Wave form in the script of *The Marionettes* is particularly pronounced in *M* and *N*, but gives a certain animation to all the letters. The sigmalike, serpentine *S* (plate 17) is especially interesting. It resembles the initials designed by van de Velde and seems to spring from the same *art nouveau* sensibility which inspired Josef Váchal's woodcut, *The Little Elf's Pilgrimage* (plate 18).

Faulkner's illustrated poem *Nocturne* (plate 2), published in the 1920–21 *Ole Miss*, is a variant of one of the poems in *Vision in Spring*, a cycle written in the summer of 1920 and dedicated to Estelle Oldham. Like *The Marionettes*, *Vision in Spring* is a handmade (although not handwritten) volume and demonstrates the breadth of Faulkner's Arts and Crafts affinities. Blotner describes it as follows: "It was another carefully crafted gift volume. He had covered the thin 5½-by-8-inch boards with a brownish-green mottled paper. On a small square of white linen paper in the upper righthand corner in India Ink he had lettered the title *Vision in Spring*, and his name. He had pasted a strip of white parchment or vellum over the spine. The white pages within were stapled together."[19]

An interesting poem itself, *Nocturne* also deserves attention

Faulkner's Graphic Work in Historical Context   157

Plate 15. Henry van de Velde, woodcut for Max Elskamp's *Dominical*
Plate 16. William Faulkner, drawing for the Organizations section of *Ole Miss* XXIV (1920)

Plate 17. Example of Faulkner's calligraphy: the sigmalike letter S
Plate 18. Josef Váchal, *The Little Elf's Pilgrimage*

as an example of *art nouveau* illustration. In the same way as other *art nouveau* artists, Faulkner attempted to realize Morris's aesthetic ideal of the unity of a page comprised of word and picture. The figures and motifs important in the poem (Pierrot, Columbine, dance, moon, and candles) appear as the main graphic motifs in the illustration. Furthermore, Faulkner's stylization is in accord with Wilde's call for two-dimensional representation; the graphic motifs do not disturb the effect of the script through excessive realism. The two blocks of the text are integrated into the design by means of the supporting candlesticks and the outstretched arms of the two dancers, who themselves rise arabesquelike out of the candleflames. Words, standing out against a white background, do not only impart subject matter, but are just as important as decoration; they have the same function as the irregular placed stars in the background of the illustration. Faulkner's effective use of black-white mirroring is altogether worthy of attention.

Obviously influenced by Beardsley, the illustrated *Dramatis Personae* of *The Marionettes* is indicative of the way Faulkner went about stylization (plate 3). His handling of the garlanded rose motif with its emphasis of individual roses is reminiscent of the Beardsley illustrations *Design for the Title Page of Salomé* (plate 19) and *Contents Border Designs*. Despite his amateurish simplification, Faulkner undoubtedly strove to give organic unity to picture and text. This is best demonstrated by the way he integrated the text into the main design. Rose garlands enclose the white background of the text and at the same time connect it to the black background below. Apart from the structure of the illustration, the affinities between the stylized letters and the roses contribute substantially to the fusion of picture and text.

In *art nouveau*, graphic motifs tend to ignore and even escape borders and frames, breaking out into the decoration as a whole. Like O. E. Eckmann, a leading German *art nouveau* artist (plate 20), Faulkner avoids a hard-edged border at the top of the page by use of asymmetrical, organic patterning. At the bottom of the

Faulkner's Graphic Work in Historical Context 159

Plate 19. Aubrey Beardsley, title page from *Salomé*

page, the edge of the border is broken by the protrusion of the depicted figures. On the sides, the two flanking figures make up nongeometric boundaries in the same way as the flower stalks in Eckmann's design and in the 1917 cover vignette in *Ole Miss* (plate 5). The structural importance of these statuesque figures lies in the lateral support they give to the illustration and in the counterbalance their softly swinging verticals lend to the two rounded, garlanded backgrounds.

The flanking figures have two additional characteristics which merit attention: their symmetrical positioning and the dissolution of their corporality into a pattern of vertical lines. This tendency towards symmetry and the accompanying transition

Plate 20. Otto Eckmann, design for Wilhelm Hegeler's *Sonnige Tage (Sunny Days)*

Faulkner's Graphic Work in Historical Context 161

Plate 21. Aubrey Beardsley, *The Eyes of Herod*, from *Salomé*

from three dimensions to two-dimensional linear ornamentation and patterned surfaces exemplify the historical position of *art nouveau*, halfway between the representational art of the nineteenth century and the abstract art of the twentieth. One of the most important of these transitional figures was Beardsley, and much of what Faulkner took from *art nouveau* he could have easily found in Beardsley's *Salomé* illustrations. Behind the symmetry of the candlesticks in *Nocturne* lie symmetrical effects like those of the torches in Beardsley's *The Eyes of Herod* (plate 21). Illustrations like *The Woman in the Moon* or *John and Salomé* (plates 22 and 23) are likely points of inspiration for Faulkner's transformation of the symmetrical figures in his *Dramatis Personae* into linear ornaments and decorative patterns.

A discussion of the *Dramatis Personae* would not be complete without mention of the miniature portico. It makes the transition between the black background and the depicted figures Pierrot and Marietta, who, in introducing the marionette motif,

Plate 22. Aubrey Beardsley, *The Woman in the Moon*, from *Salomé*

Plate 23. Aubrey Beardsley, *John and Salomé* from *Salomé*

Faulkner's Graphic Work in Historical Context 163

use the bottom of the illustration as a proscenium. This classical portico is also important to the overall structure of the page, because its geometric, centered form counterbalances both the organic, rounded backgrounds and the swing of the vertical lines. At the same time, its horizontal, rectangular shape mirrors graphically the vertical columns of the text. Furthermore, the portico reappears throughout *The Marionettes* as a graphic leitmotif. It corresponds to the metamorphoses of an image in the text of the play itself, the colonnade: "The twin poplars . . . are like two blind virgins swaying before a colonnade, and the nine white columns of the colonnade are nine muses standing like votive candles before a blue mountain."[20]

While space does not permit a detailed analysis of the relationship between Faulkner and Beardsley, the final illustration in *The Marionettes* provides a graphic example of both the affinities and the considerable differences between the two artists. Like his model Beardsley in *Salomé*, Faulkner brings *The Marionettes* to a close with a final vignette (plate 24). A horizontally and vertically well-balanced composition presents the narcissistic Pierrot standing in front of Marietta's bier, staring into a mirror. The thematic conception and design are both sound; the mirror and the Chippendale couch upon which the dead Marietta lies enhance the scene. Yet a mere glance at Beardsley's tailpiece (plate 25) demonstrates that Faulkner's is no more than the work of a talented amateur. Beardsley's grotesque genius reveals itself in an elegant inspiration: a satyr and a degenerated Pierrot lift a hermaphroditic Salome into a rococo powder box. The composition of the scene as a whole and imaginative details like the overproportional powder box leave no doubt as to Beardsley's superior artistic genius.

Such comparison is unfair, however, Faulkner never having made any pretense of being a second Beardsley, and for a proper evaluation of his drawings, it is necessary to return to *Ole Miss*. At the beginning of this excursion into the no-man's-land between the graphic arts and literature, the annual served as a mirror of the general tendencies of the period; in closing, the

Plate 24. William Faulkner, vignette from *The Marionettes*

Plate 25. Aubrey Beardsley, tailpiece from *Salomé*

Faulkner's Graphic Work in Historical Context 165

focus shifts to Faulkner's own contributions to *Ole Miss*. Most of Faulkner's drawings are by definition applied art, and it is necessary to judge them according to the way they go about fulfilling specific social functions. Consequently they are here reproduced and discussed in terms of their original context. The importance of such "lesser arts" had been greatly revaluated as a result of Ruskin's vision of a new kind of humane and harmonious life, put into practice by Morris.[21] William Bradley and countless other American and European *art nouveau* artists aligned themselves with this tradition and brought about an unprecedented flourishing of the applied and commerical arts.[22] These artists felt the need to beautify everything with which they came into contact; they found nothing—be it esoteric books and magazines or cartoons and advertisements—unworthy of their attention.

As analysis of the graphic work in the student annual *Ole Miss* shows, this fascination for the interaction of picture and text was not limited to serious artists; students at the University of Mississippi were also caught up in the same general trend toward ensembles and ensemblelike effects. In light of this background, Faulkner's contribution to the decoration of *Ole Miss* takes on a new perspective. Within the bounds of the annual format and his own talents, he made every effort to give his work the versatility of other *art nouveau* artists. A sketch like that for his own theater group The Marionettes (plate 26), indebted to Beardsley (plate 27), comes close to *art nouveau* poster art. Others show the influence of contemporary cartoonists like Richard Boix or John Held, Jr. Of particular interest is the way Faulkner adapts Beardsley to the spirit of the Jazz Age and combines him with modernist tendencies.

Like many other of his drawings in *Ole Miss*, Faulkner's sketch for the Organizations section displays a mixture of modernistic and *art nouveau* elements (plate 16).[23] While his ironic depiction of a windblown couple perfectly captures the flavor of the twenties, the waving lines of the woman's dress show signs of *art nouveau*. Through the accentuation of wave forms, he also

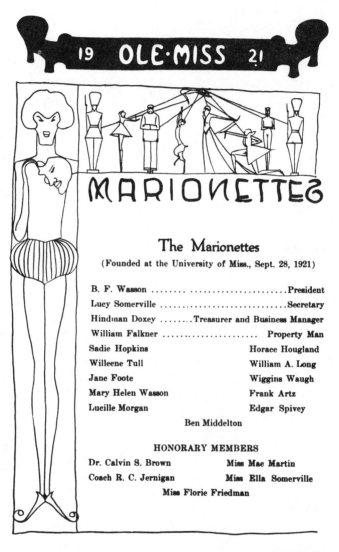

Plate 26. William Faulkner, drawing for the theater group Marionettes, from *Ole Miss* XXV (1921)

Faulkner's Graphic Work in Historical Context 167

Plate 27. Aubrey Beardsley, Avenue Theatre poster for *A Comedy of Sighs*

succeeds in integrating the script into the whole of the design. The leaves dancing over the heads of the figures link them and their fluttering clothing to the script. By continuing the curve of the letter *n* and by giving a twist to the tails of *q* and *s* and to the dash of the *t*, Faulkner sets the individual letters into motion—a motion which catches them up and is itself the theme of the sketch. The heavy lettering of certain others, particularly the *O*, links the script to the black clothing of the figures, further reinforcing the structure of the sketch.

Although there is no direct evidence that Faulkner knew such classical works of American poster art as Bradley's bicycle advertisement, there is no denying certain stylistic affinities between *art nouveau* posters and a number of his drawings. Of note in this regard is the immediacy of the interrelationship of graphic and script forms. By way of their delineation, the figures in *Red and Blue II* (plate 28) dancing to the jerky steps of the Charleston provide direct illustration of the program announced in the script.[24] The rectangular lettering perfectly suits the design and its thematic emphasis on a couple dancing. The diagonally placed, ornamentally lengthened hyphen mirrors the abrupt and elongated position of the dancers. Such detailed correspondences work toward unifying script and sketch.

Everywhere in America during the Jazz Age, people were dancing. *Ole Miss* sketches like Faulkner's *Red and Blue III* (plate 29) and M. B. Howorth's *Cotillion Club* (plate 30) testify to the fact that Oxford was no exception. They also provide a good basis for comparison. Howorth's sketch is placed near the top of the page, above a long membership list and directly below an arabesque combining neorococo and *art nouveau* and reappearing throughout the volume; Faulkner's sketch is positioned in the middle of the page. Both sketches depict a couple dancing in front of a jazz band, but in moving his couple slightly left of center, Faulkner gives his sketch compositional momentum from the very beginning. The motion which he imparts is fully developed in the dancer's dress, which extends from the left-hand side to the middle in long *art nouveau* curves; the out-

Plate 28. William Faulkner, drawing for the Red and Blue Club, from *Ole Miss* XXIV (1920)

Plate 29. William Faulkner, drawing for the Red and Blue Club, from *Ole Miss* XXV (1921)

Plate 30. M. B. Howorth, drawing for the Cotillion Club, from *Ole Miss* XXVI (1922)

stretched arms of the dancers carry the motion even further to the right. The animation of the musicians finds a focus in these long, flowing lines. In comparison to Howorth, Faulkner brings his sketch alive through an astonishingly versatile, completely authentic depiction of the bearings and gestures of the individual musicians. The figure of the bassplayer, who physically embodies the vibrations of jazz, is especially original.

The arrangement of the musicans plays a large part in producing the motion in Faulkner's sketch. In contrast to Howorth, who distributes his musicians evenly on both sides of the dancers, Faulkner avoids strict symmetry and places two on the left, four on the right. Their bouncing heads, at different levels and turned up, down, to the front, and to the side, add a final element of motion to the sketch. The effect they make results largely from a clever distribution of black and white derived from Beardsley. As his illustrations for *The Marionettes* demonstrate, Faulkner learned from Beardsley how to set small, black forms (heads, hands, legs, and feet) within larger areas of white; Howorth's sketch lacks this effect, because he makes use predominantly of black. Faulkner's black piano works as a contrasting surface behind the dancers, counterbalances their motion, and provides structural support for the sketch as a whole. Furthermore, this larger, black area gives the smaller, black forms of heads and hands the reinforcement they need in order to assert themselves within the composition.

Their handling of clothing is a final basis for comparison between Faulkner and Howorth. While Howorth reproduces tails and tie with pedantic realism, Faulkner deals with clothing in a much more abstract way. The tendency here toward abstraction, also evident in the depiction of clothes and feet, is the same tendency which manifests itself in *The Marionettes*—there closely connected to Beardsley's *Salomé* illustrations. Given that relationship, it is possible to see Beardsley's hand in Faulkner's striking treatment of the curving hem of the dancer's dress and to associate it with that of the gown in *The Woman in the Moon*.

In terms of the *art nouveau* ideal, the swinging curves are more important than the clothing they define.

There are of course significant differences. In place of the Beardsleyesque delight in decoration still found in *The Marionettes*, this *Ole Miss* drawing displays a new austerity of form—the influence of modernism. The dancer is no Salomé, no *femme fatale*, but a flapper of the twenties. The music in the background is no longer that of Wagner, who had cast his spell over Beardsley and the Decadents, but that of the Jazz Age.[25] Faulkner was much later to return to these memories of the Jazz Age—almost as if he were reworking this early drawing into prose—in the ball scene in *The Town*.[26] There, as so often in his mature prose, the early experiments with poetry and graphic art have been made an integral part of Faulkner's own work:

> It was Professor Handy, from Beale Street in Memphis. His band played at all the balls in north Mississippi and Gowan said how the hall was all decorated for Christmas and the Cotillion Club ladies and their escorts all lined up to receive the guests.

NOTES

1. Carvel Collins deserves the credit for first making a large collection of Faulkner's drawings generally accessible in *Early Prose and Poetry* (Boston: Little, Brown and Company, 1962). Joseph Blotner includes a number of drawings in the first volume of *Faulkner: A Biography* (New York: Random House, 1974). Noel Polk includes the accompanying illustrations in his facsimile edition of *The Marionettes: A Play in One Act* (Charlottesville: The University Press of Virginia, 1977).

2. See Addison C. Bross, "*Soldiers' Pay* and the Art of Aubrey Beardley," *American Quarterly*, 19 (1976), 3–23.; Timothy K. Conley, "Beardsley and Faulkner," *Journal of Modern Literature*, 5 (1976), 339–56.

3. I would like to thank members of the staff of the Faulkner Collection of the University of Virginia Library, of the Humanities Research Center at the University of Texas at Austin, and of the John Davis Williams Library at the University of Mississippi for their kindness and help during the research of this material; I also want to acknowledge the kind permission of these libraries to reproduce work by Faulkner, by fellow students in *Ole Miss*, and Carl Sandburg. Drawings by Beardsley are reprinted, with the permission of Dover Publications, from *The Early Works of Aubrey Beardsley* (New York, 1967); drawings by Henry van de Velde and Otto Eckmann, with the permission of the Keysersche Verlagsbuchhandlung, from Helmut Seling, ed., *Jugendstil: Der Weg ins 20. Jahrhundert* (Munich, 1979), Ills. 125 and 139; J. Váchal's *The Little Elf's Pilgrimage*, with the permission of the Holle-Verlag, from Hans H. Hofstätter, *Jugendstil: Druckkunst*, 2nd ed. (Baden-Baden, 1973), 256.

4. *Ole Miss* XXV (1921) 170, 129.

5. *Ole Miss* XXV (1921), 153.

Faulkner's Graphic Work in Historical Context 173

6. *Ole Miss* XXVI (1922), 29.
7. *Ole Miss* XXIV (1920). 257.
8. Howorth's *femme fatale* appeared in *Ole Miss* XXVI (1922), 215.
9. For a discussion of the considerable influence Japanese art had on the development of modern Western art, see Robert Schmutzler, *Art Nouveau: Jugendstil* (Stuttgart, 1977), 22–4 ("Japanismus"); in the abridged English translation, *Art Nouveau* (London, 1978), 21.
10. *Ole Miss* XXIV (1920), 125.
11. *Ole Miss* XXV (1921), 111.
12. *Ole Miss* XXV (1921), 31.
13. *Vanity Fair* XIII (1919), 127.
14. Quoted from *Carl Sandburg, Philip Green Wright, and the Asgard Press, 1900–1910: A Descriptive Catalogue of Early Books, Manuscripts, and Letters in the Clifton Walter Barrett Library*, comp. Joan St. C. Crane (Charlottesville: The University Press of Virginia, 1975), 108; I am indebted to Joan Crane herself for pointing out the similarity between Faulkner's and Sandburg's Arts and Crafts books and for directing me to this catalogue.
15. Roger B. Stein, *John Ruskin and Aesthetic Thought in America: 1840–1900* (Cambridge, Mass., 1967).
16. Oscar Lovell Triggs, *Chapters in the History of the Arts and Crafts Movement* (Chicago, 1902; repr. New York, 1973). Triggs discusses Maria Longworth Storer's Rockwood Pottery in Cincinnati (1880) under the heading: "Rockwood: An Ideal Workshop" (157–62). Two appendices, "A Proposal for a Guild and School of Handicrafts" and "The Industrial Art League," follow the last chapter, "The Development of Industrial Consciousness," and take up concrete questions concerning the organization of Arts and Crafts in America.
17. See Lothar Hönnighausen, *Grundprobleme der englischen Literaturtheorie des neunzehnten Jahrhunderts* (Darmstadt, 1977), 151–52.
18. For a discussion of *art nouveau* types and scripts, see Roswitha Baurmann, "Schrift," in *Jugendstil: Der Weg ins 20. Jahrhundert*, ed. H. Seling (Munich, 1979), 169–214. Baurmann's analysis of van de Velde's script could be applied to Faulkner's without any difficulty: "The lines of the letters seem . . . as if drawn with a trembling pencil, so that straight lines make little S-curves . . . The entire script has a soft, uncertain touch" (183, my translation).
19. Blotner, 307. Although *Vision in Spring* is in typescript, it was typed, as Blotner emphasizes, decoratively, with some thought as to its appearance: "This time he [Faulkner] (or perhaps Stone's secretary) had typed the poems neatly, using a purple ribbon and making few overstrikes or erasures."
20. *Marionettes*, 6–7.
21. *The Lesser Arts* was the title of a lecture delivered by William Morris in 1873 and a term he often used for the decorative arts.
22. The very same motifs were often used for both illustrations and advertisements. For example, the floral ornamentation with which Bradley decorated the title page of Doddridge's *Fringilla* (1895), he reused in a bicycle advertisement in which appear three Beardsleyesque, Pre–Raphaelite women (see the respective plates in Schmutzler, 162 and Seling, *Jugendstil*, 223).
23. *Ole Miss* XXIV (1920), 105.
24. *Ole Miss* XXIV (1920), 157. Altogether, Faulkner illustrated the Red and Blue Club page three times; this is the second illustration. *Red and Blue III* appeared in *Ole Miss* XXV (1921), 137.
25. For Faulkner's familiarity with contemporary jazz, see Blotner, *Biography*, 155, 176. "W. C. Handy or Bynum's band" played at the Red and Blue Club dances which Faulkner attended.
26. *The Town* (New York: Random House, 1957), 72–73.

Teaching Faulkner
in the Soviet Union

M. THOMAS INGE

During the fall semester of 1979, I served as a Fulbright Lecturer at Moscow State University in the Soviet Union, where I offered two courses—a large lecture course on regionalism in American literature and a small seminar in American humor. While I paid some lip service to the literature of New England and the Midwest in the regionalism course, I paid a good deal more attention to writing from the American South, a major interest of mine, and in particular, the work of William Faulkner. There were only two texts at hands, copies of which I had brought with me—the novel *Light in August,* and "The Nobel Prize Acceptance Speech."

I often use the Nobel Prize address as a useful method of summarizing the intention and achievement of Faulkner. It allows me to emphasize the extent to which his basic theme, "the human heart in conflict with itself,"[1] fits many of the classic works of Western literature from Shakespeare's *Hamlet* and Cervantes's *Don Quixote,* through Hawthorne's *The Scarlet Letter* and Twain's *Adventures of Huckleberry Finn,* to Faulkner's own fiction. I can also stress the positive and affirmative philosophy underlying his works, a faith in the possibility of man's survival, unlike so many of his contemporaries who were members of the Lost Generation and then experienced the postwar disillusionment of the existentialism of the 1940s. Hemingway offers a convenient point of comparison—a writer who had rejected the words "sacrifice . . . glory, honor, courage, or hallow"[2] as obscene, words which Faulkner would attempt to rescue and

Teaching Faulkner in the Soviet Union   175

reaffirm as a part of the glory of man along with several others—
"love and honor and pity and pride and compassion and
sacrifice."³

I usually wax eloquent and enthusiastic when giving this lecture and a good deal of my own passion for Faulkner shows through, but I was not prepared for the applause that followed my conclusion and the number of people who came up to congratulate me on what they considered the best lecture of the series. One woman asked me if I was as truly moved by Faulkner as I seemed to be. I assured her it was an honest emotion.

While I like to think that my enthusiasm and effectiveness as a teacher were partly accountable for the response I received, I also discovered another probable cause. My comments were falling on very receptive ears. Faulkner has been undergoing a renaissance in the Soviet Union in the past two decades, and it seems to be culminating in a genuine acceptance and recognition of Faulkner as a major American writer. Hemingway may still hold first place in the hearts of Russian readers, and they still dutifully read London, Dreiser, and O. Henry, but I encountered a number of people for whom Faulkner is becoming a passion.

They were not all university faculty and students. I was invited one evening to accompany a friend to the apartment of an editor of one of the trade journals. Knowing I was an American, but not that I was a student of Faulkner, he proudly took me to his study and displayed his collection of Faulkner's works and several framed photographs—a veritable shrine to the Mississippi author. When he discovered our interests were mutual, we spent a most pleasurable evening of extensive conversation about the man, the works, and the world in which he lived and worked. I had by then, however, grown not to be surprised by the discovery in unexpected places of the Russian love of things American.

Official Soviet critical recognition of Faulkner has been a long time coming, even though his work has always been amenable to the approach of "critical realism," in which the writer "expresses a kind of 'loyal opposition,' since he examines the prevailing atmosphere and trends of society from the viewpoint of one who shares in its myths and believes in its highest goals. He discloses injustice and ugliness, displays anger and indignation over the shortcomings he perceives, and implicitly pleads for humanness and sanity."[4] This may partially account for the choice of the first Faulkner story to be translated into Russian in a 1934 anthology of American short stories, "That Evening Sun," an account of the abuses a black woman has suffered at the hands of white men and the total indifference of a Southern aristocratic family to the genuine fears she has for her life, all made more horrible by being viewed through the eyes of a child entirely innocent of the meaning of the events.

The second story selected for translation a year later was less explainable, "The Artist at Home," one of Faulkner's little read and known pieces. It is about a middle-aged fiction writer whose home is threatened by a young, languishing poet who falls in love with his wife and then commits suicide when she rejects him. It is a story about the sources of art in that the events give rise to the poet's best piece of work and a marketable novel for the writer. It is a story too about the tensions that exist between a writer's public and personal lives, between the ideal world of pure art and the practical world of reality. It is the practical view of art that survives, and this may have been the story's appeal to the Russians at the time.

The third story to be translated was "Victory" in 1936, the kind of antiwar story that would interest the Soviets. Alec Gray, a young soldier in the British army during World War I, is severely punished for failing to shave before inspection though he is not old enough to shave. He kills the reporting sergeant-major, becomes a decorated hero in battle, is unable to adjust to the postwar world, and ends up a penniless beggar on the streets of London. Thus the disillusionments of war, in which petty formalities become more important than causes, render people helpless and unable to cope with normal existence.

Despite the implicit criticism of the social structures found in two of these stories, at least one Soviet critic labeled Faulkner, in the year of the first published translation, as a writer who was "preoccupied with psychological sadism and the twitchings of a sick consciousness."[5] Then there was almost complete silence about his work and no further translation for almost two decades, except for a couple of brief attacks in the late 1940s. In a public lecture delivered in Moscow on April 20, 1947, on "Soviet Interpretation of Contemporary American Literature," Maurice Mendelson labeled his work "degenerate" and noted that "the aimless cultivation of horror, an absorption of life as a nightmare, the celebration of monstrosity and sexual perversion are ubiquitous in Faulkner's work."[6] In an essay published the following year, Mendelson recognized that Faulkner was repelled by the social problems of America but was incapable of offering intelligent solutions because his ideal was a "slaveholding South," and he wanted merely to suspend time and prolong his "putrid, dying world." He found that "in almost all of Faulkner's books there are represented decomposed corpses, lunatics, triumphant prostitutes, sadists, idiots."[7]

Another critic, V. Rubin, surveying the state of American letters in a 1948 essay, felt that while Faulkner occasionally drew an image that reflected reality, his art was "permeated with motifs of madness and death." He went on to describe Faulkner's fictional world in these terms: "This is a world of rot and carrion. It oppresses the reader, paralyzes his will. The novels of Faulkner are the brood of rotting capitalist society with its noxious, putrid morals. The moods and motifs cultivated by him serve the aim of demoralization, the perversion of the reader. They inoculate him with a feeling of the most complete indifference to surrounding reality. Human passions, joy, love, strong characters are alien to Faulkner as are images of fighters for the right and dignity of man. His world is a world of dying and dissolution."[8]

Of course, such comments could not be further from the truth, but in fairness to the Soviet critics, Faulkner's American critics in the 1930s and 1940s often condemned him in not un-similar vocabulary, especially those who could not forgive the publication of *Sanctuary* in 1931 and mistook Faulkner for a shocking naturalist who dwelt upon Southern decay, degeneracy, and insanity for the simple love of wallowing in filth. Such a critic as Clifton Fadiman, who relentlessly reviewed each Faulkner novel with comments of ridicule and condemnation, also failed to perceive that beneath the world of dissolution and disillusionment created in the fiction was an affirmative belief in the capacity of man for survival. Not, in fact, until the Nobel Prize address in 1950 did many readers come to understand his intention and look beyond the subject matter for his meaning.

Suddenly, in the late 1950s, a dramatic reversal occurred in Soviet critical opinion and in attention to translation. It was prepared for by an essay in December 1955 in the sixth number of a new journal called *Foreign Literature (Inostrannaya literatura)*. Elena Romanova, upon publication in the states of *A Fable*, had gone back to *Soldiers' Pay* and the story "Victory" to trace Faulkner's attitude toward war through his work and had discovered a strong antimilitarism. In his early work about World War I, he portrayed soldiers as tragic victims of forces beyond their control, but in *A Fable*, he not only protested the cruel bloodletting of war but "accused and exposed those who are responsible for imperialist war." Despite the morbidity in his work, she felt that Faulkner's intention was to "raise the value of the human personality in the eyes of his contemporaries, to defend the right of man to personal inviolability."[9]

The same journal began to publish translations of the stories once again and published another significant essay in 1958, the same year that a small collection of seven stories appeared. Raissa Orlova and Lev Kopelev took a lengthy look at *The Hamlet* and *The Town* (the latter had appeared in the states the year before) and with an eye on his entire corpus agreed that the "stylistic fence" he had constructed was worth crossing for the territory beyond, "a new world of ideas and passions."[10] But they faulted him for not understanding "the basic laws of social-historical development" and not recognizing in Flem Snopes a perfect embodiment of the values of capitalism and in Eula Varner Snopes a victim of bourgeois marriage in the tradition of Anna Karenina and Emma Bovary. Despite his lack of the socialist vision and his abstract moral notions, Faulkner's integrity and sincerity eventually led him, they felt, to the truth.[11]

The generous attitude of Orlova and Kopelev brought forth a volley of criticism from other commentators who had read of Faulkner's gradualist stand on civil rights for blacks and could not see him as a "seeker of the truth and champion of justice."[12] In September 1959 Alfred Kazin was reported to have feigned shock at the neglect of Faulkner when talking to a group of Soviet writers, and in November, *New York Times* correspondent Max Frankel noted from Moscow that "hardly anyone in this part of the world which prides itself so on familiarity with American literature has ever heard of William Faulkner."[13] Writing about the state of Faulkner studies a year later, Deming Brown indicated that "as of 1960 there was no way of knowing how Faulkner would fare in the Soviet Union. . . . To understand and appreciate Faulkner the critics would indeed have to display much greater ideological elasticity than they had heretofore shown in their judgments of American writing and would have to become receptive to moral subtleties and psychological and social interests which they have traditionally scorned."[14] Nevertheless, the debate was started and Faulkner in the next decade became a central topic for discussion.

During the 1960s six major works appeared in Russian—*The Mansion*, "The Bear," *The Hamlet, The Town, Soldiers' Pay*, and *Intruder in the Dust*, as well as another sixteen short stories and selections from various published interviews with Faulkner and letters to Malcolm Cowley. Along with this wealth of new material, indicating a fairly substantial interest on the part of the Soviet reader, came detailed assessments by Soviet critics. One of the best examples was collected by Carl R. Proffer in his anthology of Soviet criticism of the 1960s.

In "Faulkner's Road to Realism," Pyotr V. Palievsky found that like "a genuine provincial looking to the capital for truth,"

Faulkner looked to Joyce for a new method of relating truth, and like Joyce, he "was interested in the internal motives and actions, the only things which could make this external canvas sensible and coherent." In *The Sound and the Fury*, however, unable to express the truth by entering the stream-of-consciousness of three characters, Faulkner resorted to becoming in the last section a narrator himself and thus, in a sense, rediscovering traditional realism. He saw man "in one continuous plane from the past and the present, which means that he also has a future which cannot be stopped." Like Balzac, he constructed a fictional world or cosmos unified by "an unbroken chain of human values" and became a "universal writer" as "he slowly and painfully showed the alienated world his kinship to it and the importance of humanity's foundations." Clearly reflecting a careful reading of the fiction, Palievsky has nothing but praise to offer and, interestingly enough, prefers Faulkner to Hemingway because the latter's heroes are unable to overcome their destiny by fierce attack and effrontery, as do Faulkner's.[15] Other critics joined Palievsky in a chorus of praise which can be exemplified by one writer's summary: "He is unequivocally one of the greatest writers of this century, a powerful and original epic writer, a man who has gone through hell with his characters and so has all the more ground for saying to us: 'I believe that man will not merely endure: he will prevail'."[16]

The 1970s witnessed no abatement of interest in translations or criticism. In the early part of the decade, five more major works appeared in Russian, *Requiem for a Nun*, *The Reivers*, *Sartoris*, *The Sound and the Fury*, and *Light in August*. Short stories also appeared with increasing frequency, climaxed in 1978 by the publication of a handsome edition of *Collected Stories* containing all the works in the 1950 American edition with critical essays, explanatory and bibliographic notes, a chronology of Faulkner's career, and twenty photographs of the author and his world. Two examples of criticism of the 1970s are found in the anthology issued by Progress Publishers, *20th Century American Literature: A Soviet View*, a collection of papers prepared for what was the first annual conference on American Studies held in Moscow in January of 1975 under the leadership of Americanists Yasen Zasursky and Yuri Kovalev of Moscow and Leningrad Universities, respectively.

Georgy Zlobin's essay, "A Struggle Against Time," is a thorough analysis of *The Sound and the Fury*. While he disparages the approach, Zlobin has produced what is largely a formalist analysis of plot and characterization. "If Yoknapatawpha is a model of the American South," he says, "*The Sound and the Fury* is a model of Faulkner's work. All the ingredients of Faulkner's touted, controversial art are included in this thin volume. . . . Once [the reader] overcomes the muddy jumble of Faulknerian words and the mannered rhetoric characteristic of Southern prose, he strikes a golden vein of genuine talent moving from gothic depths to the actual truth of life and art."[17] The critic's main concern is with the concept of time in the novel: "The novel's structure reflects the stoic struggle against time which Faulkner pursued on all levels, philosophically, historically, and linguistically."[18] The end result, Zlobin concludes, has less relationship to the work of Joyce than to the horrors of Poe, the sarcastic comedy of Twain, and the gothic fiction of Warren, McCullers, and O'Connor.

Mikhail Landor, the author of several earlier studies of Faulkner and Faulkner criticism, contributed an essay on "Faulkner's Creative Method in the Making," a broad survey of the development of artistry in the fiction with specific attention to *The Sound and the Fury* and *As I Lay Dying*. Although he recognizes the strong influence of the *Old Testament*, Shakespeare, Balzac, Flaubert, Dostoevsky, Gogol, Tolstoy, Joyce, and Sherwood Anderson on his fiction, Landor praises Faulkner for asserting his own "artistic self-determination" and working out his independent concept of the modern novel.[19] Landor acknowledges that "he spoke as an artist, with no pretensions to the role of an ideologist" and that one "cannot evaluate the scale of Faulkner's thought without understanding his humanism."[20] Neither Landor's nor Zlobin's essay provides new insights, but each reflects an appreciation for the latest criticism in the states and indicates an effort to take Faulkner on his own terms and especially deal with his style and artistry. For a type of criticism more at home with ideology and political content in literature, these at least represent steps in the right direction and suggest that Soviet critics have developed some of the sensitivity and sophistication Deming Brown identified in 1960 as necessary to a full appreciation of Faulkner.

What I have traced so far, on the basis of the limited information I have, is the official Soviet view of Faulkner as expressed in approved critical documents. But what about the average Russian reader? What is there about Faulkner's work that strikes a responsive chord, that attracts interest and encourages appreciation? One can only speculate, of course, but I wish to make a few suggestions.

Carson McCullers felt, with some logic, that there was a strong affinity between Southern and Russian writers. In a 1941 essay for *Decision* on "The Russian Realists and Southern Literature," McCullers found similarities in their use of cruelty, a technique she described as "a bold and outwardly callous juxtaposition of the tragic with the humorous, the immense with the trivial, the sacred with the bawdy, the whole soul of a man with a materialistic detail," which she then exemplifies by parallel scenes in Dostoevsky's *Crime and Punishment* and Faulkner's *As I Lay Dying* in which farce and tragedy are successfully if uncomfortably fused. It is rare, she felt, "except in the works of the Russians and the Southerners, that they are superimposed one upon the other so that their effects are experienced simultaneously."[21] Unlike Gogol, who had no trace of passion, Dostoevsky and Tolstoy turned in their art to metaphysical and universal problems and tried to bring order and understanding out of chaos. In their great philosophical novels, Russian realism reached a culmination. While she would not compare their achievements, McCullers felt that in the realism of Ellen Glasgow, Erskine Caldwell, and William Faulkner, a similar effort was underway: "They have transposed the painful substance of life around them as accurately as possible, without taking the part of emotional panderer between the truth as it is and the feelings of the reader."[22] Here, then, are two possible cords between Faulkner and the classic Russian writers—an ability to balance the comic with the tragic, the farcical with the cruel, and an effort in his finest work to address the fundamental questions of existence, the worth of man, the meaning of life, and the values by which we live.

Another affinity may be Faulkner's own high regard for and absorption of Russian literature and culture. When asked by a student at the University of Mississippi in 1947 which were the greatest novels of the nineteenth century, he replied. "Probably Russian—I remember more Russian names than any others."[23] When called upon by interviewers and students to list his favorite writers or those he continued to read, he included Dostoevsky, Chekhov, Tolstoy, Turgenev, Gogol, and Artzybashev.[24] Chekhov he cited over and over again as the absolute master of the short story because of his ability to tell his tale with such disciplined brevity.[25] When a friend requested an inscribed copy of *The Mansion* to be hand delivered to Boris Pasternak, Faulkner replied, "Nonsense. Pasternak is a good writer, of the 1st class, and no first-rate writer wants strangers scribbling and scrawling on his books. I wouldn't want Pasternak or Shakespeare either writing on mine, and I believe he feels the same way."[26] He claimed a "spiritual kinship" with the Russia which produced these great writers.[27]

It was Dostoevsky with whom Faulkner felt the greatest affinity and who had the most profound influence on his writing. "He is one who has not only influenced me a lot," he confessed, "but that I have got a great deal of pleasure out of reading, and I still read him again every year or so. As a craftsman, as well as his insight into people, his capacity for compassion, he was one of the ones that any writer wants to match if he can."[28] He was famliliar with *Crime and Punishment*, but his favorite, the one he reread most often, was *The Brothers Karamazov*, which he reported "I go in and out like you go into a room to meet old friends, to open the book in the middle and read for a little while."[29] The direct influence on *The Sound and the Fury* of Dostoevsky, as well as that of James, Flaubert, and Conrad was acknowledged in one version of an introduction he wrote during the summer of 1933 for a new edition of the novel:

> I wrote this book and learned to read. I had learned a little about writing from Soldiers' Pay—how to approach language, words: not with seriousness so much, as an essayist does, but with a kind of alert respect, as you approach dynamite; even with joy, as you approach women: perhaps with the same secretly unscrupulous intentions. But when I finished The Sound and The Fury I discovered that there is actually something to which the shabby term Art not only can, but must be applied. I discovered then that I had gone through all that I had ever read, from Henry James through Henty to newspaper murders, without making any distinction or digesting any of it, as a moth or a goat might. After The Sound and The Fury and without needing to open another book and in a series of delayed repercussions like summer thunder, I discovered the Flauberts and Dostoievskys and Conrads whose books I had read ten years ago. With The Sound and The Fury I learned to read and quit reading, since I have read nothing since.[30]

Two years after he published *The Sound and the Fury*, he even speculated about revising the structure of *The Brothers Karamazov* in the pattern he had originated in that novel: "Dostoevsky could have written the *Brothers* in one third the space had he let the characters tell their own stories instead of filling page after page with exposition. In the future novel, or fiction . . . there will be no straight exposition, but instead, objective presentation, by means of soliloquies or speeches of the characters, those of each character printed in a different colored ink."[31] It will be recalled that Faulkner had originally wanted *The Sound and the Fury* to be published in just that fashion with colored inks.

Source hunters have demonstrated that two crucial scenes in *Sanctuary* may have made use of images from *The Brothers Karamazov* and *Crime and Punishment*.[32] There are also striking parallels between the characterizations, situations, and actions of Raskolnikov of *Crime and Punishment* and Quentin Compson of *The Sound and the Fury*, although "what chiefly equates Raskolnikov and Quentin is the common characterization of the compulsive man, psychopathically searching for his own identity, romantically attempting to rise above ordinary human ethics, clinging to ridiculous theories in the face of hard facts, and doomed to punish himself and others in the process. And underneath these attitudes and symptoms lies the basic motive of all the thought and action of both youths—the will to suffer."[33]

Quentin Compson is not the only character in Faulkner to share the monomania and idiosyncrasies of Raskolnikov, as the French critic Jean Weisgerber has amply demonstrated in his exhaustive study entitled *Faulkner and Dostoevsky: Influence and Confluence*,[34] the most thorough comparative analysis we have of Faulkner and any major world author. Moving through the entire corpus and considering every major character, Weisgerber finds a multiplicity of parallels, a few clearly an influence and others a coincidental falling together of great minds. Yet it is clear that Dostoevsky is an extremely useful writer to study alongside Faulkner as a guide to the themes and philosophic considerations of the Mississippi author, another example of the shock of recognition that occurs when one genius encounters another.

While there is no evidence that Faulkner read any of the works of Mikhail Sholokhov, their only conjunction being that they were contenders for the Nobel Prize for literature the same year, there are noteworthy parallels between the two. In his essay "Faulkner's Road to Realism" cited earlier, the Soviet critic Pyotr V. Palievsky noted several of the similarities:

> For example, there is an unquestionable similarity between his world and the artistic world of Sholokhov. Begin with the fact that Yoknapatawpha is an Indian word meaning "quiet flows the water across a plain." This is the epic idea of a large river, the flow of life, which is also embodied in the title *The Quiet Don;* besides this, the word "quiet" in both cases masks the opposite which it contains. The American South portrayed in Faulkner's Yoknapatawpha plays a role

similar to Sholokhov's Don; here it is taken as a special patriarchal society which has been preserved, but simultaneously as a reactionary portion of a larger whole which is confronted by the necessity for drastic changes. The idea of Mother Earth, so strong in Sholokhov, is very noticeable here too. And the transition, the disruption of its norms is accompanied by gains and by irrevocable losses. The movement is toward change and sharp contradictions which demand for their expression special devices: characteristic of both Faulkner and Sholokhov are completely uncapricious transitions from humor to tragedy and back, wherein one feels not contrast, but on the contrary, the natural "polarity" of life. They also have much in common in style, in maintaining the individuality of each character, and so forth.[35]

In his short story "Man's Fate," Sholokhov stated, "A man of unbending will . . . will predominate, and at the side of the father will grow up the son, who when he is mature will be able to bear all burdens and overcome all obstacles which lie in his path,"[36] a view of human nature close to that expressed by Faulkner when he received the Nobel Prize and asserted that man will not merely endure but prevail.

The matter of Mother Earth, which is so prominent in Sholokhov and other Russian writers, is another important link between Faulkner and Russian literature. Although not directly related to the movement, Faulkner partook of the general attitude and philosophic disposition of the writers known as the Southern or Vanderbilt Agrarians, led by John Crowe Ransom, Donald Davidson, Allen Tate, and Robert Penn Warren, who in the 1930s attempted to encourage a return in the South to the agricultural economy of the past and resist the destructive forces of industrialism and technology.

They, of course, were but providing a Southern expression of what has been a dominant strain of thought in America from its founding, and in Western civilization at least as far back as classical times, which we now identify as "agrarianism." Agrarians generally believe that the cultivation of the soil and contact with nature encourage the development of honor, morality, and courage; that only farming offers complete economic independence and social self-sufficiency; that the farmer has a sense of harmony, identity, and place that counteract modern tendencies towards alienation and abstraction; that industry, capitalism, and technology create huge cities destructive of dignity and integrity; and that the brotherhood of labor and cooperation in the agricultural community provides a potential model for an ideal social order.[37] These ideas permeate Faulkner's fiction, and the conflict between the agrarian rural ideals and the forces of urban technology can be seen when Ike McCaslin lays aside the gun, watch, and compass to encounter Old Ben on his own turf; when Popeye is described as being made of stamped tin and thus a symbol of the amoral, faceless spirit of destruction loose in modern society; when the citizens of Yoknapatawpha County at first resist but then give in to the purchase of a sewing machine or automobile; or whenever the new materialistic schemes of Flem Snopes prevail over the traditional integrity and trusting innocence of the town folk. Faulkner himself once asserted, "I'm a countryman. My life is farmland and horses and the raising of grain and feed. I took up writing simply because I liked it . . .; my life is a farmer."[38]

One is likely then to find numerous parallels between Faulkner and Sholokhov and all the others who were among the "village writers" movement in the Soviet Union which celebrated the Russian countryside and the peasant life. Their fiction and personal sketches portrayed the rhythms and spiritual qualities of rural life and contact with the land, the liveliness of folk speech and wisdom of folk thought, and the importance of the peasant character to the psychological makeup of the nation. Like their agrarian counterparts, these writers also feared that increased mechanization and central management would threaten the independence and integrity of the peasant soul and village way of life. In their return to tradition and historic continuity, they participated in the national quest for the ultimate definition of Russian character and culture.[39] Soviet readers who have enjoyed their work would find some of the same concerns and qualities to admire in Faulkner.

A contemporary Russian writer who partakes of this tradition to a certain extent and who offers some interesting parallels to Faulkner is Fazil Iskander, a native of the constituent republic of Abkhazia located in Georgia in the Southeastern European part of the Soviet Union between the Black Sea and the Greater Caucasus. Most of his stories are set in this subtropical agricultural region where tobacco, tea, and citrus fruit are the leading crops and the major traditions are Orthodox Christian and Muslim. Like Faulkner, he decided to make his own "little postage stamp of native soil" the main source of inspiration and subject matter for his fiction.

Their careers have followed similar paths. Both were inattentive, lazy students who learned a good deal more by experience than formal education. Just as Faulkner headed for New York to initiate his literary career, Iskander headed for Moscow, but both returned home finally as unhappy cosmopolitans. Both encountered early on a collected volume of Shakespeare's plays. Faulkner said, "We yearn to be as good as Shakespeare and the only way to get better is through studying [literature]."[40] In his last years, he came to prefer *The Tempest* as his favorite play.[41] Iskander has noted, "Shakespeare's tragedies seemed to me muddled and pointless. On the other hand, the comedies fully justified the author's efforts at composition. I realised that it was not the jesters who depended on the royal courts but the royal courts that depended on the jesters."[42] Both decided on a literary vocation because, in Iskander's words, "it dawned on me that it would be more interesting and more profitable to write one's own books than deal with other people's."[43] And both began their careers as poets but finally achieved distinction in fiction.

A reading of the collection of Iskander's stories *The Thirteenth Labour of Hercules* indicates that he prefers a semi-autobiographical narrative in which events are related from the point of view of a young boy. Boyhood adventures predominate—playing the neighborhood detective, swimming and treasure hunting in the summer, staying with relatives in the mountains and fighting the family cock for control of the barnyard, dealing with a stern and sarcastic schoolmaster in an effort to avoid ridicule before the class, learning about the treacheries of childhood pride and envy, and discovering that the handsome boyhood idol has feet of clay—all in a series of experiences designed to instruct the narrator in the meaning of life and initiate him into the perilous passage to adulthood. The effect of using the innocent, common sense point of view of the child is to highlight the stupidity and cruelty of the adult world, a technique used by Faulkner with great skill in such works as *The Unvanquished*, "That Evening Sun," and *Intruder in the Dust*.

Iskander tells a marvelous tale called "Through the Night" in which his narrator undertakes his first journey through the mountains alone to tell his mother the news of his brother's being wounded in battle. He gets lost, stumbles into an open grave, finds himself trapped there with a goat, and yells for help. When a villager responds to the call and throws in a rope, the boy without warning sends up the goat first for rescue. The rescuer, as could be expected, abandons the task when he seems to be bringing up a horned devil from the gates of hell. The story is told with the kind of deadpan humor and graveyard comedy that both Mark Twain and Faulkner appreciated, and it incorporates much of the kind of country lore, character, and customs which were Faulkner's stock in trade in the Yoknapatawpha stories.

Iskander's tales are filled with the queer, eccentric folk of the rural village—the idiots, the con men, and the local characters. There is the memorable Old Crooked Arm in the story of that name, a man who once ridiculed a prince and received the wound that gave him his nickname, who was the butt of a joke that rumored his death but returned home to enjoy his funeral feast and maintain his open grave (the one into which the boy stumbled that dark night), and who succeeded in outwitting his oldest friend and rival from beyond the grave with a trick that proved he knew more about horses than his friend. Actually near death this time, Old Crooked Arm made his friend promise to jump his horse across the coffin three times before the burial to demonstrate his superiority through survival. What the friend did not know, until he attempted the deed, was that, in the words of a local proverb, "A good dog won't bite his master's hand and a good horse won't jump over a dead man."[44] Old Crooked Arm won again, conclusively and irrefutably. His impudent laughter even beyond death, his daring bravado on several occasions, and his heroic attitude toward the adverse circumstances of life ally Old Crooked Arm with numerous Faulkner characters of a similar foolishly brave disposition, such as Colonel John Sartoris, young Bayard Sartoris, Gail Hightower's grandfather, and "Miss" Rosa Millard.

Other similarities might be mentioned—their use of folk materials from the oral tradition, their skill in using raconteurs and recreating engaging conversation, or their descriptions of animals in the rhetoric of epic and romance—but most importantly, they share a recognition of the necessity for humor and comedy in their work. A strong believer in the saving grace of comedy, of laughter in the face of despair, Faulkner, I believe, would have agreed with Iskander who has said, "I believe that to possess a good sense of humour one must reach a state of extreme pessimism, look down into those awful depths, convince oneself that there is nothing there either, and make one's way quietly back again. Real humour is the trail we leave on the way back from the abyss."[45]

My intention here is not to demonstrate influence, of which there are no signs in Iskander's work, and I do not know that he is even aware of Faulkner. I simply wish to suggest that the elements which have made Iskander popular among Russian readers are to be found in Faulkner, and that Faulkner shares in many of the matters of style and content that are a part of Russian literature. To my knowledge, Faulkner's influence in the Soviet Union is an entirely unexplored subject, although it has been reported that the great film director Eisenstein was intrigued by the complex structure of Faulkner's novels and his use of "flashbacks" in the interior monologues and exterior narratives, just as he was fascinated with applying the fictional techniques of James Joyce to the art of film.[46]

There is a puzzle I want to leave you with before concluding. One of Faulkner's favorite characters and representatives of the traditional society was V. K. Ratliff, the sewing-machine agent, of whom Cleanth Brooks writes, "Insofar as curiosity, intelligence, sensitivity, good sense, and good humor are concerned, Ratliff is an individual, and an exceptional individual at that. . . . He is perfectly easy in his world, but he also stands a little outside it and a little above it. He is the detached sage of the folk society, which he knows, expresses, and yet judges. Ratliff is wise in his own right, but his wisdom is tinctured with the values of the Southern folk society whose intelligence and conscience he is."[47] Throughout most of the fiction in which he appears, we are not told what V. K. stand for until, almost as an afterthought in *The Town*, Faulkner reveals that the initials stand for Vladimir Kyrilytch, a name always assigned one son in the family since the first ancestor came to these shores as a soldier in the British Army during the American Revolution and was captured at Saratoga. Now why has Faulkner assigned this distinctly Russian name to his best representative of wisdom and good sense?

Intrigued by this discovery, one Soviet critic, Abel Startsev, has noted, "Documents have recently been found in our archives which show that Russian people were actually present in the United States during the period of the American War of Independence. Here, as usual, Faulkner displays his excellent acquaintance with the oral traditions of his native parts, which evidently also preserved the memory of a Russian settler."[48] Mikhail Landor also speculates, "in our view the surprising deciphering of the name reveals a genuine feeling of sympathy for Russian literature which the author nurtured during his whole writing career."[49]

Whatever his reasons were for this waggish riddle, it is clear that Faulkner was a great admirer of Russian literature, that he sought inspiration and consolation in the classic Russian writers, and that his own work displays a sympathetic identification with the great philosophic issues that concerned them in the epic sweep of their works. In the magnitude of his spirit and the greatness of his talent, Faulkner is fit company for Dostoevsky, Tolstoy, Chekhov, and the rest, and the Russian interest in his accomplishment is but verification of this fact.

NOTES

1. "Address upon Receiving the Nobel Prize for Literature," *Essays, Speeches, and Public Letters*, ed. James B. Meriwether (New York: Random House, 1965), 119.
2. Ernest Hemingway, *A Farewell to Arms* (New York: Charles Scribner's Sons, 1929), 191.
3. "Address upon Receiving the Nobel Prize for Literature," 120.
4. Deming Brown, *Soviet Attitudes Toward American Writing* (Princeton: Princeton University Press, 1962), 11.
5. *Ibid.*, 68–69.
6. *Soviet Interpretation of Contemporary American Literature* (Washington, D.C.: Public Affairs Press, 1948), 20. A translation published as a pamphlet by the American Council of Learned Societies in the "Current Soviet Thought Series."
7. Brown, 157–58.
8. *Ibid.*, 157.
9. *Ibid.*, 180.
10. Max Frankel, "The Worldwide Influence of William Faulkner: Reports from Six Capitals—Moscow," *New York Times Book Review* (November 15, 1959), 53.
11. Brown, 181–82.
12. *Ibid.*, 182.
13. Frankel, 52.
14. Brown, 182–83.
15. "Faulkner's Road to Realism," in *Soviet Criticism of American Literature in the Sixties: An Anthology*, ed. Carl R. Proffer (Ann Arbor: Ardis Publishers, 1972), 155, 156, 161, 164–65.
16. Mikhail Landor, "Faulkner in the Soviet Union," in *Ibid.*, 180. This essay and another by Landor, "William Faulkner: New Translations and Studies," *Soviet Literature*, 8 (1968), 180–85, are useful surveys in English of Soviet criticism in the 1960s as seen by another Soviet critic.
17. "A Struggle Against Time," in *20th Century American Literature: A Soviet View* (Moscow: Progress Publishers, 1976), 286–87.
18. *Ibid.*, 291.
19. "Faulkner's Creative Method in the Making," *Ibid.*, 311.
20. *Ibid.*, 314, 313.
21. "The Russian Realists and Southern Literature," in *The Mortgaged Heart* (Boston: Houghton Mifflin, 1971), 252–53.
22. *Ibid.*, 258.
23. *Lion in the Garden: Interviews with William Faulkner*, ed. James B. Meriwether and Michael Millgate (New York: Random House, 1968), 58.
24. See, for example, *Faulkner in the University*, ed. Frederick L. Gwynn and Joseph L. Blotner (Charlottesville: University Press of Virginia, 1959), 50; and *Lion in the Garden*, 217, 251, 284. See also Joseph Blotner, *William Faulkner's Library—A Catalogue* (Charlottesville: University Press of Virginia, 1964), 81–83.
25. *Faulkner in the University*, 48, 145, 207.

Teaching Faulkner in the Soviet Union 193

26. *Selected Letters of William Faulkner*, ed. Joseph Blotner (New York: Random House, 1977), 439–40.
27. *Ibid.*, 413.
28. *Faulkner in the University*, 69.
29. *Ibid.*, 150.
30. James B. Meriwether, ed., "William Faulkner: An Introduction for *The Sound and the Fury*," *Southern Review*, 8 (October 1972), 708.
31. *The Lion in the Garden*, 18.
32. Edward Wasiolek, "Dostoevski and *Sanctuary*," *Modern Language Notes*, 74 (February 1959), 114–17.
33. Frederick L. Gwynn, "Faulkner's Raskolnikov," *Modern Fiction Studies*, 4 (Summer 1958), 171.
34. First published in French as *Faulkner et Dostoïevski: confluence et influence* (Bruxelles: Presses Universitaires de Bruxelles, 1968) and translated by Dean McWilliams (Athens: Ohio University Press, 1974).
35. "Faulklner's Road to Realism," 166.
36. *Ibid.*, 167. For a brief comparison of Faulkner and Sholokhov as representatives of attitudes towards modern regionalism, see David H. Stewart, "Faulkner, Sholokhov, and Regional Dissent in Modern Literature," *Proceedings of the Comparative Literature Symposium*, 6 (1973), 135–50.
37. M. Thomas Inge, ed., *Agrarianism in American Literature* (New York: Odyssey Press, 1969), xiv.
38. *Lion in the Garden*, 169.
39. See Deming Brown, *Soviet Russian Literature Since Stalin* (Cambridge: Cambridge University Press, 1978), 218–23.
40. *Lion in the Garden*, 276.
41. Joseph Blotner, *Faulkner: A Biography* (New York: Random House, 1974), II, 1787.
42. *The Thirteenth Labour of Hercules* (Moscow: Progress Publishers, 1978), 31.
43. *Ibid.*, 11.
44. *Ibid.*, 128.
45. *Ibid.*, 14. For a perceptive brief discussion of Iskander's fiction, see Deming Brown, *Soviet Russian Literature Since Stalin*, 206–209.
46. Mikhail Landor, "William Faulkner: New Translations and Studies," 184.
47. *William Faulkner: The Yoknapatawpha Country* (New Haven: Yale University Press, 1963), 28.
48. Cited in Mikhail Landon, "Faulkner in the Soviet Union," 179.
49. "From Whitman to Hemingway," in *20th Century American Literature: A Soviet View*, 437.

The Perception of William Faulkner in the USSR

ALEXANDRE VASHCHENKO

The amount of material that was used only partially during the preparation of this paper clearly shows that the history of the perception of the works of William Faulkner could become a subject of a two-volume study, the first of which could include a multifaceted evaluation of this phenomenon while the second could serve as a bibliographical guide. Perhaps it would be premature on my part to consider the following treatment as a chapter in such an edition or even as an introduction to it. Let it stand as a preliminary summary of what might be called "The Current Perception of William Faulkner in Russia."

The traditions of literary perception as they have developed in Russia are fairly old and well-defined; they include the peculiarities of connection or contact between the writer and the reader, the tradition of editing foreign fiction, the schools of translation, and the like. Taken altogether, it is a huge complex, which has to be borne in mind when speaking of the impact of such an important phenomenon of twentieth-century literature as William Faulkner. One may generalize when analyzing the process of Soviet-American literary contacts of the last two decades (the '60s and the '70s especially) that the role of Faulkner as a master of literary narration, as a humanist, and as a deeply-rooted national writer is becoming more and more apparent. Both as a unique artist and as the head of the "Southern" school of writers, he has already become an important event in our lives; and in his democratic aspects with each passing day he

Perception of Faulkner in the USSR 195

comes into new relationships with the art of word imagery on many levels.

The limits of the present study will not permit me to cover all the aspects and nuances of these relationships. Still, striving for a more or less complete picture, I shall dwell further on four items: the characteristics of various types of editions of Faulkner's works and their chronology; the reaction to Faulkner of the average nonprofessional reader in Russia; some notions about the publication process of Faulkner in languages other than Russian; and, finally, the question of Faulkner's contemporary "dialogue" with the works of postwar Soviet writers.

Soviet Editions of Faulkner's Novels and Stories

It is fairly well known that William Faulkner became acknowledged as a writer of merit in the later years of his life. This peculiarity of his career resulted in the late arrival of Faulkner's novels in the USSR. Thus, Faulkner has entered our consciousness separately—after the other writers of experimental prose in American literature. Still, this notion holds true only if we are speaking of the time when he became a popular phenomenon— when Soviets found themselves applying to him the expression "Russian Faulkneriana," analogous to only the greatest masters of literature (as, for example, "Russian Shakespeariana" or "Russian Pushkiniana"), demonstrating the dramatic response to his work.

I should like to stress the fact that, starting from 1917 on, the basic principle of the cultural and editorial policy of the Soviet state has been responsiveness to all major and democratic phenomena of world culture. This means that editors tried hard to follow literary developments both in "cool" and "mild" political times. This, to my mind, might be one of the answers to the question, why does an average Soviet reader possess better knowledge of American culture and literature than the other way around. The tradition of reading serious American literature goes back to the last century—to the times of A. Pushkin and

V. Belinsky. Because of this tradition our interest in Faulkner manifested itself at a surprisingly early date: the first translations of Faulkner's short stories were published in the '30s. "That Evening Sun" was included in the anthology *American Short Stories of the Twentieth Century* (1934). At that time other stories were also translated: "The Artist at Home," "Victory," and an extract from *Pylon* (1938). All Faulkner's major works, as they were being written and published in America, were coming to the attention of the Soviet reader during the '30s and '40s, at least in the form of reviews in periodicals.

The problems of wartime postponed the work of translating Faulkner's novels; and so the next stage in the process of disseminating Faulkner's works in the Soviet Union occurred in the '50s. An edition of the collection entitled *William Faulkner: Seven Short Stories* was the landmark; it appeared with an introduction by the leading Soviet Americanist of the time, Ivan Kashkin, the correspondent of Hemingway and the translator of "Barn Burning," "A Justice," and "Victory" (1958).

Starting then and continuing to the present, not a single year has passed without the publication of either one or more new translations of Faulkner's works in the Soviet Union. This active and even systematic process (for by this time Faulkner had captured the attention of literary critics and translators) of studying Faulkner's works—an intense labor of more than twenty years— has culminated in the present situation, when it is much easier to list those Faulkner works which have not been translated into Russian than those which have. We possess translations of all the works of the Yoknapatawpha cycle except *Sanctuary,* now being translated, and all the other works except *Mosquitoes.* A recent translation of *Absalom, Absalom!* (1981) has elicited responses from Soviet readers almost tantamount to the publication of *The Sound and the Fury* in 1973—when many readers and critics responded vehemently, either for or against.

The bold challenge that Faulkner presents to the translator is so compelling that very often, in accordance with the traditional method of translating classical literature, almost simultaneously

Perception of Faulkner in the USSR   197

several different translations of one story are published. This occurs as a result of the general tradition of discontent with existing translations of fiction, a discontent from which Faulkner is not an exception. Translators especially tend to return to the short stories like "Dry September," "A Rose for Emily," "That Evening Sun," and even "The Bear," which, according to our concepts of the genre, is not a short story, but something close to the Russian standards of "povest," like, for instance, Gogol's "Mirgorod" or Aitmatov's "The White Steamboat." Some stories are known in two or three versions; there exist, for example, two versions of *The Unvanquished.* In trying to explain this phenomenon, one might cite the fact that, to date, the Russian translations of Faulkner are to a certain extent "interpretations." The past tense—principally used by Faulkner—is richer in grammatic specification in the English language than in Russian; and to compensate for this difference, the translator must always look for some other means.

There exist certain peculiarities in the process of editing foreign fiction. The translation of a new novel as a rule appears on the pages of one of the major popular magazines issued in approximately half a million copies—such as *Inostrannaya literatura* (as was the case with *Intruder in the Dust, The Sound and the Fury*) or *Novii Mir (Absalom, Absalom!)* or *Zvezda (The Reivers).* Soon after, the novel is published in book form. This procedure usually provides a very large audience of readers for these "best-sellers"—a term which does not correspond to the Russian "novinki," but which, for lack of an English equivalent, I would render as "the latest books of serious prose worth reading and discussing."

Editorship in the USSR is centralized, which to a certain extent helps the leading publishing houses to specialize among themselves. For instance, the first translations of Faulkner were published mainly by Progress Publishers as "novinki," or as contemporary literature, while Faulkner's earlier works (corresponding chronologically to "modern literature"), or those which soon became to be regarded as classics, belonged to the domain of "Khudozhestvennaya Literatura" publishing house (e.g., the Snopes trilogy).

Besides, there exist a number of specialized and serial editions, and Faulkner's continued inclusion among them demonstrates that he is considered an established classic not only of twentieth-century fiction, but of world literature. In considering editions of Faulkner one must mention a volume in the series *The Library of World Literature* (200 volumes altogether), which includes *Light in August* and *The Mansion* (303,000 copies). The very first volume devoted to representative American literature in the series *The Masters of Contemporary Prose* was dedicated to Faulkner and includes *Sartoris*, "The Bear," and *Intruder in the Dust*.

A celebrated event was the publication in 1977 of *The Collected Stories* (25,000 copies) in the academic series *Literary Monuments*, the name of which speaks for itself. In this series, texts generally appear with elaborate documentation, accompanied by abundant reference material. The series is a bit reminiscent of the Dover Editions, but is more scholarly in its principles of selection and is strictly literary in its orientation. Faulkner appears here along with the *Song of the Campaign Waged by Igor*, Montaigne, Plutarch, Dante, Thoreau's *Walden*, *The Complete Short Stories of Edgar Allan Poe*, the novels of Henry James and Herman Melville, to name only a few.

Despite the fact that Soviet Americanistics is younger than Germanistics or Anglistics and started almost with the beginning of the Soviet state, it still attracts the special attention of our scholars as well as the interest of Soviet readers. This can be proved by the publication of the biobibliographical volumes specially dedicated to American literature in Russian and American literature studies. These guides are compiled by the members of the A. M. Gorky Institute of World Literature and the Institute of Scholarly Information on the Humanities, both of the Academy of Sciences of the USSR. The extensive chapters dedicated to Faulkner illustrate his special popularity among Soviet

Perception of Faulkner in the USSR 199

literary specialists. I might even say nowadays Faulkner has become "the fashion."

Faulkner's Reception Among Soviet Nonprofessionals

Since the time of Belinsky it has become a cliché to speak of the average Russian reader as unusual because of the vast numbers of these readers and because of an eagerness and craving among Russians for printed matter and for serious literature in particular. As a rule, indeed, the Russian reader is not abstract and hypothetical but quite real and demanding; he responds actively to literature and is often motivated by the question— who should be read nowadays, or who among contemporary writers is to be regarded as a candidate for the classical pantheon? Still, the reading audience in the USSR, thanks to the obligatory system of school education, is constantly growing. As a matter of fact, the last two decades were characterized by an unimagined book boom and "book hunt," which at present still does not show any evidence of declining. Although large numbers of copies of classical editions are published, today these are not enough. The reason for this is not a matter of individual tastes, but rather a deeply-rooted tradition of personal involvement in world affairs—a tradition instilled by classic Russian literature. Probably, this literature is also responsible for the widespread readiness of Russians to perceive a "lesson" from this or that classic—to perceive the writer as a teacher of life and to see his heroes as examples for imitation.

The experiences of the Revolution, the Civil War, and World War II helped to sustain and further develop these traits and to foster respect for the heroic theme, which has dominated Soviet literature of the first half of the century and was readily perceived by our readers in the writings of certain American contemporaries, like Jack London and Ernest Hemingway. It was also more habitual for the general Russian reader to comprehend traditional forms of narration which in many ways are reminiscent of the experiences and modes of our own literature (e.g., Galsworthy and Dreiser). I am inclined also to think that even the Snopes trilogy was more easily understood by the Soviet reader ahead of the rest of Faulkner's novels (it appeared in the USSR in the '60s) not only because, in a sense, it was the summit of all of Faulkner's productions, but also because of the broad panorama of sociopolitical life outlined in *The Mansion* and because of the sharp opposition embodied, on the one hand, in the bourgeois Snopeses and, on the other, in the character of Linda, an ideal individual living in harmony with the private and the social worlds.

Seeking to discover how Faulkner is perceived in the Soviet Union today, I have tried to apply a sociological approach in my analysis. A short list of questions was prepared and distributed to the members of the readers' seminars on contemporary foreign literature in several district libraries of Moscow; I also included the audience of the Central Lectorium and the readers of the Union Library of Foreign Literature. The questions were composed in such a way so as to give no indication that Faulkner was of special interest, but rather to present him in the context of modern American literature. The results of this experiment together with the analysis of readers' letters to the editors of Faulkner's novels lead to the following conclusions, which nevertheless must be considered only approximate.

The most popular American authors among Soviet readers today are Hemingway, Dreiser, and London. The latter two have long been prominent names among Soviet readers and date back to Gorky and Kuprin. Hemingway is attractive to Soviets because of his more "European" outlook and context and because of the tragic heroism and the strong antiwar sentiments in his fiction. Dreiser is considered to be the most characteristically "American" of all U.S. authors and a critic of the so-called "American way of life."

To these readers the narrative style of William Faulkner presents a greater level of difficulty. This is proved by frequent laments of an inability to comprehend Faulkner; the confessions that "it is hard to share the common experience with his

Perception of Faulkner in the USSR 201

[Faulkner's] heroes." Such impressions are drawn, however, from contact with the texts of *The Sound and the Fury, Light in August,* "The Bear," *Sartoris,* and the Snopes trilogy. One must conclude, naturally, that these novels are the most "popular" with the mass reader, who may or may not like them but finds it necessary to read them.

It certainly is not an easy task to establish an age criteria for readers' perception; still, in quite a number of cases the approving responses to Faulkner came from young people between twenty and thirty-eight years of age, which may signify a turn of the younger generation towards Faulkner. The complex controversies of life, as reflected by Faulkner, appeal to their age, for "the thoughts of youth are long, long thoughts," as Longfellow puts it. Many of these young people, expressing their approval and disapproval of Faulkner, concentrate on the former and stress his mastery of psychology and philosophy and point out that in terms of depth of analysis Faulkner reminds them of Dostoevsky. Even more revealing in this respect is a longer response from a representative of an older generation, a pensionnaire who is sixty-one years old: "I like the energetic, international Hemingway, but I am presently feeling more and more inclined towards Faulkner, and consider him to be the most 'American' among others. . . . Faulkner is characterized by the same moral position as Dostoevsky. He strives to uplift man, to help him become better." But at the same time the reader cannot help admitting that "the way to Faulkner's fiction is very difficult."

A twenty-eight-year-old engineer states: "Faulkner especially appeals to me by the profound study of the psychology of an individual under extreme situations." It is perhaps interesting that he, as some others do also, names, along with Faulkner, Robert Penn Warren as the most characteristically "American" author of the present time.

Some responses are especially oriented to aspects of Faulkner's literary style: "One feels the powerful depth of the general idea; everything in the narration is concentrated upon it, 'works' to its end; it is the characteristic of the great novelist. Rereading him each five to ten years, one is able to find something new for himself," said a thirty-five-year-old whose profession is not specified.

The "Multinational" Faulkner

The chronology of editions of Faulkner in different languages within the USSR demonstrates that the process was started in the second half of the '60s and strengthened during the next decade. Among the smaller nationalities of the USSR, the reader's acquaintance with Faulkner depends very often on the peculiarities of the specific tradition and culture. In those republics where the national languages are more closely related to Russian (e.g., Belorussia), the process of reading Faulkner quite naturally continues in this language. This is also the case in such regions as Khasakhstan, where both Russian and the native language are spoken equally. In all other cases, with the exception of the Middle-Asian republics, we may find variant translations of Faulkner as well as the list of accomplished translations, which originally were made mainly from Russian.

Still, each particular case is different. Thus, the Ukranians, possessing their own version of *Inostrannaya literatura*, the *Vsesvit* magazine, seek to translate Western classics from the original even, if possible, before they are edited in Russian. During the '70s, in Kiev, where we have an important center for the study of American literature, some of the Yoknapatawpha novels were published (under one cover) and, later, the collected short stories of William Faulkner. The Lithuanians were among the first to translate Faulkner; they translated *Light in August* in 1965, and some of the short stories and *As I Lay Dying* in 1965, ahead of the Russian translation. The Latvians attempted to translate *Sartoris*, "The Bear," and *Intruder in the Dust* into their tongue; while the Estonians have succeeded in translating *The Sound and the Fury* (1972), *As I Lay Dying* (1971), and the collected short stories. There is a somewhat peculiar situation regarding Faulkner in the Caucasus. So far as I know, Azerbaijan reads Faulkner in Russian; the Georgians were especially active during the last decade and had accumulated a number of translations, *The Hamlet, The Town,* and *The Bear* among them. Armenians still possess only one translation of a short story, "Turnabout" (1965), but this paucity of translations does not point to the lack of interest towards Faulkner in Armenia; rather this interest takes different forms—a problem which I shall address later.

The average number of copies of "multiethnic" editions of Faulkner is considerably large: from 15,000 to 60,000. One may summarize, by way of a conclusion, that there are indications that Soviet readers' acquaintance with Faulkner's works will grow; and although Soviet readers may argue with some of Faulkner's ideas, still argument is dialogue; and many aspects of his stories and novels (e.g., the ethics of the land, the depiction of different types of ethnic consciousnesses, the rural daily life) must appeal to the multinational Soviet audience.

Faulkner and Contemporary Soviet Writing

The process of understanding Faulkner in the USSR has become closely connected with the processes of developing Soviet literature during the past three decades. The literature of the Soviet Union both geographically and ethnically is so widely dispersed that in the East a number of newly-born literatures are reminiscent, in some ways, of the literatures of Latin America and Africa, while in the West—for example, in the Baltic republics—old traditions of urban prose show the influence of Western classics.

In the last few decades Soviet literature has had to achieve a tremendous goal: using the tradition of classic literature as its model (I must say that the attitude toward tradition in Soviet literature is basically different from that in American literature), Soviet literature has had to grasp the essence of contemporary times, with all the changes which have taken place in Soviet society, and discover the national roots of all the major cultural processes going on in the country.

The unifying basis appeared unexpectedly in the early '60s in so-called "village" or "rural" prose, which derives, in reality, from the development of the traditions of classic Russian literature and the tradition of Mikhail Sholokhov, traditions which emphasize how the whole world can be found in a single human individuality living in the smallest portion of the world. Some of the most urgent problems of contemporary life have propelled this trend to the prominent place it now occupies in Soviet literature; such problems include ecological, moral, and educational issues as well as a need to bring to the body of the main literature all the regional geographical areas, Russian as well as others, which prior to this time had remained merely "the virgin soil unupturned." This is why to Soviet literature, which has been always on alert to discover its own literary content, Faulkner, of all the Western writers, seems most appealing. As in Soviet literature, Faulkner incorporates in himself the whole world of heroes, the world of rural provincial life, upon which the most important problems of human life are projected.

Jack London, in the introduction to the American edition of Gorky's novel *Foma Gordeev,* wrote that Gorky's hero is unable to live unless he discovers the essence of living. Such painful efforts to discover the essence of life have always been the national tradition of Russian as well as Soviet literature; they are an intrinsic aspect of all the major Russian classics of the nineteenth century, from Pushkin to Dostoevsky. It is natural, therefore, that William Faulkner, the writer who struggled hard to meet face to face the problem of the essence of life, of human nature, and sought to accomplish this on the basis of national material, was most enthusiastically received by the contemporary Soviet prose writers.

Broad comparisons between Soviet literary material and the major events in contemporary Western literature, be it Faulkner or Gabriel García Márquez, have become the natural and necessary process for us. Such comparisons may help us to shed additional light on the development of Soviet prose in the first half of this century, to grasp more deeply the meaning and influence of such developments. More specifically, the novels of the Yoknapatawpha saga, together with the narrative heritage of Sholokhov, helped Soviet writers of the '60s and '70s to define their artistic manner and individuality. Some striking proofs of this phenomenon are perhaps worth mentioning.

Among contemporary writers, i.e., "after Faulkner" as well as "after Sholokhov," whom should we look to as the next possible candidate for the classical pantheon? The nature of the present time, I believe, is not amenable to this kind of evaluation. But we could agree perhaps that among the most prominent prose writers of the present time (I am speaking of Soviet literature) one must name Valentin Rasputin, the author of *The Money for Maria, To Live and Remember, A Farewell to Matiora,* and other novels.

Speaking to students at Moscow State University on December 17, 1976, Rasputin especially dwelled on the '50s as the period in the development of Soviet literature when many young writers initially became acquainted with contemporary Western literature in Russian translations. "I had been in the Irkutsk University at the time when the rich quantity of translations of the Western classics came to us (1956–1958)," he said. "We threw ourselves on it avariciously. But very soon we were fed up, although certain influence did take place, and I have shared it. Thank God, I escaped it later, and in this process my native ground, my native roots became strong helpers."[1] The meeting took place just after the publication of Rasputin's new novel, *A Farewell to Matiora.* It is worth mentioning, in light of what follows, that in an answer to a student's question, Rasputin spoke of the river symbolism in his narratives: "I was born and lived in the village on Angara River, and that is why I write about Angara. Before *To Live and Remember* I did not name it in my narratives. It was just 'the river,' on which the steamer comes and goes, and my heroes live. I believe that the right to call the river by its own name has to be earned, as it was done by Sholokhov in *And Quiet Flows the Don.*"[2] The writer had in mind not only Sholokhov, though, but also Faulkner as he said then and elsewhere, and the following comment from E. Evtushenko serves as an additional proof. He mentions Rasputin's saying to him in private conversation: "There had been a time when I was all for Hemingway and Remarque. . . . They have come to our reader rather late, and that is why they were so craved for. . . . Whom do I love now among the foreign writers? I am still grateful to Hemingway, but lately Faulkner is the most important with me. He is much more broad and deep."[3]

Similarities in the creative consciousnesses of Faulkner and Rasputin have already been noticed by Soviet literary critics. Thus, for example, Galina Belaya in a recent article focuses primarily on a detailed comparison of Faulkner's and Rasputin's world views and narrative techniques. Finding some similarities, Belaya then discusses differences between the two and finds that the two authors differ in the way they define man's relationship with nature. In Faulkner, "man, once an organic part of nature, is today the creature both born of it and thrown away by it, already an alien to it."[4] The land in Faulkner may be either wild or conquered, but in the process of conquest man is destined to lose. On the other hand, in Rasputin's works, nature is not oblivious and not alien to man: "from birth till death he feels his blood relationship with it."[5] This ethical and moral dimension of the man-land relationship is very old in our literature, going back as far as pre–Christian times among Slavonic nations, and continues today even among many non–Slavonic nations of the USSR, who live by the land and with the land: the Georgians, the Armenians, and the like.

But it is not my aim to dwell on differences; what is common to both Faulkner and Rasputin is a sense of the necessity to make evident the moral dimensions inherent in human affairs and to examine the bonds—social or tribal—which link the individual to a larger whole; both writers also invoke the idea of responsibility of man toward mankind and the compassion which is so very powerfully manifested in the writing of Dostoevsky, Tolstoy, and, one might add, even in Russian philosophy of the period (e.g., Nikolai Fedorov). Belaya summarizes it in the following way: "Now when the leading writers the world over express their ideas capable, in their opinion, to save mankind from the threat of physical and moral destruction, the essence of the ethical program, which is formulated by Soviet contemporary prose, may become clear only through its comparison with other concepts. That is why the time has come when we not only can, but must compare ethical ideas springing, say, from such authors as V. Rasputin, V. Astafiev, Ch. Aytmatov, and G. Matevosyan, with foreign philosophic and ethical concepts."[6]

Belaya's article is characteristic and provocative, for it encourages one to draw further parallels—e.g., between *As I Lay Dying* and *The Last Time* by Rasputin. And while reading passages like the following one taken from *A Farewell to Matiora*, one is compelled to remember Faulkner: "Besides he [the imaginary host, the spirit of the village] didn't like to look up into the sky; it put him into an unclear and undefined restlessness, and frightened him with its terrible powerful vastness. Let the humans look at it and become quiet; but all that which they consider to be dreams are in fact only remembrances, even in the most remote and sweetly drawn thoughts—just the remembrances. No one is given the possibility of dream."[7] (The translations of the texts are mine.—A.V.)

But this comparison theatens to become a separate treatment. Let me pass on to some other instances of the literary interrelatedness. To all the previously mentioned authors who spoke in interviews about Faulkner's significance for them, I must add Vassily Belov, who spoke on this subject this very year in the broadcast series called "The Reading Circle." The number of such direct references to Faulkner might be prolonged at will; but even in the absence of such clear-cut avowals, the influence of Faulkner's narrative style can be detected in the work of many Soviet writers. Thus, Faulkner's mastery of the regional theme and psychology did not escape the attention of Victor Astafiev, a fact which is especially evident when one is acquainted with his collection of stories, *The Queen Fish*.

Taken together, the characters of Astafiev, along with other functions they perform in the narrative, delineate a picture of man within a social system and within the environment—in this case in the specific area of the Enisei River. Astafiev strongly makes the point that man is responsible for his own troubles because no one but he brings about his own destruction. Such themes are familiar to Faulkner's readers. One might add, perhaps, that Astafiev—consciously or unconsciously—uses a characteristic Faulknerian device: the stories are brought together into the larger epic unit by means of the same characters, manifesting themselves here as the background, there as the leading hero, and, in some other cases, just briefly mentioned. Of course, one may argue that this particular device goes back as far as Balzac; but it came to Astafiev's prose (if it did) naturally, through his contemporary Faulkner.

The influence of Faulkner's style on contemporary writers could be the subject of a separate study. For the moment, it will suffice to point only to one clear instance where Faulkner's impact is unmistakably evident in the familiar lengthy phrasing, the periods, and the effort of each sentence to encompass both past and present. To a certain extent, this is also an example of parallelism in creative thinking.

All the short novels and stories written by Grant Matevosyan, a talented young Armenian writer, take place in one of two small mountain villages, and for this reason the whole cycle has already been called "the Antaramech saga" or "the Tsmakut saga." In an interview with me, Matevosyan said that until 1965 or so William Faulkner was completely unknown to him; and even when the publication of *The Sound and the Fury* in Russia aroused so much interest, he was still not inclined to read Faulkner. Later, nevertheless, he read some Russian translations of Faulkner's Yoknapatawpha works, and although he now calls his relationship with Faulkner "a late marriage," he does acknowledge Faulkner's influence on the "Antaramech saga." Indeed, the evolution recently undergone by Matevosyan would seem to indicate Faulkner's increasing influence. The original impulse for the creation of the initial story of the "August" cycle (a part of the whole saga) is somewhat reminiscent of the process of creating *The Sound and the Fury*. Matevosyan originally attempted to write a short novel, which did not come off somehow; so he decided to tell a short story, and then discovered other stories behind each story; he continued in this way and soon found himself in possession of one great story, which, as he says, "still does not let me go."

Faulkner and Matevosyan might be compared in terms of characters or plot, general ideas (e.g., the "August") or the functional importance of the past. It might be more illuminating, however, to examine the text itself and feel the atmosphere; for example, in these final paragraphs of the story called "Under the Clear Sky the Ancient Mountains," the death of a dog is depicted.

The children asked the forester for a gun, but the forester came himself. One of the children said "a pity," but here Antonyan Zaven said: "Still more a pity for my children." His house was nearest to the graveyard, and Zaven said: "My children you do not pity, only the dog?" The forester came to the graveyard, stopped in front of the dog, took the gun from his shoulder, put the muzzle between the dog's eyes, and the dog wailed: "Wau-u-u . . ." The dog stayed lying on the grave—its head on its paws—although it knew all about the gun.

After the war, when I was young, when in the meadows on the mountains I had stolen some dogs for Vani, when the wolves were many, and for all the shepherds there was left only one dog, the old Chambar, when Vani was married, when Asatur came from the army, when yet the grandfather Danelanz Artyom played the flute, when the household of the Azbaijanian went by on and on and had no end, that spring the shepherds were given the guns, and each shot scared the dogs away—from that spring on this dog has known all about the gun and feared it, but now it didn't run away, it stayed there on the grave.[8]

Some of the ways which Soviet authors have assimilated Faulknerian modes and techniques were discussed by the Azenbiajan writer and literary critic Ch. H. Huseinov, the author of *Mohammad-Momet-Momish*. In an interview with me, he stated that although Faulkner's early works, *The Sound and the Fury* and *Light in August,* arrived comparatively late in the USSR, they have had the greatest impact on Soviet writers. Perhaps, he said, we should speak not of influences, but of the awakening of creative impulses among writers. With regard to this awakening, the following four items might be specified:

1. The device of the so-called "model situations." Presently a comparatively new trait in Soviet literature, this appears in the selection of place of action and of surroundings, which most often is a fictitious village, the country, the town, or even a house where the main conflict will develop. In general, there has been a marked shift among Soviet writers of prose fiction from "real" surroundings to symbolic ones.

2. Many contemporary novels, Huseinov's included, could not have been written in their present form without the example of Faulkner's "stream-of-consciousness" technique, which seems, externally, nongoverned chaotic narrative but which reveals, with subtle internal logic, the heart of the story. Of course, this technique is the general achievement of twentieth-century literature, but it has come to contemporary Soviet prose particularly by way of American experimental writers and by way of Faulkner especially.

3. Another feature of Faulkner's narrative skill is his daring freedom of composition, his willingness to take risks with characterization as, for example, in *Light in August* when Percy Grimm, a character of some importance to the narrative, is successfully introduced in the novel's closing chapters.

4. Finally, Faulkner's special characteristic, his original handling of narrative time, has influenced Soviet writers. Of course, many writers have contributed to the development of each of these narrative features. One has only to remember Tolstoy or Dostoevsky, for instance. But in the twentieth century Faulkner's imaginative powers and his story-telling ability predominate, for his "moments" of existence include so much that it is next to impossible to imagine such a reality—but it is a unique literary reality nevertheless.

The reaction of Soviet prose writers and Soviet readers to

William Faulkner is best summarized by one of our academic literary critics, L. N. Arutjunov. Following a lengthy comparison of Faulkner's heritage and the contemporary literary situation in Soviet Russia, Arutjunov concludes: "Faulkner has re-created a world which in many respects is different from ours: but the wish itself on the part of this American writer to overcome, on the level of general relationships, the atomized existence of bourgeois individuality manifests in itself an experience that cannot be neglected, disregarding the real attitudes of Soviet writers towards him. The problem is not in the emulation of Faulkner, but in the understanding of the fact that such a way of literary development and such a fictional reality are perspective. . . . The experience of our literatures is not alien to such tendencies, and it may even define their future life."[9] Using this quotation as my final point, I would reiterate that my task has been to discuss the reception of William Faulkner's works in the Soviet Union; I hope I have indicated the seriousness and eagerness with which Faulkner has been received in Russia and also the fruitfulness of this cultural dialogue.

NOTES

1. E. I. Zakharova, "Eto stanovitsa traditsiei. Valentin Rasputin v MGU," *Vestnik MGU*, 3 (1977), 79.
2. *Ibid.*, 80.
3. E. A. Evtushenko, *Talant est chudo nesluchainoe* (Moscow: Sovetskiy Pisatel, 1980), 280.
4. G. Belaya, "Na glubine. Rasmishlaya nad prosoi V. Rasputina," *Literaturnoe obozrenie*, 1 (1982), 12.
5. *Ibid.*, 13.
6. *Ibid.*, 11.
7. V. Rasputin, *Povesti* (Moscow: Molodaya Gvardiya, 1976), 54.
8. G. Matevosyan, *Zelenaya dolina* (Erevan: Sovetakan Groh, 1981), 229.
9. L. N. Arutyunov, "Opit mnogonatsionalnoi literaturi i mirovoi literaturnii protsess," in *Sovetskaya literatura i mirovoi literaturnii protsess* (Moscow: Nauka, 1975), 203.

William Faulkner
in Soviet Literary Criticism

SERGEI CHAKOVSKY

The study of Faulkner's creative work began in Soviet criticism almost fifty years ago if we assume that this work began in 1933 when the first review of *The Sound and the Fury* was published. Real and serious interest in Faulkner, however, manifested itself in Soviet criticism only in the middle fifties; one after another a considerable number of articles appeared in print and these publications drew the attention of Soviet readers to the new (or rather "omitted") phenomenon of paramount importance in American literary culture.

The Soviet reader's first-hand acquaintance with the art of Faulkner's novels (some of his short stories had been published in the '30s) occurred only in 1961, when the journal *Foreign Literature* published a translation of *The Mansion*. Since then the relations between Soviet readers and Faulkner have become more and more intimate each year, although this relationship was not devoid of a certain drama; Faulkner's creative career as a whole assumed for the Soviet reader a somewhat enigmatic quality, like the "reverse" Faulknerian novel, whose action only begins when, to all appearances, everything has already happened. So to many it would seem that everything had already taken place in *The Mansion*, which was apprehended as a more or less typical example of a novel in the Balzac-Dreiser tradition. (Although the author's social criteria seemed to some people to be a little vague and the style somewhat unusual). Then the writer began to reveal to Soviet readers his "current" faces: *The Hamlet* (1964), *The Town* (1965), *Soldiers' Pay* (1966), *Intruder in the Dust* (1968), *Go Down, Moses* (1969), *Requiem for a Nun* (1970), *The Reivers* (1972), *Sartoris* (1973), *The Sound and the Fury* (1973), *Light in August* (1974), *The Collected Stories* (1978), *Absalom, Absalom!* (1980), and *Sanctuary* (1981). The reaction to these later novels was far from uniform; enthusiasm mixed with a certain amount of puzzlement, and finally a general feeling arose that this kind of fiction was both necessary and inevitable.

I wonder if there is anything exceptionally peculiar in this mode of becoming acquainted with a writer, provided the writer is William Faulkner. Even in America, Faulkner had remained an "omitted" figure up to the '50s; familiarity with his novels developed unevenly, from a chronological point of view, although for different reasons. I mention this, not once more to shame critics and publishers (which is always easy to do retrospectively), but to try to give an idea, however schematic it may be, of the specific attitudes to Faulkner in the USSR and to suggest that these attitudes are of wider significance not only insofar as the history of tastes and history of criticism are concerned, but also because they reflect the specific nature of the artistic phenomenon we are trying to come to terms with.

However different the ideological and methodological backgrounds, however dissimilar the terminology, and despite the absence of a final agreement concerning the criteria of artistic values, both the serious American and the serious Soviet critics of Faulkner from the very start were concerned with more or less the same set of problems. What is he? An imitator of Joyce or a descendant of Mark Twain? An enterprising "retailer of sin" or a traditional moralist, a decadent formalist or a preacher—or all these together? American criticism was earnestly trying to answer these questions in the 1940s and had scored a number of successes. But at the same time their approach was somewhat pragmatic; the questions were dealt with as they came up, very often in isolation from one another. For Soviet criticism these questions were closely interconnected as parts of a more general problem, the problem of the artistic method of a writer. I know that many Western critics do not understand, or pretend not to understand, this term as well as such literary categories as, for example, realism or modernism when what is meant is not historically local schools or directions but a certain type of artistic vision and artistic recreation of the world. We concede that these terms are not perfect; more often than not they require a detailed commentary when used before a multilingual audience (unfortunately, literary criticism does not possess a common metalanguage, which makes it so often the target of caustic remarks from representatives of more exact sciences). What is important, however, is to agree on the essentials; whom are we talking about? Does this artist assume the absurdity of existence and the impotence of man before the faceless forces of oppression (irrespective of whether the artist models the absurdity through the completely distorted structure and style of the work or imposes it in a most lifelike shape)? If we return to the terminology accepted in our country, do we mean a modernist or an artist who himself is looking for and tries to help us to find a way out of the apparent chaos of existence (whether it is a traditional novel which appears to be cast from life itself or some kind of arbitrary allegory which concerns itself not so much with the "outer" as the "inner" man while making use of all known—and yet unknown—forms of literary expression)—our definition of the realist? What we are concerned with here is bringing to light the cardinal attitude of the author toward life and art and not a mere inventorizing of the artistic devices used by the author in question; trying to understand the artistic intention—the primary impulses that drive the author and inform his creation. This task is not scholastic at all; it is practical. Unless we are aware of the larger artistic and ideological framework to which the author belongs and the specific scale of values according to which the author and his achievements should be evaluated, we shall be doomed to roaming in the wilderness of approximate and nonobligatory information.

The attitude of Soviet critics toward Faulkner has undergone a certain evolution which reflects not only a change in the Soviet

Faulkner in Soviet Literary Criticism 215

approach to world literature as a whole but also the evolution of Faulkner's works. In the '20s and '30s Faulkner was almost uniformly regarded in the USSR as a decadent or modernist writer. This attitude was based, on the one hand, on insufficient knowledge of Faulkner's objectively "difficult" texts; on the other, on the unduly schematic, sometimes almost vulgar conception of the relationship between the reactionary and the progressive, the realistic and the modernist in art. The '50s produced a number of works which clarified aspects of Faulkner's creative work. Such works include Elena Romanova's "Antiwar Motives in Faulkner's Prose" and Ivan Kashkin's "Faulkner—the Story Teller"—which, although they did not achieve broad generalizations, did nevertheless discover new aspects in a literary phenomenon as yet quite mysterious, and thus laid the groundwork for a more dialectical understanding of Faulkner. It was in the '60s and in the '70s, however, that Faulkner was at last really discovered. This discovery was perhaps one of the most remarkable events in the course of the last two decades for Soviet readers of foreign literature, and this reaction of Soviet readers appeared to Soviet critics as a kind of challenge.

In a work by a veteran Soviet Americanist—M. O. Mendelson's *The Contemporary American Novel* (1964)—Faulkner's literary work was given for the first time comparatively full treatment. It is noteworthy that the chapter on Faulkner, who at that time was known as the author of a single novel, appeared side by side with the chapters devoted to "celebrities" of American literature, who can be said to have found a second life in the Soviet Union because of the enormous print runs of the Russian translations of works by Sinclair Lewis, Ernest Hemingway, John Steinbeck, and Erskine Caldwell. When Mendelson writes of Faulkner, he is sufficiently discrete and analytic. He doesn't try to force a certain opinion of the writer on his reader. His aim is rather to show the objective complexity of Faulkner's prose, on the one hand, while at the same time trying to dispell popular myths of the allegedly premeditated obscurity and the impenetrability of his novels.

Faulkner's books can and must be understood. His novels are certainly not at all "tales told by an idiot." This is what Mendelson succeeds in showing in a brilliant way; nevertheless, the attempt to explain Faulkner "to the very end" in order to convey his meaning as clearly as possible to the reader often brings about a certain "straightening out" of the purport of the novel, "bending" it either in the direction of "decadence" or "social criticism." According to Mendelson,

> As for Faulkner's world view in the course of the better part of his life it was characteristic of him not to accept the bourgeois modern reality and also to be addicted to the "proud," the writer's favourite word; very dear to him was the past of the Southern States at the same time as he was conscious of the decomposition and death of the old way of life. If we are to add that Faulkner in actual fact did not see any real approaches to the solution of the Negro problem we shall not fail to see the very important sources of the feeling of fear before reality, the philosophy of hopelessness which contributes to some of the writer's books, however rich they may be in their realistic content, a distinct modernist flavour.[1]

Some of Mendelson's evaluations were qualified by subsequent critics who argued against them, not without reason. Nevertheless, in Mendelson's work we find the main directions along which the study of Faulkner's work will follow. He has given us a blueprint of those phenomena which could serve as typological counterparts to Faulkner, and he has formulated the concept of evolution in Faulkner's art. The importance of this work will be quite clear if we consider that it is the problem of evolution, its ideological and artistic direction, and the dynamics of its development, which has for a long time remained the primary subject of the most important Soviet works on Faulkner.

This subject is brought out in the title of the well-known article by Pyotr Palievsky, "Faulkner's Road to Realism," which to a considerable extent has served, together with Mendelson's research, as the basis of the dialectical comprehension of Faulkner's work, which is characteristic today of Soviet literary criticism. In his study, Palievsky suggests a framework within which Faulkner's works can not only be read adequately but can also be understood in their indispensable connection with the main ideological and artistic processes, which constitute the distinctive character of twentieth-century literature.

Faulkner's movement towards realism is shown by Palievsky to be conditioned not by certain extraneous circumstances; rather, it was for the writer the way towards himself, the inevitable and difficult way of discovering his own artistic identity. Palievsky's work is not beyond criticism in certain parts. Reading it today, we notice, for example, that the author takes perhaps too literally Faulkner's words concerning the history of the creation of *The Sound and the Fury*. As if in accordance with Faulkner, Palievsky perceives the first three parts of this novel as consecutively unsuccessful attempts to "tell the same story" or, stretching it a bit further, as illustrative of the struggle between talent and "the method-of-the-flow-of-consciousness" which was voluntarily accepted by the author. Only when Faulkner passes on to the fourth part to the objective narration, according to the Palievsky, does Faulkner go beyond the limits of avant-garde literature.[2] Had this been so, however, then this step would have been taken by Faulkner earlier in his first two books, which despite their traditional style, are supremely marked by the influence of aesthetic models which are alien to him in their very nature. Besides, Palievsky himself remarks most penetratingly that there could not be a final and unique way of "telling the story" in *The Sound and the Fury*, for the uncertainty and the search for something became organically rooted in the very structure of his artistic thought.[3] And further on, speaking of Faulkner's later works, Palievsky remarks: "In every story, wherever and whatever may happen we find that there is always the unknown that takes part. Man here is only the projection of a distant and enormous life which has no beginning; but all that was in there is, nevertheless, present and makes itself known, opening up unforeseen possibilities, a kind of all-illuminating discharge of fate."[4] It is this "all-illuminating discharge" combined with the undying belief that man "not only will endure but he will prevail" that leads Faulkner beyond the framework of modernism with its proclamation of the chaotic nature and tragic destiny of human existence. This is Palievsky's basic premise which is not merely declared, not merely stated, but is pursued and investigated by the critic in all its most complex artistic transpositions.

William Faulkner, Palievsky contends

> . . . had a colossal power for growth, not only with respect to his literary system and the environment he chose to write about, but also with respect to the whole of reality of his time. In this sense he differs from many of his colleagues—writers of the West in the twentieth century—who knew very well, too well perhaps, what it meant to look at things realistically, i.e., who knew how to adapt the potentialities of their humanism to existing conditions, and were not too optimistic about man's ability to change these conditions. William Faulkner went, in this sense, much further. He completely negated the power of circumstances. . . . For him man's ability to alter circumstances to his advantage has always been much more real than the circumstances themselves. That was why his realism was full of "sound and fury," of muted and horrendous blows which make you think of a prison wall being pounded on and torn down from within.[5]

Another very important component in Palievsky's conception was the amalgamation of the national and the general human elements in Faulkner's creative work. If writers like Aldington, Dos Passos, Remarque, and Hemingway became "international writers" who "were very quick to radiate around themselves the waves of modern problems," Faulkner, "unquestionably national, even parochial, became rather a writer of universal appeal, who slowly, ponderously was proving to the disjointed world the importance of purely human principles."[6] On the one hand, Faulkner is probably the most American artist of the twentieth century, who discovered America anew, America which seemed to have lost its "Mark Twainian" identity in the "mad, mad world" of victorious commercialism. Faulkner's books, however, according to Palievsky, help make clear that Huck and Tom are not dead, to see what "the life of that colossal people is founded on," to "discover points which cannot be found either in reference books, or in current facts, or, alas, in modern novels: America as a whole, its general image, its atmosphere."[7]

This discovery, on the one hand, of the roots of Faulkner and, on the other, the globality of his ethical and aesthetic search, enables Palievsky to draw literary parallels which, although unexpected at first sight, are internally well grounded and eloquent. It is certainly very interesting, for example, to compare artistic worlds of Faulkner and Mikhail Sholokhov. What basically determines the deep-rooted affinity of the two writers despite all their nationally and historically conditioned differences is the triumphant faith, belief in man, who is capable not only of enduring but also (to a greater or lesser degree) of changing, recreating the world. "To begin with," says the critic,

> "Yoknapatawpha" is an Indian word, which means "quiet flows the river on the flat plain." This is the epic idea of a big river, the flow of life, which is embodied also in the title of *Quiet Flows the Don;* in addition, the word "quiet" in both cases is pregnant with the opposite meaning.... The idea of mother earth, which is so powerful with Sholokhov, is also most clearly pronounced here. It should also be mentioned that transcending, giving up its norms, is accompanied by a number of acquisitions and an irretrievable loss; the movement expresses itself in a change of sharp contradictions which require for its expression special devices: characteristic of both for Faulkner and Sholokhov is a completely natural transition from humour to tragedy and back.[8]

In Yasen Zasursky's seminal study *American Literature of the Twentieth Century* (1966), Faulkner's work is considered on two main planes: from the standpoint of the influence which avant-garde aesthetical canons had on his artistic method—in particular, the literature of the "flow of consciousness"—and from the standpoint of the writer's subsequent ideological and artistic evolution. Although, on the whole, Zasursky is inclined to place Faulkner's creative method of the '20s and '30s within the categories of modernism, he nevertheless remarks that "even then through the dimness and obscurity . . . of Faulkner's concepts and pronouncements, through the intricacies of his formal experiment could well be traced the passionate desire of the artist to get to the elemental causes of the tragic and dark sides in human life to which he has dedicated his work."[9]

Considering *The Sound of the Fury* within the genre of the "stream-of-consciousness" novel, Zasursky makes a detailed analysis of the philosophic, psychological, and aesthetic genesis of this literary form and studies its realizations in different national and individual creative variants. At the same time, Zasursky does not overemphasize the dependence of Faulkner on the masters of European modernism. According to Zasursky, Faulkner's novels grew on American soil and reflect the historical fate of the country as a whole as well as that part of it—the South—with which Faulkner is connected by indissoluble social and spiritual ties.[10]

As emphasized by Zasursky, "flow of consciousness" can be used as a device by writers of completely different aesthetic orientations. As a device, it is neither "good" nor "bad." It cannot in itself bring about the success or failure of a work of art. At the same time, as the author notes, although as a genre the flow-of-consciousness novel was not viable on American soil, what is usually called the "technique" of the flow of consciousness has played a considerable role in the development of American literature. It has widened the range of artistic devices, which to a greater or lesser degree are used by the greater part of realistic writers.

Many pages of *The Sound and the Fury* are greatly admired by Zasursky, and he particularly marks the brilliantly individualized inner monologues, although on the whole, in his opinion, the novel does not achieve its primary objective. This happens not because the narrative method is inappropriate; Zasursky identifies another cause: "Having marked the tragic character of the fates of the Compsons, Faulkner cannot reveal the causes of this tragedy. He can't do it because his novel does not reveal the breath of history."[11] At first sight this remark may seem paradoxical: both Faulkner and his characters do "breathe" history; moreover, they do not merely think of the past, they recognize it as their present. At the same time, however, this idea of Zasursky is quite plausible. Both in *Sartoris* and in *The Sound and the Fury* history is to a greater or lesser degree mystified, viewed as the arena of the struggle between the eternal and faceless doom and man who is eternal, in spite of his historically conditioned outer caul. And Faulkner himself seems to have been subconsciously aware of that. It is no accident that fifteen years after *The Sound and the Fury* was published he attached to it as an "Appendix" a brief resumé of quite a different novel, perhaps *The Sound and the Fury* as he would have been willing to write it then: a historical novel with social psychological motivations clearly presented and sharply set off.

The source of Faulkner's creative development Zasursky sees in the fact that "a characteristic intoxication with life causes Faulkner stubbornly and sometimes in a tortured way to look for ways and means of learning more about it, and to express his knowledge in art."[12] This persistence necessarily led Faulkner beyond the confines of modernist literature. In his subsequent works, including the Snopes trilogy, he "used . . . many of his findings which were first made in *The Sound and the Fury*, but he gave up the main distinctive feature of the novel of the "flow of consciousness, the split with the historical development, subjectivized representation of the inner world isolated from real life and the basic assumption of the absurdity of the world."[13]

During the ensuing years a number of Soviet scholars have expressed doubts about the validity of such a "basic assumption" even for Faulkner's earlier works. Literary criticism shifted its approach; instead of contrasting different stages in his artistic career, scholars began to search for unifying premises.

"It is obvious that Faulkner has gone a long way," says Tamara Motyleva, the author of *The Novel Abroad* (1966). "At the same time it is obvious that his creative work is marked by great inner unity. We cannot mechanically sever the later Faulkner from the earlier one."[14] The methodological implications of Motyleva's concept become evident when she analyzes *The Sound and the Fury*:

When considered in the general context of Faulkner's creative work, we become convinced that it was not simply a bold literary experiment but something which was much more serious. In spite of its intricate form, the novel did reflect actual processes of real life. It was the first sketch of a monumental picture of the multivolumed tragical saga of the fate of the American South. . . . Young Faulkner's tale of the fate of the Compsons is connected not only insofar as the community of characters and place of action are concerned, but also by the community of the anti-bourgeois pathos with the global narration of the mature Faulkner about the rise and fall of the Snopses.[15]

According to Motyleva, all the innovations of style and genre introduced by Faulkner "were aimed not at turning away from the tempestuous and extremely complex social reality of the twentieth century but at the fearless investigation of it. These strivings resulted in greatly enriching the realistic prose of our time."[16]

Although anticipating something which will be discussed in greater detail later on, we nevertheless should emphasize here that following the publication of *The Sound and the Fury* in Russian in 1973 a number of serious articles were published which interpreted the novel as trying to come to terms with the multiplicity of its potential meanings, both its exterior and interior connections. When considering *The Sound and the Fury* against the background of the classical European family novel, Alexei Zverev, the author of the provocative article "Literature in the Deep," remarks:

> *The Sound and the Fury*, as essentially an innovatory work (and this is the reason why it has given rise to so many interpretations by so many critics), is part of those phenomena which in his time were characterized by Y. Tinyanov as "literature in the deep," the inalienable peculiarity of which is furious struggle for a new kind of vision. . . . The peculiar complexity of the style and general structure of *The Sound and the Fury* were determined by the attempt to look beyond the surface and to contemplate the depth—not to produce another tale of the absurdity of Being but to find a language which could grasp the actual complexity of tendencies of time and history as reflected in Faulkner's Yoknapatawpha.[17]

Faulkner in Soviet Literary Criticism 223

Using Zverev's expression, we can say that Soviet, and not only Soviet, criticism of Faulkner for a long time was faced by the problem of working out "the language" which would correspond to an object so unusual and specific. It was necessary to find relevant categories which would express the essence of the artistic phenomenon without substituting for it other phenomena which had already been discovered and understood.

To recognize the inner unity of Faulkner's creative work did not at all mean substituting the study of immanent laws of self-realization of artistic individuality for a study of objective literary-historic phenomena. Our criticism was aimed at a synthesis of the two approaches. The idea of evolution in Faulkner's creative work was not relinquished. It was made more precise. It was detailed on the basis of a more dialectical and objective analysis of the texts of Faulkner's novels as well as of his short stories, essays, and public speeches. The scope of research was also broadened by monographic publications and books which began to appear from the late '60s and onwards. Among these works are V. Kostyakov's *William Faulkner's Trilogy* (1969), Yu. Palievskaya's *William Faulkner* (1970), N. Anastasiev's *Faulkner* (1976), B. Gribanov's *Faulkner* (1976), A. K. Savurenok's *William Faulkner's Novels of the 1920–1930s* (1979); in addition, numerous articles devoted to specific aspects and problems of William Faulkner's creative works were authored by V. I. Bernatskaya, B. A. Gilenson, M. Landor, G. Zlobin, T. L. Morozova, A. N. Nikolyukin, N. I. Samokhvalov, and many others. Very active academic investigation of Faulkner's work began in the early '70s.

To give an idea of the number of topics which have attracted the attention of Soviet researchers let us name some recent dissertations: A. A. Iskoz-Dolinin, "The Problem of the Literary Tradition of F. M. Dostoevsky in William Faulkner's Prose" *(Sanctuary, Requiem for a Nun)*; M. A. Pavilenene, "The Concept and Image of Man in the Works of William Faulkner"; L. I. Serdyukova, "On Certain Peculiarities of the Syntax of Sentence in William Faulkner's Novels"; O. N. Shevlyakova, "The Poetics of the Snopes Triology by William Faulkner"; K. A. Stepanyan, "Types and Functions of Narrators in the Novels of F. M. Dostoevsky and W. Faulkner."

New comprehension of Faulkner which was characeristic of this period found reflection also in a number of publications by D. Zatonsky, a well-known researcher in the field of Western literature and culture. The chapter which is devoted to Faulkner in Zatonsky's book, *The Art of the Novel and the 20th Century* (1973), is titled "The Discovered Man." Zatonsky's metaphor is ambivalent: the "discovered man" is Faulkner himself; and discovering man in the heart of the artistic universe of Yoknapatawpha is a decisive breakthrough in the evolution of Faulkner criticism. Zatonsky studies Faulkner as a complex of ideological and artistic-genealogical ties and connections. He is no longer a "stranger" who evokes only a kind of unquiet curiosity. Faulkner, for Zatonsky, is naturally connected with the traditions of European (Balzac) and American (Dreiser) critical realism. At the same time, he is the organic heir of romanticism (Melville); in this, Zatonsky is not inclined to see Faulkner's realism as flawed (thus polemicizing with Mendelson), but rather he sees this mixture of romanticism and realism as an indispensible trait of Faulkner's originality. Faulkner for Zatonsky is simultaneously local and universal. The South for Faulkner as an artist is certainly an exclusive but not "the last reality"—it is also an observation point from which the world opens in its broad and exciting perspective. Following Mendelson, Zatonsky speaks of the characteristically Southern "clairvoyance" of Faulkner. But even this does not place Faulkner in a kind of "one man" party. The same kind of clairvoyance, Zatonsky penetratingly observes, was one of the "characteristic features of Russian classical literature (Tolstoy, Dostoevsky)." "And its causes," continues Zatonsky, "in a certain sense are akin to those which reinforced the clairvoyance of the writers of the Southern Renaissance. Tolstoy and Dostoevsky looked at the modern world from the perspective of their own country—of a country of a so-far underdeveloped but already regressive capitalism. In approximately the same way but only almost a century later Faulkner looks at the American North: from the perspective of the American South."[18]

Here of special importance is not only the essence but also the scale of the comparison: Balzac, Dostoevsky, Tolstoy. Most important is conjoining Faulkner with that artistic level, with those artistic goals without which Faulkner could not imagine himself as a writer and which he pursued recklessly all his life again and again running the risk of "failure." The Balzac–Faulkner axis is central to the research. Like the creator of *Human Comedy*, Faulkner, according to Zatonsky, "constructs a model," but "not an intellectual one as in *The Magic Mountain* by Thomas Mann but one that is almost a copy of real life, while still remaining a model."[19] The author emphasizes though that Balzac, for Faulkner, was "first of all a creator of a certain specific 'universe' of the novel, a riotous, sparkling, wild genius of catastrophies, and only secondarily the chronicler of the economic adventures of the nouveaux riches of the epochs of Empire and Restoration." The necessity of that kind of qualification is accounted for by the fact, as Zatonsky remarks, that "attempts are sometimes made to reduce Faulkner to the well-beaten track of the descriptive analytic Balzacian-Dreiserian tradition. And most important—they are trying to evaluate his victories and failures on the basis of the system of Balzacian-Dreiserian coordinates."[20] In search of the roots of Faulkner's artistic originality, Zatonsky reads the Snopes trilogy as well as a number of early novels *(Sanctuary* and *The Sound and the Fury)* anew, trying to discover not only the differences with which earlier criticism was mainly concerned but also the genetic relationship which makes each of Faulkner's novels into parts of a complete and unique artistic world. The basis of Faulkner's originality, according to Zatonsky, is Faulkner's combination of realistic and romantic traits. The echoes of a romantic mode of thinking the critic hears even as Faulkner is explicitly identifying himself as a member of the only literary school—the "School of Humanists." "That which Faulkner's critics take for chaos," notes the researcher, "that which looks like chaos is very often only a means of breaking through to manhood, to honour, to hope and pride, to compassion, pity and sacrifice, to all which Faulkner believes and which is measured for him by the only criterion, Man. Hence that special slant, the special tendency of Faulkner's creative work which distinguishes him from the critical realism of the 19th century. Faulkner is less intent on criticizing capitalist reality than on the passionate rejecting, even 'annihilating' it. For this reason, Faulkner does not analyze it in detail in all its concreteness. He only gives an idea of it as something unthinkable, unnatural, void."[21]

"A characteristic feature of Faulkner's prose," remarks Zatonsky in a more recent work, "is not so much profound analysis but symbolic synthesis."[22] It does not, however, follow from this that Faulkner is "asocial."[23] "It is sometimes thought," says Zatonsky, "that Faulkner was interested not in society, not in social phenomena but in the human soul. A certain degree of truth we find here, but in my opinion, not the whole of it. Dostoevsky too (whom Faulkner names among the most important of his foremost teachers) was interested first of all in the human soul. This did not, however, prevent the author of *Crime and Punishment* from being a social writer, a social critic. The individual, for Faulkner, is not an aim in itself—the individual is also the prism which refracts the social facts."[24]

An evolution in Soviet thinking about Faulkner's creative work is clearly shown in two works by Abel Startsev, one of the founders of the Soviet school of Americanistics: "William Faulkner's Trilogy" (1964) and "Difficult Faulkner" (on *Absalom, Absalom!*) (1979).

In his early work the emphasis is on "a dark concept of the world and man which sets Faulkner apart by a tangible screen from living social reality. In the important novels of the late twenties and the first half of the thirties, *The Sound and the Fury* (1929), *Sanctuary* (1930), *Light in August* (1932), *Absalom, Absalom!* (1936), Faulkner's characters are driven by blind passions, are obsessed by fixed ideas. Cruel crisis in these novels do not do too much to solve anything: rather they bring out the futility of men's efforts to mange the deadly chaos within themselves and without."[25]

Fifteen years later Startsev published an article which was specially devoted to *Absalom, Absalom!* and which is generally recognized as the best essay that has ever been written in our country about *Absalom.* The article begins with a very characteristic declaration: "Now when Faulkner's life is over and can be apprehended globally as a whole his creative work is clarified by the humanistic idea which is its basis—the belief in the dignity of man and his eventual triumph."[26] In actual fact, however, it is not a matter of a declaration which in some form or other now appears in almost every paper on Faulkner, rather it is a matter of the quality of profound and precise analysis which supports the declaration. By accepting Cleanth Brooks's definition of Thomas Sutpen as someone who is neither a Southerner nor a Northerner but "an American in general," Startsev comes to the remarkable conclusion that "essentially this novel is devoted to the American tragedy, to the tragedy of man who was born and bred by American bourgeois civilization and who is blindly devoted to the 'American dream.' "[27] Thus, the scene of Sutpen's destruction at the hands of the "poor white," Wash Jones, is no longer apprehended as a piece of Gothicism, but occupies an appropriate, although not at all self-evident place in the typological sequence with the death of Flem Snopes at the hands of Mink at the conclusion of the Snopes trilogy. This observation, as we think, shows the connectedness and unity of Faulkner's canon, and answers those early Soviet critics who found an abrupt change in Faulkner's world view in the early and later novels.

The implicit social character of *Absalom* some critics (such as N. Anastasiev, A. K. Savurenok) connect with the atmosphere of the "red thirties." Startsev does not argue against this connection, but at the same time he emphasizes the tie between Faulkner and the tradition of American romanticism, an idea which he presents not in a general statement but as part of an analysis of the metaphorical structure of *Absalom*. If Zatonsky compares Faulkner with Melville, for Startsev (as well as for Zverev), priority should be given to the most "cryptic" of the American romantics—Edgar Allan Poe. Startsev sees similarities between Poe and the author of *Absalom* because of "the soberness of the artistic plan in conjunction with the boundless flight of imagination and the obsession of both with the curse of the South which nourishes their creative work."[28] Particularly interesting is the comparison of the mirrorlike endings of *Absalom* and "The Fall of the House of Usher." "Sutpen's house," according to Startsev, "is cursed and collapses as a result of the ordinary horrors of a completely realistic South. In this now dilapidated, formally magnificent palace there are also a brother and sister. But they are not the victims of evil spells, the magnificient Ushers, but a pitiful old man, Henry Sutpen, who is driven to murder of a beloved brother because in his brother's veins flows Negro blood."[29] In concluding, Startsev brings a historical perspective to concrete textual analysis: "If we perceive this picture in the general artistic and ideological context of the novel and regard it as a historically grounded interpretation of the 'closed' symbolism of Poe, we'll have to consider it a bold attempt on the part of modern American literature to interpret its romantic heritage."[30]

I should like to end my remarks with a discussion of two comparatively recent monographs (both published in 1976) which can be said to mark a certain stage in Faulkner's "life in the USSR." One of them, *Faulkner: An Essay on His Creative Work*, is by N. Anastasiev and was published by one of the best known houses—Khudozhestvennaya Literatura—which, incidentally, previously had published many of Faulkner's works in translation. B. Gribanov's *Faulkner* appeared in the series *The Lives of Outstanding Men and Women* (Molodaya Gvardiya is the publishing house), begun in 1933 by Maxim Gorky, who planned to compile a library of literary portraits of the most outstanding figures of national and world science, culture, and politics.

The underlying theme of Anastasiev's book consists of a

polemic with an "either/or" methodology: he develops further the productive dialectical approach to Faulkner's works. This approach presupposes among other things the rejection of "logical short cuts" which may often seem tempting but are all the more hazardous in Faulkner's case, i.e., when applied to artistic phenomena of so much originality. That Faulkner is a great writer is taken for granted by Anastasiev. Similarly, Anastasiev accepts that the driving force of all Faulkner's creative work is a passionate concern with the fate of the world and fate of man, a profound humanistic idea which he strove to convey. These ideas were more slowly grasped by other Soviet critics. Discussing Soviet critics' comprehension of Faulkner, Anastasiev notes that "sometimes trying to make their way through the chaos of events, to arrange events in a regular sequence, to discover the hidden system," critics at the same time little by little impose upon Faulkner's work "the absolutely alien idea of chronological orderliness," or, we would add, the initially intended thematic unity. But, as Anastasiev aptly points out, Faulkner's world and Faulkner's ideas can be adequately perceived only in "the sound and the fury" of their natural aesthetic condition. Anastasiev is not, we must understand, adverse to the idea of analyzing "chaos." What he really objects to is that "chaos" should be treated as some kind of alien outward caul of the idea, or as a consciously paradoxical device of its embodiment. Anastasiev is interested, to use M. Bakhtin's term, in "the place of the idea" in Faulkner's novel and the specific nature of its embodiment, the peculiarity of its concrete artistic ontology.

Considering all the novels and the short stories against a broad historical backdrop, Anastasiev concentrates on the realization and development of Faulkner's artistic idea in an effort to discover its inner tension and drama. Although, according to Anastasiev, the chronological principle should be applied to Faulkner's creative work only very cautiously, his own analysis with good reason begins with the "beginnings"—with the first novels—*Sartoris* and *The Sound and the Fury*. This, perhaps, should be stressed for the following reason. The question "to be or not to be" of Faulkner in our criticism has ceased to be a question quite long ago. He is. He is an indispensable part of our culture. Nevertheless, people still go on trying to divide the "dark" Faulkner from the "bright" one, the "good" from the "bad." And there may be a certain reason for this. Anastasiev himself recognizes that Faulkner's creative work is uneven, that his creative development is in a constant turmoil of doubts, intuition, and backward steps in which only the undying belief in man was discovered once and for all. Nevertheless we ought to read Faulkner and learn to understand him as a whole, globally, even if it is not always easy. This is what Anastasiev's book is really about.

While paying tribute to the monumental Snopes trilogy, at the same time, Anastasiev is not at all inclined to regard Faulkner's previous work as a kind of "preparatory stage." For example, a separate chapter is devoted to the analysis of *The Sound and the Fury* in his book. More than that, this early novel is the source of the "central metaphor" of Anastasiev's research, both the blueprint and the starting point. It is the general blueprint because already in this novel, which is often considered to be involved and difficult, Faulkner's artistic credo is presented quite unequivocally. Man and humanity will "endure and prevail," they will break through the "sound and fury," through the cold darkness to light and warmth. And this is also the starting point, because trying to understand and overcome the cruel chaos of life (which is the mainspring of the whole novel, determining its system of images and moods) is not only a "constant" of Faulkner's artistic thinking; it is also its main impulse, the dialectical kernel, the nucleus of its development, from which later, during the '40s and '50s, spring the artist's burning desire to achieve "greater clarity" and his attempts to give an unambiguous answer to the perennial question of the human condition.

The incompleteness, the chaotic character, the contradictions, on the one hand, and, on the other, the singlemindedness and obstinacy in pursuing as an artistic aim an outline of a modern realistic saga which appears before our eyes quite unexpectedly in all its grandeur—this, according to Anastasiev, is the core of Faulkner's artistic originality—on the one hand, the historically and sociopsychologically conditioned limitations of his world view; on the other, "the wonderful power of his talent," which has allowed the author to make an important contribution to the realistic art of the twentieth century. The contradictions, the complexity of Faulkner's creative career must also be addressed not only so that we may be scientifically accurate and correct, but also so that we may understand the necessity and the sense of that difficult evolution, which, as the years went by, his artistic work was undergoing.

The second of the previously mentioned publications of 1976 about Faulkner is B. Gribanov's biographical work which came out in the series *The Lives of Great Men and Women*. The genre of biography claims to be not merely scientific but popular as well, and thus gives no license to the writer to invent anything. The genre requires humility and tact on the part of the researcher. Ideally the image of the writer must be understood not only historically and psychologically, but also aesthetically, and his life must be "read" as a work of art. In Faulkner's case many complications repeatedly arise. First of all, his life is not an adventure novel. The most important and difficult of Faulkner's journeys was his journey "back," "inside," "to the postage-stamp" of the all-enduring Southern land, to the depths of its history, to the great theme which was hidden there. At the same time, Faulkner's books are extremely "personal," not to say autobiographical, in nature. But in order to appreciate this aspect of Faulkner's fiction, it is not enough simply to research more deeply the annals of Faulkner's family chronicle; rather, following his steps, we must look at the artist as "the sum total of the past and the present" of his country, his land. Only in this way can we accurately assess Faulkner because Faulkner's past—as is justly remarked by Gribanov—is the past of the American South. For this reason, Faulkner's roots are undestructible, deep, solid roots which cannot be torn out. Only by becoming fully aware of this indissoluable connection can one hope to read and understand both: the writer's books and "the long and often highly cryptic story of his life."

Faulkner never intended that the story of his life should be publicized. According to Faulkner, "only a writer's work is in the public domain, to be discussed and investigated and written about. . . . But . . . until the writer committed a crime or ran for public office, his private life is his own."[31] Journalists and critics who vainly solicited interviews with Faulkner often saw in his persistent refusals only the whimsicality of a celebrity, the highhanded snobbishness of the descendants of Southern aristocrats. (Some expressed their irritation in "pirated" biographical essays and psychological exercises of doubtful taste.) There is no doubt that Faulkner refused interviews for reasons other than mere whimsy. As we see it, it was a paradoxical manifestation of protest against the system of "all for sale," against the all-embracing commercialism and hypocrisy of the American way of life, which proclaimed freedom as an inalienable right of man, while at the same admitting that "any organization or group, simply by functioning under a phrase like Freedom of the Press or National Security or League Against Subversion, can postulate to itself complete immunity to violate the individualness . . . of anyone who is not himself a member of some organization or group numerous enough or rich enough to frighten them off."[32] Protest against the attempts of the crowd or the lonely eavesdropper to violate the sovereignty of the inner world of the individual is expressed powerfully in Faulkner's novels; and the most repulsive Faulknerian "eavesdroppers" are also embodiments of the spirit of cold commercialism, which, if allowed to spread, could lead mankind to degeneration and death. Finally, also reflected in these images, in addition to all else, is the tragic experience of an artist trapped in the "kingdom" of a commercialistic spirit. This experience is recreated in Gribanov's book with a documented precision that convinces us of the great courage of Faulkner's otherwise unassuming life; he was not sucked in by Hollywood as so many American writers were; in the course of all his life he never wrote a line which he did not believe sa-

Faulkner in Soviet Literary Criticism 233

credly, although compelled, almost to the end of his life, to ask publishers for meager allowances and loans.

The biographer does not dwell on the details of Faulkner's private life, does not rely on the doubtful (although very often quite interesting in themselves) "opinions of his contemporaries." This is, no doubt, a great merit of his work. Faulkner for Gribanov is not a "private person," but primarily and predominantly an artist. It would appear, however, that this "inertia of style" works against Gribanov when he passes to Faulkner's artistic work. Because he attempts to deal with "well-established" facts, his analytic discretion sometimes turns into a kind of factographic description. At the same time, however, the little known materials which have been adduced by Gribanov, especially in connection with the history of the creation of certain Faulkner's works, are of a considerable interest. Thus, for instance, in a letter from Faulkner to Hal Smith, the creative genesis of *Absalom, Absalom!* is clarified; a letter to Robert Haas, dated December 1938, convinces us that the book about the Snopeses in actual fact was conceived as a trilogy (this having been a debated point in Faulkner criticism).

The publication of the two *Faulkner*s by Anastasiev and Gribanov, as we have already said, marks a new stage in the study of the author's creative work. We are no longer trying to find out "who is who" in Yoknapatawpha or to establish the place of the mythical Faulknerian kindgom on the map of the literary history of the twentieth century. We are no longer simply "taking Faulkner apart," we begin to "assemble" him. Nevertheless, before we come to a synthesis of this kind, it is essential that many more problems should be solved.

"The number of 'white spots' on the map of Faulknerology is quite considerable," says the Soviet critic A. K. Savurenok. "First of all it is necessary to mark the absence of a scientifically acceptable edition of his complete works, which is especially important if we take into consideration the complexity of the Faulknerian text, as well as the history of creation and publication of a number of his novels. We are conscious of the urgent need for textological research without which we cannot solve a large number of controversial aspects of his ideological and artistic evolution. Practically uninvestigated are the main problems connected with the specific character of the language and style of Faulkner's works."[33]

This inventory could be continued. We could, for example, allude to the comparative typological study of Faulkner's creative work, which is only in its formative stage, or to the investigation of Faulkner's works within the framework of historical poetics. But, I should like to conclude by stressing only one idea: all these problems, so I believe, could be successfully solved if studied in their mutual relationships and, most importantly, if broad, unlimited international cooperation of literary critics could be achieved.

NOTES

1. M. Mendelson, "Uil'yam Folkner," in *Sovremennyy amerikanskiy roman* (Moscow: Nauka, 1964), 201.
2. P. V. Palievsky, "Put' Folknera k realismu," in *Literatura i teoriya* (Moscow: Sovzemennik, 1978), 221.
3. *Ibid.*, 222.
4. *Ibid.*, 226.
5. *Ibid.*, 213
6. *Ibid.*, 232.
7. Palievsky, "America Folknera," in *Literatura i teoriya*, 244.
8. Palievsky, "Put' Folknera k realismu," 233-34.
9. Ya. N. Zasursky, *Amerikanskaya literatura XX veka* (Moscow: MGU, 1966), 396.
10. *Ibid.*, 255.
11. *Ibid.*, 253.
12. *Ibid.*
13. *Ibid.*, 254.
14. T. Motyleva, "O yavlenyakh slozhzykh i neodnorodnykh Uil'jam Folkner," in *Zarubezhnyy roman segodnya* (Moscow: Sovetkiy Pisatel, 1966), 178.
15. *Ibid.*, 181.
16. *Ibid.*, 212.
17. A. Zverev, "Literatura na glubinye," *Inostrannaya literatura*, 8 (1973), 202-208.
18. D. V. Zatonsky, "Obnaruzhyennyy chelovek," in *Iskusstvo romana i XX veka (Moscow: Sovetkiy Pisatel, 1973)*, 359.
19. *Ibid.*, 361.
20. *Ibid.*, 362.
21. *Ibid.*, 370.
22. Zatonsky, "Uil'yan Folkner—novellist," in *V nashe vremya* (Moscow: Sovetkiy Pisatel, 1979), 302.
23. *Ibid.*, 283.
24. *Ibid.*, 296.

25. A. Startsev, "Trilogiya Uil'yama Folknera," in *Ot Uitmena do Khemingeya* (Moscow: Nauka, 1981), 330.
26. Startsev, "Trudnyy Folkner" (o romanye *Avessalom, Avessalom!*), in *ibid.*, 374.
27. *Ibid.*, 371.
28. *Ibid.*, 373.
29. *Ibid.*, 373–74.
30. *Ibid.*, 374.
31. William Faulkner, "On Privacy (The American Dream: What Happened to It?)" in *William Faulkner: Essays, Speeches, and Public Letters*, ed. James B. Meriwether (New York: Random House, 1967), 66.
32. *Ibid.*, 70.
33. A. K. Savurenok, *Romany U. Folknera 1920–1930s godov* (Leningrad: Nauka, 1979), 3–4.

The Hound and the Antelope: Faulkner in China

H. R. STONEBACK

My subject is more than a little overwhelming, for I aim to emblazon the name of Faulkner, easily the most important twentieth-century American novelist, across the map of China, easily the most populous nation on earth, and to *some* Western minds, at least, the most enigmatic place on earth. But the subject is overwhelming in ways that we might not initially reckon, for the problem is in large part a matter of scarcity of information and documentation, of paucity of translation, of lateness of introduction to Chinese audiences. Thus one might hazard the opinion that there would be more to say on the subject of Faulkner in Rhode Island, or Faulkner in Casey County, Kentucky, than on the subject of Faulkner in China. Or, to alter the image, to borrow a celebrated Buddhist metaphor, it might be said that the scholar on the trail of Faulkner in China is a bit like the hound on the trace of the antelope hanging by its horns ("ling-yang kua chiao"). Tao-Ying, a celebrated Chinese literary figure who died in A.D. 902, expressed the matter this way to a disciple: "You are like the well-trained hunting dog who understands only how to follow traces on the ground. If he were suddenly to meet an antelope hanging by its horns . . . he would not even recognize the scent."[1] I must confess I have felt in recent months somewhat like this hound after elusive quarry; nevertheless, I stand here today to bear witness that in the very near future the situation will be vastly improved. Indeed, even as I speak, major efforts of Faulkner translation are going forward in China, and a

Faulkner in China 237

great wave of interest in Faulkner is breaking and washing over that ancient civilization. I labor here with the conviction that this is an historical moment in the record of Faulkner studies, comparable only to the French discovery of Faulkner, and that this development holds forth the promise of deepening and illuminating *our* sense of Faulkner and his work, here and in all the lands from which we have heard the good news of Faulkner studies this week. I propose to tell something, then, about the translations, the critical reputation, and the teaching of Faulkner in China. I will also venture a few notions about Faulkner and his influence on and affinities with Chinese writers of fiction.

First, the matter of Faulkner translations into Chinese. Here the historical record is thin. In 1961, in *The Literary Career of William Faulkner: A Bibliographical Study,* James B. Meriwether listed no Chinese translations of Faulkner. In his general commentary Professor Meriwether observed that he offered his translation check-list "unhappily, and with apologies," since the list was "quite certainly both incomplete and inaccurate." That he missed some Chinese translations is to be expected, for it is particularly difficult, given the language problem as well as the recent history of China, to determine just what translation has occurred, what has appeared in book form, in wrappers or in cloth, what has appeared in periodicals, and what has appeared in anthologies of works by several foreign authors. I quite agree with Meriwether when he says: "These problems call for final resolution, I believe, by individuals working within the countries of origin of the translations."[2] That very process has been initiated in China, and with the assistance of scholars at Peking University I hope to be able to make a complete and precise report on the question of Faulkner translation in the near future. But for now, with due apologies and recognition of the intricacies of the task, I offer the following incomplete returns.

On the evidence of hearsay alone, it would appear that the first Faulkner to be translated into Chinese was "A Rose for Emily," and that this was done in the late 1940s. After this, there was apparently nothing else until 1958, when, in the Chinese review for translations entitled *I Wen,* there appeared two Faulkner short stories along with what may be the first critical essay on Faulkner's work to appear in Chinese. The essay was by a Soviet scholar, Yelena Romanova, and it was concerned with antiwar themes in *Soldiers' Pay,* "Victory," and *A Fable*.[3] One of the stories was "Victory," which was obviously selected for translation because the editors felt that it exemplified the ideas discussed in Romanova's essay. Unfortunately, the other story, as of this writing, cannot be identified. I have not yet received answers to several inquiries sent to Chinese scholars regarding the identity of this story. Just as I left New York to attend this conference, I thought I had made a breakthrough by long distance telephone. A bibliographer informed me that the other story appeared to be entitled "Dragging a Dead Dog." To this learned audience, then, I propose the question: could this be "The Hound?" or "All The Dead Pilots"? Or through some larger difficulty of translation, could it be "Death Drag"? We shall soon know, perhaps, but for now that's the best I can do. So much for that antelope hanging by its horns.

At any rate, there is some evidence, however sketchy, of Chinese interest in Faulkner in the 1950s. Further evidence of this interest is indicated by the fact that Faulkner—along with Pearl Buck, Waldo Frank, Paul Robeson, and Carl Sandburg—was invited by the Chinese government to come to Beijing to celebrate the 100th anniversary of the publication of Whitman's *Leaves of Grass* in 1955. Faulkner, however, declined the invitation.[4] Other evidence of early Chinese interest in Faulkner may be seen in the 1961 translation of *Wild Palms (Yeh Yeh)* and the 1969 translation of "The Bear" *(Hsiung),* both published in Taiwan. Thus the rather remarkable fact noted by Meriwether that, as of 1961, *Wild Palms* was, after *Sanctuary,* the most frequently translated Faulkner novel is reinforced by the Chinese situation. Another volume—apparently the first Faulkner to be published in Taiwan—is the *Selected Stories* (1959). An interesting anomaly is the 1976 Taipei English-text publication

Faulkner in China   239

of "The Bear," complete with extensive line-by-line annotations in Chinese.

It is regrettable to note that *Index Translationum*, the International Bibliography of Translations published by UNESCO, tells us nothing else about Chinese translation of Faulkner. For a few years, Taiwan was listed and it is from this source that the *Wild Palms* and "The Bear" translations are noted. From the Taiwan listings for the few years covered, it is instructive to observe that Fitzgerald and Hemingway are more popular subjects for translation, as we might guess, for these two writers preceded Faulkner in translation almost everywhere. We might be surprised, however, to learn that, at least in Taiwan, interest in Art Buchwald, Howard Fast, Ian Fleming, and Alfred Hitchcock was greater than interest in Faulkner.

With the onset of the 1960s, there seems to be a suspension of interest in Faulkner, and with the beginning of the "cultural revolution" in 1966, the rest is silence.[5] At least until a few years ago. And here, at last, we are on firm ground. The impetus for the current phase of Faulkner translation seems to derive principally from the efforts of Chen Bingyi, editor of *Shijie Wenxue* (*World Literature*) magazine and vice-director of the Institute of Foreign Literature of the Academy of Social Sciences of China; Li Wenjun, the leading Faulkner scholar in China; Professor Tao Jie of Peking University; and other Chinese scholars who have been teaching and translating Faulkner in the last few years. The first and to date the only Faulkner novel to be translated and published in Beijing is *The Sound and the Fury*, translated by Li Wenjun and published, in part, in 1981. It is reported that rendering this work in Chinese presented considerable difficulty, and that many Chinese readers are now puzzling as we have done for decades over the mysteries of Benjy's section and Quentin's tortured consciousness. I have just heard, last week, that a second translation of *The Sound and the Fury* is about to be published, though I have no details at present. Three stories—"A Rose for Emily," "The Bear," and "Wash"—have been translated and published this year in *Shijie Wenxue*. Tao Jie has completed her translations of "Spotted Horses" and "Shall Not Perish" and the former has just appeared in the journal *Foreign Literature*. Professor Luo Jing Guo of Peking University has completed his translation of "Shingles for the Lord," which will soon be published. In addition, the shorter *Saturday Evening Post* version of "The Bear" is about to be published, and there are plans to translate and publish *Go Down, Moses, As I Lay Dying*, and *Light in August*.[6] Finally, there is the scheduled publication in late 1982 of a volume entitled *Selected Stories of William Faulkner*. This will not be a journal publication, but a separate volume in the World Literature series of the Institute of Foreign Literature. This is the volume, of course, about which I may speak with some certainty. The project was initiated by Professor Tao Jie of Peking University during the time when she and other Chinese scholars participated in my Faulkner seminars at the State University of New York in 1979–1981 and in the Beijing editorial offices of the Institute of Foreign Literature. I am responsible for story selection, for the introduction and appendix to the volume. I was guided in the selection of the stories by the reactions, responses, and enthusiasms of the visiting Chinese scholars, as well as by my sense of Faulkner and the desire to present a broad spectrum of Faulkner themes and concerns. Reports from China indicate that the translations are nearly finished and the volume is on schedule. Reports also indicate that the volume is awaited there with considerable excitement, and that it promises to be a cornerstone of the present Faulkner awakening in China. Since I find this first person rather awkward I shall proceed without further ado to list the stories which will be included in the book: "A Justice," "Red Leaves," "My Grandmother Millard," "A Rose for Emily," "Spotted Horses," "Barn Burning," "Shingles for the Lord," "The Tall Men," "Shall Not Perish," "That Evening Sun," "Pantaloon in Black," "Ad Astra," "All the Dead Pilots," "A Bear Hunt," "Wash," and "Carcassonne." The second section of the book will include, with all due textual and critical caveats, "The Bear" and "Old Man."

As you may well imagine, this business of introducing Faulkner to millions of new readers has been both an immense pleasure as well as an awesome responsibility. It has required diplomacy as well as scholarship. It is not appropriate here to explain or clarify or defend the story selection for this volume, but on the chance that some of you may be wondering about some of the titles you have just heard, on the chance that you may indeed be astonished at a few of the titles, as some of my Faulkner colleagues have professed to be, let me say a few words about the matter. Ideally, perhaps, this volume would have included all of the stories from the *Collected Stories*, although a good case may be made that such a course would do Faulkner's nascent Chinese audience—and Faulkner's reputation—a disservice. In consultation with Chinese editors it was decided that it would be best to present a cross-section of Faulkner's stories in the first volume and possibly to translate the rest of the stories in a later volume. Moreover, it was felt that the selection should include representative stories from Faulkner's "Country," "Village," "Wilderness," "Wasteland," "Middle Ground," and "Beyond" categories. More than this, however, it seemed essential to select stories that presented all or most of Faulkner's voices and characters, stories that included all of Yoknapatawpha—the townspeople, the Frenchman's Bend folk, the hill-people, the Indians, and the blacks. There was also, perhaps, eccentric taste, as in the selection of "Carcassonne," one of my favorite Faulkner pieces—a whimsical choice, maybe, but one that I am prepared to defend as an immensely important Faulknerian portrait of the artist as a young man. Finally, there were the choices made, ultimately, because I was convinced of the absolute correctness—what we may wish to call the historical necessity—of their selection by the unanticipated and most enthusiastic responses of Chinese scholars. Three such stories were "The Tall Men," "Shall Not Perish," and "Shingles for the Lord."

In the case of "The Tall Men," for example, I still recall vividly the interchange among Chinese and American students over this neglected Faulkner masterpiece. It was manifestly clear to the Chinese readers that this tale presented straightforwardly the fundamental tenets of Faulkner's code, the values and verities expressed a decade later in the Nobel Price address, as well as his vision of the people, the decent country folk as represented by the McCallums. The emphasis on pride and honor and discipline, the notions of work and patriotism, duty and history, all struck a responsive chord. Likewise, with the McCallum rejection of the New Deal notion that "the only way they could raise cotton was by the Government telling them how much they could raise and how much they could sell it for, and where, and when, and then pay them for not doing the work they didn't do."[7] And there is the vision of the modern world:

> All full of pretty neon lights burning night and day both, and easy, quick money scattering itself around everywhere for any man to grab a little, and every man with a shiny new automobile already wore out and throwed away and the new one delivered before the first one was even paid for, and everywhere a fine loud grabble and snatch of AAA and WPA and a dozen other three-letter reasons for a man not to work. (58)

Then, too there was the marshall's memorable summation:

> Yes, sir. We done forgot about folks. Life has done got cheap, and life ain't cheap. Life's a pretty durn valuable thing. I don't mean just getting along from one WPA relief check to the next one, but honor and pride and discipline that make a man worth preserving, make him of any value. That's what we got to learn again. Maybe it takes trouble, bad trouble, to teach it back to us. (60)

It is not hard to see, in the light of recent Chinese history, why this story should be so compelling. For indeed, those American readers who consign this story to the waste heap of Faulkner's so-called reactionary phase notwithstanding, "The Tall Men" provides one of the clearest statements, one of the most effective embodiments of the Faulknerian code; and, in 1982, it is most timely, for audiences here as well as in China and much of the world.

Once again, in the case of the selection of "Shall Not Perish," I

Faulkner in China 243

was convinced by the responses of Chinese readers that this, one of the most neglected of all Faulkner stories, evoked powerfully certain crucial Faulkner notions about place and community, about the dignity and pride of the country people or the peasantry, as the Griers would be called in China. In the peroration of the story, we are told that the great wheel of human experience is:

> . . . hubbed at that little place that don't even show on a map, that not two hundred people out of all the earth know is named Frenchman's Bend or has any name at all, and spoking out in all the directions and touching them all, never a one too big for it to touch, never a one too little to be remembered:—the places that men and women have lived in and loved whether they had anything to paint pictures of them with or not, all the little places quiet enough to be lived in and loved and the names of them before they were quiet enough, and the names of the deeds that made them quiet enough and the names of the men and women who did the deeds, who lasted and endured and fought the battles and lost them and fought again because they didn't even know they had been whipped. (114)

This passage and others were singled out for elucidation and praise by Chinese readers and I watched in quiet amazement as American students learned something about Faulkner that the Chinese are discovering and that we, perhaps, will thereby rediscover.

As for the selection of "Shingles for the Lord," it did not take much persuasion that this story should be included, as it has always been a favorite of mine. As I listened, however, to Chinese readers praise the story for its humor and pathos, its profound understanding of the sense of community among country people, and its delight in shrewd trading—a pastime and subject dear to Chinese peasants and writers, too—it was clear that it had to be included. Indeed, I look forward to the time when my Chinese is sufficiently accomplished to read such passages as the following in Chinese:

> "You don't seem to kept up with these modern ideas about work that's been flooding and uplifting the country in the last few years."

"What modren ideas?" pap said. "I didn't know there was but one idea about work—until it is done, it ain't done, and when it is done, it is." (30)

And I am curious, too, as to how work-units and one-man-hour units and dog-units will sound in Chinese, as I am about that quintessential Southern and perhaps Chinese country litany: "I am jest a average hard-working farmer trying to do the best he can" (30–31). But the point is that with regard to these more or less neglected stories, as well as with others, the process of story selection for this volume was illuminating and the inspiration came as much from fresh and insightful Chinese readings as it did from American canons of taste. In brief, then, this tells the story of the making of this volume of Faulkner translations.

But before we leave the matter, perhaps a word or two on specific problems of translation is in order. First of all, it should be clearly stated that the work of translation has been done by a team of translators at various Chinese universities, most of them American literature scholars, some of them Faulkner enthusiasts. I have discussed various problems with some of the translators, in person and in correspondence, and other translators have found assistance from Americans teaching at their institutions in the past year. One of the first decisions to be made concerned the matter of folk speech, of dialect. The translators discussed the possibility of using local dialect in their renderings but discarded the idea on the grounds that they should use a language easily understood by the broadest possible audience. There were other difficult decisions to be made as to how certain technical devices and innovative forms should be handled and the result remains to be seen, although it would appear that most of the decisions have leaned in the direction, once again, of simplification and broad communication. This is a problem, perhaps, that can only be resolved by a later phase of translation. As for my advising of translators, it has been a matter of linguistic and sometimes thematic clarification. One small but typical instance that comes to mind is the confusion over the use of "ere a" and "that ere" in "Spotted Horses," as in the following: "It wasn't ere a man knowed yet" . . . "That ere baby had done gone on to the field." Such problems are understandable, of course, and somewhat old hat, as I have over the past decade had to explain similar locutions even to New York audiences. Other instances that come to mind include the clarification of what exactly it was that Rider and other Faulkner characters drink, that corn or bust-skull liquor, white mule or lightning or moonshine, that "fierce duskreek of uncured alcohol," that "chill liquid tamed of taste or heat" (see "Pantaloon in Black"). This was easily and vividly accomplished by the production of a mason jar of that illustrious folk product which I keep in my file cabinet for educational purposes (this, too, sometimes necessary for New Yorkers as well as other outlanders). Then there was the necessity of projecting a clear image of the kind of hound dog that often appears in Faulkner's work—a problem solved by introducing one of the translators to my bloodhound and to other hounds in the neighborhood. Or there was the clarification of squatting on one's haunches. These moments fall under the rubric of the joy of translation, I reckon, as does the finest moment of all, when the translator of "Shingles for the Lord" wanted to know precisely the positions of the men as they worked at splitting the shingles, and exactly what tools were used. I solved this problem by taking the Chinese scholar to our archive of Folk Objects and Tools, where we spraddled on the floor with mauls and froes and old wooden shingles and the text of the story in front of us. As we worked the passage out, sitting there on the floor surrounded by tools and text and shingles, a bemused administrator looked in the door. Little did he know that he was witnessing a landmark translation, and, indeed, a veritable act of community. Such have been the joys of this project.

As I have said, the volume includes a substantial introduction, an appendix with notes on individual stories, and the text of the Nobel Prize address. When it came time to focus my introductory essay, beyond the general summary of Faulkner's life and work, I found myself agonizing a bit overmuch about just what to say about the burden of the past, the problem of evil, sense of place and community in Faulkner. Once again, the matter was solved for me by visiting Chinese scholars. They had heard a series of lectures in which I addressed such topics as Faulkner's Sense of Place, Sense of Evil, Sense of Community, and Faulkner's Role in the Southern Renascence. It was clear that what I and others have had to say about evil, especially the notion of Original Sin, was quite alien, quite mystifying to my Chinese audience. It was likewise clear that the business about a sense of place seemed either too romantic or too provincial for their taste and that they were not yet ready to deal with the contexts of the Southern Renascence which might tend, at this phase, to suggest limitations to Faulkner's significance, his universality. Fortunately, the indecision was dissipated by their unanimous declaration that they hoped I would say in the introduction what I had said in my lecture on Faulkner and Community. One problem remained: the translator of that essay had difficulty with the rather intricate notion of community evinced in Faulkner's work. At last, after much searching, an appropriate term was found, a Chinese idiom which meant, roughly: "neighborhood, people and their customs and sentiment, speaking in and through and bound to place." Just the thing, I declared, and I trust Faulkner and the notion of community are well-served.

One last point about this volume, which touches upon the matter of diplomacy, I reckon, and tells us something about the state of literary affairs in China. In my introductory essay I dealt with the matter of Faulkner as regionalist, his "little postage stamp of native soil" image, and I quoted by way of illumination Allen Tate's well-known apothegm: "Regionalism is limited in space but not in time. Provincialism is limited in time but not in space." I went on to say that this notion has immense consequences, for literary as for human identity. By way of praising Faulkner, I then wrote:

> Thus, in this view, a Walt Whitman, a John Dos Passos, a John Steinbeck, anyone who reaches for the universal by embracing abstractions, by presuming to embrace everything, anyone who pur-

ports to write the great American novel by extensive catalogues and inventories of the vastness of the American continent and its people, is doomed to provincialism. Embrace the continent, embrace it all, and you embrace nothing. The place to hear the universe sing, after all, is in the single street, the single community, where you are rooted or choose to be rooted in time, place, family, history. Mere space, mobility, vastness yield no crop of the particular. They yield instead the flat wine of a book such as Steinbeck's *Grapes of Wrath*, which is concerned with some of the same themes and people as Faulkner is in his work, but which, for a variety of reasons—principal among them its provincial and non-rooted will to embrace it all—fails and distorts the truth of human experience.

I went on to allude briefly to Arthur Mizener's essay on Steinbeck entitled "Does a Moral Vision of the Thirties Deserve a Nobel Prize?" I must confess I was rather fond of this passage, but when my Chinese readers informed me that the Chinese would not understand this, that indeed it might stifle their receptivity to Faulkner, I chose to follow their advice and delete the references to Steinbeck, who remains, for all the wrong reasons perhaps, a rather popular writer in China. It may be that such a deletion is an act of diplomacy; it may be that it is, as some of my more rigorous colleagues tell me, an act of critical bad faith; but if it served the end of bringing Faulkner to a wider, more receptive audience, then it is sound and just scholarship.[8]

At the beginning of this essay, I promised to say something about the critical reception and reputation of Faulkner in China. It would appear that the initial response to Faulkner in China was conditioned by early Soviet views rather than first-hand readings and criticism. Thus, to catch the flavor of this, we must take a brief look at widely promulgated Soviet views from the 1940s and 1950s. If one were to consult M. Mendelson's pamphlet *Soviet Interpretation of Contemporary American Literature*, from the late 1940s, one would reach the bizarre conclusion that the major contemporary American writers were Theodore Dresier, Howard Fast, and Upton Sinclair. Faulkner is mentioned briefly, in connection with the "ascendancy of decadence in American literature," and his work is generally associated with "reactionary bourgeois ideology."[9] We are told that the "aimless cultivation of horror . . . the celebration of monstrosity and sexual perversion are ubiquitous in Faulkner's work" (20). The only Faulkner work mentioned by name, of course, is *Sanctuary*, which is characterized as the "most odiously decadent" book written by an American. Other views from the 1940s regard Yoknapatawpha County as a "world of rot and carrion . . . the brood of rotting capitalist society with its noxious, putrid morals." The aim of the work, it is asserted, is to demoralize and pervert the reader: "Human passions, joy, love, strong characters are alien to Faulkner, as are images of fighters for the rights and dignity of man. His world is a world of dying and dissolution."[10] I am told that such representative early Soviet views of Faulkner were shared by the Chinese into the 1960s. The Soviet view, of course, began to shift somewhat in the late 1950s, when Faulkner was declared no longer a "decadent" but a writer worthy of serious study. (See, for example, the Romanova article cited above, as well as the essays of P. V. Palievsky, one of which is cited below.) Yet even though the Soviet view of the late 1950s and after may be said to deepen in sympathy and understanding, it is quite clear that it was still felt that Faulkner's "conception of good and evil" was terribly confused, that his work was "extremely gloomy," and that what he really needed was a good course in Marxism.[11] As late as the mid-1970s I heard these views echoed by a Soviet teacher of American literature when I made the return voyage from Europe on board the Soviet ship *Lermontov*. I was informed, too, that the only bright spot, the only valid "proletarian optimism" to be found in Faulkner's work resided in the person of V. K. Ratliff. The gentleman's argument seemed to rest on the fact that Ratliff's initials had, after all, been revealed by Faulkner to stand for the Russian given names, Vladimir Kyrilytch; thus, this indicated that Faulkner was on the correct road. Perhaps this was said in jest.

At any rate, much of this found its way into the early Chinese view of Faulkner, and some of it may remain as lingering after-effect, especially the notions about Faulkner's confused sense of evil, his lack of optimism, and so forth. But other views have been revised, such as the belief that Faulkner was a racist, an apologist for slavery; or that his early innovative style and narrative forms were decadent and inferior to the more traditional narration of the Snopes Trilogy. There are reports that such views as the latter found their way into a handful of Chinese critical essays in the early 1960s. Once again, the information is sketchy and may not be verifiable. Indeed, such criticism may have disappeared during the "cultural revolution." But since those "years of chaos" there are many signs of a deepening of Chinese critical engagement with Faulkner's works. Indeed the chapter on Faulkner in the recent and authoritative *Concise History of American Literature* is a balanced and judicious reading of Faulkner's life and work, which clears away many of the earlier misconceptions.[12] The author writes with admiration for Faulkner's stylistic achivement, his moral vision and he speaks well of such positive characters as Dilsey—"the only healthy person in the book, whose loyalty, perseverance, endurance and compassion constitute a resurrection of humanity." He concludes that while Faulkner presents a vivid picture of the South he also "explores the major problems of modern man: man's relationship with society, sin and redemption, the burden of the past and how to deal with this burden, the corruption of modern civilization and how to maintain one's spiritual purity, etc." He also notes that "these are issues often discussed by the middle class and its intellectuals in the West," that Faulkner "takes the stand of a sensitive intellectual, the stand of humanism and democracy" and thus embodies the "spirit of his age"; therefore, he asserts, Faulkner is crucial for Chinese readers who would understand the "major problems of the West." Concerning style, he notes that Faulkner's stream-of-consciousness method is a "step forward from James Joyce," that his "works of many dimensions and their complex narrative methods further reflect the complexity of modern life." Then he suggests that "it is still too early to say whether his methods are the best. But, at least, he offers some experience for us in the development of technique in writing." Clearly, all this is a long way from the view of Faulkner's work held before the "cultural revolution." There are still other positive signs such as the recent volume, *A Collection of Faulkner Criticism*.[13] This volume includes important essays and excerpts from books by names familiar to all of us: George Marion O'Donnell, Malcolm Cowley, Robert Penn Warren, Conrad Aiken, Warren Beck, Cleanth Brooks, Jean-Paul Sartre, Michael Millgate, R. W. B. Lewis, and Joseph Blotner (the names are given in order of appearance). Also, there is one essay, "Faulkner's Road to Realism," by the Soviet Faulknerian, P. V. Palievsky.

Directly related to the question of Faulkner's critical reception is the matter of his influence on Chinese writers. Of all the antelopes hanging by their horns, this is the most difficult one to trace. Trying to get at this quarry from as many vantage points as possible, I have talked and corresponded with Chinese writers and readers, asking them about Faulkner's influence and about themes, methods, and concerns he shares with important twentieth-century Chinese writers. First, a word about the writers who were contemporaneous with Faulkner, where the question of influence is doubtful. One of the first of these, mentioned by most respondents as one of the greatest Chinese writers of fiction was Lu Xun (1881–1936). It is clear that Lu Xun had a vast sympathy for and a profound understanding of the rural and village folk of China; that he had a good ear for folk speech, a sharp eye for folk ways, and the shrewdness of the peasantry, as well a lively contempt for bureaucrats and treacherous intellectuals. That he "drew his inspiration from . . . the bizarre fantasy of Chinese folklore" and yet was very much a modern writer is generally acknowledged.[14] That he was preoccupied with "darkness," the darkness of China in particular and humanity in general, is another facet of Lu Xun that, according to some of my respondents, is reminiscent of Faulkner. One of his oft-quoted passages, summing up the mood in China in the 1920s, is the following; "Let the awakened man burden himself with the weight of tradition and shoulder up the gate of darkness."[15] That might be taken as a fairly accurate description of Faulkner's sense of vocation in the late 1920s. One of Lu Xun's stories mentioned as a possible parallel to Faulkner is his classic, "The True Story of Ah Q." If Faulkner gave a word to the language in Snopesism, Lu Xun gave an equally renowned phrase to his language in Ah-Q-ism, defined by one observer as a "blend of wiliness and stupidity, arrogance and cowardice, self-importance and servility, cynicism and naivety."[16] That might do, for a start, as a definition of Snopesism. In any case, whether Ah-Q-ism closely resembles Snopesism or not, the widespread admiration for Lu Xun, I am told, may well have a good deal to do with preparing Chinese readers for Faulkner.[17]

Another writer often mentioned in this context is Shen Congwen (b. 1902), a writer of the Chinese countryside who has been compared to Faulkner as a committed and unsentimental regionalist, a man deeply rooted in his "little postage stamp of native soil." In writing about his country, one critic maintains, Shen Congwen "uncovers beneath its dirty and often bizarre surface the life-giving stream of emotional integrity and instinctive honesty . . . [he holds] the firm conviction that, unless certain pieties and attitudes persist, China and, by extension, the rest of the world will become increasingly brutalized. The pastoralism of Shen Ts'ung-wen therefore is on the same moral plane and speaks with the same urgency to modern man as that of Wordsworth, Yeats, and Faulkner."[18] In the story "Hsiao-hsiao" (1935) we find a country girl (whose name gives the story its title) whose innocence and life-giving powers of renewal are celebrated and who, according to the same Chinese critic, "reminds one forcibly of Lena Grove. . . . It is not at all coincidental that Shen Ts'ung-wen and Faulkner have evinced a similar interest in this kind of innocence and have often tested it against the absurd or cruel codes of society: in their loyalty to the earth and to the common man, they both regard it as the foundation for the more difficult virtues of charity, gallantry, and courage."[19] While I have not discovered any brief held for Faulkner's direct influence on Shen Congwen, the parallels are considerable and the possibility exists.

Still another Chinese writer, roughly of Faulkner's generation and sometimes mentioned in connection with Faulkner, is Lao She, the popular author of the well-known *Rickshaw Boy* and numerous other works. There are many similarities of mood and theme in the works of Lao She and Faulkner. According to one scholar, Lao She's overarching general theme was: "Why was China losing the coherence and homogeneity of traditional society?" The answer, it appears, is money.[20] Lao She, it is reported, was dispatched by the Red Guards during the upheavals in 1966.

As for the younger contemporary Chinese writers, one detects here and there, perhaps, a phrase, a rhythm, an image, a character that may owe something to Faulkner. In Gao Xiaosheng's "The River Flows East," for example, the rendering of the quality of family life in a rural village has something of a Faulknerian flavor, as does the character of the peasant Liu Xingda and the use of imagery.[21] In Li Binkui's recent story, "A Soldier in the Tianshan Mountains," we read: "The fierce wind roared over the Gobi desert, as a sandstorm devoured the land. Vision was restricted in the brown, swirling void. . . . The wind howled all night vehemently shaking the low hut."[22] This is the kind of vaguely Faulknerian language we did not find in Chinese stories ten and twenty years ago. Again: "At night, lying in bed, I felt as if I was on a rudderless boat floating aimlessly on a vast misty sea. I did want to change my life, but how? The 'gang of four' had been overthrown. I had toiled in the countryside for six years, and now it was thought a futile sacrifice. . . . My volunteering to go to the countryside was all a joke now." With that very contemporary instance of Chinese fiction, which I cite as much for its indication of the mood in China now as for any trace of Faulkner, I abjure influence-hunting and urge you to continue the quest by having a look at the young Chinese writers appearing, in English, in the monthly magazine *Chinese Literature*.

Now let us turn finally for a brief glance at the related ques-

Faulkner in China 253

tion of the teaching of Faulkner in China. For, ultimately, it is the teaching of Faulkner that will get his style and rhythm and vision flowing in the blood of the next generation of Chinese writers. We have already discussed, in other contexts, the fact that many Chinese scholars and students are studying Faulkner at institutions in this country. The first to do so came to the State University of New York in the late 1970s. They, in turn, went back to China and now teach Faulkner in their American Literature courses—which formerly covered Hawthorne to Twain to Dreiser, and sometimes Fitzgerald and Hemingway, but never Faulkner. Also, graduate seminars in Faulkner are springing up everywhere in Chinese universities. In addition, there are the lecturing and advising activities of American Fulbright scholars in Chinese institutions. It is my understanding that one of the most requested specializations is Faulkner.

In the *New York Times Book Review* several weeks ago, André Schiffrin's "Letter from China" appeared, in which he purported to tell America what was being read in China now, and managed to leave millions of readers with the impression that everyone in China is reading and talking about Herman Wouk and Sidney Sheldon.[23] He made no mention of Faulkner, and quite clearly, is utterly unaware of the wave of enthusiasm for Faulkner, the teaching and translating and publishing activity now taking place. Thus I am compelled to include here another "China Letter," from a Chinese correspondent in Beijing:

> I think you will be interested to hear that many Chinese students are enjoying Faulkner's works. I taught "Spotted Horses" and "Pantaloon in Black" to my students here last semester—they liked them very much. And they all think Faulkner is greater than Fitzgerald or Hemingway. These two stories have started them on their way to further readings. I have recommended *The Portable Faulkner* and *Light in August*. I don't want them to feel frustrated after reading *The Sound and the Fury*. It is a bit too difficult for them at present.

And from another letter:

> Last semester a Fulbright professor gave a Faulkner seminar at Beijing University. This semester another Fulbright professor is giv-

ing a seminar on Cather and Faulkner, and teaching *The Sound and the Fury* and *Light in August* in her novel course. She is also supervising graduate students working independently on Faulkner. I continue to work on my translations of the stories and teach various Faulkner stories in my classes.

And from a letter received just the other day:

> Faulkner's achievement in style is now highly acclaimed here and, as you know, there are many brave attempts to introduce him to the Chinese reader. . . . Aside from all the translation, critical essays on him are coming out, too, on his style and his themes. Two graduate students at my university want to write about his technique and the initiation problem in his works. These are ambitious topics. They are young people full of original ideas and some of them very good. I've learned a lot from them. . . . As for other American writers, I like some of Hemingway and Fitzgerald but I prefer Faulkner because he has more depth. My students feel the same way, too. . . . Fitzgerald's prose is graceful and his stories are affecting and touching. But they are a bit shallow, and they are concerned with very trivial matters, maybe too personal. But Faulkner had a deep understanding of human beings with all their vice and virtue. I think I can understand Sutpen's design after what he suffered at the door of the aristocrat's house, and Joe Christmas' frustration in trying to find out who he really was. They are grander than life, but they are credible. Also, the collapse of a big family is a familiar and recurrent theme in Chinese literature. So is the burden of the past, though not racial problems or original sin, but the sin committed by one's ancestry. . . .

Such are the other China letters coming in from Beijing, Nanjing, Shanghai, and elsewhere. They tell, perhaps more effectively than I have been able to do in these pages, the story of Faulkner in China today.

In conclusion, allow me to quote a passage with a familiar ring: "I am a countryman. . . . A countryman has as a rule his deep-seated stubborn rustic ways and conforms to a pattern of loves, hatreds, sorrows, and joys entirely different from that of the man of the city. A countryman is conservative; he is obstinate; he loves the earth." No, this is not Faulkner, but Shen Congwen, speaking a half century ago. This passage reminds me

Faulkner in China 255

of what a Chinese friend suggested to me the other week: that it is precisely because China is still in large part a rural country that Faulkner will soon have a vast audience there, that particularly because China is a rural country on the brink of modernization Faulkner will be "very necessary" and extremely popular over the coming decades. This may well prove to be so, but for today, what we do know is that Faulkner is being read, taught, translated for the first time in China, truly. We know, too, that there are Lena Groves and V. K. Ratliffs, Bundrens and McCallums and Compsons and Sutpens in China, and we might surmise that the next great master of Chinese fiction will profit from Faulkner's example. But until that happens we may rest secure in the knowledge that Faulkner is at last being read and discussed in China, in Chinese; that the eternal and universal verities which he addressed with such precision and passion—courage, honor, pride, pity, compassion, and endurance—are as compelling in China as in Carolina, and that the illumination for which we all hunger is as accessible in Beijing as in Holly Springs.

NOTES

1. For this version, see *Literature East and West*, Vol. 12, December, 1968.
2. (Princeton: Princeton University Library, 1961), 123–24.
3. The Romanova essay was originally published in Russian. See "Antivoyennyie motivy v tvorchestve Vilyama Folknera," *Inostrannaya literatura*, 6 (1955), 170–76.
4. Joseph Blotner, *Faulkner: A Biography* (New York: Random House, 1974), 1579.
5. I follow throughout the current Chinese practice, as in the journal *Chinese Literature* and other publications, of using lower case and putting quotation marks around the term "cultural revolution." It might be preferable to follow the practice of some current Chinese writers and refer to the period as the "years of chaos," but for the sake of Western audiences, I shall use the more familiar term.
6. For these facts, as for other information presented throughout, I have relied on conversation and correspondence with a number of Chinese scholars.
7. William Faulkner, *Collected Stories* (New York: Random House, 1977), 57. All further references to this work are indicated in the text.
8. By way of anecdote, I might add that Steinbeck has had his revenge. A recent note in the *U.S.-China Review* erroneously announced that Professor Stoneback of the State University of New York was playing a major role in bringing Steinbeck's work to the attention of Chinese audiences. I was then deluged with letters from all over the world, wanting to know what translations of Steinbeck were in progress, what Steinbeck was being read and taught in China today, what my views about Steinbeck's contemporary social relevance were, etc.—all of these matters of no concern to me, about which I have not the faintest notion.

9. (Washington: Public Affairs Press, 1948), 19.
10. Deming Brown, *Soviet Attitudes Toward American Writing* (Princeton: Princeton University Press, 1962), 157–58, 180–82.
11. See Brown, 180–82.
12. The Faulkner chapter of this work is by Li Wenjun, whose work with Faulkner translations has been cited above. This volume was published in Beijing in 1979. The translation was generously supplied for me by Professor Tao Jie.
13. This collection was edited by Li Wenjun and published in Beijing, 1980.
14. See Tsi-an Hsia, *The Gate of Darkness: Studies in the Leftist Literary Movement in China* (Seattle, 1969) and H. C. Chuang's review of this work in *Literature East and West*, Vol. 13, December, 1969.
15. See Chuang, 440.
16. Simon Leys, *Broken Images* (London, 1969), 34.
17. For a recent Chinese view of Lu Xun, see the Centenary essays in *Chinese Literature*, January, 1982. At a week-long symposium in 1981, some 160 papers discussing Lu Xun were given in Beijing. Incidentally, his birthday is September 25, the same as Faulkner's.
18. C. T. Hsia, *A History of Modern Chinese Fiction* (New Haven: Yale University Press, 1971), 191. In this work, the older rendering of the name is used: Shen Ts'ung-wen.
19. *Ibid.*, 202.
20. Ranbir Vohra, *Lao She and the Chinese Revolution*, Harvard East Asian Monographs, No. 55 (Cambridge, 1974).
21. *Chinese Literature* (Beijing, October, 1981), 49–73.
22. *Chinese Literature*, August 1981.
23. "Window on the West," July 18, 1982.

"Native Soil"
and the World Beyond:
William Faulkner and Japanese Novelists

KENZABURO OHASHI

It is doubtful if Japanese young people—especially those who wanted to become writers—really understood what William Faulkner meant by his message, "To the Youth of Japan," which he sent them just before his departure from Japan in late August 1955. When Faulkner compared, for example, the human situation in postwar Japan to that of the South in America after the Civil War, and said that through man's endurance and toughness "something very like that [the resurgence of good writing in the postbellum South] will happen here in Japan within the next few years—that out of your disaster and despair will come a group of Japanese writers whom all the world will want to listen to, who will speak not a Japanese truth but a universal truth,"[1]—young Japanese would-be writers may have accepted Faulkner's words, though with a deep appreciation, as being merely a generous encouragement given them by a great writer representing a powerful nation that had conquered their own country not so long before. And they must have been quite at a loss as to what relationship there might be between their own literary situation and that of the American South after the Civil War. At that time, they did not yet know America and her literature well enough to understand the comparison.

However, we can now look back over the thirty long years since that time and see that something of "a resurgence of good writing" has become a reality in Japan, producing one Nobel Prize novelist through a "universal" acceptance of Japanese literature in the world. And although we can never know if the "resurgence" would have satisfied Faulkner himself or not, it was at about this time—or, more strictly speaking, from 1951 (just after Faulkner was awarded the 1949 Nobel Prize for Literature) to 1955 (when he visited Japan)—that the impact of Faulkner's literary works began to show heavily on several important young Japanese novelists[2] and, indeed, that Faulkner's comparison of the postbellum South with postwar Japan really began to have a deeper significance in the development of postwar Japanese literature.

The influence, of course, as is always the case with any literary influence, was neither a one-sided nor a conspicuous one because all true artists "steal from any source," as Faulkner himself admits,[3] and integrate what they steal into their own works of art. But a most significant fact is that quite a few important novelists began, during and after this period, either to refer directly to Faulkner's works in their literary essays or to confess openly that they were influenced by him, or even to try to set up their own Yoknapatawphas in their novels, or to liken some places which are set as backgrounds in their works to Faulkner's Yoknapatawpha. A notable example is Takehiko Fukunaga (1918-1979), poet and novelist, who was deeply influenced by Faulkner—especially by his techniques—through French translations of his works as early as in the late 1930s, and who, after World War II, gained many young admirers by modernistic novels that often adopted Faulknerian techniques of disorganizing time sequences and of interior monologue. In his three short works which appeared in 1956, 1959, and 1961, Fukunaga actually began to set "Sabishiro" and "Iyahate," two fictitious lonely towns in the back country of Hokkaido (the big island at the extreme north of the Japanese Islands), as a kind of Yoknapatawpha. This attempt, however, proved abortive, the last story having been finally left unfinished,[4] but, as we shall discuss later, the fact that even Fukunaga, who was never a local-color writer, nor a folkish one, but instead an out-and-out modernist, would follow the example of Faulkner in trying to set up some

Faulkner and Japanese Novelists 259

imaginary place which was to be deeply rooted in the native soil of Japan shows that there *was* some important kinship, even if quite remote, between the workings of imagination of these two quite different writers. It goes without saying that there is an essential difference between the two with such different geographical, historical, and cultural backgrounds, and the difference probably explains why Fukunaga failed in his attempt in spite of his deep sympathy toward Faulkner and his novels. Nevertheless, there must be some kinship, something fundamentally similar, at bottom, between the two, such as Faulkner himself intuited prophetically when he visited Japan.

We have not only Fukunaga, but also some other more conspicuous examples of this kinship. But before entering into a full discussion of them, which will make up the main issue of this paper, we should trace briefly the history of the acceptance of Faulkner's works on the literary soil of Japan from its beginning until the period discussed above, which marked the turning point of the history. That will make the importance of the main issue clearer and the discussion easier.

It was quite reasonable that Faulkner should have been first introduced to Japanese literati as a kind of modernistic vanguard writer, mainly through French translations of his works and through criticism of them by French critics (as in the case of Fukunaga, who was a student of French literature and a translator of Baudelaire). This was because in Japan before the last war—in the 1920s and '30s—American literature was not known so well as French literature, and the modernistic phase of new literature came to the country mostly via the French route. Before Fukunaga, Yukio Haruyama (b. 1902), a well-known modernist poet, who early introduced Faulkner in Japan, once wrote in a literary essay entitled "William Faulkner," published in 1932: "The American literature we like reaches our hands via Siberia; in other words, it is sent to us from Paris just like the vogue of the world. William Faulkner, though an American, is a writer imported here from Paris—a writer whom we can read in the French language."[5] Haruyama's knowledge of Faulkner seems to have come chiefly from such French literary magazines as *n.r.f.*, which published a translation of "Dry September" in January 1932, and *Commerce*, in which appeared a translation of "A Rose for Emily" in the same month, although Haruyama must have read *As I Lay Dying* in the first American edition at that time.

Of course, Faulkner had a sufficient amount of modernism in himself, which by itself must have been quite challenging and inspiring to young Japanese poets and writers of the period, who, as their predecessors and successors always did, sought for some fresh literary stimuli from the Western world. But unfortunately, first the sudden change of the literary trend in Japan in the '30s, as in other countries, from modernism to Marxism and next the gradual transition from the liberal atmosphere of Japan in the '20s into that dark, inhibitive, and savage militarism of the '30s and the early '40s, put an end to the inflow of new literary currents of the Western countries, especially to direct communication with the American literary world, America and Japan being enemies; and that communication came to a complete halt during the unfortunate war between the two countries. Haruyama himself, though he published in September 1932, in the magazine he edited a translation of "A Rose for Emily" by Naotaro Tatsunokuchi ([1903–1979], who later became a well-known translator and introducer of American literature) must have been greatly shocked by the event—even so, he soon moved on to interests other than Faulkner, and the introduction of Faulkner's works came to be interrupted for quite a long time.

So, it must be said to have been, indeed, a kind of miracle that Takehiko Fukunaga, together with his literary group named "matinée poétique," could have read Faulkner in French translations as well as in the original and have been influenced by him, even in that darkest period of the last phase of the war. At this time in a withdrawn, quiet corner of the University of Tokyo, he read with a secretly throbbing heart the French translations of *Sanctuary* (with André Malraux's introduction) and *As I Lay Dying*, already published then, and Jean-Paul Sartre's essays on

Sartoris and *The Sound and the Fury*, which had appeared in *n.r.f.* in 1938 and 1939, and was captivated by Faulkner as well as by James Joyce and Virginia Woolf.[6] And, indeed, it was already "l'age du roman américain" in France then, which was to culminate about the time when Claude-Edmonde Magny would publish her epoch-making book on the new American novelists under that title, including Faulkner as the foremost. It is no wonder then that Fukunaga, as soon as he was liberated from the oppression of the war with the defeat of Japan, should have expressed what he really wanted to do as a writer. Reaccepting Faulkner as one of his most important literary models or ideal novelists, he wanted to create a literature which embodies a "universality," "the cosmic" or "the archetypal" in its particularity, not a literature just written about some "particular" environment, manners, and life, and nothing more, as did the Japanese literature as he saw it then.[7] Actually, a little later in 1951 he wrote a penetrating essay entitled "Notes on Faulkner,"[8] and at the same time began to publish novels richly reminiscent of Faulknerian technique and theme.

Meanwhile, however, that great turning point in the history of the acceptance of William Faulkner in Japan—the turning point in the early 1950s when Faulkner's influence on Japanese writers began to become real and serious—had arrived. Faulkner had received the 1949 Nobel Prize for Literature in 1950, and he visited Japan five years later. Japanese writers, we must say, were not influenced directly by these actual literary events, few of them being interested in literary events as such; however, Japanese publishers, incited by the news of the Nobel Prize, began to publish translations of Faulkner's works, so that many writers, who had encountered the difficulty of Faulkner's English, now had easier access to his works through translations. Although the translations of *Sanctuary* and *The Wild Palms* had appeared before 1950, it was after 1950 that translations of *Intruder in the Dust* (1951), *Knight's Gambit* (1951), *Soldiers' Pay* (1952), *The Sound and the Fury* (1954), *Pylon* (1954), *Absalom, Absalom!* (1957), and *As I Lay Dying* (1959) were published successively, together with translations of short stories such as "Dry September," "Red Leaves," "That Evening Sun," and others. In translating these works, Japanese scholars of American literature played an important role, together with professional or semi-professional translators such as Naotaro Tatsunokuchi, previously mentioned, and Yasuo Okubo (b. 1905). Among those scholars, we should mention especially Masami Nishikawa who early translated *Sanctuary* (in collaboration with Tatsunokuchi) and some short stories of Faulkner, and also Masao Takahashi and Kichinosuke Ohashi who did the most difficult tasks of translating, respectively, *The Sound and the Fury* and *Absalom, Absalom!*.

No doubt, these translations had an important effect on those writers who were eager to read Faulkner, though many of them seem to have tried to read him in the original English text. The most important thing, however, was not just that many translations of Faulkner's novels became available about this time. Without feeling a deep sympathy toward the works of this American writer, which was born from the awareness of some basic human condition in the present world common to them all, Japanese writers would not have been influenced so much by Faulkner as to declare openly his influence in their writings or to try to set up their own Yoknapatawphas in their works, as we have pointed out before.

And here we really begin to understand what Faulkner meant when he compared the human and literary situation of postwar Japan, especially its impact upon "the Youth of Japan," to that of the postbellum American South. One of the most important reasons why young Japanese writers felt such a sympathy toward Faulkner was that in this first postwar decade they were confronted with the disorder and confusion of the world to be depicted in their fiction, just as Faulkner, in those rapidly changing decades of the 1920s and the 1930s, was caught between the traditional or conventional society of the South, to which he belonged by birth as well as by kinship, and that overwhelming wide world beyond, which both attracted and oppressed him;

and they found in Faulkner's modernistic way of writing a novel—especially that unique technique of his, represented by interior monologue and the disorganization of the time sequence—the fittest means to truly represent their own relation to the world in the form of prose fiction. In this case, for them the technique was the first appeal, the first charm, and fascination—not, it must be admitted, the theme, the subject matter—but that was not all. Even Fukunaga, who especially in his early stage appears to have followed mainly Faulkner's technical innovations, was not just a superficial pursuer of technique but was always searching, through it, for some solid ground on which he could stand in the midst of the confused world, the world that was "out of joint" in some baffling way. His attempt at setting up those two fictional towns as a kind of Yoknapatawpha, to which we referred before, was, indeed, an attempt to build up the integral imaginative world of his fiction on a basis deeply rooted in the soil of reality.

Only he failed in the attempt, because he, like his young contemporary Japanese writers suddenly thrown out by the defeat of their country in World War II into the collapse and subsequent confusion of cultural and moral values, could find no such solid ground and community, no such powerful tradition or popular solidarity to fall back on, as Faulkner's Deep South, which, despite the erosion of the old values following the Civil War, still continued powerfully to sustain the writer's imagination. Fukunaga, without having his "mother earth" to fall back on, ultimately ran to the extreme of pursuing rather abstractly the theme of "love and death" of the uprooted man in a rootless society, although he retained to the last that painful effort to search almost in an apocalyptic way for a true home, or "native climate" as he called it.[9] Yet, at least he tried to fill the deep gap between his "own little postage stamp of native soil," which was Japan, and the overwhelming wide world beyond, which was mainly the Western world, just as Faulkner did in America and in his own unique characteristic way. And even Faulkner did not always find a solid basis to stand on: did he not himself often go to the extremity of the abstract "love-death" theme, too, which suggested an apocalyptic ultimacy and urgency, as in *The Sound and the Fury* or *The Wild Palms*?

But the difference is greater, of course, than the similarity. The young Japanese writers, who, like Fukunaga, tried to set up their own Yoknapatawphas in their own way, were doomed to fail in the attempt, except perhaps one, Kenji Nakagami, a very young writer born just after the end of the war, who was to begin to write novels in the 1970s (whom we shall discuss later). Another example is Mitsuharu Inoue (b. 1926), a novelist of a quite different type from Fukunaga. In his novels and stories since 1950, he has written persistently about the small coal-mining area in Kyushu, an island southwest of Honshu, where he had worked as a young man, concentrating on the conditions of life in the postwar period, full of contradictions, friction, and absurdities symbolically seen in that small, local area, and came to liken the area to Faulkner's Yoknapatawpha probably about the time when he wrote *The People of the Land (Chi no Mure*, 1963*)*, which described the postwar struggles and sufferings of the common people in a local town. He even adopted some of Faulkner's techniques—frequent changing of points of view in a novel, for example, which, by frequently cutting up the sequence of a story, represents appropriately the confused state of man's mind and his existence in a confused world. But after all, Inoue's coal-mining area was not Faulkner's Lafayette County, first of all because the latter was an area with agriculture as its social and economic background, while the former was characterized by a declining coal-mining industry. To the Japanese novelist was given nothing but barren ground where people struggled in a vacuum, as it were, colliding with each other self-destructively, instead of that kind of community of close human relationships which was Faulkner's, and which, despite rapidly loosening ties, still retained in it some strong moral power for a writer to fall back on. And Inoue recognized that fact. He soon struggled to elude Faulkner's influence, even criticizing Faulkner's repetitive imaginative pattern or "formula" (Inoue's term) of turning back from the time present to the time past, which Inoue thought "would not satisfy sufficiently those readers who search for a strength by which to live on."[10] In this sense we can say that Inoue came nearer Sartre than Faulkner, as probably he himself was aware. He did not see—nor did Sartre himself see—Faulkner's belief in man's future evident in his idea of "endurance" and "prevailing."

And yet, in the same essay in which he criticized Faulkner, Inoue also wrote: "Nevertheless, for example, when I smell the odor of verbena again after having sailed round the shores of seas and lakes of other contemporary writers, I irresistibly feel at home. That is probably because I think then, 'Ah, at last I have come back to the home of literature.'"[11] And this kind of nostalgia for the imaginative world of William Faulkner is shared by many other contemporary Japanese writers. It is not just nostalgia, but an aspiration, a thirst for a solid foundation for a novelist's imagination to stand and work on. Paradoxically, Faulkner created this foundation in his fictional world through that very repetitive pattern or "formula" Inoue criticized, which contained, in spite of his criticism, some moral force that *would* "satisfy sufficiently those readers who search for strength by which to live on."

This solid foundation for the imaginative power and the moral force, we can assume, was derived from Faulkner's deep vision of the power of nature as against civilization, which is embodied in the physical appearance of nature, the big woods, big rivers, or the earth itself, and in the people who retain the primitive power of life rooted deep in the "mother earth," the inhabitants of Frenchman's Bend and the black people in Yoknapatawpha County; the pattern of nature vs. civilization forming another important imaginative pattern of Faulkner's which contributed to his deeply symbolical works of art. And there is one powerful Japanese novelist who has long been seriously concerned with the symbolic image of a conventional village community as against the destructive power of encroaching civilization, and who has written remarkable symbolic novels which bring into deep relief the conditions of human existence in postwar Japan. The novelist's name is Kenzaburo Oe (b. 1935), and his works have been translated into English and probably have been read in the United States.

It is difficult to trace the evidences of Faulkner's influence accurately in Oe's novels, which are quite numerous, because he is quite an energetic and omnivorous writer, and has been drawing literary sustenence from various writers, either foreign or Japanese—among whom are included such American writers as, for example, Norman Mailer and Saul Bellow, together with Faulkner. However, in the case of Faulkner, not only has Oe expressed his admiration for Faulkner in several of his literary essays (recently he even published in a literary magazine a unique essay on Faulkner's Snopes trilogy),[12] but also we can actually hear in some of Oe's novels the deep echoes of a Faulknerian way of seeing man and the world and of writing about them.

For example, in *Football in the First Year of Man'en (Man'en Gannen no Futtoboru)*[13] which was published in 1967, quite effectively he employed two Faulknerian literary devices, or devices reminiscent of those of Faulkner. One is setting up, as we have hinted above, the country community of a village which symbolizes the typical conservative and conventional Japanese mind hidden at the bottom of the superficial modern civilization; and the other is a kind of superimposition of time elements, of the past and the present—i.e., "The First Year of Man'en" corresponds to the year of A.D. 1860, just a hundred years before the time of the novel's action[14]—giving the present events a historical perspective, deepening their symbolic meaning. The "football" signifies an interchangeable relationship between two historical eras, just as a football is kicked to and fro between two goals. And the novel's main theme is to find some ultimate "roots" of the Japanese people, especially the young people of the present age (the family name, "Nedokoro," of the brothers who are the protagonists of the novel, literally means "the place of the roots") in some hidden corner of the Japanese society,

Faulkner and Japanese Novelists   267

which is caught between traditional values and the new industrialization and mechanization. Such "roots," Oe indicates, might have been, and still might be, in such a small country village as "Okubo Village" of the novel (which is modelled after a village of Shikoku Island where Oe himself was born and brought up), and might give strength and will power to the dejected modern young people. Such strength and power might be rooted in the people of such a community, surrounded by a symbolic "woods": nature, which is at once creative and destructive, might bring real salvation and healing and at least give people strength to try to build up a new world of their own.

The ending of the novel is ambivalent. The younger of the Nedokoro brothers fails in an attempt to organize a riot against the monopolizing "supermarkets" run by some Korean people of the neighborhood, and because of the failure, finally kills himself; while the older brother, who as the narrator of the whole story takes the point of view of the novel upon himself, is at first skeptical and even cynical about his brother's enthusiasm since it derives its force from the memory of an insurrection led by the brothers' great great-uncle a hundred years before. But in the end, shocked by the brother's death, he rejects his former skepticism and thinks of beginning a "new life" as an interpreter for an African expedition for catching animals, which as yet is nothing but just an "expectation" and a mere wish. But here Oe is trying to grasp symbolically, or even mythically, the whole meaning of human existence in the modern world through pictures of young people's struggles depicted against the background of a small, local, agricultural Japanese community juxtaposed against the overwhelming tide of modern industrial civilization with all its destructive powers, political, economical, and moral. And Oe, while confessing reservedly that "the greatness of Faulkner cannot be an actual norm for us," expresses his deep sympathy toward the American writer so warmly, that we cannot but think of some undeniable kinship, or at least some common human ground, between the two in spite of all their superficial differences:

But Faulkner brings me an impression of salvation, even on his most bloody, cruel, terrible side. It must derive from our sense of the unmistakable existence of the deep roots Faulkner has taken in the American people in general, though he himself is just one personally biased novelist. Travelling in America, I got an impression that the American South is America itself rather than just a region, or at least one of the two faces America has; and Faulkner's South is exactly the sum total of America, giving him naturally the glory of a national writer. . . . And because Faulkner creates the universal town and people of the Yoknapatawpha Saga, by just taking deep roots in his own closed and personal inner world, here is probably an achievement of literary effectiveness, it must be said, which transcends all social and personal differences, and which, therefore, fascinates every novelist.[15]

Oe has continued into the present writing about the same theme originally set forth in *Football in the First Year of Man'en*, gradually enlarging and deepening the theme until it has culminated in his recent powerful novel, *A Game for the Contemporaries (Dojidai Geimu*, 1979), a bold experiment in a thorough mythification of the history and the reality of the life of the people in Japan through the image of a typical Japanese village just like "Okubo Village" in Oe's earlier novel.

It is quite remarkable that two other important contemporary novelists, who also feel deep sympathy toward Faulkner, have been more or less consistently writing novels and short stories the backgrounds of which are set in certain country areas of Japan—one of these writers even lives in the very area about which he writes. And, interestingly and significantly enough, the two contrast with each other, both in their theme and in their style. Kunio Ogawa (b. 1927), who lives in Fujieda, a small city between Tokyo and Nagoya on the Pacific coast of Japan, writes in some of his novels and stories about the people of the area surrounding the city, trying to make their stories symbolic of contemporary Japanese life with its own fate historically determined, somewhat like Kenzaburo Oe in the novel discussed above. For example, in his beautiful novel entitled *The Shore of Temptations* (*Kokoromi no Kishi*, 1972), he depicts the tragic fate of a young man, who, coming down from the mountain area just behind the Pacific coast, is lured by the charm of the ocean which, because of its vast free openness, seems to promise him a brilliant future. But the promise proves to be only illusion, and the young man is severely punished by fate, so to speak: having been robbed of all the metal materials from the ship he had bought with all the money he had, the young man persists in searching after the criminals and, when he finds and murders two of the criminals, is put into jail and is put into almost utter despair.

Here, the narrow, closed area "on the eastern seacoast" is implicitly contrasted with the wide foreign world full of both promise and danger, which is symbolized by the ocean, or natural forces, at once benevolent (creative) and retributive (destructive). Though some Catholic Christian symbolism is intended by entitling the novel *The Shore of Temptations*—Ogawa having a Catholic affiliation—what this symbolism ultimately brings out is not religious problems such as sin and salvation but the critical conditions of man's life in the present world, which, faced with modern industrial civilization, is on the verge of losing its essential human and natural qualities, not unlike the relationship between Yoknapatawpha and the larger world outside. And Ogawa himself is well aware of the similarities between Faulkner and himself. He not only has discussed Faulkner, though briefly, in several of his literary essays, but also he once used quite effectively an interior monologue technique like Faulkner's in the Benjy and Quentin sections of *The Sound and the Fury:* in the third section, titled "Shizunami Village," of *The Shore of Temptations,* the heroine, who drowns herself, narrates in her *monologue intérieure* the story of her unrequited love, mixing present actions and several past events alternately like a deranged person. This adaptation and integration of Faulkner's technique into Ogawa's own imaginative world suggests not only that there is a natural, partial affinity between the two writers, but also that Faulkner's themes and techniques have universal adaptability. Probably Faulkner anticipated long ago the literary situation of the present-day world, as could also be surmised from his prophecy about the future of Japanese literature referred to earlier in this paper.

As for his literary style, apart from the themes of his novels, however, Ogawa has much more affinity with that reticent side of Faulkner which tends toward "understatement" or "silence," rather than with his loquacious side which tends toward "storytelling" volubility or comprehensiveness.[16] In this respect Ogawa is nearer Hemingway than Faulkner, who was, however, capable himself of a Hemingwayesque simple style, as is seen, for example, in Benjy's section. On the other hand, Kenji Nakagami (b. 1946), the youngest of the Japanese novelists we are discussing here in relation to Faulkner's influence, is definitely like Faulkner as an out-and-out storyteller, in sharp contrast to Ogawa. He goes even further. In *The Sea of Kareki* (*Kareki-nada*, 1977), not only has he set up his native area, the city of Shingu and its vicinity on the Kii Peninsula in the middle-south part of Honshu, as his own Yoknapatawpha, but he also drew up a map of the area and a genealogical chart of the fictional families that appear repetitively in his novels, much as Faulkner did with the completion of *Absalom, Absalom!* And Nakagami goes on telling story after story about the families who live in the area—they are, however, not families with an agricultural background, aristocratic or plebeian, like Faulkner's Compsons and Bundrens, but small country-town entrepreneurs and laborers, who live in a kind of narrow, closed society of their own—and transforms these people into important symbolic figures who reveal the truth about the mind of the Japanese people in the crisis of the contemporary world. Because these figures are shut up within this particular, limited, and closed area of the local city and its vicinity in an implicit contrast to the great changing tide of the world outside, they represent all the more deeply the universal critical conditions, spiritual and physical, which the Japanese people endure, just as Faulkner's symbolic figures reflect the true human conditions in the midst of the wide world and its long history. In *The Sea of*

Kareki, for example, the father by blood of the young protagonist, one of whose sons by another women (i.e., a half-brother) is murdered by the young man because of his suppressed hatred toward the father, is a demon-like man like Thomas Sutpen (a comparison which Nakagami himself has noted)[17] and seems to represent some brutal force, both destructive and creative, that always lurks behind the diffident, tender, and introverted mentality of Japanese people.

And this indicates further a mythopoeic trend which has become more and more conspicuous in Nakagami's writings. Indeed, he has been trying with some success to create a kind of "mythical kingdom," like the one which Malcolm Cowley found Faulkner's Yoknapatawpha world to be. Thus, in his travel book, *A Story of Kishu, Country of the Trees and the Roots* (*Kishu: Kinokuni, Nenokuni Monogatari*, 1978), he declared:

> The Kii Peninsula, or Kishu, I feel, is just another country.
> It is precisely a country sunk in the dark, beaten again and again by the enemies since the time of Jimmu.[18] "A Country Sunk in the Dark" seems to be just another name of Kumano, the Hidden Country of Kishu. To write stories as if to raise the spirit of the land by putting down the name of Shingu, for example, is the method of *Kiki*.[19]
> I say again and again that this is neither just a tourist guide nor a book on a cultural climate. Rather, it resembles the way William Faulkner, the American writer, draws up the map of Jefferson, Yoknapatawpha, Mississippi, and writes on it "William Faulkner, Sole Owner & Proprietor."[20]

We have to remind ourselves here again, as we did in the beginning of this paper, that, needless to say, Faulkner is not the only foreign writer who has influenced young Japanese writers during those long years from the end of the last war to the present. Many European and American writers have been translated and discussed in Japan and have had an impact on the Japanese literary mind. And as compared with such other prominent literary figures as Jean-Paul Sartre, Albert Camus, Ernest Hemingway, Norman Mailer, Saul Bellow, and others, Faulkner is, strange to say, rather the one who has been the least discussed by Japanese literary critics and has seldom become a focal point of the literary current in Japan at any time. But, stranger still to say if we come to think of it, there seems to be no other postwar foreign novelist who has been, and still continues to be, read by Japanese *novelists*, even though small in number, so seriously and so earnestly as William Faulkner. When the Japanese translation of *The Complete Works of Faulkner* (twenty-five volumes, of which twenty have appeared so far) began to be published in 1967, many novelists, including Fukunaga, Inoue, and Ogawa, together with a few critics, contributed essays on individual works of Faulkner, so that this *Complete Works* has become a mirror in which what Japanese writers want to do in their own writings can be vividly seen reflected in their reactions to the literary works of a foreign writer. This, we can presume, is precisely the case of a most real, a most essential literary influence, if there can be such a thing as literary influence at all.

Moreover, as we have seen already, Japanese writers' interest in Faulkner not only has continued ceaselessly, but also has deepened and widened, from their earlier interest in Faulkner's technical innovations to their more recent one in his whole vision of the contemporary world. Just recall again those writers and their works we have discussed so far, and arrange them roughly in chronological order—Yukio Haruyama and his early essay on Faulkner (1932), Takehiko Fukunaga and his interest in Faulkner's technique (culminating around 1951), Mitsuharu Inoue and his *The People of the Land* (1963), Kenzaburo Oe and his *Football in the First Year of Man'en* (1967), Kunio Ogawa and his *The Shore of Temptations* (1972), and Kenji Nakagami and his *The Sea of Kareki* (1977)—and do we not clearly see, especially after Faulkner's visit to Japan in 1955, a deepening and widening of Japanese novelists' sympathy toward, and assimilation of, Faulkner's imaginative world? True, these writers and their works are only a few out of many in the postwar and contemporary Japenese literature, but they *are* among those very important writers and important literary works which steer powerfully in the middle of the main currents of the literature.

And also there are, although we do not have space to discuss them here, many other writers and critics, including some female novelists, who, even though they have their own writing styles, quite different from a Faulknerian style, have been impressed by Faulkner's works and have expressed their admiration and appreciation for them in very clear words. (We have also some brilliant scholars of American literature whose articles on, and translations of, Faulkner's works have contributed considerably to the understanding of the American writer in Japan.) Their heartfelt response to Faulkner must have been incorporated into their literary works at some deep level, which, far from contradicting numerous other levels of theirs which make up their wide and free world of imaginative possibilities, seems actually to support and reinforce them solidly at the bottom.[21] In other words, the Faulknerian trend in recent Japanese literature is in a way really symbolic of its whole trend—other influences besides Faulkner merge with his and make up one big current, which has been marked by some outstanding works of art, including several of those referred to in this paper—and we can now see the truth of Faulkner's prophecy, in his address "To the Youth of Japan," that postwar Japanese literature, like the postwar literature of the American South, would flourish.

Faulkner died in 1962, and, strictly speaking, he is not a contemporary of ours. The literary trend, not only in his native country but also in a foreign one like Japan, has been, and is, changing. But despite such change, there must be something of him, of his works, which is very important and fundamental to the contemporary literary situation, and which helps in making up continuously a new, meaningful literature in the world of today and tomorrow. Even recent trends in Japanese literature, as we have seen in this paper, show this unmistakably.

NOTES

1. William Faulkner, "To the Youth of Japan" in James B. Meriwether, ed., *William Faulkner: Essays, Speeches and Public Letters* (New York: Random House, 1966), 83–84.

2. We do not include here Faulkner's influence on Japanese scholars of American literature—to discuss which would require another full-length paper—except briefly about the translations of Faulkner's works which they did, which must have had important effects on the writings of the novelists.

3. "Interviews in Japan" in James B. Meriwether and Michael Millgate, eds., *Lion in the Garden: Interviews with William Faulkner, 1926–1962* (New York: Random House, 1968), 128.

4. About these facts, see Fukunaga's own account of them in his essay, "Faulkner and Myself" (in Japanese) in *William Faulkner: Materials, Studies, and Criticism* (Tokyo: Nan'undo), Vol. 2, No. 1 (June 1979), 69–74.

5. Haruyama's essay, "William Faulkner" (in Japanese) was originally published in *Literature (Bungaku)*, a quarterly literary magazine, in 1932, and is reprinted in *William Faulkner: Materials, Studies, and Criticism*, Vol. 2, No. 1, 36–39.

6. Fukunaga, "Faulkner and Myself," 70.

7. Takehiko Fukunaga, "The Interchange of Literature" (in Japanese), originally published in *Generation (Sedai,* a literary magazine), July 1946; reprinted in Shuichi Kato, Shin'ichiro Nakamura, Takehiko Fukunaga, *1946: Literary Reflections* (in Japanese—Tokyo: Shinzenbi-sha), 1947. The quotations are from the paperback edition of the book in the "Fuzambo Hyakka Bunko" (Tokyo: Fuzambo, 1977), 23–24.

8. Originally published in *Literature, 51 (Bungaku, 51)* in 1951; reprinted in *The Works of Takehiko Fukunaga: Critical Essays A* (Tokyo: Bunjido, 1966)—all in Japanese.

9. Fukunaga published the novel *Native Climate (Fudo)* in 1952 in an imperfect form. It was republished in 1957 in its complete text.

10. Cf. Mitsuharu Inoue, "Faulkner's Formula: The Meaning of Influence" (*The Shukan Dokushojin,* March 21, 1966) and "Faulkner and Myself" (*Sekai Bungaku*—Tokyo: Gakushu Kenkyusha, 1978)—both in Japanese.

11. From "Faulkner and Myself" reprinted in *The Third Collected Works of Mitsuharu Inoue,* Vol. 4 (Tokyo: Keiso Shobo, 1980), 155.

12. "Reading Faulkner from a Writer's Point of View" (*Bungakukai* [*The World of Literature*], July 1981). This was originally prepared for a special lecture at the 53rd Anniversary Convention of the English Literary Society of Japan, which was held in May, 1981.

13. Translated into English by John Bester under the title, *The Silent Cry* (Tokyo: Kodansha International, Ltd., 1974).

14. The year 1860, by the way, is also the year when the first official Japanese envoys visited America, whose "Broadway Pageant" Walt Whitman witnessed.

15. "What Is Literature to a Writer Himself?," originally written for his *Complete Works* 6 (Tokyo: Shinchosha, 1966), and included in *Contemporary Essays of Kenzaburo Oe* 7 (Tokyo: Iwanami Shoten, 1981), 6–20. The quotation is from 19–20 of the latter.

16. Concerning these two sides of him, we may well call to mind the following words of Faulkner himself, stating about them quite meaningfully: ". . . That is, music would express better and simpler, but I prefer to use words as I prefer to read rather than listen. I prefer silence to sound, and the image produced by words occurs in silence. That is, the thunder and the music of the prose take place in silence."—"Interview with Jean Stein vanden Heuvel" in *Lion in the Garden,* 248.

17. See "Modern Literature Getting Multilateral," Nakagami's interview with Kenzaburo Oe (in Japanese), in *All the Utterances of Kenji Nakagami,* 2 (Tokyo: Shueisha, 1980), 500.

18. The half-mythical first Japanese emperor.

19. Two books of the Japanese classic myth: *Kojiki* and *Nihonshoki,* recorded in the 8th century.

20. Kenji Nakagami, *Kishu: Kinokuni, Nenokuni Monogatari* (Tokyo: Asahishim-bunsha, 1978), 10.

21. To give a few names of such writers: Shin'ichiro Nakamura (b. 1918), novelist and critic, who, though writing his own novels in a quite different manner, has written several excellent essays on Faulkner; Nobuo Kojima (b. 1915), who has written some important novels which remind us of Faulkner at some depths, though not explicitly; Hiroshi Sakagami (b. 1936), who has a sincere interest in the American writer, and has published novels which describe close blood relationship in a family; two prominent female novelists, Minako Oba (b. 1930) and Yuko Tsushima (b. 1947), both of whom understand, and feel a deep sympathy for, Faulkner's works.

Il Penseroso and L'Allegro:
The Poetics of a Faulkner Collector

LOUIS DANIEL BRODSKY

I

The first of an unprecedented three-auction series to liquidate the fabulous modern rare books from the Jonathan Goodwin Collection was slated to be held on March 29, 1977, at the New York galleries of Sotheby Parke Bernet. Margie Cohn, legendary proprietress of House of Books, Ltd., and I had spent weeks prior to that first sale discussing listings #80 through #101, which represented the most impressive run of unique Faulkner books ever offered at one time. Among the items for sale were presentation copies, three of which Faulkner had inscribed for Malcolm Cowley. Also included was a complete run of the signed, limited deluxe editions and #25 of a numbered, boxed edition of *Salmagundi*, a potpourri of early Faulkner fiction, poetry, and criticism dating 1919 through 1925. This particular copy of the rare 1932 book was one of the original twenty-six copies retaining an incorrect trim and binding that was distributed before the binder's error was discovered and the remaining 499 copies could be rebound and trimmed.

Systematically I selected which items should be bid and a range for each that seemed realistic, even generous to the extreme, to insure that none would elude me. As sale day approached, I began to have misgivings about my eventual success. Time after time I would flash the list on my mind's display and erase the carefully chosen figures with the imaginary depression of a silent button, then replace the figures with newer, morer inflated ones. Finally my list included just five items, with an estimated retail value of approximately $15,000.

Speaking with Margie Cohn three days before the event, I learned that, although she would gladly bid almost exclusively for me, she would be forced to abstain on one Faulkner item. It seemed she had a moral obligation to bid, sans commission, for the University of Virginia on *The Portable Faulkner*, the classic item on my "list of lists." I was crushed. Even as we spoke, alternatives without solutions began to flash across my imagination: who else at this late date might I get to bid this item for me? How might I go about bidding it myself? All my blind groping proved futile once she relayed that they had given her a firm bid of $3,500, a figure that both astounded her and made me wince and gasp. At that time, a figure of such magnitude for a Faulkner book was reserved for the two "Grand Rarities," *The Marble Faun* (a pristine copy in dust jacket, with double inscriptions) and *Go Down, Moses and Other Stories* in the very scarce issue of 100 signed, limited deluxe copies. Quickly my hostility subsided to disappointment. How strange it seemed that even though I had not yet entered the auction, my mind had settled on the certainty that all the desired items belonged to me; my imagination had appropriated them on sheer missionary zeal. That most precious association copy, *The Portable Faulkner*, had surely been at the eye of my appropriation's storm; that special copy which the author had mailed to its editor, Malcolm Cowley, shortly after having received his own publisher's copies; that book on whose free front endpaper Faulkner had inscribed: "For Malcolm Cowley. / in appreciation. / William Faulkner / Oxford, Miss/3 June 1946" and on whose title page he had signed his name; that sensational collector's item regarded as even more significant in hindsight, although of signal importance then, since Cowley had almost single-handedly seen this little book through to publication during a time when Faulkner's reputation was, with the exception of French readers and critics and a few isolated voices in America, at a decidedly low point. That this book should have been so impersonally scratched off my list pained me immeasurably. Despite the importance of the other items, their glitter was tarnished; at one moment, I even considered aborting the entire notion of entering the auction, but reminded myself that I was an adult playing adult games. Ironically, the disappointment this news created indeed might have been just the anodyne I needed to salve the monetary wound my good fortune in the auction would bring three days later.

The auction arrived and I was unable to stay in one place for more than a few minutes, dying to make that phone call to Margie Cohn's home "any time after 7:00 P.M.," as she had advised, to learn the outcome. Finally, I gathered in the oracular message, discovering that the Brodsky Collection had become considerably more robust for its most recent acquisitions purchased at a cost of just above $14,000. Once my stomach and nerves quit their pugilistics, my hand cooperated in jotting down: *The Marble Faun*, with dust jacket, inscribed to Joe Parks (the presumable prototype for Faulkner's Flem Snopes of "The Trilogy" fame); *Soldiers' Pay*, with dust jacket, inscribed and dated by Faulkner for Kenneth Godfrey, "William Faulkner/ New York/7 Nov. 1931"; *Salmagundi*, #25, in slip case; and *Light in August*, inscribed, "For Malcolm Cowley/William Faulkner/Sherman, Conn/25 Oct. 1948." I had been victorious; four out of four bids had been successful. Already I had steeled myself to the inevitability of *The Portable Faulkner* being placed on the shelves of the Alderman Library at Charlottesville, a conclusion which cut two ways. It annoyed me in that now the book would be forever out of circulation, "under glass," never within my reach, regardless of the funds I might amass. I would forever be "too late." On the other hand, it comforted me in a vague way knowing that this special "collector's item" would not exist in any other private collection. My rationalization, selfishly motivated or not, derived from the same mentality that motivates large corporations to secretly attempt to gain majority stock in other unsuspecting companies. To gain controlling interest in the world of Faulkner book collecting was precisely what I had outlined for myself a few years earlier. If the book could not be mine, at least no other private collection would ever boast of its presence. In any event, I felt very confident that I had finally begun to execute my plans. Naturally, it was my single-minded intention to enter the second and third Goodwin sales, which had been announced for late 1977 and mid-1978.

As our conversation drew to a close, sparked by my nagging curiosity, I queried Margie Cohn concerning the price University of Virginia had ultimately been obliged to pay for *The Portable Faulkner*, hoping, as I did so, that it had not been so low a figure that I would always carry with me doubts as to whether or not I might have succeeded going head on with that institution. "You won't believe it, L. D.," she stammered. "I mean, you just can't imagine. The book sold for $5,000." There were two extended silences. "I mean, I was bidding for Virginia and I never even got a chance to bid a second time. A West Coast dealer sitting in the back of the room bought the book—for someone—a customer—I have no idea whom. Warren Howell of John Howell-Books in San Francisco bought it, and word has it he had an open bid from a private individual to purchase at any cost." My face had turned to heat no amount of sunburn could equal. "Your books will go out in a few days," Margie said. I was too stunned to repeat how pleased and appreciative I was to her for her expertise and efforts (implied was a special thanks for her 5 percent fee, rather than the usual 10 percent commission) on my behalf.

The grapevine that entwines itself about the trellis made up of dealers and collectors in this rather narrow and inward-focused field of modern book collecting sooner or later ripens into gossip of every bouquet; and it was not long before I learned as a result of its fructification that Mr. Howell's "mysterious customer" had actually paid in the neighborhood of $6,000 to $7,000 for the same book which had done such a splendid solo at auction, *The Portable Faulkner*. This pained me all the more because I just knew that despite my enormous desire to excel and my "intuitive rightness," I never would have exercised the option to spend that kind of money for one book—not even for a "Faun";

there still remained some semblance of rationality in my nature. So the book was gone; gone in a way even more final than it might have seemed to me "under glass" at Virginia in that it was, by virtue of its terrific cost, at a value I could not, nor ever would be able to touch.

Furthermore, it was a "plum," or "grape," I suspect (assuming one must always be precisely concerned with keeping his metaphors undiluted), that would always stand (hang) in a class by itself; it would always be a major attraction, always be a symbol of my collection's "incompleteness." Still, it might also serve, I reassured myself, to help me develop the necessary tools with which to counter future disappointments. It could help create in me an awareness of, if not temperance, at least, restraint, without which a person, certainly a collector, is doomed.

October 1977, like April 1978, yielded something transcendent: both months were characterized by additional sales of the Jonathan Goodwin Collection. When Parts II and III were concluded, the Brodsky Collection was richer by yet another group of unique items, including three more books inscribed by Faulkner to Malcolm Cowley, all on the same date, October 25, 1948, this occasion being the author's one visit to Sherman, Connecticut: *Absalom, Absalom!*, *The Unvanquished*, and *Go Down, Moses and Other Stories*, the latter of which Faulkner had deferentially inscribed and presented to Cowley's wife, Muriel, as a token of his gratitude for her having tended to him in her home.

As a sidelight, one additional book, *Pylon*, which I had failed to bid on during one of these last two auctions, ended up in the next catalogue of another West Coast book dealer, Maurice Neville. Although I had not known to whom this and the few other inscribed Cowley books had gone, I recall being disappointed at the time by that old Nemesis, Completeness, which had always nagged me. By the end of November 1978, through a complicated trade in which many of my duplicates (but not a single dollar) changed hands, I was able to acquire *Pylon*, also inscribed to Malcolm Cowley on October 25, 1948, and thus bring to five the total of Faulkner–Cowley inscriptions. Missing in the Brodsky Collection from the run Cowley originally sold to Henry Wenning were the colossal *Portable,* as well as *Dr. Martino and Other Stories* and *Intruder in the Dust,* which I had simply not been able to afford in the three Goodwin sales.

I had made a major accomplishment based not only on a tangible outlay of funds, but more significantly on the fact that now the collection boasted a total of fourteen new one-of-a-kind rarities that gave distinction to the entire collection of books and manuscripts. The Cowley associations were especially sweet. Triumphantly, I returned to Oxford, Mississippi, on July 30, 1978, to attend the annual Faulkner and Yoknapatawpha Conference (my third such visitation), and with immense excitement on the prospect of getting a chance to meet in person one special participant, the keynote speaker, a man who would speak on the "Magic" in Faulkner's "The Bear": Malcolm Cowley himself.

Sunday evening was all Malcolm Cowley; white hair shimmering above his reddish spectacled face, he read from his typed lecture with a kind of reverence and awe for the author from whose work he was slowly quoting, pausing occasionally to make a personal aside or critical comment. At one point, having just completed an attenuated passage from "The Bear," Cowley pounded his fist on the lectern and apostrophized: "Now that's Prose!" There was an authoritarian finality to his statement which everyone in the audience assimilated and bowed to without standing up, though they did that too with enormous exhilaration when he finished his paper. I stormed the stage afterwards and sat beside him with an armful of books, waiting until he had received another's encomiums to beg of him his signature in each of the eight or ten volumes which I had brought with me from Farmington for just such an opportunity.

The party that followed was in honor of Cowley's eightieth birthday. I saw him only from a distance that evening. Next morning, however, when I glimpsed him sitting alone at a table in the Alumni House cafeteria on the Ole Miss campus, I eagerly turned the occasion to my advantage. We sat and talked over toast and coffee and eggs; I described to him the nature of my most recent acquisitions; those presentation copies which Faulkner had inscribed to him thirty years earlier in his home in Sherman, Connecticut. He perked up at once, set his newspaper aside, and proceeded to describe in detail the occasion those books documented: Faulkner's convalescence in his home when he brought the sick author to recuperate from a severe drinking bout in New York; that period in late October 1948, which Cowley had substantially recreated in his *Faulkner-Cowley File*. He also recalled how he had sold all those books when he had been "hurting" for money, a condition he confided to me had dogged him all his days as a professional writer and critic. He clearly remembered selling them to Henry Wenning, "a fine book dealer" in New Haven, not far from his home in Sherman. I responded that this man had been my mentor while I was a student at Yale between 1959 and 1963. Wenning had bought these books, along with much Hemingway material from his library and files, Cowley recalled. He seemed pleased not only about my acquaintanceship with Wenning, but learning that I now possessed many of his inscribed Faulkner books and that I cherished having them in my collection.

We ended our breakfast on a high, if somewhat vague note. It seemed that Cowley was returning East within a few hours, called away unexpectedly, to attend the funeral of a dear, longtime friend, Allen Tate. When I questioned him as to whether he might yet have any materials from that period surrounding creation and publication of *The Portable Faulkner*, he answered cryptically that he would "do some checking"; possibly, he suggested, there might be "a few things" still on his shelves. I would be welcome to write him, he mentioned, as he stiffly removed himself from the table and shuffled back toward his room.

The remainder of the week's lectures and encounters engaged my attention, but none could slake my raging excitement to know more about what might yet be in Mr. Cowley's possession. The day I returned home from Oxford, I wrote to him; within a

The Poetics of a Faulkner Collector 283

week I had an answer, which got my immediate response. He, in turn, wrote a detailed response which read in part:

> I mulled over your very kind offer for my copy of *The Sound and the Fury*. I measured it against the lively memories that the copy rekindles in me, and I decided that, no, I cherished the memories more than I needed a thousand dollars. The book does have a history; I'll write it out sometime. I used it in putting together *The Portable Faulkner*. Then Faulkner, before or after writing his "Appendix" for me, complained that he didn't own a copy of *The Sound and the Fury* and couldn't find one in Oxford, so I sent him this one. That was, I think, in the fall of 1945. Sometime in 1946, after the *Portable* appeared, Faulkner sent it back to me with two inscriptions, one on the title page (just his signature and "Oxford, 1946"), the other, the longer inscription on the half-title page, with the ". . . robbed me of what was to have been the leisurely occupation of my old age." You can see why I want to keep the book. But if, at some future time, the need for money becomes more pressing and with the prospect of death nearer, I promise that I'll get in touch with you before approaching anyone else. It would be nice to have this book with the others.
>
> I do have one other book inscribed by Faulkner; an "association copy," though the association is more with me than with Faulkner. It is the copy of *The Portable Faulkner*, first edition, first printing, that I have used in teaching Faulkner at various universities. Battered. Passages underlined. Notes in the margins. Still has that lavender dust jacket, but the jacket is worn out and patched in many places with Scotch tape. Faulkner inscribed the title page when he was here in 1948 and the copy was still not too much thumbed. Thirty years later I think it should be retired. Have you any interest in it? This one I would sell. . . .
>
> Sincerely,
> Malcolm Cowley

As I laid the letter down after the first reading, I was aware that I had just experienced one of life's remarkable ironies; there it was, typed out before my eyes. The phrase, coming as a coda to the denigrating description of the little book's condition, continued to reverberate in my disbelieving ears: "Have you any interest in it?" If ever I had a rhetorical question put to me, it was this one referring to Malcolm Cowley's personal copy of *The*

Portable Faulkner. I reread the letter, incredulous even after assuring myself that this was an authentic letter from an authentic person, that there could be still another copy of *The Portable Faulkner*; and not only another copy, but one which I might place after all in the collection as a kind of "crowning glory" to the other Cowley inscriptions, a capstone since this little book had come to symbolize, realistically or not, the pivot on which Faulkner's waning career had turned around and begun spinning back up the rarefied plane to public as well as critical adulation.

I wrote back at once. Possibly a week later, a registered package arrived from Sherman, Connecticut, and I carefully disentombed the book from its flimsy sarcophagus and held it, ratty dust jacket to be sure, under the light, staring at the title page on which in uncharacteristic oversized scrawl, Faulkner had written: "For Malcolm Cowley/William Faulkner/Sherman Conn/25 Oct. 1948." That Malcolm Cowley had not sold this along with the others to Henry Wenning, but rather had kept it for sentimental and pragmatic reasons as a copy from which he would teach Faulkner until retiring from academia, that ultimately I might discover it and place it with its sisters and brothers, most of them, anyway, was miraculous to me. And as I stood there cradling the precious book, a note written entirely in Malcolm Cowley's hand, which on first glance I had missed, caught my attention in the package:

> This beat-up copy of *The Portable Faulkner* is the one I used for many years in teaching and lecturing. Faulkner autographed it for me when he was at our house in 1948. It is first edition, first printing. It traveled with me to the University of Washington, 1950, Stanford, 1956, 59, 61, 65, Minnesota, 1971, the University of Warwick, 1973, and other campuses. Sometimes I made notes in the margins. When the lavender dust jacket wore out, I mended it with Scotch tape. The book deserves an honorable retirement; give the old racehorse plenty of oats and hay and a warm stall.
>
> Malcolm Cowley

Until this moment, I had felt almost like Milton's pensive man in his poem "Il Penseroso," browsing among admired books in a "high lonely Tower" by night, wallowing by day in "the studious Cloister's pale." Now, suddenly, and in sharp contrast, I, like the cheerful protagonist of Milton's companion poem "L'Allegro," found myself floating through an idealized day in the country, followed by a night of ecstasy in the "tower'd cities" of my most grandiose dreams.

That today there exist two "Portables" inscribed to Malcolm Cowley neither diminishes the value of the books, nor detracts from the uniqueness of each. Both are precious gems; the one belonging to the "mysterious California collector" is a relic of Faulkner's initial exuberance and appreciation. The copy in the Brodsky Collection is a souvenir of the one and only meeting the author and editor shared; it remains as a memento of that meeting, a gift of friendship.

II

For almost exactly two years, no significant auctions brought to the surface any unusual Faulkner books or documents or manuscripts. During this hiatus, however, I had been quite active making and developing contacts among persons who had known Faulkner personally or indirectly. The collection continued to expand in directions I had been unsuccessful in tapping previously.

One such area was what has been termed "Faulkner in Hollywood." I had been well aware that much of Faulkner's time, if not his best literary efforts, had been spent, perhaps squandered, in Hollywood as a screenwriter for various movie studios during at least four separate stints occurring between 1932 and the mid-1950s. But I had not been able to unearth any materials for the collection to document his sojourns: treatments, screenplays, letters, photographs, contracts, posters, stills, lobby cards, campaign manuals. The collection suffered a few voids; Hollywood was certainly one.

Among the most exciting aspects of collecting modern rare

books is the very unpredictability of the avocation; simply, one never knows what is hiding just beneath the surface of that great anonymous "out there." I can't help but believe that there are people still residing in Los Angeles, Memphis, Santa Monica, Glendale, Oxford, New Orleans, and Manhattan who knew Faulkner and may still retain valuable treasures given them personally or handed down by family members; indeed, persons who may yet be unaware of their preciousness. With book collecting, as in everything from Fashion to Health to Creativity itself, success runs in cycles from deluge to drought.

When it rains in Faulknerland, it pours Hollywood contracts; or so it seemed in February 1980. The first inundation after my nearly twenty-year wandering in the wilderness of Hollywood materials came with an offering from Maurice Neville of Santa Barbara, California. It seemed that one of his "pickers" or "scouts" had uncovered a small diffusive trove of movie items from someone, unnamed, who apparently had been associated at one time with Metro-Goldwyn-Mayer Studios. Despite my immediate awareness that these materials were not of particular literary importance or content, as a group they intrigued me. They represented my entry into the varied world of Faulkner's movie career. Among the four legal contracts, each signed by Faulkner, two concerned sale of the short story "Turn About," retitled "Turnabout," and its renewal of copyright, dated 1932 and 1959 respectively, and the other pair documented the sale of movie rights to *The Unvanquished* to Loew's Incorporated, MGM's successor, in 1938 and renewal of copyright for three of the short stories comprising this volume in 1962. Eventually "Turnabout" was retitled *Today We Live*; it enjoyed brisk notoriety, more because of Faulkner's recent celebrity from his "corncob" novel *Sanctuary*, than by virtue of its having Gary Cooper, Joan Crawford, Robert Young, and Franchot Tone in its cast. *The Unvanquished* was never developed. In addition, almost as an afterthought, Maury Neville mentioned that he also had a mimeographed in-process script alternately entitled "Wooden Crosses/Zero Hour" on which originally Faulkner and Joel Sayer had collaborated in 1935 and early 1936. This was accompanied by a publicity shot of Howard Hawks, the film's director, seated with its star Fredric March; the photograph was signed by Hawks.

The dry spell had definitely ended. As if to reinforce my determination to spend so much money on items of this caliber, I can still recall asking Maury Neville repeatedly: "Have you ever had materials of this kind come around before?" "Yes, and No" was always his answer, and each time I would ask him to qualify his response he would retort: "These are the first *Faulkner* documents I've ever had, other than for a few scattered later screenplay adaptations of his own works written by others. In fact, I can't recall any ever coming up before—not even at auction. Of course, I've had plenty of contracts—Chaplin, Marx Brothers, Abbott and Costello. Sure, but no Faulkner stuff!" And each time he would repeat what he knew to be truth, I was all the more certainly convinced that I needed to have these documents.

Less than a month later, the skies of good fortune opened up again, not a little to my amazement. Maury Neville had heard again from his "picker" who apparently realized he'd found an inexhaustible source of "good weal"; he was willing (anxious? Who will ever know?) to sell more documents originally part of Metro-Goldwyn-Mayer's legal files. Maury's letter to me read: "Enclosed you will find some copies of Faulkner contracts. These relate to his first trip to Hollywood for Metro Goldwyn Mayer. I believe that you already have material dealing with TURNABOUT. You will find from looking at Blotner that MANSERVANT is based on Faulkner's own work and was his first project." I phoned immediately; Maury assured me that when he had obtained the first "batch" of materials he'd recently offered and sold to me, he positively had had no idea that there was more to come. I believed him. Actually, belief had nothing to do with it. All that I had to do was read those lines in Maury's letter, "I believe that you already have material dealing with . . . ," and I realized I was hooked, doomed not so much by my own greed as by that ancient Nemesis again, Completeness; that irrepressible mirage or illusion which never disappears for very long, but returns improvidently to nag away at my lesser angels, blinding me to the irrefragable truth that there is always another "one-of-a-kind item" after the last one, and even another dozen after the next dozen. Abiding by questionable wisdom, I called Maury Neville again and told him that I would take all four contracts: "Man Servant," "Flying The Mail," "Turnabout," and "Louisiana Lou."

Less than a week after this agreement was verbally consummated, I received from The Scriptorium, a Beverly Hills firm specializing in autographs, an invitation to purchase three William Faulkner MGM contracts. The letter was accompanied by xerox copies of contracts for "Louisiana Lou" and "Mythical Latin-American Kingdom," as well as a more comprehensive agreement by which Faulkner signed away all his rights to anything he might produce while under MGM's employment, be it his fiction or their movie properties. All three appeared to be from the same cache as those Maury Neville had just sold to me. In fact, "Louisiana Lou" was a duplicate original of the Neville copy. Praying that these items had not been sold out from under me, and discovering they remained untouched by other desirous hands, I offered to purchase them all without the slightest quibble about the asking price. When I was told that because my check would be forthcoming at once they would deduct 10 percent from the total, I could only chuckle to myself, knowing in my heart that had they required an additional 10 percent over the asking price for "allowing me to buy these items" I would have been equally eager to take them at their word.

Now, I had a seemingly "complete" run of MGM materials; and what an impressive grouping it was! Yet, something besides the need to make funds materialize to pay for these extravagant plums bothered me. Would there still be more? Had an endless pleasure principle been set in motion unbeknownst to me? A resourceful collector must be able to manufacture at will not only useful justifications for his actions, but bold qualifications by which he can always expiate himself from heinous selfishness. This, to my good fortune, I was able to accomplish by magnanimously deciding to beg off Maury Neville's copy of "Louisiana Lou" in favor of that same contract which The Scriptorium had offered (the latter was, coincidentally, $150 cheaper); but not before I had called my admired collecting friend, Carl Petersen, who I was absolutely certain would not only appreciate having the contract, but would consider my gesture "good sportsmanship," both of which he did.

While all of these intricacies were working themselves out, one more element was at that very moment inexorably directing itself on a collision course toward my overly active acquisitive instincts; it took the shape of an auction to be held April 9, 1980, at Sotheby Parke Bernet. And I had only learned of its existence at the "midnight hour" from Margie Cohn, who had hastily ripped the germane page from her catalogue and sent it to me more out of habit than concern. It arrived with her familiar doodlings decorating the margins, perhaps five days before the auction was to take place.

As I read entry #207 for the April 9, 1980, "Afternoon Session," I realized that neither my resourcefulness nor my malleable sense of propriety, my flexible probity and "right reason," had any heart left in them to ACT. Yet, I read on:

> 207 FAULKNER, WILLIAM. Typed contract signed, 5 pages 4to, 20 December 1935, notarized and countersigned.
> A carbon typescript (marked "duplicate original") of the contract between Twentieth Century-Fox Film Corporation and Faulkner by which Faulkner agreed to work on the script of a war movie called Wooden Crosses, later titled Zero Hour. Upon completion of the script on 7 January he returned to Mississippi to finish *Absalom, Absalom!*

The auction house's estimated price customarily provided at the back of each catalogue had been scribbled to the left of the entry by Margie Cohn: $1,200–$1,800. Even had I not owned the screenplay for this movie, the mere existence of the contract would still have been sufficient to activate my obsessive drive toward completeness. That I did, however, coupled with the notion that this contract was the only Faulkner item in the entire sale, made it loom especially large. Also, the document's placement in the catalogue between a 2½-page autograph letter of Charles Darwin and a most extraordinary 47-page typescript short story, "The Freshest Boy," by F. Scott Fitzgerald, didn't do anything to lessen the desirability of Faulkner's lone contract either.

Nor could I be consoled by congratulating myself on having just acquired six more contracts for less than half, and in some cases one third, the estimated value that had been placed on this as-yet unsold document: my collector's psyche had never been assuaged by such basic "good-business" principles; rather, it lamented that which it did not have and needed in order to fill another gap. In fact, contemplating this contract, I almost forgot entirely that not a year before, the collection could not even list among its desirable holdings a solitary piece of Faulkner's "Hollywood."

Ashamedly, against every principle I had held sacred, I submitted to the way of all flesh, called Margie Cohn, and sheepishly directed her to enter a bid of $1,000 for me. I suppose that when I had directed Margie Cohn to take my intentions into the auction room, it was because I realized that in collecting there is virtually no such thing as redemption when you let an item slip away into other hands; almost always, what you've lost is irrevocably gone when the stakes are this rarefied. While waiting for Margie's call the next day, I realized palpably the meaning of the proverbial "rock and the hard spot." I sat between them as she began to speak, then, with salutary, if ambivalent, relief, extricated myself as she proclaimed: "I told you you'd never get it; everyone's gone crazy . . . it's just crazy . . . but then, I won't be around when the bust comes . . . so why should I care. My husband Louie always used to say it only takes two crazies in an auction room." What Margie was trying to tell me was that the contract, which had sold for $1,600 face value, had actually cost the buyer, whoever he was, almost $2,000; not only was there an additional 10 percent commission for the dealer bidding the object, but another 10 percent of the price bid to be paid directly by the successful bidder to the auctioneering firm itself, a twist instituted since I had last been in any auction house in 1978.

Characteristically, I failed to congratulate myself on making a paper profit on my six recent acquisitions, let alone on the other four from 1979 which had been even less expensive than those from the second and third groups. Instead, I could only inquire of Margie Cohn as to who she suspected might have purchased the contract. Not knowing bothered me. All she knew for certain was that the West Coast dealer Warren Howell, owner of John Howell-Books of San Francisco, had received the winning nod: "Oh, I'm sure he would not have bought that item for stock; obviously he had a commissioned sale for it or he would not have continued raising the bid so assertively, raising the bid, raising the bid . . . and L. D., if you had been in the competition against him, you could have gone to $3,000 and still not got it . . . that I can assure you."

I felt immediately better and worse: better, because I not only didn't have the original $1,000 which I had instructed Margie to enter, but never would have been able to deal with the embarrassment of trying to find $1,600 or $2,000 or $3,000; and worse, because I now knew that someone out there had actually caused my defeat. He must be one hell of a high roller, I thought; a power (Power) to be reckoned with. Until now, and for at least the past four years, I had virtually had my own way in the New York auction houses—or almost, I reminded myself with noticeable annoyance. Once before, in August of 1977, when it had come time to pull out all the stops in trying to acquire Malcolm Cowley's inscribed copy of *The Portable Faulkner*, I had met my match.

And now that it was all over and I had time to sort things through, it dawned on me that this was the same dealer who had intercepted me before, and, both times, apparently, on behalf of the same "mysterious California collector."

III

On Wednesday, November 11, 1981, I read selections from my most recently completed book of poetry, *Mississippi Vistas*, at the University of Mississippi's Center for the Study of Southern Culture on the Ole Miss campus in Oxford. In attendance was Thomas Verich, archivist and head of the University's rare book collection. Later, Thomas happened to ask whether I had seen the Faulkner materials which were coming to auction in New York sometime soon. I replied with a nervous negative, feeling sure that Margie Cohn would have informed me had there been anything of special interest. "I'm not sure what it is, but I did see something—can't even remember where I saw it; we get so many catalogues. But when we go back to my office, I'll see if I can locate it." Thomas was unable to find the catalogue, but he did proffer the use of his phone and the recollected data that he might have seen the reference in a Sotheby Parke Bernet sale catalogue. My phone call assured me the auction was forthcoming and that a copy of their catalogue would be in that day's priority mail. In my excitement, I failed to jot down the description of the two Faulkner listings read hastily to me. Two days after my arrival home to Farmington, Missouri, I had the catalogue in hand.

Slightly more than a year and a half had passed without a single Faulkner item of note coming to auction. Now, Sotheby Parke Bernet had issued catalogue number 4771E to announce and describe their November 24, 1981, sale of "Fine Books and Manuscripts." Among the listings consigned by "various owners" were numbers 134 and 135, two signed contracts executed by Twentieth Century-Fox Corporation and William Faulkner between the months of February 26, 1936, and July 17, 1937. As I stared at the listings, digesting their descriptive annotations, I could sense myself catching fire.

Next day, I phoned Margie Cohn. She apologized for her oversight; actually she had not even noticed the items and was determined not to participate in this auction regardless of my decision to go after the contracts or not. In fact, she lectured me, moralizing that it was a fatuous endeavor. I already had "too much." "Let someone else have a crack at it, L.D.," she said. Her resolve echoed in my ears for days, a week, right up to the day of the auction.

All that day I was unusually attentive to my work at the factory. I almost completely forgot that there was an auction progressing somewhere else just out of reach and range; almost forgot, until I came back in to work the following morning and discovered that the urge to phone Sotheby Parke Bernet was so irresistible that I never even got an hour into my morning before calling to learn that the two contracts had each sold for $900. The sum, considerably below that of the last contract sold at Sothebys, created a source of irritation for me all day. I couldn't help wondering whether I might have purchased them for that price had I been bidding. I assured myself repeatedly that had I entered the contest the price would have gone to the moon. Regardless, at this time, nothing would have really mattered because the cupboard was not only bare, but outsiders were threatening to come into the kitchen, unscrew it from the wall and cart it off. Above all, I had clearly shown restraint.

And that was that! The pain was so clean, so impersonal that I couldn't do a thing except file the catalogue away on the shelf. And that really was that! Lately I had begun to learn a new lesson; and it was not just that no one person, or even a consortium (not even the Hunt brothers) could corner the market on anything, rather that if he tried and did, he would actually eviscerate the very goose that laid the golden books, because by obtaining everything, were it possible, he would have created such a vacuum in the market that his ingatherings would have both all value and no value simultaneously.

So, as the days passed, I determined that my collection was all the more valuable because others had fine collections; because each of the other collections had items not found in mine. My contracts, for instance, were more attractive precisely because others presumably existed elsewhere with the possibility, no matter how unlikely, of someday surfacing. Wisdom was a very consoling balm! And I remained satisfied in my wisdom from the time of that auction in late November 1981 until just about the very first day of February 1982 when, working in my writing office on the Farmington square, I answered a phone call which lifted me completely out of my poetic musings.

"Hello, Mr. Brodsky. This is Jackie Barron from Abilene, Texas. I don't know if you remember me or not . . ."

"Sure, I do. We talked about collecting Faulkner for a good long while one afternoon last August in Oxford."

"And you signed your book for me. It's been so helpful to me and my husband. And that's sort of why I'm calling. I wanted to ask you for your advice on a few things that have come up."

"I'm so happy to hear from you again. You know I'll be glad to help."

"Well, most importantly, I would like to know what you feel about two items I have a chance to buy . . . Should I get them? Are they too expensive? etc."

I waited, unable to imagine what she might be alluding to, suspecting it might be an option on a copy of *The Marble Faun* or one of the signed, limited copies of *Go Down, Moses and Other Stories*, both of which I thought she might still be missing.

"I have been offered two Faulkner contracts from 1936 and 1937; they were made between him and Twentieth Century-Fox Corporation."

So thorough had been my reverse psychology and self-imposed debriefing at the time of Sotheby's November 1981 auction that on hearing her refer to these documents (the same ones that had sold for $900 apiece), I failed to connect; rather, without hesitation, I gave her my most candid expression: "Jackie, both contracts sound very fine; they have to be quite unique. And how much are they asking for them?"

"$1,500 each."

Suddenly I surmised that these were the same contracts that I had let pass without a fight. I remarked their sale price from the auction, then reassured her that even at this price, I felt they were a fair value. "But," I admonished her, "you might be better off waiting for the two big books and trying to find pristine copies of the remaining three or four signed, limited editions you're still missing. I think that for you, a complete run of the first editions might be a much more significant accomplishment than having a few scattered ephemeral pieces of exceptional quality and an incomplete set of the books."

I assured her that my advice was not in any way based on selfish motives. She would do well, I said, whether she decided to accept the contracts or hold off. I learned that she had been given a formal option by John Howell-Books of San Francisco; they had sent it to her unsolicited, knowing her keen interest in putting together a first-rate Faulkner collection.

Also, we spoke about matters regarding lesser, though no less necessary items she required to "complete" her collection. Then we voiced polite goodbyes.

Once I found my way back to my poetic musings, I discovered that they no longer seemed nearly as motivating as those which our conversation had generated. So! I thought. Warren Howell had bought those contracts, too! Later that morning, I drew his phone number from my files (I had never done business with him before) and called him. Diplomatically I explained to him that I had just spoken with a friend of mine who had asked my advice about the two contracts his firm had optioned to her. I made absolutely certain he understood just exactly how I had advised Mrs. Barron, and that I felt the items were fairly priced, if high; that she could not go wrong purchasing them because, if she ever regretted her purchase, they could be quite easily disposed.

In closing, I mentioned to Mr. Howell that if for any reason Mrs. Barron decided not to purchase the contracts, I would be pleased to do so. At that juncture, he began a lengthy admission; there had been a big mistake! The contracts had actually been acquired specifically for a good customer, and held pending the man's return from an extended trip abroad. In his own absence,

Mr. Howell said, one of his salespersons had taken it upon himself to xerox the documents and make them available on binding option to the lady in Texas. He assured me he would try to dissuade the lady personally from purchasing the contracts. He also felt that she needed to concentrate on other items first. When we hung up, I realized, though Mr. Howell had not said so definitively, that the contracts would not come my way regardless, but would be redirected into the channel they originally had been meant to go—to the "mysterious California collector."

Next morning, I phoned Mrs. Barron. I felt an imperative to let her know that I had called Mr. Howell, and to reassure her my intention had not been to wrest the materials from her. She fully understood. Furthermore, she and her husband overnight had determined that my advice to continue systematically searching to complete a run of Faulkner "firsts" was by far more prudent and potentially satisfying. Purchasing the contracts would only divert money more advisably put toward the final grand purchases which inevitably would be required to secure *The Marble Faun* and the special 1-of-100 copy of *Go Down, Moses and Other Stories:* together these might cost as much as $10,000 to $12,000, assuming that they could be found!

She described to me in detail how Mr. Howell had used every argument he could muster to get her to decline the option, finally, in anger, demanding that she make her decision on the contracts by this very evening, or he would cancel it.

"L.D., I want you to know how much your Faulkner work has meant to me, and your kindness in taking time to help guide me. Furthermore, I want you to know that I am calling Mr. Howell now to tell him I am purchasing the contracts anyway and that I shall be sending him out today a check for the full amount."

"That will really upset him; I'm certain from my conversation with him yesterday that he'd bought them especially for his collector out there." In my heart of hearts, I was happy for her, happy for myself; it had become quite obvious from my conversation with Mr. Howell that I would have had no chance at the documents even if Mrs. Barron had declined gracefully. Although I would not have enjoyed admitting it to myself, I suspected that a portion of my happiness derived from the fact that Jackie Barron had inadvertently stalemated and stymied the "force" which had twice outclassed me. I was actually proud of her.

"L.D., I also realized that if I refused them, Mr. Howell would have sent them elsewhere, bypassed you. Today, I am dealing a blow for the Brodsky Collection."

I had no idea to what she was referring.

"You know," she continued, "how in your article 'The Collector as Sleuthsayer' you talked about piecing together a Faulkner map out of a jig-saw geography, and how you had brought your collection together from all parts of the country?"

I, of course, recalled the metaphor which I had used as a pivot in that published lecture. But I waited anxiously for her to finish her thought.

"Well, today, I am striking a blow for Texas. I want you to put Texas on your map. I am buying the contracts so that you may have them for your splendid collection; they belong there. You can send me a check whenever you're ready. No hurry! I shall send the contracts on to you the day they arrive."

From the World to Jefferson

JOSEPH BLOTNER

It is a great pleasure for me, as always, to be back here at Ole Miss, a special pleasure too, to participate in my third Faulkner and Yoknapatawpha Conference, the pleasure balanced only by the anxiety at having come to a conference, for the first time in my life, knowing I was going to present a formal talk, without having written one word of it in advance. It gave me a feeling vaguely like that of the dream in which you are walking down a street feeling properly attired except for the sudden awareness that you are wearing everything but your trousers. But I could not write a talk which would in some sense provide a kind of summing up, as Professor Harrington asked me to do, until I had heard the other talks. That I have now tried to do, updating it day by day and lecture by lecture, writing far from the security blanket of my books. And so I hope you will forgive any inaccuracies and infelicities resulting from these special circumstances or my own shortcomings, though I can assure you I have been doing more assiduous notetaking during this past week than at any time since I was a graduate student.

The titles of Professor Brown's talk and my own are like two bookends. We were both thinking of the same beautiful passage in *The Town,* both of us considering its relevance to Faulkner's work—Calvin Brown thinking of the way Faulkner, from his place here in Oxford-Jefferson, voyaged out to the uttermost reaches of the world in his reading and returned with precious cargo for the microcosm he created. In approaching that microcosm from a compass point 180 degrees different, I remembered something Phil Stone said, relayed to us by his wife, Emily. One summer day in the early 1920s, William Faulkner's Uncle John was holding forth, according to Stone, to a group of men in front of the First National Bank, his father's bank (in which, as we know, William Faulkner worked briefly and unhappily as a clerk). Uncle John was discussing his nephew.

"That damn Billy is not worth a Mississippi goddam," he declared, "and never will be. Won't hold a job; won't try! won't do anything! He's a Falkner and I hate to say it about my own nephew, but, hell, there's a black sheep in everybody's family and Billy's ours. Not worth a cent."

Phil Stone had approached during the end of the diatribe. "No, sir, Judge Falkner," he said. "You're wrong about Bill. I'll make you a prediction. There'll be people coming to Oxford on account of Bill who would never have heard of the place except for Bill and what he writes." John Falkner remained unconvinced.[1]

Phil Stone had no better luck with William Faulkner's father. "Mr. Murry," he said, "Bill may not make a lot of money for you in your time, but he's got the stuff." And Stone would shake his head at the disbelief he met. "I'm a male Cassandra," he would say. Murry Falkner would remain unconvinced to the end of his life. His son once said that when he received an advance from Metro-Goldwyn-Mayer to go to Hollywood and write scripts in the spring of 1932, his father had to see the check in order to believe it. And there were times when even he, normally supremely self-confident, found himself at a low ebb. After the disappointing sales of his early novels he said to Stone one day, "I think I not only won't make any money from my writing, I won't get any recognition either."

But our presence here this week, coming to Oxford-Jefferson from the world, shows how right Phil Stone was over half a century ago. One feels like saying, "rest, perturbed spirit!" You were indeed right.

In the years since Faulkner's death, his reputation in his home country has not suffered the decline that marks so many literary careers. Rather, interest in his work has increased with each passing year by all sorts of measurements. Each year the *International Bibliography* of the Modern Language Association of America lists work done—essays, articles, monographs, books—on English and most other living languages. Unsurprisingly, in the *International Bibliography* for 1980 (the most recent) the largest number of works listed comes under the name of William Shakespeare. The next is the body of scholarship and criticism devoted to the work of James Joyce. Next is that on William Faulkner, 156 items in all, including seven books of various kinds and thirteen doctoral dissertations. (Several years ago Faulkner scholarship reached the point at which entire books were being devoted to individual Faulkner works, just as one scholar will write a book on *King Lear*, another on *The Tempest*, and so on.) This kind of numbers game—like the kind of evaluation Robert Frost used to call quotations on the literary stock exchange—is not the most reliable, and the figures do vary from year to year. In an earlier year, for instance, there were more items listed about Faulkner's work than Joyce's. But though these numbers constitute no reliable index to literary immortality, they do indicate the way in which William Faulkner's work continues to speak to increasing numbers of readers the world over.

Many of us have favorite Faulkner abroad anecdotes or illustrations. Several years ago we met our friend, Paul Theroux, at a conference in Copenhagen. He had just come from Turkey, where he had visited a writer he particularly admired. Paul had been somewhat surprised to learn that the Turkish writer and many of his colleagues valued Faulkner's work very highly. "Don't you find him difficult and strange?" Paul asked. "No," replied his friend. "You should remember two things: tobacco is our staple crop, and we live in a highly stratified society."

When we went on from Copenhagen to France, we traveled to Strasbourg, where I was to give a lecture. My host, André Bleikasten, was escorting me through a quadrangle at the University when we met one of his colleagues, a historian. He told me about his interest in Faulkner. I said it was good to know that his work continued to have relevance for French readers. "Oh," said the historian, "if you want to know what a French village is like, you should read Faulkner."

Last year, one of my students who is doing a dissertation on Faulkner and certain South American writers showed me an interview in which Gabriel García Márquez said that *The Hamlet* was "the best South American novel ever written."[2] He showed me another, a dialogue between García Márquez and Mario Vargas Llosa which quoted García Márquez as saying that "the only unique thing" between his generation of Latin American novelists and that of their grandparents was Faulkner. "He was the only thing that took place between those two generations."[3] Even if this is part hyperbole or part courtesy, it still testifies to the power that has brought us here to Jefferson from the world.

I suppose that one of the reasons why some readers might not have expected Faulkner's work to be so accessible and suggestive to foreign readers is the early emphasis on the regional qualities in his work. He is not a regionalist in the narrow sense that term implies, though one of his greatest strengths is in conveying the sense of place which is a hallmark of Southern writing, the kind of setting of a work in geography and history too which writers such as Eudora Welty and critics such as Louis Rubin have described so well. There is certainly that, and I think there is very little question that Faulkner, like Antaeus, is strongest when his feet are planted firmly on his own earth. This was one of the things Phil Stone observed in his Preface to Faulkner's first book, *The Marble Faun*. And, of course, Sherwood Anderson's advice emphasized this quality. "You're a country boy," the older man had told him. "All you know is that little patch up there in Mississippi."[4] He ought to write about it. I think that Anderson may well have been projecting something of his own situation onto that of his younger friend, but Faulkner took his advice to his profit, as we know. Parenthetically, in this international context, it is interesting to recall that Sherwood Anderson was once called, by some, "the American Chekhov."

But we have to be cautious. Faulkner was a country boy only in the sense that he was not a city boy and that he came from an agricultural rather than an industrial region. He lived in two county seats before he came to Oxford at age five, and he spent his formative years in a town where he had not only the resource which Professor Brown mentioned, a university library, but also the other advantages which a university town confers such as, for instance, the drama—the plays of masters such as Shakespeare and others by then-contemporary playwrights.

From some of his earliest writings, Faulkner showed signs of the voyaging in imagination which he had also done in his reading. If the poems in *The Marble Faun* followed the models of the Greek pastoral with an overlay of English diction (recent research has revealed other more particular borrowings and imitation in that book), the poems which he wrote after the composition of the cycle showed him venturing even further afield. When he went to New Orleans in 1925 and began selling pieces to *The Double Dealer* and *The Times-Picayune*, he began to envision a whole series. It was to be called *Sinbad in New Orleans*. He was hardly a Sinbad even when he sailed for Italy in July of 1925, but the use he made of that journey—setting one story in the Italy of "Divorce in Naples," another in the Switzerland of "Mistral," his unfinished novel, *Elmer*, in several countries—showed him voyaging in fact and feeding his fiction thereon, as he had done in imagination not long before his trip in a story called "Yo Ho and Two Bottles of Rum," set quite unmistakably in the Malaysia of Joseph Conrad. One could go on, moving forward in time and outward in geography to the England of his story, "The Leg" or the Caribbean of "Black Music," with its action set in a place identified only as Rincon. That place name of course suggests his strangest and most suggestive story, "Carcassonne," evoking at once medieval France and then-contemporary Puerto Rico, or perhaps Cuba (where he once thought he might go as interpreter in a bankruptcy case) or perhaps simply some place in the Caribbean. But one thinks of the central character in that plotless story, the poet who sees himself galloping through the skies on a buckskin pony with a mane like tangled fire and eyes like blue electricity. Faulkner would often say he thought of himself as a failed poet. (He once spoke of himself as "the cat that walks by himself," but to me it seems that his totem animal should have been the horse.) I think he must have thought of himself as that poet, voyaging through the cosmos of his imagination, in a way that suggests a character created by that poet Faulkner greatly admired, Conrad Aiken, the title character of the story "Mr. Arcularis," whose spirit leaves his body in a vast trip that presages his death—something which resonates with the condition of the nameless poet of "Carcassonne."

Before he was twenty-one, Faulkner's travels had taken him from the Gulf of Mexico to Lake Ontario. As I have said, he had seen four European countries before he was thirty. Before he had become a world figure he had traveled the North American continent from Mexico to New England, and afterwards, when he was still a productive novelist and now a world figure speaking out on many issues, his travels took him to the South American continent, and as far as Asia, Africa, and Iceland. If there was an artist one could call Faulkner the Provincial, he existed only when the artist chose, for his own purposes of privacy or evasion, to play that role. Because a Mississippi farmer could not be away at harvest, he told the American Academy that he could not accept their Howells Medal in the spring and the Swedish Academy that he could not accept their Nobel Prize in the fall. "I'm just a farmer," he would say. "I ain't a literary man." But if he was not a literary man in the way that Thomas Mann or André Gide was, he was a literary artist who wrote in English and spoke a universal language. (I must immediately pause to qualify or amplify that last sentence. As you know, he studied French and Spanish in the classrooms of Ole Miss. He wrote and spoke French, perhaps with more enthusiasm and flair than accuracy, and one of the last things he did was to draft a letter in French to a Frenchwoman, an Ole Miss faculty wife. After his last trip abroad, he sent a thank-you letter to one of his hosts in Spanish, expressing particular pleasure in, among other things, "el puncho con ron agrariano" that had been served at a party in the country. Once again, for all I know, the rendering may have been faulty, but the sentiments were sincere.)

Given all of the above, why is it that he is now translated so widely, particularly in view of the complexities of style which make him for some, as Professor Díaz-Diocaretz has told us, "Faulkner, the untranslatable demon"? (He used to say that the writer wrote because he was "demon-driven." He must have thought it only fair that the translator should feel the same pitchfork.) The answer is, of course, both obvious and complex. He would speak of "the same griefs grieving on universal bones," of a literature of the heart and not of the glands, of (and he may have gotten this from Balzac) the human heart in conflict with itself. Although he was a writer firmly based in the particulars of his own region, writing out of a sense of history which was for him most vivid over the hundred-year span between 1850 and 1950, he was nonetheless an artist concerned with the human condition, one who heard the sounds which Arnold's speaker in "Dover Beach" heard, knowing that they were also heard on the Aegean by Sophocles "long ago." He was a writer who asked what Dostoevsky called "The Eternal Questions." And if he had begun his career in the ancient pastoral mode, he was a modernist who learned from the Symbolist poets and Eliot and Joyce and Mann and then developed his own art to push the technical frontiers still further for those who came after him. A restless and tireless experimenter, he was an artist who sought always, in handbook language, for the form to fit his content. This is not to ignore the fact, as several speakers have pointed out, that Faulkner the modernist also used to the full the resources of the tall tale, of myth, and the richness of the oral narrative tradition.

He was fond of metaphors from carpentry: he reached back into the lumber room for whatever materials he needed; he grasped whatever tool was required to build the chicken coop. When he wanted straight narrative he could write with clarity and directness that evoked the Old Testament quite as much as did similar elements in Hemingway's famous style. As Joyce learned (he said) from Dujardin, as Eliot learned (some have said) from Tennyson, so Faulkner learned from both of them. He came along at a good time, a time of artistic ferment. Increasingly we are learning about his interest in the visual arts, not only as seen in the watercolors he did for *Mayday*, the line drawings in the style of Aubrey Beardsley and John Held, Jr., for *The Marionettes* and *Ole Miss*, as Professor Hönnighausen so interestingly showed us, but also in his interest in the Impressionists and the Cubists, explored revealingly by Professor Ilse Lind, among others. (Jo Pagano said that when he complimented Faulkner on his technique—Pagano then an admiring junior screenwriter—Faulkner answered, "Have you noticed that it's all done with mirrors?") What should one call our literary period—Modernist, Post-Modernist? No matter what one calls it, writers today still find in Faulkner ways of approaching their material that are new to them. Mr. Edwards described this experience when he read *As I Lay Dying*. One could go on to name many others. When I wrote William Styron to tell him how much I admired *Sophie's Choice*, he replied that he was pleased, adding that early in his career he had learned from Faulkner and thought that his new book showed him in mastery of his own style and voice.

I will not belabor Faulkner's qualities as what one critic has called an "epic poet in prose." I will cite another, however, who says that *As I Lay Dying* is a novel which "tends toward being a poem."[5] Faulkner said that he thought the writer wanted to distill all the poignancy of human experience into fourteen words. (I think he meant lines, although he may have been thinking of something like a haiku.) If the writer could not do that, he said, he tried to do it in two thousand words as a short story. If he could not do that, he took a hundred thousand and wrote a novel. To me, one of the crucial things about Faulkner's style is that he adapted many of the things he had tried to learn as a poet for the purposes of prose. In its density, its condensation, its allusiveness, its use of irony and paradox and many rhetorical devices, his prose tends toward the condition of poetry, and sometimes, as when Miss Rosa Coldfield speaks to Quentin Compson in one of her more frenetic flights, the lines scan like blank verse. Equally, the haunting ruminations of Darl Bundren could be printed as free verse.

This willingness to use every voice and stop in the console is a manifestation of Faulkner's intensity and dedication as a writer. He once said words were "meat and drink" to him. He said of the writing of *The Sound and the Fury* that it was something he began for himself alone, that he had closed the door against all thought of publishers' lists. His daughter would say that if it ever came to a choice between his family and his work, he would not have hesitated. For many writers who came after James Joyce, Joyce became for them a kind of archetypal artist figure, the Dedalus figure, leaving his homeland to fulfill himself as a priest of art through the use of exile and cunning if not silence. There was much of this in Faulkner. And I think that even for non-American writers who may not know a great deal about the price Faulkner paid for his art, there is something of this same archetypal quality about him which cannot but appeal to other artists. (It is certainly there in his artist figures, whether they are sculptors or poets.) His way was not Hemingway's way—becoming a literary celebrity, someone has said, unparalleled since the time Byron paraded "the spectacle of his bleeding heart across the face of Europe." That was not Faulkner's way, but his example, as a screenwriter with most of his books out of print, writing things in which he did not believe in order to be able still to write the things in which he did, this example, I think, must be a deeply compelling one.

Here is not the place to launch into a further catalogue of his technical achievements: his mastery of the interior monologue, his manipulation of point of view, his breaking up of chronology, his treatment of time. But that last element, the question of time, helps me to make a transition to the few things I should not fail to say about Faulkner's content. He treats time not only as it impinges on consciousness such as that of Quentin Compson, but also in the way it stretches out behind his other, individual people and their land. He presents man in history. Scholars such as Lewis Simpson have spoken brilliantly on this subject (here at a Faulkner conference, as a matter of fact) and written on it. I think of a particular novel by that writer Faulkner admired so much—Joseph Conrad—as he said of *Nostromo* that he thought it would always remain his "broadest canvas." When we think of the panoramic history of Costaguana over the course of its evolution as a nation, we have the sense of seeing whole epochs presented before us from pre-colonial times to the present. Faulkner does the same thing in extended form in the Snopes trilogy and in condensed form in the three introductions to the acts of *Requiem for a Nun*. And again, though he talks in *The Hamlet* about Yoknapatawpha County, he gives us a kind of paradigm of the transition from the rural and agrarian to the modern. (And in this sense I think it can be said that Faulkner is more an anti-modernist [as well as anti-materialist] than a modernist.) In *Requiem*, in a characteristic tour de force, he begins his account in prehistoric times, before the primeval lava has even cooled. It is no wonder to me that his work should prove interesting to a writer such as the author of *One Hundred Years of Solitude*.

But always, there in the foreground, against whatever panorama of history, is the figure of man, talking in "his puny, inexhaustible voice," as Faulkner would put it, and if he is sometimes embodied in such dashing figures as that of the Carolina Bayard Sartoris or such more quietly heroic ones as that of Bayard's nephew and namesake in Yoknapatawpha, he is also embodied in those of far humbler ones, the Wash Joneses and the Mink Snopeses, men seeking, as Professor Chakovsky pointed out, nothing more than justice and human dignity. One thinks especially of Mink Snopes, at the end of *The Mansion*, feeling the pull of the earth and now about to enter it, "himself among them, equal to any, good as any, brave as any, being inextricable from, anonymous with all of them: the beautiful, the splendid, the proud and the brave, right on up to the very top itself among the shining phantoms and dreams which are the milestones of the long human recording—Helen and the bishops, the kings and the unhomed angels, the scornful and graceless seraphim."[6] And as these figures suggest the quest for human dignity and justice, so too, among the many qualities which Professor Gresset pointed out, we see in *A Fable* the overpowering sense of the universal human longing for peace. And we know that, again and again, in writing and in conversation, Faulkner said how essential a part of this book, for him, was its message that, after the great wars of the twentieth century, man might not have another chance to abjure that tragedy for the sake of his very survival. What artist could not feel his own mind and heart resonate with that same cry?

I have been describing elements in Faulkner's work which I would have tried to characterize in much the same fashion if I had not come to this conference. I would like now to reflect on some of the ways in which the lectures and discussions I have heard have changed my sense of Faulkner beyond the bounds of this country. It has been a healthy as well as an informative experience for me. Because I have been so immersed for so long in Faulkner studies, I think I have been in danger of becoming a literary chauvinist. It has become very easy for me, when asked about the status of Faulkner studies, to roll off my tongue the kind of statistics from the MLA *International Bibliography* I mentioned earlier, almost in the way Faulkner described the child glibly reciting the same verse from scripture before breakfast each morning until one day he found himself fixed by the kindly blue eye but inflexible expression of Grandfather Murry.[7] In our first panel discussion, one member of the conference asked if Faulkner studies had peaked. I said that I thought they had not, that the curve was still rising. But later, as Professor Gresset traced Faulkner's reputation in France, I learned about the way in which his reputation in some quarters reached its zenith in 1952 and actually had declined somewhat, for political reasons, when he received the Nobel Prize and gave the acceptance speech which further elevated his reputation in Scandinavia and the Soviet Union. This is not to say that criticism and scholarship have declined in France—far from it, as the splendid work of "the new wave," led by Professor Gresset, so clearly shows. My conception of Faulkner's popularity there was fixed at a certain time, and now I have been brought up to date. I did not entertain any exaggerated ideas of Faulkner's popularity in Britain, if only from the reviews of *Uncollected Stories of William Faulkner* sent to me by Random House. (As for Irish reactions, parenthetically, the single notice from an Irish journal made the least cordial British ones seem hospitable.) So Professor Gidley's lecture kept my feet on the ground, as it were, helped to keep my chauvinism in check in that quarter. I can't help thinking that it's a melancholy irony that England should have proved in large part cool to Faulkner's work when he was such an Anglophile—from calling people blokes to tucking his handkerchief in his sleeve. And I regretted what Professor Hönnighausen called "the sad state of affairs" in West Germany, where all of Faulkner major works have been available for twenty years, but at the hands of twenty-five different translators, all of them mediocre and the Yoknapatawpha they present providing little relevance for most readers in a heavily industrialized modern state beset by economic problems and understandably fearful of international ones. What a happy result, though, that Faulkner should have been taken to so many Gallic hearts in the country which he regarded as the prime nurturer of the human spirit.

We knew that he had been much admired by Latin American writers at least from the time of the São Paulo quadricentennial and his subsequent visit to Venezuela. Now we know that the interest was strong even earlier, and we know too about the problems for the reader confronted with so many translations, at least of certain works, of such varying quality. It is good to see that work goes forward elsewhere, often at the hands of very gifted translators, as in Italy, where the house of Mondadori some time ago undertook the publication of the Opera Omnia edition of Faulkner's works, an ambitious project that would be expensive and lengthy in the completion even in the best of times for commercial publishers. (Faulkner, incidentally, was at some pains to help in this, writing to Livio Garzanti asking that he make available to Mondadori the rights to the early Faulkner novel Garzanti had published. In his letter he told Sr. Garzanti how much at home he had felt since the time of his first visit to Italy, that he had felt himself to be Italian too, sentiments expressed with a warmth almost as great, I think, as that in Browning's famous declaration.)

What has come to me as a special revelation, however, is the fact that of a projected edition of twenty-five works of Faulkner's in Japan, twenty have already been completed. This seems to me to be quite remarkable. As Professor Ohashi has said, in 1955 Faulkner found in Japan conditions closely analogous to those in his own region ninety years earlier. In his interviews and classes in Japan he was at particular pains to emphasize resemblances between the two cultures and even circumstances of his own life. (He said, among other things, that he felt a deep sense of connection to all of his family, including his ancestors, he said, from whom he had inherited his land. [He had complained to Malcolm Cowley ten years earlier that he had received nothing from anyone not even a stick of furniture, since his first pair of long pants.]) Naturally, the hospitable Japanese responded warmly, so much so that one reporter said that Faulkner reminded him of nothing so much as a shy and virtuous Japanese old man of an earlier generation. I was interested to hear Professor Ohashi say that Faulkner's influence is no longer so strongly evident in the work of contemporary novelists as it was a few decades ago. I think this may indicate a familiar process, particularly when seen in the light of the near-completion of the edition of his collected works in Japan: he is being as-

From the World to Jefferson 311

similated, I take it, into the Japanese pantheon of world figures in literature, with Cervantes, Balzac, and Dostoevsky.

What I have learned about Faulkner in the Soviet Union was another eye-opener for me. Professor Deming Brown is one of our friends and neighbors in Ann Arbor, and I once served on a committee with Professor Carl Proffer there at the University of Michigan. So I should have known from sheer proximity to these Slavic specialists more about Faulkner in the Soviet Union than I did. But I have been trying to cultivate new growth in my own garden to such an extent that I have not often lifted my eyes to see what the workers were doing in the neighboring vineyard. And so my ideas were gleaned chiefly from items such as had appeared, for instance, in the *New York Times*. I remember a colorful account in which, as I recall it, one reader first encountered Faulkner when he read an imperfect edition of *The Sound and the Fury* in Siberia. (Come to think of it, that is not altogether bizarre if we remember the Quentin Compson of *Absalom, Absalom!* shaking in the "cold iron dark" of Cambridge, Massachusetts.) And so I was very glad to learn from Professor Vashchenko and Professor Chakovsky and Professor Inge about the extensive and changing history of Faulkner criticism and the increasing tempo of translation of Faulkner's works in the Soviet Union.

I knew even less about this subject in the life of that other colossus, the People's Republic of China, and so I was fascinated to hear Professor Stoneback say that a great wave of interest in Faulkner in China is about to break. He mentioned the large press runs sometimes produced in China. I tried to visualize what might happen if any of Faulkner's books should be printed and approved for dissemination and study in the school system of a country whose population may exceed one billion by the end of the century. I was fascinated, too, by the interests he pointed out which are shared by Faulkner and certain contemporary Chinese writers, in the land and its people, for instance, call them peasants or country people (Faulkner did both) or agricultural workers. It was provocative too to think of Faulkner studies at this early juncture in China, and of the coming years when Faulkner scholarship will emanate increasingly from that land too.

One observes the scholarly process as it goes on, manifested in many ways. Here are two examples. Not long ago in Ann Arbor I received an advertisement for Y. Yoshizaki's new book, *Faulkner's Theme of Nature*, published by Yamaguchi Shoten in Japan. (His title reminds me of another element I might have mentioned that also bespeaks his universality: his use of nature, the role of nature in his work, an element more important now in an increasingly mechanized and dehumanized world, than in earlier times when, for the mass of mankind, the pastoral was the mode in which they lived.) And here is another item. It is from a review of seven new Faulkner books provided by James G. Watson, a participant in a recent Faulkner conference here. (It is a review which also includes a discussion of *Faulkner's Intruder in The Dust: A Critical Study of the Typescripts* by Patrick Samway, another recent participant, happily among us again now.) The particular item that struck me, in our immediate context, was Watson's discussion of a book entitled *William Faulkner and the French New Novelists*, published in Virginia and written by Tran Qui-Phiet, whom I take to be of Vietnamese origin. Watson writes, "Tran argues that Faulkner is the writer of the Modernist tradition who most inspired individual talents such as Alain Robbe-Grillet, Nathalie Sarraute, Michel Butor, and 'the French Faulkner,' Claude Simon, all of whom carried his experiments in fiction to their own extremes."[8] And just this afternoon we learned from Professor Menasseri about Kateb Yacine, called "the Algerian Faulkner," who called Faulkner, without regard to geographical boundaries, I take it, "the greatest writer of our time."*

---

*Editors' Note: Hocine Menasseri, Senior Inspector of English in Algiers, told conference participants about Kateb Yacine, an Algerian writer whose major work, a novel called *Nedjma*, shows the influence of Faulkner in both style and themes and has numerous parallels to *The Sound and the Fury*. *Nedjma* was published in Paris by Editions du Seuil in 1956; an English version translated form the French by Richard Howard was published in New York by G. Braziller in 1961.

I have come to see more clearly, I think, how one must take the long view of Faulkner studies abroad, as one sees a historical process at work. Once again, the French provide a model for us, admirably set forth in the chronology of the French translations of Faulkner's novels and the bibliography, "The French Face of Faulkner: Some Landmarks in the History of A Literary Acculturation," which Professor Gresset has so helpfully provided. After a solid decade of work by "The Heralds" of Faulkner and his art, "The Explorers" strike out to take measurements of this apocryphal new-found land during the following two decades. Then comes the "New Wave" which begins to create nearly half a century after the first sightings of the Heralds. What next? I think now of Professor Lombardo's history of Faulkner's career in Italy, and what strikes me almost overpoweringly is not just that all of Faulkner's novels and many of his stories have been published in Italy, or even that there are innumerable courses and seminars on his work and numerous dissertations, nor even that his influence should be seen in the work of such a major writer as Cesare Pavese, but that Faulkner became the mediator between the new novel and Italy, *before* James Joyce and Virginia Woolf, and even more that he "touched the very heart of our culture," as Professor Lombardo put it, that he "*has become a part of our culture.*" That is the final step, I think, not simply for the artist to be recognized as belonging to the pantheon of classical artists, but also to be assimilated into the culture of the nation. (It is almost enough to make me think I was not being a chauvinist but perhaps just a realist.) Thinking beyond the Americas and Europe, I am bemused at the idea of the future impact of this large and extraordinary body of work on other continents, in another hemisphere. And I say this realizing that in most countries he is not likely to be read by large numbers of readers but rather, perhaps, as Matthew Arnold put it, by those concerned with "the best that is known and thought in the world."

Parenthetically again, gazing with the mind's eye at the riches in existence and yet to come, I think about a group I have not mentioned: the collectors, people such as Messrs. Boozer, Brodsky, and Petersen—such as my late loyal friend, Linton R. Massey—and I think of the debt scholars and critics owe to them.

It is not easy even to begin the effort of summing up when so many facets of such an extraordinary literary phenomenon have been approached with such stimulating diversity. I'll try though with part of the passage that Professor Brown and I both were remembering, I'm sure, when we titled our talks. Near the end of *The Town* Gavin Stevens tell us,

> There is a ridge; you drive on beyond Seminary Hill and in time you come upon it: a mild unhurried farm road presently mounting to cross the ridge and on to join the main highway leading from Jefferson to the world. And now, looking back and down, you see all Yoknapatawpha in the last of day beneath you. . . . And you stand suzerain and solitary above the whole sum of your life. . . . First is Jefferson, the center, radiating weakly its puny glow into space; beyond it, enclosing it, spreads the county, tied by the diverging roads to that center as is the rim to the hub by its spokes, yourself detached as God Himself for this moment above the cradle of your nativity and of the men and women who made you, the record and chronicle of your native land proffered for your perusal in ring by concentric ring like the ripples on living water above the dreamless slumber of your past; you to preside unanguished and immune above this miniature of man's passions and hopes and disasters—ambition and fear and lust and courage and abnegation and pity and honor and sin and pride—all bound, precarious and ramshackle, held together by the web, the iron-thin warp and woof of his rapacity but withal yet dedicated to his dreams.[9]

Gavin Stevens stands there looking out over Yoknapatawpha, and beside him stands the spirit of William Faulkner looking out over his apocryphal county, his cosmos, as he called it. Its roads reached out to the world. We have traveled them and they have brought us here.

W. H. Auden used a powerful spatial metaphor in his poem, "In Memory of W. B. Yeats." He wrote,

> . . . for him it was his last afternoon as himself,
> An afternoon of nurses and rumors;

> The provinces of his body revolted,
> The squares of his mind were empty,
> Silence invaded the suburbs,
> The current of his feeling failed: he became his admirers.

Twenty years ago last month William Faulkner died. If we agree with Auden, we can say that he lives not only in his work but also in us. And he will live particularly in the work of those of us who have the gifts to be translators. Professor Stoneback mentioned the importance of teaching in the continuing process by which Faulkner's work is made available to new generations of readers. The scholars and critics perform their function, but I think now particularly of the labors of the translators and those who will teach the ones to come, the translators who will know that there are two Quentins in *The Sound and the Fury* and that Dilsey was a woman, the translators who will not use one verb for eight different bird images, who will not dispense with the more troublesome tenses, who will not, as Professor Díaz-Diocaretz put it, disambiguate a complex text to produce a monotone.

Faulkner's last work had a mellow valedictory tone that one thinks of here, now, just after the twentieth anniversary of his death. One thinks how unlike the tone of *The Reivers* was that of one of Yeats's last major works, "Under Ben Bulben." One thinks particularly of that stanza (like the others so well recalled stylistically in Auden's tribute), that stanza in which the dying Yeats looks to the future and writes,

> Irish poets, learn your trade,
> Sing whatever is well made,
> Scorn the sort now growing up
> All out of shape from toe to top.

Fortunately, the translators now growing up are not, like the examples cited by Professor Lombardo and Professor Díaz-Diocaretz, all out of shape from toe to top. And it is thanks to the example and instruction of several among us, such as Professor Ohashi, to name only one. As I think of us gathered here, soon returning to our students, I find certain kinds of phrases drifting through my mind, phrases such as this one, for instance,

> Go ye out into the world, to all the nations,
> And proclaim unto them the Word.

(Please don't be offended. I'm not being irreverent or even blasphemous. Those lines are not from the New Testament or the Old, I just made them up.)

I am thinking too of the title of Professor Gresset's forthcoming *The French Face of William Faulkner*. Being aware of the multiplicity of translations and titles in single languages, one might even think of the faces of William Faulkner, within a single language, for his visage will inevitably change at the hands of each one who attempts to render it. This reminds me of his response to a student who asked about the true character of Thomas Sutpen: "In *Absalom, Absalom!*, does any one of the people who talks about Sutpen have the right view, or is it more or less a case of thirteen ways of looking at a blackbird?" This time Faulkner answered without his characteristic pause. "That's it exactly," he said. "I think that no one individual can look at the truth. It blinds you. You look at it and you see one phase of it. Someone else looks at it and sees a slightly awry phase of it. But taken all together, the truth is in what they saw though nobody saw the truth intact."[10] This makes me recall the comments of Professor Brown and Professor Lombardo about the limits of translation and the impossibility of achieving the dream to which the translator aspires. It is tempting to think of all the translations of a novel in some fashion achieving collectively (perhaps in the mind of some extraordinary comparativist) some approximation, some sort of Platonic form of the ideal translation.

I think it is very likely that Faulkner knew that preface of Joseph Conrad's which was published with the title "The Artist's Creed." You will remember that he begins, "A work that aspires, however humbly, to the condition of art should carry its justification in every line. And art itself may be defined as a single-minded attempt to render the highest kind of justice to the visible universe, by bringing to light the truth, manifold and one, underlying its every aspect." Then, towards the end, Conrad continues, "In a single-minded attempt of that kind, if one be deserving and fortunate, one may perchance attain to such clearness of sincerity that at least the presented vision of regret or pity, of terror or mirth, shall awaken in the hearts of the beholders that feeling of unavoidable solidarity; of the solidarity in mysterious origin, in toil, in joy, in hope, in uncertain fate, which binds men to each other and all mankind to the visible universe." I think that William Faulkner would have subscribed to these sentiments. And I think that this describes the kind of vision and feeling that each of us—readers and writers, collectors, scholars, critics, editors, teachers, translators of the work of William Faulkner—have glimpsed and perhaps felt here, as now we prepare to make our return journey from Jefferson to the world.

NOTES

1. Susan Snell, *Phil Stone of Yoknapatawpha* (Ann Arbor: University Microfilms International, 1978), 329.
2. William Kennedy, "The Yellow Trolley Car in Barcelona and Other Visions," *The Atlantic*, 213 (1973), 57.
3. *La Novela en America Latina: Dialoga* (Lima: Carlos Milla Batres, 1968), 52–53.
4. *William Faulkner: Essays, Speeches & Public Letters*, ed. James B. Meriwether (New York: Random House, 1965), 8.
5. André Bleikasten, *Faulkner's "As I Lay Dying"* (Bloomington: Indiana University Press, 1973), 43.
6. *The Mansion* (New York: Random House, 1959), 435–36.
7. *Lion in the Garden: Interviews with William Faulkner, 1926–1962*, ed. James B. Meriwether and Michael Millgate (New York: Random House, 1968), 250.
8. *Modern Fiction Studies*, 27 (Summer 1981), 368.
9. *The Town* (New York: Random House, 1957), 315–16.
10. *Faulkner in the University*, ed. Frederick L. Gwynn and Joseph Blotner (Charlottesville: University Press of Virginia, 1959), 273.

Appendixes

A.
Selected Recent British Writing on Faulkner
MICK GIDLEY

NB: This list does not include items cited in "Faulkner and the British."

Beaver, Harold. "The Count of Mississippi," *Times Literary Supplement*, No. 3,821 (May 30, 1975), 600–601. Lengthy review of Joseph Blotner's *Faulkner: A Biography* (1974).
Bennett, J. A. W. "Faulkner and A. E. Housman," *Notes and Queries*, New Series, 27 (June 1980), 234.
Duncan, Alastair B. "Claude Simon and William Faulkner," *Forum for Modern Language Studies*, 9 (1973), 235–52.
Gidley, Mick. "Another Psychologist, a Physiologist and William Faulkner," *Ariel: A Review of International English Literature*, 2 (October 1971), 78–86.
———. "William Faulkner and Willard Huntington Wright's *The Creative Will*," *Canadian Review of American Studies*, 9 (Fall 1978), 169–77.
———. "William Faulkner and Some Designs of Literary Naturalism," *Studies in American Fiction*, 7 (Spring 1979), 75–82.
Godden, Richard. "William Faulkner, Addie Bundren, and Language," *University of Mississippi Studies in English*, 15 (1978), 101–23.
———. "Addie Bundren's Words with God," *Essays in Poetics*, 3 (April 1978), 25–46. Enlargement of item above.
———. "William Faulkner and Benjamin Compson: The Voices that Keep Silence," *Essays in Poetics*, 4 (April 1979), 1–19.
———. "'Call Me Nigger!': Race and Speech in Faulkner's *Light in August*," *Journal of American Studies*, 14 (August 1980), 235–48.
Gray, Richard. *The Literature of Memory: Modern Writers of the American South*. London: Edward Arnold, 1977, 197–256.
Jarrett, David. "Eustacia Vye and Eula Varner, Olympians: The Worlds of Thomas Hardy and William Faulkner," *Novel*, 6 (Winter 1973), 163–74.
Jarrett-Kerr, Martin. *William Faulkner*. Grand Rapids: Eerdman's Contemporary Writers in a Christian Perspective Series, 1969. A brief treatment.
Leaf, Mark. "William Faulkner's Snopes Trilogy." In Warren French, ed., *The*

319

Fifties: Fiction, Poetry, Drama. Deland, Florida: Everett-Edwards, 1970, 51–62.

Mottram, Eric. "Mississippi Faulkner's Glorious Mosaic of Impotence and Madness," *Journal of American Studies*, 2 (April 1968), 121–29.

———. *William Faulkner.* London: Routledge, Kegan & Paul, Profiles in Literature Series, 1971. A brief introductory anthology.

Tallack, Douglas G. "William Faulkner and the Tradition of Tough-Guy Fiction." In Larry N. Landrum, Pat Browne, Ray B. Browne, eds., *Dimensions of Detective Fiction.* Bowling Green: Popular Press, 1976, 247–64.

B.
Faulkner in Spanish
MYRIAM DÍAZ-DIOCARETZ

1934 *Sanctuary*

Santuario. Trans. Lino Novás Calvo. Introd. Antonio Marichalar. Madrid: Espasa-Calpe, 1934.

———. Trans. Amando Lázaro Ros. In *Obras escogidas*, Vol. II. Madrid: Aguilar, 1960.

1940 *The Wild Palms*

Las Palmeras Salvajes. Trans. Jorge Luis Borges. Buenos Aires: Sudamericana, 1940; 2nd ed., 1944; 3rd ed., 1949; 4th ed., 1951; 5th ed., 1956.

———. Trans. Jorge Luis Borges. Introd. Juan Benet. Barcelona: E.D.H.A.S.A., 1970; 1983.

1942 *As I Lay Dying*

Mientras yo agonizo. Trans. Introd. Max Dickmann. Buenos Aires: Santiago Rueda, 1942. Reprint 1952, 1969.

———. Trans. Max Dickmann. Buenos Aires: Santiago Rueda, 1969.

Mientras agonizo. Trans. Agustín Caballero Robredo and Arturo del Hoyo. Introd. not signed. Madrid: Aguilar, 1954.

———. Trans. Agustín Caballero Robredo and Arturo del Hoyo. In *Obras escogidas.* Vol. I. Madrid: Aguilar, 1956.

———. Trans. Agustín Caballero Robredo and Arturo del Hoyo. In *Obras Completas*, Vol. II. Barcelona: Caralt, 1962.

———. Trans. A. Fornet. Habana: Editorial Nacional de Cuba, 1965.**

---

*An asterisk indicates that there are additional and subsequent reprints which I have excluded because the bibliographical information for those entries was incomplete.

**For the information on the edition of *As I Lay Dying* published in Cuba I am indebted to M. Thomas Inge who, after the 1982 Faulkner and Yoknapatawpha Conference, kindly shared with me his article "Contemporary American Literature in Spain," in *Tennessee Studies in Literature*, 16, ed. Richard Beale Davis and Kennett L. Knickerbocker, Knoxville: The University of Tennessee Press, 1971, 155–67.

Faulkner in Spanish 321

1942 *Light in August**
Luz de agosto. Trans. Pedro Lecuona. Buenos Aires: Sur, 1942.
———. Trans. Pedro Lecuona. Buenos Aires: Goyanarte, 1957.

1944 *These Thirteen*
Victoria y otros relatos. Trans. José Blaya Lozano. Buenos Aires: Corinto, [Colección Nivola], 1944.
Estos trece. Trans. Aurora Bernárdez. Buenos Aires: Losada, 1956.

1947 *Pylon*
Pylon. Trans. Julio Fernández Yáñez. Barcelona: Caralt [Colección Gigante], 1947. Reprint 1956.
———. Trans. Julio Fernández Yáñez. In *Obras escogidas*, I.
———. Trans. Julio Fernández Yáñez. In *Obras completas*, II.
———. Trans. Julio F. Yáñez [sic]. Barcelona: Caralt [Serie Novela, 1st ed.], 1978.

1947 *The Sound and The Fury**
El sonido y la furia. Trans. not given. Buenos Aires: Ed. Futuro, 1947.
El ruido y la furia. Trans. Amando Lázaro Ros. In *Obras escogidas*, II.
El sonido y la furia. Trans. F. E. Lavalle. Buenos Aires: Libros del Mirasol, 1961. Contains Faulkner's "Appendix."
———. Trans. Floreal Mazía. Buenos Aires: Libros del Mirasol, 1963.
———. Trans. Mariano Antolín Rato. Barcelona: Bruguera, 1981.

1947 *The Hamlet**
El villorrio. Trans. Raquel W. de Ortiz. Buenos Aires: Ed. Futuro, 1947.
———. Trans. Napoletano Torre and P. Carbó Amiguet. Barcelona: Caralt, 1953. Reprint 1959.
———. Trans. Napoletano Torre and P. Carbó Amiguet. In *Obras escogidas*, I.
———. Trans. Napoletano Torre and P. Carbó Amiguet. In *Obras completas*, I.
———. Trans. Santos Merino. Buenos Aires: Libros del Mirasol, 1961.
———. Trans. Napoletano Torre and P. O. Carbó Amiguet. Barcelona: Caralt [Serie Novela], 1978. "Primera edición." [sic]

1950 *Absalom, Absalom!**
¡Absalón, Absalón! Trans. Beatriz Florencia Nelson. Buenos Aires: Emecé, 1950. 2nd ed., 1951, 3rd ed., 1952. 4th ed., 1958.
———. Trans. Amando Lázaro Ros. In *Obras escogidas*, II.
———. Trans. Beatriz Florencia Nelson. Madrid: Alianza Editorial [Buenos Aires: Emecé], 1971.

1951 *The Unvanquished*
Los invictos. Trans. Alberto Vilá de Avilés. Barcelona: Caralt, 1951.
———. Trans. Alberto Vilá de Avilés. In *Obras escogidas*, I.
———. Trans. Alberto Vilá de Avilés. In *Obras completas*, II.
———. Trans. Alberto Vilá de Avilés. Barcelona: Caralt [Serie Novela], 1975. 1st ed.

1951 *Knight's Gambit*
Gambito de caballo. Trans. Lucrecia Moreno de Sáenz. Buenos Aires: Emecé,

1951. 3rd ed. [1st ed. Colección Piragua], 1964.
———. Trans. Lucrecia Moreno de Sáenz. Madrid: Alianza Editorial, 1972.

1951 *Intruder in the Dust*
Intruso en el polvo. Trans. Aída Aisenson. Buenos Aires: Losada, 1951.
Colección Los grandes novelistas de nuestra época.
———. Trans. Aída Aisenson. Buenos Aires: Losada, 1959. 2nd ed.

1952 *Requiem for a Nun**
Réquiem para una mujer. Trans. Jorge Zalamea. Buenos Aires: Emecé, 1952.
2nd ed., 1956. 4th ed., 1962. 6th ed. [2nd, Collección Piragua], 1968.
Réquiem para una reclusa. Trans. Victoria Ocampo. Buenos Aires: Sur, 1960.
Translation of Albert Camus, *Requiem pour une nonne.* Paris: Gallimard, 1956.

1953 *Sartoris*
Sartoris. Trans. Francisco Garza. Buenos Aires: Editorial Schapire, 1953.

1953 *Soldiers' Pay**
La paga de los soldados. Trans. Francisco Garza. Buenos Aires: Schapire, 1953.
Reprint 1956, 1959.
———. Trans. not given. Barcelona: Caralt, 1954.
———. Trans. Francisco Garza. Mexico City: Continental, 1955.
———. Trans. not given. In *Obras completas,* I.

1955 *Go Down, Moses**
¡Desciende, Moisés!. Trans. Introd. Ana María de Foronda. Barcelona: Caralt, 1955. Reprint 1959.
———. Trans. Ana María de Foronda. In *Obras escogidas,* I.
———. Trans. Ana María de Foronda. In *Obras completas,* I.
———. Trans. Ana María de Foronda. Barcelona: Argos Vergara [1st ed. Colección Libros Vivos], 1980.

1955 *A Fable*
Una fábula. Trans. Antonio Ribera. Introd. Agustí Bartra. Barcelona: Éxito, 1955. Reprint 1956, 1962.
———. Trans. Antonio Ribera. Introd. Agustí Bartra. México, D. F.: Ed. Cumbre, 1955.
———. Trans. Antonio Ribera. Introd. Agustí Bartra. Buenos Aires: Editorial Jackson de Ediciones Selectas, 1956.
———. Trans. Amando Lázaro Ros. In *Obras escogidas,* II.
———. Trans. Antonio Ribera. Introd. Agustí Bartra. In *Obras completas,* II.

1956 *Mosquitoes**
Mosquitos. Trans. Jerónimo Córdoba. Buenos Aires: Ediciones Siglo Veinte, 1956.
———. Trans. Domingo Manfredi. Barcelona: Caralt, 1959.
———. Trans. Domingo Manfredi. In *Obras completas,* I.

1960 *The Town*
En la ciudad. Trans. Ramón Hernández. Buenos Aires-Barcelona-Mexico City: Plaza & Janés, 1960.
———. Trans. Ramón Fernández [sic.]. Barcelona: Ediciones G. P., 1960. This edition includes works by other authors.
———. Trans. Ramón Hernández. Barcelona: Ediciones Cisne, 1963.

Faulkner in Spanish 323

1960 *The Mansion*
La mansión. Trans. Jorge Ferrer Vidal. Buenos Aires-Barcelona-Mexico City: Plaza & Janés, 1960.
———. Trans. Jorge Ferrer Vidal. Barcelona: Ediciones G. P., 1964.

1963 *The Reivers**
Los rateros. Trans. Jorge Ferrer-Vidal. Buenos Aires-Barcelona-Mexico City: Plaza & Janés, 1963.
———. Trans. Jorge Ferrer Vidal. Barcelona: Ediciones G. P., 1964.

1963 *New Orleans Sketches*
Historias de Nueva Orleans. Trans. Fracisco Elías. Barcelona: Caralt, 1963.

1970 *The Wishing Tree*
El árbol de los deseos. Trans. not given. Barcelona: Ed. Lumen, 1970.

Obras escogidas, I. Madrid: Aguilar [Biblioteca Premios Nobel], 1956. 2nd ed., 1958. 3rd ed., 1962. 4th ed., 1965. 5th ed., 1967.
CONTENTS:
Mientras agonizo (As I Lay Dying). Trans. Agustín Caballero and Arturo del Hoyo.
Pylon. Trans. Julio Fernández Yáñez.
Los invictos (The Unvanquished). Trans. Alberto Vilá de Avilés.
El villorrio (The Hamlet). Trans. J. Napoletano Torre and P. Carbó Amiguet.
¡Desciende, Moisés! (Go Down, Moses). Trans. Ana María de Foronda.

Obras escogidas, II. Trans. Amando Lázaro Ros. Madrid: Aguilar [Biblioteca Premios Nobel], 1960. 2nd ed., 1962. 3rd, 1967.
CONTENTS:
Novelas (Novels):
Una fábula (A Fable); El ruido y la furia (The Sound and The Fury); ¡Absalón, Absalón! (Absalom, Absalom!); Santuario (Sanctuary)
Novelas cortas (Short stories):
"Quemando Establos" ("Barn Burning"); "Un techo para el Señor" ("Shingles for the Lord"), "Los hombres altos" ("The Tall Men"), "Dos soldados" ("Two Soldiers"), "Una rosa para Emily" ("A Rose for Emily"), "Elly" ("Elly"), "Todos los pilotos muertos" ("All the Dead Pilots"), "El Doctor Martino" ("Doctor Martino"), "Estación Pennsylvania" (Pennsylvania Station"), and "Un artista en el hogar" ("Artist at Home").

Obras completas. I. Introd. Mariano Orta. Barcelona: Caralt, 1959.
CONTENTS:
La paga de los soldados (Soldiers' Pay). Trans. not given.
Mosquitos (Mosquitoes). Trans. Domingo Manfredi.
El villorrio (The Hamlet). Trans. J. Napoletano Torre and P. Carbó Amiguet.
¡Desciende, Moisés! (Go Down, Moses). Trans. Ana María de Foronda.

Obras completas, II. Barcelona: Caralt, 1962.
CONTENTS:
Pylon. Trans. Julio Fernández Yáñez.
Los invictos (The Unvanquished). Trans. Alberto Vilá de Avilés.
Mientras agonizo (As I Lay Dying) Trans. Arturo del Hoyo and Agustín Caballero.
La fábula (A Fable). Trans. Antonio Ribera. Introd. Agustí Bartra.

Given that Faulkner's works have existed in three continents, it is extremely difficult to give conclusive information about all the editions and reprints. Included are only the entries I have been able to confirm. This bibliography does not include the publications of Faulkner's individual short stories as they appeared in collections of works by other authors.

C.
Spanish Criticism of Faulkner 1932-59
MYRIAM DÍAZ-DIOCARETZ

Benedetti, Mario. "William Faulkner, un novelista de la fatalidad." *Número*, 2 (Septiembre-Diciembre 1950), 563-71.
Calvo, Lino Novás. "El demonio de Faulkner." *Revista de Occidente*, 39 (Enero 1933), 98-103.
Coindreau, Maurice E. "Panorama de la actual literatura joven norteamericana." Trans. not given. *Sur*, 30 (Marzo 1937), 49-65.
Dickmann, Max. "William Faulkner, escritor diabólico." *Revista de las Indias*, 13 (Marzo 1942), 107-16.
Frank, Waldo. "El corazón de la literatura norteamericana moderna." Trans. not given. *Sur*, 95 (Agosto 1942), 7-23.
Gide, André. "Interviú imaginaria sobre la literatura de los Estados Unidos." Trans. not given. *Sur*, 116 (Junio 1944), 7-13.
Hipwell, Herminia Hallam. "La América del Norte a través de los ojos de su juventud: Notas a las obras de Ernest Hemingway y William Faulkner." *Sur*, 5 (Verano 1932), 186-94.
Justo, Luis. "La antropología de Faulkner—a propósito de *Gambito de Caballo*." *Sur*, 206 (Diciembre 1951), 126-30.
Montenegro, Ernesto. "Interpretación de William Faulkner." *Panorama*, I, 2 (1952), 71-75.
Onís, Harriet de. "William Faulkner." *La Torre* (Octubre-Diciembre 1955), 11-26.
―――. "William Faulkner y su mundo." *Sur*, 202 (Agosto 1951), 24-33.
Portuondo, José Antonio. "William Faulkner y la conciencia sureña." In *El heroismo intelectual*. México: Tezontle, 1955, 73-81.
Sosa López, Emilio. "El problema del mal en William Faulkner." *Sur*, 247 (Julio-Agosto 1957), 55-63.
Soto, Luis Emilio. "Profecía y experimento." *Sur*, 213-14 (Julio-Agosto 1952), 85-95.
Zabel, Morton Dauwen. "La literatura en los Estados Unidos: Panorama de 1943." Trans. Frida Weber. *Sur*, 113-14 (Marzo-Abril 1944), 17-61.
Zavaleta, Carlos Eduardo. *William Faulkner, novelista trágico*. Publ. del Instituto de literatura de la Facultad de la Universidad Nacional Mayor de San Marcos, No. 7. Lima: Universidad Nacional Mayor de San Marcos, 1959.
Yndurain, Francisco. *La obra de William Faulkner*. Madrid: Ateneo, 1953.

D.
Faulkner in German
MONIKA BRÜCKNER

Light in August

1935 Licht im August. Trans. Franz Fein. Berlin: Rowohlt, 1935.
1949 ———. Trans. Franz Fein. Stuttgart, Hamburg, Baden-Baden: Rowohlt, 1949.
1951 ———. Trans. Franz Fein. Berlin, Darmstadt: Deutsche Buchgemeinschaft, 1951.
1955 ———. Trans. Franz Fein. Einmalige Sonderausgabe [new edition]. Die Bücher der Neunzehn, Vol. 13. Hamburg: Rowohlt, 1955. Titelauflage d. Sonderausgabe, 1959.
1957 ———. Trans. Franz Fein. Berlin-Ost: Verlag Volk u. Welt, 1957. 2nd ed., 1964. 3rd ed., 1975.
1962 ———. Trans. Franz Fein. München, Zürich: Droemer Knaur, 1962.
1963 ———. Trans. Franz Fein. Stuttgart, Hamburg: Deutscher Bücherbund, 1963.
 ———. Trans. Franz Fein. Zürich: Buchclub Ex libris, 1963.
1972 ———. Trans. Franz Fein. Reinbek (bei Hamburg): Rowohlt [1.–22. Tsd.], 1972. 3rd ed. [29.–33. Tsd.], 1975. 4rth ed. [34.–38. Tsd.], 1976. [39.–42. Tsd.], 1979. [43.–47. Tsd.], 1980.
1981 ———. Trans. Franz Fein. Zürich: Diogenes (detebe), 1981. Also in Faulkner, William: *Werke, Briefe und Materialien in 29 Bänden in Kassette.* Vol. 7. Zürich: Diogenes (detebe), 1982.

Pylon

1936 Wendemarke. Trans. Georg Goyert. Berlin: Rowohlt, 1936.
1951 ———. Trans. Georg Goyert. Stuttgart, Hamburg, Baden-Baden: Rowohlt, 1951. 3rd ed, 1953. 4th ed., 1955. 5th ed., 1956.
1978 ———. Trans. Georg Goyert. [New edition]. Zürich: Diogenes, 1978. Also in Faulkner, William: *Werke, Briefe und Materialien in 29 Bänden in Kassette.* Vol. 8. Zürich: Diogenes (detebe), 1982.

Absalom, Absalom!

1938 Absalom, Absalom! Trans. Hermann Stresau. Berlin: Rowohlt, 1938.
1948 ———. Trans. Hermann Stresau. Stuttgart, Hamburg, Baden-Baden: Rowohlt [4.–8. Tsd.], 1948. 3rd ed. [9.–12. Tsd.], 1956.
1974 ———. Trans. Hermann Stesau. Zürich: Diogenes, 1974. Diogenes (detebe), 1981. Also in Faulkner, William: *Werke, Briefe und Materialien in 29 Bänden in Kassette.* Vol. 9. Zürich: Diogenes (detebe), 1982.

Sanctuary

1951 Die Freistatt. Trans. Herberth Egon Herlitschka. Vorwort William Faulkner [Modern Library Edition 1932]. Zürich: Artemis, 1951.
1953 ———. Trans. Herberth Egon Herlitschka. Vorwort William Faulkner [ib.]. Köln, Berlin: Kiepenheuer u. Witsch (Ki-Wi-Taschenbücher), 1953.

1955 ———. Trans. Herberth Egon Herlitschka. Vorwort William Faulkner [ib.]. Frankfurt a. M.: Das Goldene Vlies (Bürgers Taschenbücher), 1955.
1960 ———. Trans. Herberth Egon Herlitschka. Vorwort William Faulkner [ib.]. Frankfurt a.M., Berlin, Wien: Ullstein, 1960. 2nd ed., 1965.
1973 ———. Trans. Hans Wollschläger. Vorwort André Malraux. Zürich: Diogenes, 1973. Diogenes (detebe), 1981. Also in Faulkner, William: Werke, Briefe und Materialien in 29 Bänden in Kassette. Vol. 6. Zürich: Diogenes (detebe), 1982.

Intruder in the Dust

1951 *Griff in den Staub*. Trans. Harry Kahn. Zürich: Fretz u. Wasmuth/ Stuttgart, Hamburg: Scherz u. Goverts [deutsche Parallelausgabe], 1951. Goverts (Leinen-Ausgabe), 1981.
1954 ———. Trans. Harry Kahn. Frankfurt a.M.: Das Goldene Vlies (Bürgers Taschenbücher), 1954.
1958 ———. Trans. Harry Kahn. Frankfurt a.M., Berlin, Wien: Ullstein, 1958.
1964 ———. Trans. Harry Kahn. Nachwort H. Petersen. Berlin-Ost: Verlag Volk u. Welt, 1964.
1974 ———. Trans. Harry Kahn. Zürich: Diogenes, 1974. Diogenes (detebe), 1981. Also in Faulkner, William: Werke, Briefe und Materialien in 29 Bänden in Kassette. Vol. 14. Zürich: Diogenes (detebe), 1982.

Go Down, Moses

1953 *Das verworfene Erbe. Chronik einer Familie*. Trans., Vorwort u. Genealogie Hermann Stresau. [This ed. does not include a trans. of "Pantaloon in Black"; see later trans.] Zürich: Fretz u. Wasmuth/ Stuttgart, Hamburg: Scherz u. Goverts [deutsche Parallelausgabe], 1953.
1964 ———.———. Trans., Vorwort u. Genealogie Hermann Stresau. Frankfurt a.M., Hamburg: Fischer-Bücherei, 1964.
1965 *American Short Stories.** Vol. 8. The Twentieth Century II. In *Englische Lesebogen*, 162. Paderborn: Schöningh, 1965. 1981. [Title story of *Go Down, Moses* included.]
1974 *Go down, Moses: Chronik einer Familie*. Trans. Hermann Stresau u. Elisabeth Schnack. Contents: seven stories. Zürich: Diogenes, 1974. Diogenes (detebe), 1981. Also in Faulkner, William: *Werke, Briefe und Materialien in 29 Bänden in Kassette*, Vol. 13. Zürich: Diogenes (detebe), 1982.

The Unvanquished

1954 *Die Unbesiegten*. Trans., Vorwort Erich Franzen. Zürich: Fretz u. Wasmuth/Stuttgart, Hamburg: Scherz u. Goverts [deutsche Parallelausgabe], 1954.
1957 ———. Trans. Erich Franzen. Frankfurt a.M., Hamburg: Fischer-Bücherei, 1957.
1957 *The Unvanquished: The Adventures of an Old Lady and Two Boys in the American Civil War.** Ed. Friedrich Lange. Velhagen u. Klasings

englische Lesebogen, 22. Bielefeld, Berlin, Hannover: Velhagen u. Klasing, 1957. Cornelsen-Velh.Klas., 1981.
1962 *Die Unbesiegten.* Trans. Erich Franzen. Frankfurt a.M., Wien, Zürich: Büchergilde Gutenberg, 1962.
1973 ———. Trans. Erich Franzen. Zürich: Diogenes, 1973. Diogenes (detebe), 1981. Also in Faulkner, William: *Werke, Briefe und Materialien in 29 Bänden in Kassette.* Vol. 10. Zürich: Diogenes (detebe), 1982.

The Bear

1955 *Der Bär.* Trans. Hermann Stresau. Frankfurt a.M., Wien: Forum (Forum-Taschenbücher, N.F., 19), 1955.
1958 *The Bear.** Ed. Alexander Niederstenbruch. Schöninghs englische Lesebogen, 134. Paderborn: Schöningh, 1958.
1959 ———.* Ed., Vorwort u. Anmerkungen Paul Fussell. Silva-Schulausgaben. A. Vol. 24. Verden a. Aller: Silva, 1959.
1959 *Der Bär.* Trans. Hermann Stresau. Juventus-Bücherei, Reihe 1.77. Aarau, Frankfurt a.M.: Sauerländer, 1959.
1960 ———. Trans. Hermann Stresau. Bibliothek Suhrkamp. Vol. 56. Frankfurt a.M.: Suhrkamp [1.–5. Tsd.], 1960. 2nd ed. [6.–10. Tsd.], 1961. 4th ed. [15.–18. Tsd.], 1967. 5th ed., 1973. 1981.
1969 ———. Trans. Hermann Stresau. Nachwort Günther Gentsch. Leipzig: Insel-Verlag, 1969.

A Fable

1955 *Eine Legende.* Trans. Kurt Heinrich Hansen. Zürich: Fretz u. Wasmuth/ Stuttgart, Hamburg: Scherz u. Goverts [deutsche Parallelausgabe], 1955. Goverts (Leinen-Ausgabe), 1981.
1963 ———. Trans. Kurt Heinrich Hansen. Nachwort Hans Petersen. Berlin-Ost: Verlag Volk u. Welt, 1963. 2nd ed., 1972 (Bibliothek der Weltliteratur).
1982 ———. Trans. Kurt Heinrich Hansen. In Faulkner, William: *Werke, Briefe und Materialien in 29 Bänden in Kassette.* Vol. 16. Zürich: Diogenes (detebe), 1982.

"Was"

1956 *Jagdglück.* Trans., Nachwort Elisabeth Schnack. Die kleinen Bücher d. Arche, 233. Zürich: Verlag d. Arche, 1956.
1956 ———. Trans., Nachwort Elisabeth Schnack. Bonner Buchgemeinde. Published by Verlag d. Arche as 2nd ed., Zürich, 1956.
[See also trans. by Hermann Stresau *Es war* in *Das verworfene Erbe,* 1953.]

"Mountain Victory"

1956 *Sieg in den Bergen.* Trans., Nachwort Hans Hennecke. Langen-Müllers kleine Geschenkbücher, 53. München: Langen/Müller, 1956.
[See also trans. by Elisabeth Schnack *Sieg im Gebirge* in *Gesammelte Erzählungen* IV, 1972.]

"That Evening Sun"

1956 *Abendsonne.* Trans. Erich Franzen. 3 Erzählungen "Rotes Laub" u.

"Schwüler September." München: Piper-Bücherei, 1956.
[See also trans. by Elisabeth Schnack *Wenn die Sonne untergeht* in *Gesammelte Erzählungen* II, 1972.]

1962 *That Evening Sun.** Ed. H. R. Faerber. In "Collection of English Texts," *Four American Writers of the Twentieth Century.* Vol. 82. Bern, München: Francke, 1962.

1962 ———.* Ed. O. Neugebauer. Schöninghs englische Lesebogen, 146. *Four Stories* ("Death Drag," "Pennsylvania Station," "Barn Burning"). Paderborn: Schöningh, 1962.

"Spotted Horses"

1956 *Scheckige Mustangs.* [Trans. of episode in *The Hamlet*]. Trans. Kurt Alboldt. Wiesbaden: Insel-Verlag, 1956.

The Sound and the Fury

1956 *Schall und Wahn.* Trans. Helmut M. Braem u. Elisabeth Kaiser. Zürich: Fretz u. Wasmuth/Stuttgart, Hamburg: Scherz u. Goverts [deutsche Parallelausgabe], 1956.

1964 ———. Trans. Helmut M. Braem u. Elisabeth Kaiser. München: Kindler (Kindler-Taschenbücher, 35), 1964.

1973 ———. Neu durchgesehene u. revidierte Übersetzung [revised trans.] mit e. Genealogie der Familie Compson von Helmut M. Braem u. Elisabeth Kaiser. Zürich: Diogenes, 1973. Diogenes (detebe), 1981. Also in Faulkner, William: *Werke, Briefe und Materialien in 29 Bänden in Kassette.* Vol. 4. Zürich: Diogenes (detebe), 1982.

Requiem for a Nun

1956 *Requiem für eine Nonne.* Trans. Robert Schnorr. Zürich: Fretz u. Wasmuth/Stuttgart, Hamburg: Scherz u. Goverts [deutsche Parallelausgabe], 1956.

1958 ———. Trans. Robert Schnorr. Darmstadt: Moderner Buch-Club, 1958.

1959 ———. Trans. Robert Schnorr. Sonderausgabe [from 1st ed., 1956]. Stuttgart, Hamburg: Scherz u. Goverts, 1959.

1961 ———. Trans. Robert Schnorr. [Titelauflage Moderner Buch-Club, 1958]. Berlin, Darmstadt, Wien: Deutsche Buchgemeinschaft, 1961.

1961 ———. Trans. Robert Schnorr. Zürich: Schweizer Druck- u. Verl.-Haus, 1961.

1962 ———. Trans. Robert Schnorr. Nachwort A. Haberkalt. Wien: Buchgemeinschaft Donauland, 1962.

1964 ———. Trans. Robert Schnorr. München: Deutscher Taschenbuch-Verlag (DTV, 242), 1964.

1965 ———. Trans. Robert Schnorr. Frankfurt a.M.: S. Fischer, 1965.

1982 ———. Roman in Szenen. Trans. Robert Schnorr. In Faulkner, William: *Werke, Briefe und Materialien in 29 Bänden in Kassette.* Vol. 15. Zürich: Diogenes (detebe), 1982.

A Green Bough

1957 *Ein grüner Zweig.* [Selection of 25 from 44 poems in English and German]. Sel., trans., Nachwort Hans Hennecke. Zürich: Fretz u. Wasmuth [Schweizer Parallelausgabe]/Stuttgart: Goverts, 1957. Goverts (Leinen-Ausgabe), 1981.

"Two Soldiers"

1957 *Zwei Soldaten.* Kurzausgabe. [Trans. not given]. In *Reader's Digest-Auswahlbücher.* Vol. 8, Spring 1957. Stuttgart, Zürich, Wien: Verl. Das Beste, 1955–1957.
[See also trans. by Elisabeth Schnack in *Gesammelte Erzählungen* I, 1972.]

The Hamlet

1957 *Das Dorf.* Trans. Helmut M. Braem u. Elisabeth Kaiser. Zürich: Fretz u. Wasmuth/Stuttgart: Goverts [deutsche Parallelausgabe], 1957. Goverts (Leinen-Ausgabe), 1981.
1960 ———. Trans. Helmut M. Braem u. Elisabeth Kaiser. Gütersloh: Bertelsmann Lesering, 1960.
1965 "Scheckige Mustangs." [Snopes, Auszug]. [Trans. not given]. Gelesen von Gunter Böhmer. Stuttgart: Manus-Presse (23 Blätter; 4 Beilagen), 1965.
1965 *Das Dorf.* Trans. Helmut M. Braem u. Elisabeth Kaiser. In *Snopes-Trilogie.* Nachwort Hans Petersen. Berlin-Ost: Verlag Volk u. Welt, 1965.
1982 ———. Trans. Helmut M. Braem u. Elisabeth Kaiser. In Faulkner, William: *Werke, Briefe und Materialien in 29 Bänden in Kassette.* Vol. 12. Zürich: Diogenes (detebe), 1982.

The Wild Palms

1957 *Wilde Palmen und Der Strom.* Trans., Vorwort Helmut M. Braem u. Elisabeth Kaiser. Zürich: Fretz u. Wasmuth/Stuttgart, Hamburg: Scherz u. Goverts [deutsche Parallelausgabe], 1957.
1961 ———. Trans., Vorwort Helmut M. Braem u. Elisabeth Kaiser. Sonderausgabe [Titelauflage of ed., 1957]. Stuttgart: Goverts, 1961.
1961 *Der Strom.* (Old Man). Trans. Helmut M. Braem u. Elisabeth Kaiser. Frankfurt a.M., Hamburg: Fischer-Bücherei, 1961. 2nd ed., Nachwort Elisabeth Kaiser, 1978. 1981.
1963 *Wilde Palmen.* (The Wild Palms). Trans. Helmut M. Braem u. Elisabeth Kaiser. Bibliothek Suhrkamp, 80. [6.–10. Tsd.], Frankfurt a.M.: Suhrkamp, 1963. 3rd ed., [11.–14. Tsd.], 1967. 4th ed., [18. Tsd.], 1970. 1981.
1982 *Wilde Palmen und der Strom.* Trans. Helmut M. Braem u. Elisabeth Kaiser. In Faulkner, William: *Werke, Briefe und Materialien in 29 Bänden in Kassette.* Vol. 11. Zürich: Diogenes (detebe), 1982.

"My Grandmother Millard" and "Pantaloon in Black"

1958 *Meine Großmutter Millard und die Schlacht am Harrykin-Bach* (My Grandmother Millard and General Bedford Forrest and the Battle of Harrykin Creek) and *Schwarzer Harlekin* (Pantaloon in Black). Trans. Elisabeth Schnack u. Hermann Stresau. Nachwort Helmut M. Braem. Reclams Universal-Bibliothek. Stuttgart: Reclam, 1958. 1981.
[See also trans. in Faulkner, William: *Werke, Briefe und Materialien in*

29 Bänden in Kassette. Vol. 13 ("Pantaloon," *Go Down, Moses*) and *Gesammelte Erzählungen* IV ("Millard"). Zürich: Diogenes (detebe), 1982.

Soldiers' Pay

1958 *Soldatenlohn*. Trans. Susanne Rademacher. [1.–50. Tsd.]. Hamburg: Rowohlt (Taschenbuch), 1958. 2nd ed., 1960. 3rd ed. [64.–70. Tsd.], 1962.

1967 ———. Trans. Susanne Rademacher. Nachwort Karl-Heinz Schönfelder. Reclams Universalbibliothek, 333. Erzählende Prosa. Leipzig: Reclam, 1967.

1978 ———. New trans. Susanne Rademacher. (Die Übersetzerin hat d. Text für diese Neuedition durchgesehen). Neuausgabe. Zürich: Diogenes, 1978. 1981. Also in: Faulkner, William: *Werke, Briefe und Materialien in 29 Bänden in Kassette*. Vol. 1. Zürich: Diogenes (detebe), 1982.

The Town

1958 *Die Stadt*. Trans. Elisabeth Schnack. Zürich: Fretz u. Wasmuth/ Stuttgart: Goverts [deutsche Parallelausgabe], 1958.

1961 ———. Trans. Elisabeth Schnack. Gütersloh: Bertelsmann Lesering, 1961.

1965 ———. Trans. Elisabeth Schnack. In *Snopes-Trilogie*. Nachwort Hans Petersen. Berlin-Ost: Verlag Volk u. Welt, 1965.

1982 ———. Trans. Elisabeth Schnack. In Faulkner, William: *Werke, Briefe und Materialien in 29 Bänden in Kassette*. Vol. 17. Zürich: Diogenes (detebe), 1982.

The Mansion

1960 *Das Haus*. Trans. Elisabeth Schnack. Zürich: Fretz u. Wasmuth/ Stuttgart: Goverts [deutsche Parallelausgabe], 1960.

1962 ———. Trans. Elisabeth Schnack. Gütersloh: Bertelsmann Lesering, 1962.

1965 ———. Trans. Elisabeth Schnack. In *Snopes-Trilogie*. Nachwort Hans Petersen. Berlin-Ost: Verlag Volk u. Welt, 1965.

1982 ———. Trans. Elisabeth Schnack. In Faulkner, William: *Werke, Briefe und Materialien in 29 Bänden in Kassette*. Vol. 18. Zürich: Diogenes (detebe), 1982.

Trilogy

1962 *Snopes Trilogie*. Trans. Elisabeth Schnack. [Titelauflagen der jeweiligen Erst- u. Einzelausgaben]. Stuttgart: Goverts, 1962.

Mosquitoes

1960 *Moskitos*. Trans., Nachwort Richard Karl Flesch. [1.–38. Tsd.] Reinbeck b. Hamburg: Rowohlt (Taschenbuch), 1960. 2nd ed., 1961. 3rd ed. [46–55. Tsd.], 1963.

1978 ———. Revised trans. Richard Karl Flesch. Neuausgabe. Zürich: Diogenes, 1978. 1981. Also in Faulkner, William: *Werke, Briefe und*

Faulkner in German

Materialien in 29 Bänden in Kassette. Vol. 2. Zürich: Diogenes (detebe), 1982.

Sartoris

1961 *Sartoris.* Trans. Hermann Stresau. Reinbeck b. Hamburg: Rowohlt, 1961. 1981.
1973 ———. Trans. Hermann Stresau. Zürich: Diogenes, 1973. 1981. Also in Faulkner, William: *Werke, Briefe und Materialien in 29 Bänden in Kassette.* Vol. 3. Zürich: Diogenes (detebe), 1982.

As I Lay Dying

1961 *Als ich im Sterben lag.* Trans. Albert Hess u. Peter Schünemann. Zürich: Fretz u. Wasmuth/Stuttgart: Goverts [deutsche Parallelausgabe], 1961, 1981.
1963 ———. Trans. Albert Hess u. Peter Schünemann. Bibliothek Suhrkamp, 103. Frankfurt a.M.: Suhrkamp, 1963.
1973 ———. Trans. Albert Hess u. Peter Schünemann. Zürich: Diogenes, 1973. 1981. Also in Faulkner, William: *Werke, Brief und Materialien in 29 Bänden in Kassette.* Vol. 5. Zürich: Diogenes (detebe), 1982.

New Orleans Sketches

1962 *New Orleans.* Skizzen und Erzählungen. Trans. Arno Schmidt. Carvel Collins: Zu diesen Skizzen. Stuttgart: Goverts/Zürich: Fretz u. Wasmuth [Schweizer Parallelausgabe], 1962.
1964 ———. Skizzen und Erzählungen. Trans. Arno Schmidt. Carvel Collins: Zu diesen Skizzen. Sonderreihe DTV, 30. München: Deutscher Taschenbuch-Verlag, 1964.
1964 ———. Skizzen und Erzählungen. Trans. Arno Schmidt. In Faulkner, William: *Werke, Briefe und Materialien in 29 Bänden in Kassette.* Vol. 27. Zürich: Diogenes (detebe), 1982.

CONTENTS:

Zu diesen Skizzen (Carvel Collins);
New Orleans:
Wohlhabender Jude; Der Priester; Frankie und Johnny; Der Seemann; Der Flickschuster; Schwarzer Hafenarbeiter; Der Polizist; Der Bettler; Der Künstler; Die Dirne; Der Tourist.
Aus dem Geschäftsleben von Charles Street
Damon & Pythias in Konkurs
Heimat
Eifersucht
Meinliebermann!
Geburtsort Nazareth
Das Reich Gottes
Der 'Rosenkranz'
Der Flickschuster
Ein Glückstag
Sonnenuntergang

Noch bist du Lehrling, mein Junge!
Der Lügner
Episode
Landmäuse
Yo Ho und zwei Buddeln voll Rum

Knight's Gambit

1962 *Der Springer greift an.* Erzählungen. Trans. Elisabeth Schnack. Zürich: Fretz u. Wasmuth/Stuttgart: Goverts [deutsche Parallelausgabe], 1962. Goverts: 2nd ed., 1963.

1964 ———. Trans. Elisabeth Schnack. Berlin, Darmstadt, Wien: Deutsche Buchgemeinschaft, 1964.

1969 ———. Kriminalgeschichten. Trans. Elisabeth Schnack. Frankfurt a.M.: Fischer-Bücherei, 1969.

1972 ———. Trans. Elisabeth Schnack. Volk-und-Welt-Spektrum, 41. 1st ed., Berlin-Ost: Verlag Volk u. Welt, 1972. (5 Erzählungen). 2nd ed., 1973. 3rd ed. (completed), 1977.

1974 ———. Kriminalgeschichten. Trans. Elisabeth Schnack. Zürich: Diogenes, 1974 (Taschenbücher 30, 14), 1981. 1975 (Taschenbuch, 86). Also in Faulkner, William: *Werke, Briefe und Materialien in 29 Bänden in Kassette.* Vol. 25. Zürich: Diogenes (detebe), 1982. Contents: "Rauch" (Smoke); "Monk" (Monk); "Hand auf den Wassern" (Hand upon the Waters); "Heute und morgen und in alle Ewigkeit" (Tomorrow); "Mangelnde Chemiekenntnisse" (An Error in Chemistry); "Der Springer greift an" (Knight's Gambit).

The Reivers

1963 *Die Spitzbuben.* Trans. Elisabeth Schnack. Zürich: Fretz u. Wasmuth/ Stuttgart: Goverts [deutsche Parallelausgabe], 1963. Goverts 2nd ed., 1964.

1967 ———. Trans. Elisabeth Schnack. Reinbek b. Hamburg: Rowohlt (Taschenbuch), 1967. 2nd ed., 1969.

1967 ———. Trans. Elisabeth Schnack. Berlin-Ost: Verlag Volk u. Welt, 1967. 2nd ed., 1968, 362 pp. 1978, 187 pp. Roman-Zeitung, Heft 343; Verlag Volk u. Welt.

1968 ———. Trans. Elisabeth Schnack. Sonderausgabe [Titelauflage der Ausgabe v. 1964]. Stuttgart: Goverts, 1968. 1981.

1975 *Die Spitzbuben: eine Erinnerung.* Trans. Elisabeth Schnack. Nachwort Richard E. H. Gerber. Manesse-Bibliothek der Weltliteratur. Zürich: Manesse-Verlag, 1975. 1981.

1982 *Die Spitzbuben.* Trans. Elisabeth Schnack. In Faulkner, William: *Werke, Briefe und Materialien in 29 Bänden in Kassette.* Vol. 19. Zürich: Diogenes (detebe), 1982.

Big Woods

1964 *Der große Wald.* 4 Jagdgeschichten. Trans. Hermann Stresau u. Elisabeth Schnack. Zürich: Fretz u. Wasmuth/Stuttgart: Goverts [deutsche Parallelausgabe], 1964. Goverts (Leinen-Ausgabe), 1981.

1969 ———. Jagdgeschichten. Trans. Hermann Stresau u. Elisabeth Schnack. München: List (Taschenbuch, 345), 1969.

Faulkner in German 333

1974 ———. 4 Jagdgeschichten. Trans. Elisabeth Schnack u. Hermann Stresau. Zürich: Diogenes, 1974.

———. Vier Jagdgeschichten. Trans. Elisabeth Schnack. Zürich: Diogenes, 1974. Diogenes (detebe), 1981. Also in Faulkner, William: *Werke, Briefe und Materialien in 29 Bänden in Kassette.* Vol. 26. Zürich: Diogenes (detebe), 1982. Contents: "Der Bär" [without chapter IV], "Das alte Volk"; "Eine Bärenjagd"; "Hetzjagd in der Frühe."

"Death Drag," "Pennsylvania Station," "Barn Burning," and "That Evening Sun."

1962 *Four Stories.** Selected, ed. Otto Neugebauer. Schöninghs englische Lesebogen, 146. Paderborn: Schöningh, 1962. 1981.

"Shingles for the Lord"

1962 *Five Modern American Short Stories.** Ed. H. Tischler. Frankfurt: Diesterweg, 1962.

Collected Stories

1965 *Erzählungen.* (Teilsammlung). Trans. Elisabeth Schnack. Zürich: Fretz u. Wasmuth/Stuttgart: Goverts [deutsche Parallelausgabe], 1965. Vol. 1, 2 parts, 16 stories. 1981. Contents: "Brandstifter"; "Schindeln für den Herrn"; "Die großen Männer"; "Eine Bärenjagd"; "Zwei Soldaten"; ". . . und sollen nicht untergehen";//"Eine Rose für Emily"; "Haar"; "Zentaur aus Messing"; "Dürrer September"; "Der Todesschwung"; "Elly"; "Onkel Willy"; "Maultier im Garten"; "Das wäre fein!"; "Wenn die Sonne untergeht."

1966 *Erzählungen.* (Teilsammlung). Trans. Elisabeth Schnack. Zürich: Fretz u. Wasmuth/Stuttgart: Goverts [deutsche Parallelausgabe], 1966. Vol. 2, 2 parts, 9 stories. Goverts, 1981. Contents: "Rotes Laub"; "Eine Gerechtigkeit"; "Eine Werbung"; "Und siehe da!"//"Ad Astra"; "Sieg"; "Crevasse"; "Der Reihe nach!"; "All die toten Flieger."

1967 *Erzählungen.* (Teilsammlung). Trans. Elisabeth Schnack. Zürich: Fretz u. Wasmuth/Stuttgart: Goverts [deutsche Parallelausgabe], 1967. Vol. 3, 2 parts, 17 stories. Goverts, 1981. Contents: "Wash"; "Ehre"; "Doktor Martino"; "Fuchsjagd"; "Pennsylvania Station"; "Der Künstler daheim"; "Die Brosche"; "Meine Großmutter Millard"; "Goldenes Land"; "Es war eine Königin"; "Sieg im Gebirge"; // "Jenseits"; "Schwarze Musik"; "Das Bein"; "Mistral"; "Scheidung in Neapel"; "Carcassonne."

"Dry September" [Collections]

1968 *"Dürrer September" und acht andere Erzählungen.* Trans. Elisabeth Schnack. Holzschnitte Werner Hofmann. Diogenes-Erzählerbibliothek. Zürich: Diogenes (Lizenz Fretz u. Wasmuth), 1968.

1980 *"Dürrer September": ausgewählte Kurzprosa; 1925–1939/William Faulkner.* Ed. Hans Petersen. Trans. Helmut M. Braem. 1st ed. Berlin-Ost: Verlag Volk u. Welt, 1980.

The Wishing Tree

1969 *Der Wunschbaum.* Ein Märchen. Trans. Elisabeth Schnack. Illustr. Don

Bolgnese. Stuttgart: Goverts (Lizenz Fretz u. Wasmuth, Zürich), 1969. 1981.

Collection

1970 *Meistererzählungen.* (Teilsammlung). Trans., Nachwort Elisabeth Schnack. Stuttgart: Goverts (Lizenz Fretz u. Wasmuth, Zürich), 1970.

Collected Stories

1972 *Brandstifter.* Gesammelte Erzählungen I. Trans. Elisabeth Schnack. Zürich: Diogenes (Lizenz Fretz u. Wasmuth, Zürich), 1972. 1981. [In Kassette: 1–5] 1978. 1981. Also in Faulkner, William: *Werke, Briefe und Materialien in 29 Bänden in Kassette.* Vol. 20. Zürich: Diogenes (detebe), 1982. 6 stories. Contents: "Brandstifter" (Barn Burning); "Schindeln für den Herrn" (Shingles for the Lord); "Die großen Männer" (The Tall Men); "Eine Bärenjagd" (A Bear Hunt); "Zwei Soldaten" (Two Soldiers); ". . . und sollen nicht untergehen" (Shall Not Perish).

1972 *Eine Rose für Emily.* Gesammelte Erzählungen II. Trans. Elisabeth Schnack. Zürich: Diogenes (Lizenz Fretz u. Wasmuth, Zürich), 1972. 1981. [In Kassette: 1–5] 1978. 1981. Also in Faulkner, William: *Werke, Briefe und Materialien in 29 Bänden in Kassette.* Vol. 21. Zürich: Diogenes (detebe), 1982. 10 stories. Contents: "Eine Rose für Emily" (A Rose for Emily); "Haar" (Hair); "Zentaur aus Messing" (Centaur in Brass); "Dürrer September" (Dry September); "Der Todesschwung" (Death Drag); "Elly" (Elly); "Onkel Willy" (Uncle Willy); "Maultier im Garten" (Mule in the Yard); "Das wäre fein!" (That Will Be Fine); "Wenn die Sonne untergeht" (That Evening Sun).

1972 *Rotes Laub.* Gesammelte Erzählungen III. Trans. Elisabeth Schnack. Zürich: Diogenes (Lizenz Fretz u. Wasmuth, Zürich), 1972. 1981. [In Kassette: 1–5] 1978. 1981.
Also in Faulkner, William: *Werke, Briefe und Materialien in 29 Bänden in Kassette.* Vol. 22. Zürich: Diogenes (detebe), 1982. 9 stories. Contents: "Rotes Laub" (Red Leaves); "Eine Gerechtigkeit" (A Justice); "Eine Werbung" (A Courtship); "Und siehe da!" (Lo!); "Ad Astra" (Ad Astra); "Sieg" (Victory); "Crevasse" (Crevasse); "Der Reihe nach!" (Turnabout); "All die toten Flieger" (All the Dead Pilots).

1972 *Sieg im Gebirge.* Gesammelte Erzählungen IV. Trans. Elisabeth Schnack. Zürich: Diogenes (Lizenz Fretz u. Wasmuth, Zürich), 1972. 1981. [In Kassette: 1–5] 2978, 1981. Also in Faulkner, William: *Werke, Briefe und Materialien in 29 Bäden in Kassette.* Vol. 23. Zürich: Diogenes (detebe), 1982. 11 stories. Contents: "Wash" (Wash); "Ehre" (Honor); "Doktor Martino" (Dr. Martino); "Fuchsjagd" (Fox Hunt); "Pennsylvania Station" (Pennsylvania Station); "Der Künstler daheim" (Artist at Home); "Die Brosche" (The Brooch); "Meine Großmutter Millard" (My Grandmother Millard); "Goldenes Land" (Golden Land); "Es war eine Königin" (There Was a Queen); "Sieg im Gebirge" (Mountain Victory).

1972 *Schwarze Musik.* Gesammelte Erzählungen V. Trans. Elisabeth Schnack. Zürich: Diogenes (Lizenz Fretz u. Wasmuth, Zürich), 1972. 1981. [In Kassette: 1–5] 1978. 1981. Also in Faulkner, William *Werke, Briefe und Materialien in 29 Bänden in Kassette.* Vol. 24. Zürich:

Diogenes (detebe), 1982. 6 stories. Contents: "Jenseits" (Beyond); "Schwarze Musik" (Black Music); "Das Bein" (The Leg); "Mistral" (Mistral); "Scheidung in Neapel" (Divorce in Naples); "Carcassonne" (Carcassonne).

"A Rose for Emily"

1977 *Eine Rose für Emily.* Trans. Elisabeth Schnack. Die Diogenes-Mini-Bibliothek der Weltliteratur. Zürich: Diogenes (Lizenz Fretz u. Wasmuth, Zürich), 1977. 44 pp. 1 Illustration [name not given].

1958 *American Short Stories.** Vol. 4. The Twentieth Century I. In *Englische Lesebogen*, 125. Paderborn: Schöningh, 1958. 1981.

Selected Letters of William Faulkner

1980 *Briefe.* (Samnlung). Nach der von Joseph L. Blotner ed. amerik. Erstausgabe v. 1977, ed., trans. Elisabeth Schnack u. Fritz Senn. Deutsche Erstausgabe. Zürich: Diogenes, 1980. 1981. Also in Faulkner, William: *Werke, Briefe und Materialien in 29 Bänden in Kassette.* Vol. 28. Zürich: Diogenes (detebe), 1982.

Über William Faulkner

1973 Ed. Gerd Haffmans. Ausfsätze und Rezensionen von Malcolm Cowley bis Siegfried Lenz. Mit *Essays* und *Zeichnungen* und einem *Interview* mit William *Faulkner,* Chronik und Bibliographie. Zürich: Diogenes, 1973. [Italics mine.] Also in Faulkner, William: *Werke, Briefe und Materialien in 29 Bänden in Kassette.* Vol. 29. Zürich: Diogenes (detebe) 1982.

Essays by Faulkner: [1]"Vom Schreiben"; [2]"Nobelpreisrede"; [3]"Über Kritik"; [4]"Vorwort zu 'Schall und Wahn'"; [5]"Interview." Trans. [1]Elisabeth Schnack (1971); [2]Wulf Teichmann u. Walter Hertenstein (o.J.); [3]Walter Hertenstein (o.J.).; [4]Wulf Teichmann (o.J.) [5]Wilhelm Borgers u Günter Steinbrinker (o.J.)].

From 1935 until 1982 Faulkner's works, essays, speeches, letters, and interviews have been translated into German by about thirty different translators. It is almost impossible to give conclusive information about all the editions and reprints in the four German-speaking countries, especially with regard to the translations and publications of individual short stories as well as collections, because there are also anonymous translations in magazines. Included are only the entries I have been able to confirm.

The first (almost) complete paperback edition of Faulkner's works in German is: Faulkner, William; *Werke, Briefe und Materialien in 29 Bänden in Kassette.* Zürich: Diogenes (detebe), 1982.

The year 1981 mentioned at the end of single entries indicates that the respective edition can be obtained and is listed in *Verzeichnis Lieferbarer Bücher.* German Books in Print 1981/82, 1982/83, and 1983/84. Frankfurt am Main: Verlag der Buchhändler-Vereinigung GmbH.

*An asterisk indicates that the American original has been included in an edition of American stories that are read and taught at German schools. Such editions might also cast some light on the reception of Faulkner's works in Germany.

Sources of information consulted for this bibliography are:
Deutsches Bücherverzeichnis. Eine Zusammenstellung der im deutschen Buchhandel erschienenen Bücher, Zeitschriften und Landkarten. Bibliographische Abteilung des Börsenvereins der Deutschen Buchhändler zu Leipzig, 1926–1950.
Deutsche Bibliographie. Verzeichnis aller in Deutschland erschienenen Veröffentlichungen und der in Österreich und der Schweiz im Buchhandel erschienenen deutschsprachigen Publikationen sowie der deutschsprachigen Veröffentlichungen anderer Länder. Frankfurt am Main: Buchhändler-Vereinigung GmbH. Jahresbände und Halbjahresverzeichnisse, 1953–1982.

Edith Zindel, *William Faulkner in den deutschsprachigen Ländern Europas: Untersuchungen zur Aufnahme seiner Werke nach 1945.* Diss., Hamburg, 1972. Geistes- und Sozialwissenschaftliche Dissertationen 25. Verlag Hartmut Lüdke. 552 pp. This dissertation provides the reader with detailed information about the translations and the reception of Faulkner's works in German-speaking countries up to about 1967.

For a more detailed description of the complex translation process Eberhard Boecker is recommended: *William Faulkner's Later Novels in German: A Study in the Theory and Practice of Translation.* Linguistische Arbeiten 10. Tübingen: Max Niemeyer Verlag, 1973. 236 pp.

E.
A Chronology of Faulkner Translations Into Russian

M. THOMAS INGE

The following chronology is based on information derived from Glenora W. Brown and Deming B. Brown, *A Guide to Soviet Russian Translations of American Literature* (New York: King's Crown Press, Columbia University, 1954), 39–40, 77; Deming Brown, "American Best-Sellers in Soviet Bookstores," *The Reporter*, 15 (November 29, 1956), 36–38; Max Frankel, "The Worldwide Influence of William Faulkner: Moscow," *New York Times Book Review* (November 15, 1959), 52–53; Deming Brown, *Soviet Attitudes Toward American Writing* (Princeton: Princeton University Press, 1962), passim; Carl R. Proffer, ed., *Soviet Criticism of American Literature in the Sixties: An Anthology* (Ann Arbor: Ardis Publishers, 1972), xxviii–xxxi; V. A. Libman, *Amerikanskaia literatura v russkikh perevodakh i kritike: Bibliografiia 1776–1975* (Moscow: Nauka, 1977), 277–81; and four unpublished research reports prepared by Maurice Friedburg for the Office of Research, U. S. Information Agency, Washington, D.C.: "American Literature Through the Filter of Recent Soviet Publishing and Criticism," January 22, 1976, Research Report R–3–76; "Soviet Translations and Translators of American Literature," February 10, 1978, R–4–78; "American Literature Through the Filter of Soviet Translation," December 22, 1978, R–34–78; and "Recent Soviet Criticism of American Literature," August 15, 1979, R–19–79. Irene Guseva of Moscow also provided helpful information. Libman should be consulted for full bibliographic information through 1975.

Faulkner Translations into Russian 337

1934 "That Evening Sun"
1935 "Artist at Home"
1936 "Victory"
1957 "Smoke"
1958 *Seven Stories* (includes "Barn Burning," "Red Leaves," "A Justice," "That Evening Sun," "Smoke," "Percy Grimm," and "Victory")
1959 *Barn Burning* (stories; includes "Barn Burning,", "A Justice," "Percy Grimm," "That Evening Sun," "Yo Ho and Two Bottles of Rum," and "Sunset")
1960 "By the People," "Turnabout"
1961 *The Mansion*, "A Bear Hunt"
1962 "The Bear," "Delta Autumn"
1963 "Dry September," "The Liar"
1964 *The Hamlet*
1965 *The Town*, selections from *Faulkner at Nagano* and the *Paris Review* interviews
1966 *Soldiers' Pay*, "Hand Upon the Waters," "Race at Morning," "Pantaloon in Black," "The Old People," selections from *The Faulkner-Cowley File* letters
1967 "An Error in Chemistry," "The Rosary," "Landing in Luck," "Wash"
1968 *Intruder in the Dust*, selections from the *Lion in the Garden* interviews
1969 "Go Down, Moses," "A Rose for Emily," selections from the *Faulkner in the University* interviews
1970 *Requiem for a Nun*
1971 "Mr. Acarius"
1972 *The Reivers*, "Two Soldiers"
1973 *The Sound and the Fury*, *Sartoris* (in one volume with "The Bear" and *Intruder in the Dust* under the general title "Masters of Contemporary U. S. Prose"), "The Tall Men," "Golden Land," "A Courtship"
1974 *Light in August*, "Monk," "Tomorrow," "On Privacy, The American Dream: What Happened to It?" "Upon Receiving the Nobel Prize for Literature"
1975 *Stories* (includes "Shingles for the Lord," "Fox Hunt," "Uncle Willy," and "Honor"), "An Odor of Verbena"
1976 *The Unvanquished*, "Was"
1977 "Hair," "On Literature" (addresses, articles, reviews)
1978 *As I Lay Dying, Collected Stories* (follows the exact order of the 1950 American edition bringing together earlier published translations along with the first translations of "Shall Not Perish," "A Centaur in Brass," "Death Drag," "Elly," "Mule in the Yard," "That Will Be Fine," "Lo!" "Ad Astra," "Crevasse," "All the Dead Pilots," "Dr. Martino," "Pennsylvania Station," "The Brooch," "My Grandmother Millard and General Bedford Forrest and the Battle of Harrykin Creek," "There Was a Queen," "Mountain Victory," "Beyond," "Black Music," "The Leg," "Mistral," "Divorce in Naples," and "Carcassonne")
1979 "The Fire and the Hearth"
1980 *Absalom, Absalom!*
1981 *Sanctuary*
1982 "Old Man"

APPENDIX F

Although no titles or publication data are supplied, a checklist of American authors translated into the various languages of the Soviet Union found in *20th Century American Literature: A Soviet View* (Moscow: Progress Publishers, 1976), 503–11, indicates that between 1960 and 1974, at least 15 works by Faulkner were translated into Russian, 7 into Ukrainian, 7 into Lithuanian, 5 into Georgian, 4 into Estonian, 3 into Latvian, 1 into Armenian, and 1 into Byellorussian.

F.
A Checklist of Faulkner Translations into Chinese
H. R. STONEBACK

1958	(Beijing)	"Victory" and "Death Drag" in *I Wen*
1959	(Taipei)	Selected Stories ("A Rose for Emily," "That Evening Sun," "Two Soldiers," "Red Leaves," "Wash," "Spotted Horses," "Mountain Victory")
1960	(Taipei)	*Wild Palms*
1969	(Taipei)	"The Bear"
1982	(Beijing)	*The Sound and the Fury*, trans. Li Wenjun
1982	(Beijing)	"A Rose for Emily," "The Bear," and "Wash" in *Shijie Wenxue*
1982	(Beijing)	"Spotted Horses" in *Foreign Literature*
1983*	(Beijing)	*Selected Stories of William Faulkner*, separate volume in World Literature series of the Institute of Foreign Literature. Part I includes "A Justice," "Red Leaves," "My Grandmother Millard," "A Rose for Emily," "Spotted Horses," "Barn Burning," "Shingles for the Lord," "Pantaloon in Black," "Ad Astra," "All the Dead Pilots," "A Bear Hunt," "Wash," and "Carcassone." Part II of the volume includes "The Bear" and "Old Man."

*Announced for publication

Addendum: Since this essay was prepared, many new Faulkner projects have come to my attention. In addition to the works cited here, the following works are in process of translation and publication: *Absalom, Absalom!*, *Light in August*, *The Snopes Trilogy*, *The Unvanquished*, "The Bear" (several translations), "Dry September," "Mule in the Yard," and "Centaur in Brass." The returns are still incomplete, and since with each passing month a new work is translated or published, they will remain so until the day—perhaps not far distant—when all of Faulkner's work is available in Chinese. I am told that even John Faulkner's *My Brother Bill* is being translated. As Li Wenjun, senior editor of *Shijie Wenxue*, recently remarked, "It is evident that the 'Faulkner Industry' here is as flourishing as in other parts of the work."

G.
Faulkner in Japanese
KENZABURO OHASHI

Soldiers' Pay (1926)

Heishi no Kyuyo. Trans. Saburo Yamaya. Tokyo: Hayakawa Shobo, 1952. Repr. Tokyo: Kadokawa Shoten, 1957.
Heishi no Moratta Hoshu. Trans. Ichiro Nishizaki. Tokyo: Jiji Tsushinsha, 1956.
Heishi no Hoshu. Trans. Hiroshi Hayakawa. Tokyo: Shufu no Tomo Sha, 1971.
Heishi no Hoshu. Trans. Shozo Kajima. Tokyo: Shinchosha, 1971.
**Heishi no Hoshu.* Trans. Kyoichi Harakawa. Tokyo: Fuzambo, 1978.

Sartoris (1929)

Satorisu. Trans. Nobuyuki Hayashi. Tokyo: Hakusuisha, 1965.
**Satorisu.* Trans. Tadatoshi Saito. Tokyo: Fuzambo, 1978.

The Sound and the Fury (1929)

Hibiki to Ikari. Trans. Masao Takahashi. Tokyo: Mikasa Shobo, 1954. Repr, Tokyo: Kodansha, 1972, 1975.
**Hibiki to Ikari.* Trans. Masaji Onoe. Tokyo: Fuzambo, 1970.
Hibiki to Ikari. Trans. Kenzaburo Ohashi. Tokyo: Shinchosha, 1971.

As I Lay Dying (1930)

Shi no Toko ni Yokotawaru Toki. Trans. Saburo Onuki. Tokyo: Kadokawa Shoten, 1959.
Shi no Toko ni Yokotawarite. Trans. Shoichi Saeki. Tokyo: Chikuma Shobo, 1959. Repr. Tokyo: Kodansha, 1975.
**Shi no Toko ni Yokotawarite.* Trans. Katsuzo Sakata. Tokyo: Fuzambo, 1974.

Sanctuary (1931)

Sankuchuari. Trans. Naotaro Tatsunokuchi and Masami Nishikawa. Tokyo: Getsuyo Shobo, 1950. Repr. Tokyo: Shinchosha, 1954.
Sankuchuari. Trans. Kenzaburo Ohashi. Tokyo: Kadokawa Shoten, 1962.
Sankuchuari. Trans. Masami Nishikawa. Tokyo: Chuokoronsha, 1967.
Sankuchuari. Trans. Shozo Kajima. Tokyo: Shinchosha, 1971.

These 13 (1931)

**Korera Jusanpen.* Trans. Nobuyuki Hayashi. Tokyo: Fuzambo, 1968.

Light in August (1932)

Hachigatsu no Hikari. Trans. Masao Takahashi. Tokyo: Kawade Shobo Shinsha, 1961.
Hachigatsu no Hikari. Trans. Shozo Kajima. Tokyo: Shinchosha, 1964.
**Hachigatsu no Hikari.* Trans. Shizuo Suyama. Tokyo: Fuzambo, 1967.
Hachigatsu no Hikari. Trans. Masami Nishikawa. Tokyo: Chuokoronsha, 1973.

Doctor Martino and Other Stories (1934)

*Ishi Matino, hoka. Trans. Moto'o Takigawa. Tokyo: Fuzambo, 1971.

Pylon (1935)

Sora no Yuwaku. Trans. Kenzaburo Ohashi. Tokyo: Daviddosha, 1954. Repr. as Pairon. Tokyo: Chikuma Shobo, 1959.
*Hyoshikito. Trans. Shoji Goto. Tokyo: Fuzambo, 1971.

Absalom, Absalom! (1936)

Abusaromu, Abusaromu! Trans. Junzaburo Nishiwaki and Kichinosuke Ohashi. Tokyo: Arechi Shuppansha, 1957. *Repr. Trans. Kichinosuke Ohashi. 1965. Tokyo: Fuzambo, 1968. Tokyo: Chikuma Shobo, 1974.
Abusaromu, Abusaromu! Trans. Hajime Shinoda. Tokyo: Shueisha, 1966, 1979.

The Unvanquished (1938)

Seifuku Sarezaru Hitobito. Trans. Masami Nishikawa. Tokyo: Chuokoronsha, 1967.
Seifuku Sarezaru Hitobito. Trans. Tetsuji Akasofu. Tokyo: Obunsha, 1974.
*Seifuku Sarezaru Hitobito. Trans. Hikaru Saito. Tokyo: Fuzambo, 1975.

The Wild Palms (1939)

Yasei no Jonetsu. Trans. Yasuo Okubo. Tokyo: Hibiya Shuppansha, 1950. Tokyo: Mikasa Shobo, 1951. As Yasei no Shuro. Tokyo: Shinchosha, 1954. Tokyo: Kawade Shobo, 1956.
*Yasei no Shuro. Trans. Kenji Inoue. Tokyo: Fuzambo, 1968.
Yasei no Shuro. Trans. Shozo Kajima. Tokyo: Gakushu Kenkyusha, 1978.
*The Hamlet (1940)
Mura. Trans. Hisao Tanaka. Tokyo: Fuzambo, 1983.

Go Down, Moses (1942)

*Yuke, Moze. Trans. Kenzaburo Ohashi. Tokyo: Fuzambo, 1973.

Intruder in the Dust (1948)

Hakaba eno Chinnyusha. Trans. Shozo Kajima. Tokyo: Hayakawa Shobo, 1951.
*Bochi eno Shinnyusha. Trans. Kenzo Suzuki. Tokyo: Fuzambo, 1968.

Knight's Gambit (1949)

Kishi no Kansei. Trans. Yasuo Okubo. Tokyo: Yukeisha, 1951. Repr. Tokyo: Shin'eisha, 1957.
*Komasabaki. Trans. Sho Yamamoto. Tokyo: Fuzambo, 1978.

Requiem for a Nun (1951)

*Niso eno Chingonka. Trans. Katsuzo Sakata. Tokyo: Fuzambo, 1967.

A Fable (1954)

Guwa. Trans. Tomoji Abe. Tokyo: Iwanami Shoten, 1960, 1961, 1974.

The Town (1957)

*Machi. Trans. Hiroshi Hayakawa. Tokyo: Fuzambo, 1969.

The Mansion (1959)

Yakata. Trans. Masao Takahashi. Tokyo: Fuzambo, 1967.
The Reivers (1962)
Jidosha Dorobo—Hitotsu no Omoide. Trans. Masao Takahashi. Tokyo: Kodansha, 1963. *Repr. Tokyo: Fuzambo, 1975.

Poems, Short Stories, etc.

Fokuna Sho (Selected Poems of Faulkner). Bungaku (a literary magazine), June 1933. "The Race's Splendor," "Over the World's Rim," "Gray the Day," and "Night Piece."
"Emiri no Bara." Trans. Naotaro Tatsunokuchi. *Bungaku* (a literary magazine), September 1932.
Emiri no Bara. Trans. Naotaro Tatsunokuchi. Tokyo: Kosumoporitansha, 1952. "A Rose for Emily," "That Evening Sun," "Dry September," "An Odor of Verbena," "Delta Autumn," "Barn Burning," "Turnabout," and "The Hound."
Fokuna Tanpenshu (Selected Stories of Faulkner). Trans. Naotaro Tatsunokuchi. Tokyo: Shinchosha, 1955. "Jealousy," "A Rose for Emily," "Dry September," "That Evening Sun," "Barn Burning," and "Wash."
Emiri no Bara, hoka 4 pen (A Rose for Emily, and Other 4 Stories). Trans. Naotaro Tatsunokuchi. Tokyo: Kadokawa Shoten, 1955. "A Rose for Emily," "Delta Autumn," "The Hound," "An Odor of Verbena," and "Turnabout."
Emiri no Bara: Ryoken. Trans. Masao Takahashi and Kichinosuke Ohashi. Tokyo: Eihosha, 1956. "A Rose for Emily," "Crevasse," "The Hound," "Pantaloon in Black," and "Eula."
Fokuna (Faulkner). Trans. Kenzaburo Ohashi and Naotaro Tatsunokuchi. Tokyo: Arechi Shuppansha, 1958. "The Bear" (trans. Ohashi), "A Rose for Emily" and "That Evening Sun" (trans. Tatsunokuchi), together with *Absalom, Absalom!* trans. Kichinosuke Ohashi and Junzaburo Nishiwaki.
Fokuna. Trans. Minoru Fukuda. Tokyo: Nan'undo, 1964. "Shall Not Perish," "A Rose for Emily," "That Evening Sun," "Crevasse," "Episode" and "Jealousy." (Together with Caldwell's 8 stories.)
Fokuna. Trans. Masao Takahashi. Tokyo: Shueisha, 1966. "Red Leaves," "A Justice," "That Evening Sun," "A Rose for Emily," "Wash," "There Was a Queen," "Was," and "Delta Autumn."
Maho no Ki (The Wishing Tree). Trans. Hajime Kijima. Tokyo: Fuzambo, 1967.
Fokuna. Trans. Naotaro Tatsunokuchi. Tokyo: Shinchosha, 1971. "A Rose for Emily" and "That Evening Sun." (Together with *Soldiers' Pay* and *Sanctuary,* trans. Shozo Kajima, and *The Sound and the Fury,* trans. Kenzaboro Ohashi.)
Korotachi, Kuma, hoka 4 pen (The Old People, The Bear, and Other 4 Stories). Trans. Tetsuji Akasofu. Tokyo: Obunsha, 1973. "The Old People," "The Bear," "Delta Autumn," "That Evening Sun," "A Rose for Emily," and "To the Graduating Class, University High School, 1951."
Fokuna. Trans. Kenzaburo Ohashi and Masami Nishikawa. Tokyo: Chikuma Shobo, 1974. "The Bear" and "Delta Autumn." (Together with *As I Lay Dying,* trans. Shoichi Saeki, and *Absalom, Absalom!,* trans. Kichinosuke Ohashi.)

APPENDIX G

Fokuna. Trans. Msao Takahashi. Tokyo: Kodansha, 1975. "That Evening Sun" and "A Rose for Emily." (Together with *The Sound and the Fury,* trans. Takahashi, and *As I Lay Dying,* trans. Shoichi Saeki.)

Kirisutokyo Bungaku no Sekai (The World of Christian Literature). Trans. Atsuhide Iijima. Tokyo: Shufu no Tomo Sha, 1977. "A Rose for Emily," "Dry September," "That Evening Sun," "Hair," and "The Brooch." (Together with Steinbeck's and Saroyan's stories.)

Fokuna. Trans. Naotaro Tatsunokuchi. Tokyo: Gakushu Kenkyusha, 1978. "A Rose for Emily," "Red Leaves," "Dry September," "That Evening Sun," "The Hound," "Turnabout," and "An Odor of Verbena."

Fokuna. Trans. Masami Nishikawa. Tokyo: Shueisha, 1979. "A Rose for Emily" and "Hair." (Together with *Absalom, Absalom!,* trans. Hajime Shinoda.)

**Tanpenshu I (Short Stories I).* Trans. Masao Shimura. Tokyo: Fuzambo, 1981. "Centaur in Brass," "Artist at Home," "Pennsylvania Station," "A Bear Hunt," "Mule in the Yard," "Lo!" "Golden Land," "That Will Be Fine," "Uncle Willy," "The Brooch," "Barn Burning," "The Tall Men," "Two Soldiers," "Shall Not Perish," "Shingles for the Lord," "My Grandmother Millard and General Bedford Forrest and the Battle of Harrykin Creek," and "A Courtship."

"Nippon no Insho" ("Impressions of Japan"). Trans. Naotaro Tatsunokuchi. *Mainichi Shinbun,* Aug. 20, 1955.

"Mishishippi" ("Mississippi"). Trans. Masami Nishikawa. Tokyo: Chikuma Shobo, 1959. (Together with *As I Lay Dying,* trans. Shoichi Saeki, and *Pylon,* trans. Kenzaburo Ohashi.)

"Watashi wa Ningen no Shuen o Ukeire Masen" ("Upon Receiving the Nobel Prize for Literature, 1950"). *Ondori Tsushin,* 7, iv (1951). The speech is also trans. Kyoichi Harakawa in *Wiriamu Fokuna (William Faulkner),* Tokyo: Hayakawa Shobo, 1973.

*Denotes a volume in *Collected Works of William Faulkner* (Tokyo: Fuzambo), 1967–

Contributors

Joseph Blotner has lectured extensively in the United States and Europe on American literature and particularly on the work of William Faulkner. Among his books are *Faulkner in the University*, edited with F. L. Gwynn; *William Faulkner's Library: A Catalogue; Faulkner: A Biography; Selected Letters of William Faulkner;* and *Uncollected Stories of William Faulkner.* He is Professor of English at the University of Michigan.

Louis Daniel Brodsky has published poetry in *Harper's, Texas Quarterly, Southern Review, American Scholar,* and other journals. His twelfth book of poems, *Mississippi Vistas,* and *Faulkner: A Comprehensive Guide to the Brodsky Collection, Volume I: The Biobibliography,* and *Volume II: The Letters,* with Robert W. Hamblin, were recently published by the University Press of Mississippi.

Monika Brückner compiled a bibliography of German translations of Faulkner for this volume. Her task involved collecting information from four German-speaking countries and was complicated by the loss of material at publishing houses during World War II. She teaches in Cologne.

Calvin S. Brown is Alumni Foundation Distinguished Professor of English and Comparative Literature Emeritus at the University of Georgia. His books include *Music and Literature, Repetition in Zola's Novels, Tones into Words,* and, most recently, *A Glossary of Faulkner's South.* Born in Oxford, Mississippi, he knew William Faulkner and his family intimately.

Sergei Chakovsky, a research fellow at the A. M. Gorky Institute of World Literature in Moscow, specializes in Faulkner studies as well as literary theory and the depiction of blacks in American literature. In addition to lecturing at the conference, he participated in planning meetings for a joint USA-USSR project on William Faulkner.

Myriam Díaz-Diocaretz is a Chilean poet, critic, and translator. She has participated in numerous international meetings on literature and translation theory and published extensively on American writers. Among her essays on Faulkner are "'The Waste Land' and *The Sound* *and the Fury:* Two Concurrent Interpretations of Contemporary Society." Her translations and her poems have appeared in the United States, Mexico, Uruguay, Dominican Republic, Spain, and Denmark. Her recent publications include *Que no se pueden decir,* a volume of poetry, and a Spanish edition of Adrienne Rich's works.

Jorge Edwards, a native of Santiago, Chile, entered the diplomatic service in 1957 and represented his country in Paris, Lima, and Havana. Since 1973 he has dedicated himself entirely to writing. *Persona non grata,* a non-fiction book about his experience as a Chilean diplomat and writer in Castro's Cuba, has been widely read and discussed in all the Spanish-speaking countries and published in French, Italian, and English. His recent works include two novels, *Los convidados de piedra* and *El museo de cera,* and a book of essays, *Desde la cola del dragón.*

Mick Gidley is Senior Lecturer in American Literature and Chairman of American and Commonwealth Arts at the University of Exeter, England. He has published on a variety of topics in American cultural and literary history, including *Kopet: A Documentary Narrative of Chief Joseph's Last Years.* His Faulkner work, mostly devoted to Faulkner's extra-literary reading, has appeared in *The Mississippi Quarterly, Journal of American Studies, Ariel, Studies in American Fiction,* and other journals.

Michel Gresset edited the first volume of the Faulkner Pléiade edition; coedited, with Patrick Samway, S. J., *Faulkner and Idealism: Perspectives from Paris;* and translated *Selected Letters of William Faulkner* and *Uncollected Stories of William Faulkner.* His criticism includes "Home and Homelessness in Faulkner's Works and Life" and *Faulkner ou la Fascination.* He is Professor of American Literature at the University of Paris VII.

Lothar Hönnighausen is Professor and Chairman of English and American Literature at the University of Bonn. Among his books are *Der Stilwandel im dramatischen Werk Sir William Davenants, Präraphaeliten und Fin de Siècle,* and *Grundprobleme der englischen Literaturtheorie des 19. Jahrhunderts.* In addition to articles on Blake, Wordsworth, Swinburne, Dobson, Dawson, and James, he has published "'Point of View' and Its Background in Intellectual History," "Zum literaturwissenschaftlichen Problem einer amerikanischen Mythologie im 19. Jahrhundert," and "Konservative Kulturkritik: Yeats and Eliot."

M. Thomas Inge, Professor and Head of the Department of English at Clemson University, has served as Fulbright Lecturer in Spain, Argentina, and the Soviet Union. He is editor or author of over two dozen books on American literature, including *Essays on "Light in August"* and a critical casebook on Faulkner's "A Rose for Emily." His several published essays on Faulkner include a lengthy entry for the American humorists volume in the *Dictionary of Literary Biography*.

Agostino Lombardo is Professor of English at the University of Rome, where he is also in charge of the course in American literature and is Director of the Institute of English and American Literature. His works on American literature include three collections of essays—*Realismo e simbolismo, La Ricerca del Vero*, and *Il Diavolo nel Manoscritto*—and a book on Hawthorne's stories, *Un Rapporto col Mondo*. In addition to translating and editing works by several English and American authors, he has edited the yearly journal *Studi Americani* since 1955 and the yearly journal *Studi Inglesi* since 1974.

Kenzaburo Ohashi has published *Faulkner: A Study* in three volumes, other books on American literature, and Japanese translations of *The Sound and the Fury, Sanctuary, Pylon*, and *Go Down, Moses*. He coedits *William Faulkner: Materials, Studies, and Criticism*, a biannual journal published at Tokyo, Japan. Professor of American Literature at Tsurumi University in Yokohama, Japan, he is a former president of the American Literature Society of Japan and serves on the board of directors of the Japanese Association for American Studies.

H. R. Stoneback has lectured on Faulkner in France, China, and Thailand. He served as advisor to the team of Chinese translators for *Selected Stories of William Faulkner*, recently published in China. He also edited the volume and wrote an introduction and an appendix for it. He is Professor of English at the State University of New York, New Paltz, where he is also Curator of the Hudson Valley Regional Archive and Associate Director of the Carl Carmer Center for Catskill Mountain and Hudson River Studies.

Alexandre Vashchenko, a research fellow at the Gorky Institute of World Literature in Moscow, has published works examining the literature of the American West and the mythology of North American Indians. He and Sergei Chakovsky participated in the 1982 Faulkner and Yoknapatawpha Conference as part of a project sponsored by the American Council of Learned Societies-USSR Academy of Sciences Commission on the Humanities and Social Sciences.

Index

Absalom, Absalom! (Faulkner), 13, 26, 76, 128, 133, 213, 226, 227–28, 261, 262, 280
Achievement of William Faulkner, The (Millgate), 81
"Ad Astra," (Faulkner), 102, 103, 240
"Adolescence," (Faulkner), 13
Algeria, response to Faulkner, 312
"All the Dead Pilots," (Faulkner), 102, 103, 240
American Literature of the Twentieth Century (Zasursky), 219
American studies, in England, 80–81
Anastasiev, N., 228–31
Argentina: *The Sound and the Fury,* 41; *The Wild Palms,* 35
Armenians, Faulkner translations, 203
"Artist at Home,The"(Faulkner), 176, 196
Art nouveau, See Graphic art.
Arts and Crafts Movement, See Graphic art.
As I Lay Dying (Faulkner), 16–17, 39, 63, 181, 182, 202, 260, 261, 305
Auction: books, 276–97; Hollywood contracts, 285–91

"Barn Burning," (Faulkner), 196, 240
"Battle Cry," (Faulkner), 108
Beardsley, Aubrey, 144, 148, 150, 158, 162, 163, 171
"Bear Hunt, A," (Faulkner), 240
"Bear, The," (Faulkner), 133, 179, 197, 198, 202, 239, 240
Benbow, Horace, 10, 11, 22
Benet, Juan, 38
Benveniste, Emile, 32
Bible, importance to Faulkner, 15–16
Bingyi, Chen, 239
Binkui, Li, 252
"Black Music," (Faulkner), 302

Black speech, in Spanish translation, 41, 43–45
Blotner, Joseph, 6, 82, 94, 99, 108
Borges, Jorge Luis, 32, 35, 38, 63
Brothers Karamazov, The (Dostoevsky), influence on Faulkner, 183–84

Calvino, Italo, 125
Calvo, Lino Novás, 35, 37, 63
Cambon, Glauco, 133
Camerino, Aldo, 128
Cape, Jonathan, 83
"Carcassonne," (Faulkner), 107, 240, 241, 302–3
Cecchi, Emilio, 122–23
Chaulnesmont, 114–16
Chile, impact of Faulkner, 68–72
China: influence of Faulkner on writers, 250–52; interest in Faulkner, 238–39; response to Faulkner, 247–50; study of Faulkner, 253; writings on Faulkner, 249–50
Chinese language: *As I Lay Dying,* 240; "The Bear," 238–39, 240; *Go Down, Moses,* 240; *Light in August,* 240; "A Rose for Emily," 237, 239, 240; *Selected Stories of William Faulkner,* 238, 240; "Shall Not Perish," 240, 241, 242–43; "Shingles for the Lord," 240, 243–44; "Spotted Horses," 240, 244; *The Sound and the Fury,* 239; "The Tall Men," 240, 241–42; translation problems, 244–45; "Victory," 238; "Wash," 239–40; *The Wild Palms,* 238, 239
Chinese Literature, 252–53
Chiuminato, Tony, 129
Christmas, Joe, 13, 26
Coindreau, Maurice E., 36, 37, 38
Collected Stories (Faulkner): Russian edi-

347

348 INDEX

tion, 198, 213; stories included in, 102–03
Collins, Carvel, 82
"Compson Appendix," 101
Compson, Quentin, 11, 22, 25, 49–50, 53–55, 185
Congwen, Shen, 251
Contemporary American Novel, The (Mendelson), 215
Cowley, Malcolm, 78, 276, 277, 281–85
"Crevasse," (Faulkner), 102, 104–07
Crime and Punishment (Dostoevsky), similarity to Faulkner, 182, 183, 184–85
Cultural scuttlebut, 8

D'Agostino, Nemi, 133
Dawn, an Orchid, a Song (Faulkner), 140
Dawson, Eric, 6–7
"De Gaulle Story,"(Faulkner), 107–08, 113
"Delta Autumn," (Faulkner), 19, 109
Dialect: black speech, 41, 43–45; literature and, 88–89
Dickmann, Max, 37
Dilsey, 41, 43–45, 249
"Divorce in Naples," (Faulkner), 22, 302
Dostoevsky, Feodor, 182; influence on Faulkner, 183–85, 226
Drake, Temple, 19
"Dr. Martino," (Faulkner), 26
Dr. Martino and Other Stories (Faulkner), 281
"Dry September," (Faulkner), 197, 262

Elmer (Faulkner), unfinished novel, 302
England: American studies in, 80–81; censorship of Faulkner, 82; Faulkner studies in, 81–85; reaction to experimentation, 86–87; response to Faulkner, 74–80; review of Faulkner's works, 74–76
English language: in England and America, 88–89; in Ireland, 89
Estonians, Faulkner translations, 202
Europe, Faulkner's view of, 102, 110–11

Fable, A, (Faulkner), 9, 18, 39, 88, 99, 111–18, 238, 308
Faulkner (Gribanov), 231–33
Faulkner: An Essay on His Creative Work (Anastasiev), 228–31
Faulkner, John, 299
"Faulkner's Road to Realism" (Palievsky), 216, 250
Faulkner's Theme of Nature (Yoshizaki), 312
Faulkner Studies, 79

Faulkner, William: artistic influences, 139, 144, 150; influence of literature on, 5–27; as a public figure, 122, 232; technical achievements of, 306–07; travels of, 302–03; writers/poets of importance to, 21–22
Fenoglio, Beppe, 133
Fish, Flesh, Fowl, Faulkner sketch, 145
Flags in the Dust (Faulkner), 10, 11, 12, 13, 22
Foreign Literature, Russian journal, 178, 212
France: *A Fable,* 111–18; Faulkner's response to, 97–99; in Faulkner's work, 100–115
French language: *As I Lay Dying,* 260; "Dry September," 260; *Pylon,* 36; "A Rose for Emily," 260; *Sanctuary,* 260; *Sartoris,* 261; *The Sound and the Fury,* 261; *The Unvanquished,* 36
French literature, Faulkner and, 23
Fukunaga, Takehiko, 258–59, 260–61, 263, 272
Fusini, Nadia, 133

Garnett, Edward, 83
Georgians, Faulkner translations, 203
Giannitrapani, Angela, 134
Girl of the Limberlost, A, 27
Go Down, Moses (Faulkner), 24, 39, 212
Go Down, Moses and Other Stories (Faulkner), 280, 281, 296
Graphic art, 139–72; art nouveau influences, 139, 140, 144, 146, 148, 150, 151, 158, 160, 162, 165, 168; Arts and Crafts Movement, 144, 153–55; *Dramatis Personae (The Marionettes),* 144, 151, 153, 158, 162–63; handwritten books, 140, 155–56; *The Marionettes,* 139, 140, 144; *Ole Miss,* 140, 144, 145, 146, 148, 150–51, 153, 156, 163, 165, 168, 172
Gray, Alec, 176
Greece, Faulkner's response to, 118–19
Green Bough, A (Faulkner): Poem XXI, 18; Poem XXXII, 12; Poem XXXIV, 12
Gribanov, B., 228, 231–33
Grimm, Percy, 13, 210
Guo, Luo Jing, 240

Hamlet, The (Faulkner), 9, 12, 18, 22, 39, 75–76, 92, 125, 129–30, 178, 179, 203, 212, 307
Haruyama, Yukiooo, 259, 260, 272
Helen: A Courtship (Faulkner), 12, 140

INDEX

Hill, The (Faulkner), 104, 105, 110
Hollywood, 107–08; documents from, 285–91

Images, Spanish translation, 46–48
Inoue, Mitshuharu, 264–65, 272
International Bibliography, Faulkner listings, 300, 308
Intonation, Spanish translation, 54–56
Intruder in the Dust (Faulkner), 113, 179, 189, 198, 202, 212, 261, 281
Ireland, response to Faulkner, 309
Iskander, Fazil, 188–90
Italian language: *Absalom, Absalom!*, 133; *The Hamlet*, 125, 129–30; *Intruder in the Dust*, 132; *Light in August*, 125, 131; *Pylon*, 121; *The Sound and the Fury*, 132
Italy: criticism of Faulkner, 129; Faulkner's reaction to, 310; impact of Faulkner, 126–28, 130–31, 132, 134; response to Faulkner, 121–22, 123, 129; view of America, 123–25; works on Faulkner, 133–34

Jackson, Al, 27
Japanese language: *Absalom, Absalom!*, 261; *As I Lay Dying*, 261; *The Complete Works of William Faulkner*, 272, 310; "Dry September," 262; *Intruder in the Dust*, 261; *Knight's Gambit*, 261; *Pylon*, 261; "Red Leaves," 262; "A Rose for Emily," 260; *Sanctuary*, 261; *Soldiers' Pay*, 261; *The Sound and the Fury*, 261; "That Evening Sun," 262; *The Wild Palms*, 261
Japan, influence of Faulkner on writers, 258, 260–73
Jie, Tao, 239, 240
Jones, Januarius, 13
Jones, Wash, 227
"Justice, A," (Faulkner), 196, 240

Kashkin, Ivan, 196
Khayyam, Omar, 12–13, 15
"Kid Learns, The," (Faulkner), 18
Knight's Gambit (Faulkner), 26, 261

Latin America: fiction in, 62; response to Faulkner, 309–10
Latvians, Faulkner translations, 202
Lavalle, F. E., 41
"Leg, The," (Faulkner), 27, 302
Library of World Literature, The, Russian edition, 198
Light in August (Faulkner), 13, 26, 74–75, 105, 125, 131, 180, 198, 202, 210, 212, 226, 278
Lilacs, The (Faulkner), 140
Literature, influence on Faulkner, 5–27
"Literature in the Deep," (Zuerev), 222
Lithuanians, Faulkner translations, 202
"Lizards in Jamshyd's Courtyard," (Faulkner), 12–13

Magny, Claude-Edmonde, 261
Mallison, Chick, 15
Mansion, The (Faulkner), 9, 12, 14–15, 179, 198, 200, 212, 307
Marble Faun, The, (Faulkner), 277, 278, 296, 301, 302
Marionettes, The (Faulkner), 3–4, 7, 139, 140, 144, 148, 151, 153, 156, 158, 162–63, 171
Márquez, Gabriel García, 301
Masters of Contemporary Prose, Russian edition, 198
Materassi, Mario, 122, 134
Mayday (Faulkner), 18, 140, 154
Mazía, Floreal, 41
McCaslin, Ike, 187
Mediaeval references, in Faulkner's work, 18–20
Mendelson, M. O., 215–16
Millard, Rosa, 190
Millgate, Michael, 81, 82
Mississippian, The, 144–45
"Mississippi," (Faulkner), 109
"Mistral," (Faulkner), 302
Model situations, 210
Modernism, of Faulkner, 87–88, 219, 304–05
Montale, Eugenio, 126
Morra, Umberto, 128
Mosquitoes (Faulkner), 16, 27, 39, 89–90, 196
Motyleva, Tamara, 221–22
"My Grandmother Millard," (Faulkner), 240
Mythology, 17–18

Narrative technique: duplicity of, 131; poetical elements in, 64; Spanish translation, 51–54
Nekagami, Kenji, 264, 270–71, 272
Nishikawa, Masami, 262
Nobel Prize, 98, 121, 309; Faulkner's speech, 110, 174, 242, 245
Nocturne, 144, 156, 158
Novel Abroad, The (Motyleva), 221
"Nympholepsy," (Faulkner), 10

349

Oe, Kenzaburo, 266–68, 272
Ogawa, Kunio, 268–70, 272
Ohashi, Kichinosuke, 262
Okubo, Yasuo, 262
Old Ben, 187
Old Colonel, Faulkner's grandfather, 6
"Old Man," (Faulkner), 240
"Old People," (Faulkner), 133
Ole Miss, 140, 144, 145, 146, 148, 150–51, 153, 156, 163, 165, 168, 172
"Omar's Eighteenth Quatrain," (Faulkner), 12

Palievsky, P. V., 216–19, 248, 250
"Pantaloon in Black," (Faulkner), 240
Paragraphing, Spanish translation, 54–56
Pavese, Cesare, 124, 125, 129–30, 133
Pivano, Fernanda, 121
Popeye, 77, 83, 187
Portable Faulkner, The, 102, 277, 278, 279, 283–284
Praz, Mario, 121, 123, 124, 125, 128
Provincialism, in art, 90–91
Public figure, Faulkner as, 122, 232
Pylon (Faulkner), 19, 36, 121, 261, 280–81

Raimbault, R. N., 36
Ratliff, V. K., 191, 248
Rato, Mariano Antolín, 40, 41, 52, 56
Red and Blue III, Faulkner sketch, 168
"Red Leaves," (Faulkner), 240, 262
Regionalism, British reaction to, 92
Reivers, The (Faulkner), 19, 180, 213, 315
Renaissance literature, 21
Requiem for a Nun (Faulkner), 39, 110, 113, 180, 213, 307
Romanova, Yelena, 238, 248
Ros, Amando Lázaro, 36, 41
Rosati, Salvatore, 128
"Rose for Emily, A" (Faulkner), 197; Chinese translation, 237, 239, 240; in Japanese, 260
Royal Street (Faulkner), 140
Rubáiyát (Khayyam), influence on Faulkner, 12–13, 15
Russian language: *Absalom, Absalom!*, 196; "The Artist at Home," 176, 196; "Barn Burning," 196; "The Bear," 179; *The Hamlet*, 179; *Intruder in the Dust*, 179; "A Justice," 196; *Light in August*, 180; *The Mansion*, 179; multiversions of Faulkner, 197; *Requiem for a Nun*, 180; *The Reivers*, 180; *Sartoris*, 180; *Soldiers' Pay*, 179; *The Sound and the Fury*, 180, 181, 196; "That Evening Sun," 176, 196; *The Town*, 179; "Victory," 176, 196
Russian literature: influence on Faulkner, 183–92; similarity to Faulkner, 224–25

Salmagundi (Faulkner), 278
Sanctuary (Faulkner), 19, 25, 27, 35, 39, 76, 83, 100, 105, 129, 178, 184, 196, 213, 226, 260, 262
Sartre, Jean-Paul, 48, 50, 260–61
Sartoris, Bayard, 190
Sartoris, Colonel John, 190
Sartoris (Faulkner), 180, 198, 202, 212, 261
Sartoris, John, 15
Savurenok, A. K., 233
Scandanavia, response to Faulkner, 309
Scream, The, 144
Selected Stories (Faulkner), Chinese edition, 238, 240
"Shall Not Perish," (Faulkner), 240, 241, 242–43
She, Lao, 252
Shijie Wenxue (World Literature) magazine, 239, 240
"Shingles for the Lord," (Faulkner), 240, 241, 243–44
Sholokhov, Mikhail, 185–86, 187, 219
Snopes, Eula, 15, 179
Snopes, Flem, 178, 227, 278
Snopes, Linda, 16, 25
Snopes, Mink, 227, 307–08
Soldiers' Pay (Faulkner), 12, 13, 14, 26, 39, 74, 179, 212, 238, 261, 278
Sound and the Fury, The (Faulkner), 10, 11, 18, 25, 27, 35, 40–56, 128, 180, 181, 184, 196, 202, 209, 212, 226, 261, 262, 264, 306; in Chinese, 239; in Spanish, 40–56; Soviet analysis of, 217–18, 220–22, 230
South, the, 71–72
Soviet Union: analysis of *The Sound and the Fury*, 217–18, 220–22, 230; contemporary literature and Faulkner, 203–10; criticism of Faulkner, 212–34; editions of Faulkner's works, 195–99; evolution of attitude toward Faulkner, 214–15; multiethnic editions, 202–03; recent Faulkner publications, 223–24, 226, 228, 231; response to Faulkner, 175–76, 177, 178, 179, 199–202, 210–11, 212, 214–15; reviews of Faulkner's work, 177–82; studies of Faulkner, 215–34; teaching of Faulkner in, 174–92; *See also* Russian language; Russian literature.

INDEX   351

Spain: Hispanic readers, 30–31; impact of Faulkner, 36; influence of Faulkner, 38
Spanish language: *As I Lay Dying*, 39, 63; *A Fable*, 39; *Go Down, Moses*, 39; *The Hamlet*, 39; *Mosquitoes*, 39; *Pylon*, 36; *Requiem for a Nun*, 39; *The Reivers*, 39; *Sanctuary*, 35, 39; *Soldiers' Pay*, 39; *The Sound and the Fury*, 40–56; *These Thirteen*, 39; *The Unvanquished*, 36; *The Wild Palms*, 35
"Spotted Horses," (Faulkner), 240, 244
Startsev, Abel, 226–28
Stevens, Gavin, 16, 25, 314
Stone, Phil, 6, 299, 301
"Stream-of-consciousness" technique, 210, 217, 219, 220, 249
Sutpen, Henry, 228
Sutpen, Thomas, 227, 316
Symbolists, 23, 99

Takahashi, Masao, 262
"Tall Men, The," (Faulkner), 240, 241–42
Tatsunokuchi, Naotaro, 260, 262
"That Evening Sun," (Faulkner), 176, 189, 196, 197, 240, 262
"Thrift," (Faulkner), 103
Time: in Faulkner's work, 307; in Spanish translation, 48–50
Today We Live, film, 286
Town, The (Faulkner), 25, 172, 178, 179, 191, 203, 212, 314
Translations: Chinese language and, 244–45; Faulkner's works and, 32, 34, 38; multiversions in Russian, 197; receptor-language text, 32, 33; stylistic development and, 31; translator's role, 32, 33
Turkish language, Faulkner translations, 38–39
"Turnabout," (Faulkner), 102, 103, 203; film version of, 286

Ukranians, translations of, 202
Unvanquished, The (Faulkner), 24, 36, 189, 197, 280

"Victory," (Faulkner), 102, 176, 196, 238
Vidal, Jorge Ferrer, 36
Viking Portable Faulkner, The, 78
Village prose, 204
Vision in Spring (Faulkner), 140, 156
Vittorini, Elio, 124, 125, 131, 133

War stories, 104–07; antiwar themes, 238
"Wash," (Faulkner), 239, 240
"Wednesday Night," (Faulkner), 110
Wenjun, Li, 239
West Germany, Faulkner translations in, 309
Wilbourne, Harry, 27
Wild Palms, The (Faulkner), 10, 27, 35, 38, 238, 261, 264
William Faulkner (Millgate), 81
William Faulkner: Seven Short Stories, 196
Wishing Tree, The (Faulkner), 26, 140
Wistaria (Giannitrapani), 134
"With Caution and Dispatch," (Faulkner), 103

Xiaosheng, Gao, 252
Xun, Lu, 250–51

"Yo Ho and Two Bottles of Rum," (Faulkner), 302
Yoknapatawpha, meaning of, 219
Yoshizaki, Y., 312

Zasursky, Yasen, 219
Zatonsky, D., 224–26
Zverev, Alexei, 222–23